THE
UNITED STATES
IN
WORLD AFFAIRS
1957

THE
UNITED STATES
IN
WORLD AFFAIRS
1957

By Richard P. Stebbins

AND THE RESEARCH STAFF OF THE
COUNCIL ON FOREIGN RELATIONS

Published for the
COUNCIL ON FOREIGN RELATIONS
by
HARPER & BROTHERS
NEW YORK
1958

The Council on Foreign Relations is a non-profit institution
devoted to study of the international aspects of American
political, economic and strategic problems. It takes no stand,
expressed or implied, on American policy.

The authors of books published under the auspices of the
Council are responsible for their statements of fact and expressions of opinion. The Council is responsible only for
determining that they should be presented to the public.

COUNCIL ON FOREIGN RELATIONS

OFFICERS AND DIRECTORS

JOHN J. McCLOY
Chairman of the Board

HENRY M. WRISTON
President

FRANK ALTSCHUL
Vice-President & Secretary

DAVID ROCKEFELLER
Vice-President

ELLIOTT V. BELL
Treasurer

WALTER H. MALLORY
Executive Director

GEORGE S. FRANKLIN, JR.
Executive Director

FRANK D. CARUTHERS, JR.
Assistant Treasurer

HAMILTON FISH ARMSTRONG
WILLIAM A. M. BURDEN
ARTHUR H. DEAN
LEWIS W. DOUGLAS
ALLEN W. DULLES
THOMAS K. FINLETTER
JOSEPH E. JOHNSON

DEVEREUX C. JOSEPHS
GRAYSON L. KIRK
R. C. LEFFINGWELL
PHILIP D. REED
WHITNEY H. SHEPARDSON
CHARLES M. SPOFFORD
MYRON C. TAYLOR

JOHN H. WILLIAMS

COMMITTEE ON STUDIES

HENRY M. WRISTON
Chairman

HAMILTON FISH ARMSTRONG
GORDON DEAN
BYRON DEXTER
JOSEPH E. JOHNSON

GRAYSON L. KIRK
WILLIAM L. LANGER
AUGUST MAFFRY
WILLARD L. THORP

JOHN H. WILLIAMS

STUDIES PROGRAM

PHILIP E. MOSELY
Director of Studies

WILLIAM DIEBOLD, JR.
Director of Economic Studies

JOHN C. CAMPBELL
Director of Political Studies

PREFACE

THE AIM of this volume is to present a concise record of
United States participation in international affairs during
the calendar year 1957. The preparation of such a record becomes more difficult but also, perhaps, more needful as each
new year expands the scope of America's international responsibilities. The outstanding events of 1957—the promulgation of the "Eisenhower Doctrine" for the Middle East
and the extension of the East-West rivalry into outer space
through the agency of the two Soviet "Sputniks"—are part of
a much larger evolution which demands examination as a
whole if its significance is to be rightly appreciated. Definitive analysis must await the passage of time and the disclosure
of information not now available. The present volume offers
a recapitulation of the essential facts and a first attempt to
bring out the inner coherence of the story.

Though intended to be read as a whole, the volume is so
organized as to provide a point of departure for readers whose
immediate interest is limited to a single area or topic. So far
as possible, matters pertaining to a particular theme are
treated within the same chapter, with cross references to related material appearing elsewhere in the volume. Footnote
references are grouped at the end of each chapter. Since the
specialized literature dealing with recent events is necessarily
limited, the student in quest of more detailed information is
referred in the first instance to the documentation provided
by the parallel Council on Foreign Relations volume, *Documents on American Foreign Relations, 1957,* references to
which are included wherever appropriate. Other official statements, communiqués, and speeches which are identified only
by date can be readily located in newspaper files or in the
weekly issues of the *Department of State Bulletin.* Direct
quotations have been verified wherever possible by reference
to the official texts.

In dealing with the more controversial aspects of our recent foreign relations, the author has done his best to respect the Council's established principle of nonpartisanship as well as the normal obligations of scholarly objectivity. In this endeavor he has been aided by the advice and assistance of a number of eminent authorities associated with the Council who have generously allowed him to draw upon their special knowledge and experience. Dr. Henry M. Wriston and the members of the Committee on Studies have been uniformly helpful and considerate, as have the resident staff led by Hamilton Fish Armstrong, Walter H. Mallory, George S. Franklin, Jr., and Philip E. Mosely. Among my immediate associates, John C. Campbell somehow found time to read and comment on the entire manuscript, substantial portions of which were read also by William Diebold, Jr., and other colleagues. In addition, thanks are due to Ruth Savord and the Library Staff for invaluable aid in obtaining necessary materials, and to Frank D. Caruthers, Jr., and the members of the business office for unfailing assistance in technical and administrative matters. Somewhat beyond the range of verbal expression is my indebtedness to Elaine P. Adam, who has fully shared the rigors and (I must hope) the occasional satisfactions that go with authorship.

For permission to include several of the year's best cartoons the Council is indebted to *The Buffalo Evening News, The Christian Science Monitor, The Detroit News,* the *Los Angeles Times,* the McNaught Syndicate, Inc., the NEA Service, Inc., and *The Newark News.* The editors of *Vital Speeches of the Day* and *The Current Digest of the Soviet Press* have kindly authorized the use of certain quotations which are identified by footnote references. The maps have been adapted for this volume by E. L. Weldon of the American Geographical Society.

While deeply appreciative of the varied assistance provided him from so many directions, the author retains responsibility for the entire volume and would particularly value comments and suggestions from any readers who find it useful.

R.P.S.

New York
February 7, 1957

CONTENTS

Maps

THE
UNITED STATES
IN
WORLD AFFAIRS
1957

CHAPTER ONE

INTRODUCING 1957

NINETEEN HUNDRED AND FIFTY-SEVEN will be remembered as
the year when man first overcame the limitations of gravity
and extended the range of world affairs far outward into
space. The launching of two artificial earth satellites by the
Soviet Union on October 4 and November 3 represented a
major turning point in international affairs as well as an
important advance in man's gradual conquest of his physical
environment. So startling a display of scientific and engineering prowess on the part of a power generally rated far below
the West in technical accomplishment provided the U.S.S.R.
and international Communism with a world-wide psychological victory of the first order. In addition, it raised serious
doubts about the adequacy of the military, political, and economic arrangements which the Western powers had thus far
relied upon to protect themselves and the rest of the free
world against the dangers of Communist aggression, subversion, or peaceful conquest. It thus accentuated a number
of grave problems which had already been brought into relief by the extraordinary events of the preceding twelve
months.

Seldom if ever has a new year opened on such a spectacle
of confusion and uncertainty as had characterized the international scene at the beginning of 1957, nine months before
the ascent of the first Soviet "Sputnik." Sensational developments of the recent past—the unexpected loosening of the
Soviet grip on Poland in the autumn of 1956, the bloody
suppression of Hungary's subsequent bid for freedom, the

abortive military campaign waged by Israel, France, and Great Britain against Egypt—had already disrupted the previous pattern of international society and called in question a number of widely accepted dogmas of international politics. The placid atmosphere of "competitive coexistence" which had been developing ever since the death of Stalin in 1953 had been shattered by an acute threat of world war—a war which, had it occurred, would presumably have brought into play the full repertory of nuclear destruction already available to the two leading world powers. On the morrow of this complex and harrowing experience, humanity had looked out upon a landscape heaped high with the wreckage of past illusions and shrouded in dense fogs of doubt and perplexity.

Symptomatic of the confusion prevailing at this period had been the widely varying judgments put forward with respect to some of the most fundamental aspects of world affairs. "We live in a land of plenty, but rarely has this earth known such peril as today," said President Eisenhower in the Inaugural Address that opened his second term on January 21, 1957.[1] "In too much of the earth there is want, discord, danger." One of the most farseeing of European statesmen, Paul-Henri Spaak of Belgium, wrote of "a sense of futility [that] seems to smother us": [2]

"I have said—and there is no use trying to hide it—that things seem to me to have been going badly. I am not entirely pessimistic; I do not look for a third world war. But I do fear (I must admit) that a more and more confused situation is developing in which the Western world risks losing much. It can gain only by showing unexpected courage and unity."

Yet such misgivings were by no means universal. Secretary of State John Foster Dulles, meeting with the President and congressional leaders on New Year's Day of 1957 to appraise the still threatening situation in the Middle East, was officially credited with the opinion "that the position of international communism had deteriorated throughout the world and that the United States at the same time had moved into a position of great opportunity for world leadership for peace and stability as well as for world responsibility." An equal buoyancy—in public, at least—was apparent on the Soviet side. In a New Year statement replete with Communist clichés of a sort that had grown all too familiar in the months before the crushing of the Hungarian revolt, Premier N. A. Bulganin declared:

"There is every reason to think that the coming of 1957 will be marked with important victories by [the] peoples in their struggle for the preservation and consolidation of peace, for the relaxation of international tension, for the triumph of the principle of peaceful coexistence of states with different social systems. As before, the Soviet Union will not miss any opportunity to ensure that peace and security are guaranteed."

Thus Bulganin reaffirmed a basic Soviet propaganda line which had proved serviceable to Communist interests in many parts of the world but had latterly been almost hidden from view by the smoke of conflict within Moscow's own empire.

1. APPRAISING THE WORLD SITUATION

It was in this unsettled and darkly menacing atmosphere that the United States, as it confronted the new year and the new presidential term, was called upon to review the international policies of the past decade and to effect such adjustments as might now seem necessary to its own security and that of the many other non-Communist peoples for whom Washington had come to acknowledge a measure of responsibility. "You meet in a season of stress that is testing the fitness of political systems and the validity of political philosophies," President Eisenhower told the new Eighty-Fifth Congress in his annual State of the Union Message on January 10.[3] "The forces now at work in the minds and hearts of men will not be spent through many years." The United States, the President insisted, "cannot be aloof to these events heralding a new epoch in the affairs of mankind. Our pledged word, our enlightened self-interest, our character as a Nation commit us to a high role in world affairs: a role of vigorous leadership, ready strength, sympathetic understanding."

For President Eisenhower, the underlying force which made this turbulent world of 1957 intelligible was "the spirit of freedom"—the very spirit that had inspired America's own fight for national identity 180 years before. "In the main," he said, "today's expressions of nationalism are, in spirit, echoes of our forefathers' struggle for independence." Each individual stress in the contemporary world, the President believed, stemmed in part from causes peculiar to itself; but each was the reflection of a universal phenomenon:

"In the world today, the surging and understandable tide of nationalism is marked by widespread revulsion and revolt against tyranny, injustice, inequality and poverty. As individuals, joined in a common hunger for freedom, men and women and even children pit their spirit against guns and tanks. On a larger scale, in an ever more persistent search for the self-respect of authentic sovereignty and the economic base on which national independence must rest, peoples sever old ties; seek new alliances; experiment—sometimes dangerously—in their struggle to satisfy these human aspirations."

As a key to the "sympathetic understanding" which must precede intelligent action in world affairs, this brief characterization of the contemporary epoch of world history would have been difficult to improve upon. No one who looked closely at the world situation in the winter of 1956–57 could doubt that the spirit of nationalism and the revolt against "tyranny, injustice, inequality and poverty" were among the most powerful forces at work on the contemporary scene. It was this universal insistence on the right to individual and national freedom, human dignity, an adequate standard of living, that inspired the so-called "anticolonial" movement and the bitter hostility to the West prevailing in large parts of Asia and Africa. It was the endorsement and encouragement of these aspirations by the Communist governments of China and the U.S.S.R. that gave the Communist system such an appeal for millions of human beings who knew at first hand the evils of Western "colonialism," but who remained ignorant of the degradation of human personality behind the Iron and Bamboo Curtains. And it was the systematic frustration of these same inborn sentiments by the Communist governments themselves that had produced the recent upheavals within the Communist world and set in motion a process which might, in the opinion of at least some highly placed Western authorities, lead ultimately to the overthrow of the whole edifice of Communist tyranny.

These universal sentiments might be the common birthright of all mankind. Politically, however, humanity remained no less divided and at strife with itself than had been the case before the overthrow of Nazi totalitarianism and Japanese militarism a dozen years earlier. In the earliest postwar years, the view of international politics most generally accepted in the West had made a fundamental distinction between the Communist bloc and the nations of the "free world," whose common interest in remaining free from Communism was felt to outweigh the disparity of their outlook in other respects. This fundamental opposition between Marxist-Leninist Communism and all other modes of government and social organization may yet prove to have been the most significant political phenomenon of our time. But by the early 1950's it had become obvious that the "free world" itself was not in agreement on this fundamental issue. On the contrary, this "free world" was found to comprise at least two distinct and rather inharmonious elements —on the one hand the traditional group of Western states led by the United States, Great Britain, and France, and on the other a growing number of newly enfranchised countries in Asia and Africa whose peoples refused to look at the situation through Western eyes but stressed their continuing opposition to Western "colonialism" as well as their insistence on "noninvolvement" or "positive neutrality" in the East-West struggle.

Rationalized by such leaders as Prime Minister Jawaharlal Nehru of India, and strongly encouraged by the Communist governments for reasons of their own, this attitude had been justified in the eyes of its adherents by the persistence in the postwar years of a number of unsettled "colonial" issues involving the sovereignty over such areas as French Indochina and North Africa, Portuguese Goa, Netherlands New Guinea, and various British possessions in both hemispheres. Equally offensive to "anticolonial" sentiment in Asian and African countries had been the privileged status still claimed on behalf of certain important Western economic and strategic interests such as the oil installations of the Middle East, the military bases maintained in various overseas countries, and the Suez Canal. Year by year, controversy over such matters had tended to strengthen the notion of an inherent conflict of interest between the "colonial" powers of Western Europe (with which the United States was widely viewed as inseparably linked) and the predominantly "anticolonial" countries which staged the twenty-nine nation Asian-African Conference at Bandung in 1955 and participated in the so-called "Asian-African bloc" in the United Nations.

Thus it gradually became customary to interpret world politics in terms of a continuous interplay between not two but *three* major groupings: the Communist bloc, centering around the U.S.S.R. and Communist China; the anti-Communist Western nations, particularly the fifteen governments participating in the North Atlantic Treaty Organization (NATO); and the "anticolonial," "uncommitted," or Asian-African states which were accustomed to take their cue from India or, in matters of particular concern to the Arab world, from the revolutionary government headed by Egypt's President Gamal Abdel Nasser (Abd-al-Nasir).

That this process of internal subdivision and fragmentation might be destined to go still further had been one of the important possibilities raised by the events of late 1956, which had disclosed that none of the three existing groups was as firmly knit together as had sometimes appeared. The Asian-African states, indeed, had never pretended to constitute a united front except on a few specialized issues; several of them (Iran, Iraq, Pakistan, the Philippines, and Thailand) were actually allied with the West through the Southeast Asia Treaty Organization (SEATO) or the Baghdad Pact for the defense of the Middle East. The Western alliance, too, had for some years been exhibiting internal strains and a growing tendency toward more independent action on the part of individual members; and even the supposedly "monolithic" Soviet bloc had revealed certain important lines of cleavage in the period since the death of Stalin in March 1953. By early 1956 there had been much talk of a growing "depolarization" of world politics which, it was suggested, might soon inaugurate a new era in international relations. The old power centers in Washington and Moscow, mutually neutralizing each other through a "balance of terror" inspired by the nuclear and thermonuclear weapons now available to each, had seemed to be losing their magnetism. Allies on both sides had been growing more and more tired of acting on outside orders (or advice) and increasingly in the mood to try to make policy on their own.

These tendencies had reached a climax in the events of the last autumn. Poland, under the "national" Communist leadership of Wladyslaw Gomulka, had openly defied the Soviet Union and secured a substantial retraction of Soviet authority, thus gaining at least temporarily a measure of independence not far short of that already won by Tito's Yugoslavia after 1948. Hungary, attempting to improve on this example and dissociate itself from the military arrangements imposed on the Communist bloc, had been physically crushed by Soviet armed force; but the spirit of national independence kindled by the Hungarian revolt had remained alive to plague the Soviet leaders in various sections of their domain. In the non-Communist world, meanwhile, first Israel and then Great Britain and France had attempted to safeguard what they considered vital interests by making war on Egypt, in disregard of the known wishes of the United States as well as the United Nations; and the United States had found itself unable to support its closest allies in such a venture, even though it was aware that in failing to do so it risked a serious breakdown of the Western alliance. As a byproduct of the turmoil in the Middle East, the Arab nations had also shown signs of splitting into antagonistic camps, with Egypt and Syria heading a radical and pro-Soviet movement that contrasted sharply with the more conservative tendencies still dominant in Saudi Arabia, Iraq, and Lebanon. Thus at the beginning of 1957 all three political camps, but particularly those of East and West, faced major tasks of readjustment and internal conciliation if their solidarity was to be restored and further disintegration avoided. Western attempts to capitalize on Soviet discomfiture in Eastern Europe, and Soviet attempts to exploit Western disunity in the Middle East, did not disguise the fact that both groups were now beset by dangerous internal weaknesses.

The situation of the Western alliance, traditionally regarded as the world's one indispensable safeguard against Communist military aggression, was in some respects especially painful. Unlike the Communist bloc, the association of the Western nations rested not on coercion and military force but on voluntary consent and a common feeling of solidarity in face of an identified peril. It was this sense of common interest and mutual trust that had suffered most gravely from the events of recent months. In the course of the lengthy diplomatic discussions that took place between Egypt's nationalization of the Suez Canal in July and the Anglo-French military attack in November, 1956, Great Britain and France had become convinced that they were being abandoned and betrayed by the United States in a matter bearing directly upon their national survival. The United States, in turn, had been profoundly shocked and disillusioned by the action of its allies in mounting their attack on Egypt without so much as a warning of their intentions. The scars of this episode would take a long time to heal under the best of circumstances. One step toward reconciliation was taken at the very beginning of 1957 with the retirement of Britain's ailing Prime Minister, Sir Anthony Eden, in favor of Harold Macmillan, an old associate and friend of President Eisenhower. But the confident relationship between Washington and London which had given life to the Atlantic alliance in the past would be restored slowly if at all.

There were other weaknesses in the Western position, the more disturbing because the possibility of a Soviet military attack in Europe and the North Atlantic area now seemed much more real than had been true a few months earlier. In

notes to Britain and France at the height of the autumn
crisis, Moscow had openly discussed the possibility of using
"rockets" and other destructive weapons against them if they
failed to desist from their attack on Egypt. Washington itself
had been impressed by these threats, and had since become
seriously exercised over what was described as a danger of
Communist aggression in the Middle East. Aggression in the
Middle East would in all likelihood be the prelude to world
war; yet the outbreak of world war would admittedly find
the vital Western European theater without adequate means
of defense. The long-standing NATO plans for the creation
of a defensive military "shield" on the European Continent
had been revised downward repeatedly under the impact of
economic difficulties, outside preoccupations, and changing
military technology. Great Britain had undertaken a long-
term reduction of its military forces which would entail at
least some thinning of the British divisions stationed in
Western Germany. France had already withdrawn most of its
NATO contingents from Europe for service in Algeria,
where a desperate struggle with nationalist guerrilla bands
was progressively upsetting its domestic economy as well as
incurring the bitter enmity of Asian and African peoples.
The German Federal Republic had only just begun to make
its promised contribution of armed manpower for the common defense, and would soon face a parliamentary election
which might or might not confirm the pro-Western orientation associated with the person of Chancellor Konrad Adenauer. The United States itself was engaged on a long-term
readjustment of its defense policies in the direction of increased emphasis on the "deterrent" effect of long-range air
power and atomic weapons—an emphasis which, despite official denials, was widely believed to imply a lessening concern
with the territorial defense of Western Europe and other
exposed areas. Aggravated by the current political disunity,
the persistence of these long-standing problems cast more than
a little doubt on NATO's future effectiveness as an instrument
of Western security.

It was perhaps fortunate for the West that the difficulties
it was now experiencing were equaled or even exceeded by

THE TRAVELING SALESMEN

By Crawford in *The Newark News*

those prevailing within the Communist camp. There, too, the
events of late 1956 had called in question the most fundamental aspects of the general policy pursued in recent years.
As authoritatively expounded by Communist party chief
Nikita S. Khrushchev at the Twentieth Congress of the
Soviet Communist party in February 1956,[4] Soviet policy was
still avowedly directed toward the eventual triumph of Communism throughout the world. In contrast to the tone of
Soviet policy in the Stalin era, however, the new Soviet leaders explicitly sought to advance this aim primarily by non-
violent means, by playing down the more ruthless features
associated with Stalin's dictatorship, and by strengthening the
appeal to the less sophisticated sections of humanity, partic-

ularly in non-Western countries. In relation to the outside world this policy, in its earlier manifestations at least, had proved remarkably successful. Aided by the flamboyant personal diplomacy of Khrushchev and Premier Bulganin, it had already won the Soviet Union a marked ascendancy in certain Asian and Middle Eastern countries and had evoked expressions of lively concern on the part of some non-Communist observers.

Within the Soviet empire, however, the more relaxed methods of rule that naturally accompanied such a policy had helped to produce such phenomena as the Poznań riots and subsequent bloodless revolution in Poland, the national rising in Hungary, and a state of extreme unrest throughout the world Communist movement. The disturbances in Eastern Europe had precipitated a serious economic crisis, necessitating revisions of the Soviet bloc's coordinated economic plans; the Soviet military position was similarly impaired by the now doubtful reliability of the satellite armies. The whole question of the kind of relationship that ought to prevail among Communist states had been thrown wide open as a result of Moscow's inability to keep order within its own preserve. The bloody suppression of the revolt in Hungary had cost heavily in prestige among Communists and non-Communists the world over.

Under such circumstances, further action along the lines laid down at the Twentieth Party Congress had become difficult, and the whole conception of Soviet policy expounded by Khrushchev on that occasion was thought to be under attack by an influential group within the Soviet Communist party. Even if Khrushchev eventually succeeded in quieting his critics within the party Presidium, it was uncertain whether Soviet external policy could be fully restored to its former effectiveness. Major new initiatives on the world scene would in any case have to be subordinated to the need for stabilizing conditions within the Soviet bloc itself. The "cleanup" in Hungary would have to be completed. There was an urgent need to clarify relations with the new "national" Communist regime in Poland. Some new understanding was also required with the Communist authorities in

China, who had observed the late developments in Eastern Europe with scarcely concealed distaste.

While addressing itself to these urgent tasks, Moscow in its relations with the West had seen fit to resume a tone of truculent hostility recalling the worst days of the Stalin era. "When it comes to fighting imperialists," Khrushchev had said in a sharp reversal of his former tone, "we are all Stalinists." Amid the numerous uncertainties besetting both camps, leaders on both sides could at least agree that the relations between them had become more tense than at any time in the past several years—certainly since the famous "summit conference" held at Geneva in July 1955.

Yet in contrast to certain earlier periods of tension, it now seemed to be pretty clearly appreciated both in Moscow and in the Western capitals that a resort to armed hostilities would be extremely perilous to all concerned and might easily result in a process of mutual annihilation. The condition of so-called "nuclear stalemate"—the realization that both the United States and the Soviet Union now possessed sufficient nuclear and thermonuclear weapons and means of delivery to inflict deadly damage on each other—powerfully reinforced all the other considerations that tended to discourage open warfare between them and the camps they headed.

So long as military action continued to appear mutually unprofitable, the relations between East and West might remain fundamentally hostile, but would tend to take other forms than those of active belligerency. A state of armed truce would not preclude the possibility of negotiations on matters of mutual interest—limitation of armaments, measures to eliminate the danger of surprise attack, conceivably even political issues such as the future of Germany. If experience was any guide, however, each side would be primarily interested in using any negotiations that might occur to further its own objectives and strengthen its own position relative to its opponent's. The United States would undoubtedly retain its interest in promoting the reunification of Germany "in freedom" and the eventual liberation of the "captive" countries in Eastern Europe; the Soviet Union and Communist China would be unlikely to desist from their efforts to undermine "imperialism" in overseas areas still subject to Western influence. Meanwhile it was a foregone conclusion that each side would continue to compete to the best of its ability for the support of the "uncommitted" states which might eventually swing the balance between them.

It was this inveterate tendency of the East-West struggle to become diverted from the military plane and assume the forms of what was sometimes called "competitive coexistence" that lent such extraordinary importance to the position of these more or less "neutral" or "uncommitted" countries of Asia and Africa. In its unremitting cultivation of the Asian and African nations in past years, Communist diplomacy had shown a sure awareness of their importance in the emerging world order. Despite recent setbacks, moreover, the U.S.S.R. and its allies were still rather better situated than the Western nations for promoting their interests in this part of the world. The Western powers, handicapped from the first by the heritage of colonialism, had been much less adroit than the Soviet Union and Communist China in identifying themselves with the dominant preoccupations of these formerly dependent peoples. Western energies in Asia had been largely, though by no means exclusively, absorbed by direct resistance to Communist expansionism, partly on the battlefield and partly through the formation of anti-Communist military alliances—which were not especially popular even in states which had joined them and had proved highly objectionable to some other influential governments in the area. Even the Western attempts to assist in promoting economic development and higher living standards through such instrumentalities as the American Point Four Program had given the impression of being motivated primarily by anti-Communist political aims. The Communists, in contrast, had consistently stressed the "anticolonial" theme in their Asian and African operations, and in the last year or two had come forward with a number of spectacular offers of trade and economic assistance "without strings"—i.e., without any formal obligation to adopt a pro-Communist political posture. Western policy had only begun to wake up to this challenge when the crisis over Hungary and Suez had plunged the world in confusion and imposed a virtual moratorium on long-range political thinking.

In terms of political influence, the net effect of the autumn crisis on the Asian and African countries had on the whole been rather less unfavorable to the Soviet Union than it was to the West. In Asian and African eyes, the Anglo-French attack on Egypt, as a manifestation of recrudescent "colonialism," was even more reprehensible than the Soviet repression in Hungary. True, the almost universal condemnation incurred by the British and French (and Israeli) governments did not extend to the United States, which had been widely commended for dissociating itself from their actions. On the other hand, the Soviet Union had also gained in some areas through its violent denunciation of "aggressors" in the Middle East and its open threat to intervene militarily on the side of Egypt. Among the Arab countries, where these threats were widely credited with having stopped the Anglo-French invasion, Moscow had thus gone far to consolidate the position already gained by its astute diplomacy of the past year or two.

By consistently endorsing the Arab states in their quarrel with Israel, the U.S.S.R. had long since won a psychological advantage in this area which had been unavailable to the Western nations in view of their desire to maintain good relations with both Israelis and Arabs. By supplying important quantities of modern armaments to individual Arab states—first Egypt, and more recently Syria—it had encouraged a tendency in Arab opinion to look to the Soviet bloc as the one source of ostensibly disinterested outside support. This tendency, though it caused some misgiving in conservative Arab circles, was particularly marked in left-wing and ultranationalist groups such as those that surrounded Colonel Abdel Nasser in Egypt and Colonel Abdel Hamid Sarraj, the Chief of Military Intelligence in Syria. In view of the ebullient frame of mind prevailing in these circles in the weeks that followed the cessation of hostilities in Egypt, it was not surprising that the United States should have come to regard the Middle East as the most immediately endangered of all the areas threatened by Soviet machinations.

Indeed, it was only in the Middle East that responsible American quarters at this period perceived a need for immediate action of an emergency character to counter what was considered an imminent threat to an important segment of the non-Communist world. Despite the widespread disorientation of world opinion, the situation elsewhere around the Communist periphery was still felt in Washington to be under reasonably good control, thanks in part to the continued validity of the various security pacts concluded among the non-Communist governments, and partly to the numerous internal preoccupations of the Communist powers. In the Middle East, however, it seemed that almost anything might happen. With the Suez Canal blocked, oil facilities shut down, and Israeli troops still occupying extensive areas in Egypt despite repeated admonitions from the United Nations General Assembly, the situation was delicate in the extreme. It would certainly not have been surprising if the Soviet Union, with its well-known proclivity for fishing in troubled waters, should have tried to take advantage of the "power vacuum" created by the collapse of British influence (and to cover its own embarrassment about matters nearer home) by making some overt move to extend its foothold in an area that was of great concern to it as well as to the West.

Yet despite its complexity, its emergency character, and the unusual priority accorded it in official Washington, the Middle Eastern situation was not altogether an isolated phenomenon. Similar, if less acute, problems fringed the Asian-African area from the Mediterranean to the Pacific. Everywhere there was the same underlying preoccupation with national individuality, with political and economic independence, with industrialization and higher living standards, with the achievement of a life more nearly commensurate with what was dimly felt to be the inherent dignity of human beings. These were the great popular cravings to which the Communists claimed to have the answer, and to which the West had not, as yet, provided any answer sufficiently clear-cut and convincing to win the confidence of the uncommitted third of mankind.

It was in this area of long-range positive endeavor, rather than in the meeting of temporary emergencies incident to the East-West struggle, that the foreign policy of the United States and the other Western powers would ultimately have to prove its effectiveness. As 1957 began, there was world-wide interest in learning what the United States proposed to do about these broader problems—about the issue of colonialism in places like Algeria, for example, and about the widespread clamor for increased funds for economic development. Would the American government and people perceive an opportunity for a new departure in relations with the uncommitted countries, one that might enable them to recover some of the ground lost in recent years? Would they be prepared to take whatever measures might be needed to restore the vitality of the Western alliance? Or would American action be confined to trying to counter any obvious Soviet thrusts that might develop in the Middle East or elsewhere in the wake of recent disturbances?

2. DEFINING U.S. POLICY

It was, perhaps, inevitable that the difficult situation already existing in the Middle East should have so absorbed American attention during the early months of 1957 as to leave little time or interest for these broader issues of long-range foreign policy. Despite the shocks of recent weeks, the American mood was not at the moment particularly well attuned to sustained and imaginative effort in the international field. For a number of years there had been indications of somewhat diminished popular concern with world events and of diminishing support for an active foreign policy, especially in those departments of foreign policy that involved large financial outlays. This trend the critical events in Hungary and the Middle East had failed to check. On the contrary, the recent reelection of President Eisenhower had been interpreted in many quarters as a signal for sharply reduced expenditure for international purposes. Although the President himself repeatedly called attention to the vastly increased international responsibilities now resting upon the

United States, experience in the months ahead was to show that Congress and the public were only moderately responsive to this line of thought. Action aimed at directly countering Soviet machinations in the Middle East could still count on general national support. But action aimed only at strengthening the general position of the non-Communist nations, whether allied or uncommitted, was either left in abeyance or approved with reluctance and generally on much more restricted lines than the administration itself thought desirable.

It must be added that apart from the special message on the Middle East which President Eisenhower delivered to the Congress on January 5,[5] the series of administration pronouncements that marked the beginning of a new presidential term and a new congressional session gave no indication that the administration's own thinking had been greatly affected by recent world developments. Generalizations about the interdependence of the free nations and the responsibilities of American leadership abounded in the President's State of the Union Message (January 10)[6] and still more in his Second Inaugural Address (January 21),[7] which was devoted almost entirely to foreign affairs and was hailed in some quarters as the death knell of American isolationism. But outside the Middle East, where the President sought authority to make special financial and military commitments for the specific purpose of countering an asserted threat of Soviet aggression, there was no suggestion that established forms of international action needed to be modified or intensified in any important way. Much as he deplored the ruthlessness displayed by the U.S.S.R. in Hungary, and greatly as he mistrusted its intentions in the Middle East, the President explicitly disclaimed any belief that the Russians were "hardening . . . or changing their attitude." "After all," he observed at a news conference two days after his inauguration, "we are dealing with people who are rather unpredictable and, at times, . . . just practically inexplicable, so far as we are concerned." The important thing for the United States, he implied, was to maintain stability in its own policies rather than try to gear them to the vagaries of the other side.

In seeking to apply this principle during the years of his first administration, the President had often referred to certain fundamental convictions which he now enunciated afresh in his January messages to the Congress. First, he felt, the existence of a "strongly armed imperialistic dictatorship" like the U.S.S.R. posed a continuing threat to the security and peace of the nation and the free world. Second, America under modern conditions could not survive in isolation, but must join its destiny with that of all other freedom-loving peoples. Third, economic and moral factors were as vital to national security as the maintenance of a powerful military establishment. "Any program that endangers our economy could defeat us," General Eisenhower said once again in his 1957 State of the Union message.

Inevitably, the special concern for the national economy which had characterized the Eisenhower administration since its beginnings had influenced its response both to the Soviet challenge and to the problems of association within the non-Communist world. The President often pointed out (e.g., May 14, 1957) that there was "no cut-rate price for security," that the price of peace was high, and that it was much better to pay it than to sacrifice "our sons, our families, our homes and our cities to our own shortsightedness." At the same time, Mr. Eisenhower had at all times insisted on the necessity of searching out the most economical ways of developing that measure of power and stability which he considered essential to the security of the nation and the free world. Considerations of economy, to which Congress was at least as sensitive as the administration, had profoundly influenced the nature and scope of American international policy during the previous four years. They were destined to exert an even more powerful influence in this new year when mounting inflationary pressures had begun to arouse general concern throughout the country.

The most conspicuous monument to this economy concept was a national military policy explicitly designed, to quote words spoken by Secretary Dulles in 1954 but often

echoed by the President himself, to provide "maximum protection at a bearable cost." Based primarily on the idea of
deterring any attack by maintaining the capacity to retaliate
against an aggressor with atomic and thermonuclear weapons,
this policy as originally enunciated in the winter of 1953–54
had emphasized the notion of "massive" retaliation against
enemy centers as the principal if not the only response to any
aggression. Though subsequently modified to some extent
in order to take account of the availability of "tactical" nuclear weapons designed for battlefield use, its main outlines still remained intact despite the insistence of critics at
home and abroad that it threatened to turn minor local conflicts into large-scale atomic wars, afforded insufficient protection to allied nations situated close to the probable sources
of aggression, and was bound to lose its effectiveness as the
Soviet Union built up its own capacity for long-range atomic
war.

Despite the known progress of the U.S.S.R. in the field of
nuclear and thermonuclear weapons, long-range aircraft, and
guided and ballistic missile prototypes, these considerations
had thus far exerted no identifiable influence on American defense planning. As unfolded to Congress in the State of the
Union and Budget messages, the defense program for the
fiscal year 1958 seemed if anything to accentuate the trend
toward exclusive reliance on nuclear weapons, primarily
"strategic" ones. "Our nuclear weapons and our ability to
employ them," said the President in his Budget message
(January 16),[8] "constitute the most effective deterrent to an
attack on the free nations. We shall continue to expand our
nuclear arsenal until an agreement has been reached for reduction and regulation of armaments under safeguarded
inspection guaranties." Though it was doubtless true that
America's nuclear armory remained the principal guarantee
of free world safety, this fact in itself would inevitably color
American relations with the Communist states, with allies
who had watched with misgivings the gradual reduction of
United States military manpower at home and overseas, and
with Japan, India, and other countries which were particularly alarmed at the progressive poisoning of the atmos-

phere by the testing of new nuclear devices. (See further section 5.)

A further effect of the concern with economic factors in world policy had been a progressive reduction during the last few years in the scope of American efforts to promote economic stability and growth in the non-Communist world. The massive economic aid to Western Europe undertaken under the Marshall Plan had been terminated some years previously. Economic aid to other and poorer regions had never attained a comparable scale, except in a few isolated instances such as South Korea and South Vietnam, which received special consideration for strategic reasons. Nor was any important change in this respect envisaged for the coming fiscal year, extending from July 1, 1957 to June 30, 1958. Except for a proposed item of $200 million for use in connection with the Middle East emergency, there was no plan for expanded economic operations under the Mutual Security program, the nonmilitary portion of which was estimated at $1,950 million for fiscal year 1958 as compared with $1,750 million in fiscal 1957. (Important modifications in the method of spending the money, involving the establishment of a special Development Loan Fund, were introduced at a later date. See section 6.)

A somewhat comparable trend could be discerned in the field of international trade and finance, in which United States policy of late years had shown at most a rather limited concern with the needs of the international economy and the responsibilities of the world's leading creditor nation. Here again, the President had repeatedly drawn attention to the importance of expanding world trade and helping friendly countries to remain solvent by enabling them to compete in the American market. Yet both Congress and the executive in their concrete decisions in this field had on the whole appeared to be less influenced by broad international considerations than by reluctance to disturb established interests at home. Particularly noteworthy was a growing protectionist trend which had resulted, among other things, in a marked unwillingness on the part of Congress to authorize United States membership in the proposed Or-

ganization for Trade Cooperation, a step recommended by
President Eisenhower in 1955, 1956, and now for the third
time in 1957 (cf. section 6).

Protectionism in economic matters was closely related to
isolationism in international politics; and it is paradoxical
but true that isolationist currents in Congress and the country
had continued to influence the trend of American foreign
policy even during these years when America's direct involvement in world affairs outran all previous experience.
At times the isolationist trend found expression in overt
moves to limit American participation in international activities through such devices as the proposed Bricker Amendment to redefine the constitutional powers of the executive.
At other times it motivated the resistance to specific international arrangements like the "status-of-forces" agreements
whereby American servicemen who committed certain
crimes abroad became liable to trial in the courts of allied
nations. It was in matters of this kind that President Eisenhower's personal concept of national responsibility diverged
most sharply from that of some other powerful figures on
the national scene. His view was plainly stated on May 21,
1957 when he said that American foreign policy was inspired
"not only by calculations of self-interest but also by decent
regard for the needs and the hopes of all our fellowmen. . . .
If ever we were to lose our sense of brotherhood, of kinship
with all free men, we would have entered upon our Nation's
period of decline. Without vision, without a quick sense of
justice and compassion, no people can claim greatness."

Fresh evidence of the gap between executive and legislative thinking on these matters was destined to accumulate as
Congress considered the President's 1957 program, which
included, in addition to the special resolution on the Middle
East and the routine appropriations for national defense and
mutual security, a number of measures concerned with the
fulfillment of a more general international responsibility.
Among them were approval of United States participation
in the Organization for Trade Cooperation and the International Atomic Energy Agency, some increase in the annual
appropriation for international informational activities, and

a partial revision of the immigration laws. Though neither very new nor very radical, even this program was to prove too far-reaching for Congress under the conditions of 1957. The President, who subsequently praised the handling of his Middle Eastern proposals as "bipartisanship at its best," did not conceal his disappointment at the treatment accorded to some of his other recommendations.

The reasons for this disappointment will be examined in more detail in Chapter II. In the meantime it may be useful, in a year when so much in world affairs hinged directly on the actions of the President and the executive branch of the government, to try to define a little more precisely the general aims and attitude of the President and his administration at this important international turning point. For this purpose the frank and informal comments made at news conferences are at least as revealing as the carefully wrought official pronouncements delivered to national and worldwide audiences.

Of special significance to a world which had learned to shudder at the notion of American "brinkmanship" was an unwavering emphasis in responsible American pronouncements during 1957 on the concept of "peace with justice," on the rule of law, and on the vital necessity of an international understanding which would embrace not only our friends but our enemies. "I have told you this time and time again," said the President at a news conference on June 26. "I repeat it almost in my sleep: there will be no such thing as a victorious side in any global war of the future. I believe that any time we begin to think of war as an inescapable event of some future time, . . . we have become completely pessimistic on the future of humanity, at least in the northern hemisphere, as we have known it, and it is really a tragedy that the human imagination and mind won't compass." "The great struggle of our age," he said on another occasion (July 31), "is to free men of terrible fear. Men are living—men and women—all over the world, . . . in fear of one kind or another, and I think we have got to help raise that burden." Asked by a reporter to name three or four accomplishments by which he would like his second administration to be judged, Mr. Eisenhower replied (January 23):

"Look, everything else . . . fades to unimportance beside this one: that we do make progress toward better world understanding, achieved, I would say, in several steps. First, a better understanding among the free nations of the world, that is, better and stronger confidence among them; the certainty that their economic and military strength is equal to the test, and after that, particularly better understanding with the Russians, the Russian Government; and, finally, agreements in which we could all trust them."

This insistence on the necessity for understanding and agreement even with a power like the Soviet Union, so often branded as the chief menace to peace in the world, seemed to imply a belief that the Soviet rulers were, after all, men with whom one could in due time reach agreements that would afford a basis for mutual trust. Although a great deal of American foreign policy in the last few years had in fact reflected some such assumption—the whole idea of the President's famous "open skies" plan, for example, was to generate mutual confidence as a basis for larger agreements—not everyone in official Washington took an equally hopeful view. "We cannot trust the Russians on this or anything," said Admiral Arthur W. Radford, the outgoing Chairman of the Joint Chiefs of Staff, on May 19 at a critical moment in the discussions being carried on in the United Nations Disarmament Subcommittee. "The Communists have broken their word with every country with which they ever had an agreement." To this the President in effect replied on May 22 that the pursuit of disarmament was too important to be blocked by an excess of suspicion:

"I think our first concern should be making certain we are not ourselves being recalcitrant, we are not being picayunish about the thing. We ought to have an open mind and make it possible for others, if they are reasonable, logical men, to meet us half way so we can make these agreements."

And again, in the same vein (July 17):

"I know of nothing that has occurred in our time where greater optimism . . . , or enthusiasm almost, must be maintained . . . ,

than in this whole business of beginning disarmament, of reliev-
ing tensions in the world. The alternative is so terrible that you
can merely say this: All the risks you take in advancing or in
trying to advance are as nothing compared to doing nothing, to
sitting on your hands."

In conformity with this view, the United States in the
course of 1957 was to make a number of significant concessions to the Soviet viewpoint on disarmament in the vain
hope of reaching at least a "first step" disarmament agreement (section 11). Among other things, it ceased to insist that
initial disarmament measures must await progress toward
a settlement of the great political issues dividing East
and West. Deep reductions in national armaments, Washington insisted, would still be impracticable until such time
as the great powers managed to narrow their differences on
the future of Germany, the unification of Korea, and similar
problems. But certain preliminary steps might be taken, under
proper safeguards, even without political agreements.

In thus demonstrating its concern for basic agreement
with the U.S.S.R., the American Government had no thought
of relaxing its opposition to any expansion of the Communist domain or of weakening its stand on the ultimate freedom of the peoples now under Communist domination. Not
only did the United States undertake an unprecedented unilateral commitment to oppose Communist aggression in the
Middle East, and seize every opportunity to denounce the
Soviet record in Hungary. The year was also to be marked
by solemn reaffirmations of the established American policy
on the unification of Germany, the eventual freedom of the
Eastern European "captive" states, and the nonrecognition
of Communist China. Perhaps inevitably under the circumstances, however, these declarations gave the impression of
having been made more for the record than in the expectation of early or concrete results. In practice, the American
position on dealings with the Communist countries was to
be relaxed in several particulars during the year; and any
idea of using force to promote the freedom of enslaved peoples had by this time receded very far into the background.
The tone of official pronouncements was quite different from

that of the early months of the Eisenhower administration back in 1953. "We revere and honor those who as martyrs gave their blood for freedom," said Secretary Dulles in an important restatement of American policy toward Eastern Europe on April 22.[9] "But we do not ourselves incite violent revolt. Rather we encourage an evolution to freedom. . . . When Hungary was invaded and freedom crushed, we sponsored a United Nations condemnation of the Soviet Union. And when some steps are made toward independence, as recently in the case of Poland, we show a readiness to respond with friendly acts."

For Secretary Dulles, this policy of limited encouragement of the forces of freedom was supported by a body of theory as well articulated as the contrary theories espoused by Khrushchev and his associates. "American policy," the Secretary told his news conference on July 2, "is conducted on the assumption, as a working hypothesis, that free governments in the long run are going to prevail and despotic governments in the long run are going to go under." This generalization Mr. Dulles believed to be no less applicable to the Soviet Union than it was to the satellites and to Communist China. Although we did not look for a violent revolution in the U.S.S.R., he explained, we believed it almost certain that there would be an evolutionary change there in the direction of greater internal freedom and responsiveness to the popular will:

"I don't put any dates on these things. I don't say what is going to happen in 1 year, 5 years, 10 years, but I am confident that that is a basic truth. Certainly it's an assumption that I think must be made by anybody who believes in the American tradition. It was in that belief that our nation was founded. It's expressed in *The Federalist* papers. It is expressed by Abraham Lincoln in a sentence I often quote. He said our Declaration of Independence meant liberty not alone for the people of this country but hope for all the world for all future time. It means in due course the weight should be lifted from the shoulders of all men. That is a basic American belief, and it is also the working hypothesis on which we conduct our foreign policy."

How far such a hypothesis was compatible with Washington's proclaimed aim of establishing a more trustful relationship with the existing Soviet Government would be for events to determine, although it may be noted in passing that expressions of this character were invariably badly received in Moscow. (Cf. section 11.)

The American approach to world affairs in these years had certain other characteristic aspects which failed to generate great enthusiasm, even among friendly countries. Particularly irksome to some of our allies at this period was an unprecedented official emphasis on the role of moral principle as the basic determinant of American foreign policy, toward friends as well as foes. People in France and Great Britain during early 1957 were in no mood to cheer the superior morality of America's course in the recent Suez crisis, which might have been motivated by the most laudable aims but had left them in a decidedly uncomfortable position (cf. section 12). Some American observers, too, found the administration inclined to be overly facile in its ethical judgments. "The idea that we are engaged in a crusade or mission to vindicate a vaguely and erroneously conceived 'moral law,'" wrote former Secretary of State Dean Acheson, "has led to actions which, I fear, are quite contrary to our interests." [10]

Especially questionable, in the opinion of some critics of current American policy, was the administration's apparent predisposition during the early months of 1957 to identify the moral law with the opinion of the majority in the United Nations Assembly. Washington had not always been so ready to take its cue from the world organization as it seemed to many to be doing through the late winter of this year, as the Assembly struggled with the aftermath of the Suez venture. Both at home and abroad the suggestion was heard that the administration in reality was actuated less by moral principle than by political expediency or mental laziness. Some observers went so far as to charge outright hypocrisy. Yet whatever the justice of these criticisms, America's new readiness to work through the United Nations and respect majority views had its positive aspect and helped to keep the United States in tune with at least some of the dominant currents in world opinion. After all, President Eisenhower observed (March 7), we had voluntarily joined the United Nations organization and had an obligation to operate through it as long as we could, in spite of its admitted failures and weaknesses. He doubted that any of his auditors would want the United States to take the opposite course and try to stand "up above the world, flex its muscles, say, 'I am the policeman,' and go everywhere and . . . try to compel people . . . to follow its own dictates. . . ."

It was this grasp of the psychological implications of America's stance in world affairs that had made President Eisenhower a popular figure abroad even among people who went out of their way to criticize other American representatives and found little to praise in the substance of American policy. Secretary Dulles, desperately fighting for an adequate Mutual Security appropriation, allowed himself on one occasion during 1957 to tell a congressional subcommittee that the State Department was not concerned with making friends for the United States, and that if our loans saved a people from Communism he did not care whether they liked us or hated us.[11] President Eisenhower, less involved in the day-to-day battle with Congress, invariably managed to take a more complaisant view. In one unfinished sentence pronounced at a news conference on July 17, he somehow contrived to state the whole problem of America's place among the non-Communist nations:

"I think that if the United States could only understand that we are dealing with sovereign nations whose prides, whose traditions, whose whole attitude toward their sovereign rights is just as strong as in our own country, and that these are people whom we are trying to win as friends and keep as friends, we are not trying to dominate, we are not trying to establish a new system of international imperialism of some kind."

This observation, inspired primarily by the controversy at home over the "status-of-forces" agreements (section 7), is no less applicable to the broader history of a year in which the United States was to attempt as never before to sway the course of world events in accordance with its own views.

3. CLEARING THE TRACKS

It was with such views and hopes as these that President Eisenhower, Secretary Dulles, and their civilian and military associates were now to grapple with the confused and difficult world situation left by the fighting in Egypt and Hungary. Although their detailed endeavors will be described at some length in the chapters that follow, the early months of 1957 were a time of such extraordinary complexity in world affairs that a few preliminary comments are well-nigh essential if events are to be seen in their proper relationship. In the main, the winter and spring of 1957 were devoted by all parties to recuperation from the shocks of the autumn, to struggling with the physical and political debris that encumbered the Middle East, and to reestablishing a semblance of normality in relations with allies and associates. Until these urgent tasks were under way, none of the powers could tell for certain where it stood or what kind of world situation it was going to face.

An essential requirement from almost every point of view was the liquidation of the Suez war and the restoration of normal conditions in the neighborhood of the Suez Canal and the Egyptian-Israeli armistice lines. Late in December Great Britain and France had withdrawn their forces from Egypt in compliance with the resolutions of the United Nations Assembly. Israel, however, still occupied substantial areas on the Egyptian side of the demarcation line and was insisting on various international guarantees before it would consider withdrawing farther. These demands were considered highly improper by the majority of the General Assembly, including the United States, which exercised heavy pressure on Israel to withdraw without formal guarantees and to rely on the good will of the international community to protect its legitimate interests. Israel nevertheless held out until March 1, then yielded under protest. As the Israeli forces withdrew, the recently created United Nations Emergency Force was provisionally deployed along the armistice lines and the Gulf of Aqaba, where it served as a *de facto* protection to Israel against raids or blockading activities. In the meantime the Suez Canal had been cleared by a United Nations salvage fleet and was reopened in April under Egyptian management. Britain and France, whose attack on Egypt had been aimed in part at putting the Canal back under some form of international control, soon began to use the waterway again in spite of Egypt's successful insistence on its own point of view. (For details, see section 12.)

The complete frustration of British and French purposes in the Middle East further complicated the task of restoring good relations among the Western Big Three, which had been seriously impaired as a result of the Anglo-French action against Egypt. The reopening of communications was nevertheless recognized as essential by all parties. Duncan Sandys, Britain's new Defense Minister, broke the ice on a visit to Washington at the end of January; French Premier Guy Mollet, following a month later, found that he and President Eisenhower could still agree on most of the generalities of international politics.[12] A further stage in the process of reconciliation was reached in March when Messrs. Eisenhower and Dulles traveled to Bermuda for a full-dress meeting with Prime Minister Macmillan and Foreign Secretary Selwyn Lloyd—the discussions being conducted, in the language of the official communiqué (March 24)[13] "with the freedom and frankness permitted to old friends in a world of growing interdependence." A major subject at Bermuda was the plan of the new British government to reduce military expenditure still further and shift the emphasis in defense planning from standing forces to increased mechanization and reliance on the most modern weapons, including missiles. This change in British military dispositions was obviously destined to have a profound effect on allied defense arrangements in Europe, and was to be sharply questioned at a NATO Council session in May (cf. section 8). But the emergence of a fresh problem of such importance was at least helpful in diverting attention from past misunderstandings and restoring the traditional NATO practice of meeting common problems by some kind of common approach.

A similar process of clarification and reconsolidation was meanwhile going forward behind the Iron Curtain, although

its progress was less easily observed because of the secrecy in
which the Communist authorities were accustomed to veil
their most important actions. The basic problem confronting the leaders of international Communism was to find
some way of reconciling the principle of "separate roads to
socialism" espoused by such figures as Tito and Gomulka
with the necessity for some measure of central direction of
Communist efforts. With party Secretary Khrushchev apparently fighting for his own political life, a major role in this
effort devolved upon Communist China's Prime Minister
Chou En-lai, who interrupted a missionary tour of South-
eastern and Southern Asia for an emergency trip to Moscow,
Warsaw, and Budapest in January. In Poland, Chou apparently persuaded the Gomulka government that the notion
of "separate roads to socialism" must as a practical matter be
tempered with the Moscow principle of "proletarian internationalism." In Hungary, he threw his support behind the
Soviet-imposed regime of János Kádár, now engaged in stamping out the last vestiges of popular resistance to Communist
rule. Returning to the U.S.S.R., the Chinese representative
joined in a public redefinition of the permissible limits of
national individualism within the "camp of Socialism." With
Gomulka's overwhelming endorsement on January 20 in
what by Communist standards was the nearest thing to a
free election, the situation in Eastern Europe began to stabilize itself. Khrushchev meanwhile was gradually consolidating his authority at home. His general aim apparently
was to reestablish at least the broad outlines of domestic and
foreign policy laid down at the Twentieth Party Congress
the year before; but the opposition of such leading Soviet
figures as V. M. Molotov, L. M. Kaganovich, and G. M.
Malenkov would seem to have acted as a powerful restraint
up to the moment in late June when Khrushchev found it
possible to remove them from their positions of influence.
(See further section 10.)

Meanwhile the East-West struggle did not stand still but
was going forward with new intensity, particularly in the
Middle East. Scenting a threat of overt Communist aggression against that area, the United States administration at

the very beginning of the year had laid before Congress its emergency resolution designed, in Secretary Dulles' words, to erect a "stop sign" before the Russians and make clear the determination of the United States to resist an overt Communist aggression in the Middle East by force of arms. (Cf. section 4.) No such aggression in fact materialized, either before or after the final enactment of the resolution on March 9. Moscow did, however, take advantage of the irritation aroused in Arab nationalist circles to strengthen its foothold in Egypt and Syria and extend its intrigues in other Arab countries. The United States, on its part, began a vigorous diplomatic courtship of Saudi Arabia and other non-Soviet-influenced Arab countries, and in March agreed in addition to join the military committee of the Baghdad Pact organization. With the Arab world thus split apart on the issue of East-West relations, a preliminary showdown occurred in April when King Hussein of Jordan, with strong and indispensable American backing, managed to quell a military plot supported in Syria and Egypt and apparently aimed at taking Jordan into the pro-Soviet camp. (See further section 13.)

While laying chief emphasis on foiling Soviet designs in the Middle East, the United States also gave considerable attention to the problems of Eastern Europe. At the winter session of the General Assembly it took the lead in condemning the Soviet-sponsored repression in Hungary and in securing the establishment of a special United Nations committee to study and report on Hungarian developments. It also reiterated several times its interest in the eventual freedom of the captive countries, and after prolonged negotiations eventually concluded a rather modest economic aid agreement with the new government in Poland. Tito's Yugoslavia likewise continued to enjoy official favor in Washington, although a proposed visit by the Yugoslav President fell through as a result of opposition in Congress. Regarding the problem of German reunification, too, the United States and its allies continued to assert their established viewpoint, though apparently with more hope of influencing the forthcoming West German elections than of changing the Soviet attitude. (See further section 10.)

Other "cold war" fronts remained relatively inactive during this period. The United States and Communist China maintained their desultory ambassadorial contact at Geneva, with no prospect of a major change of position by either side; and the stalemate in Korea, Vietnam, and the Taiwan area persisted with little alteration (see Chapter V). A more forward-looking trend from the standpoint of Western policy was the progress of the Gold Coast (Ghana), Malaya, and other British territories toward independence within the Commonwealth, and the increased self-government being conferred on certain French colonial territories, although the impact of these latter developments in Asian and African countries was lessened by France's continuing refusal to consider independence for Algeria (section 9). Meanwhile the Soviet "trade and aid" offensive in Asian and African lands appeared to have slackened off to some extent since 1956, but could conceivably revive once conditions in the Communist world were stabilized. Latin America throughout this period continued to live its own life in comparative seclusion from the tides of cold war, though deeply concerned with the problems of economic and political growth and heavily preoccupied, as always, with the behavior and possible intentions of the United States (see Chapter VI).

Such, in broad outline, was the trend of world affairs in the months that preceded Khrushchev's victory over his principal domestic antagonists at the beginning of the summer (section 19). The gradual lifting of the fog and smoke engendered by the crisis of late 1956 had revealed a landscape not greatly dissimilar to that of the year before. Hungary was crushed, Poland was partly free, Egypt remained in possession of the Suez Canal; in other respects not a great deal seemed to be altered. Despite the excitement over Jordan, the immediate fear of war had largely passed; in its place one could again detect the atmosphere of "relaxation of tensions" which the Communist powers had cultivated with such success in past years. This was an atmosphere in which the West had found it extraordinarily difficult to maintain its own solidarity and sense of direction, and the difficulties would certainly not be less formidable in future. But it was an atmosphere that had also produced highly disturbing effects within the "camp of socialism," which was still and would continue to be torn between the need for discipline and the need to give some scope to those popular energies that Khrushchev claimed to rely upon.

It thus appeared that the basic problems confronting East and West in 1957 were not to be essentially dissimilar to those that each side had so spectacularly failed to master in 1956. Peace still hung precariously upon a "balance of terror." Enveloped by the sultry climate of "nuclear stalemate," each side still sought to advance its own objectives in the world and at the same time to avert the constantly threatened deterioration of its own political and military position. Even the advent of the two "Sputniks" would not alter this picture in any fundamental way, greatly as it was to modify the outlook and the relative diplomatic position of the two camps (Chapter VII). The ultimate question would still remain: Would mankind eventually destroy itself in the pursuit of irreconcilable political and ideological goals, or would it find ways of assuring the survival of the race while still preserving the millenary human ideal of freedom and peace with justice? It was this question that lent such extraordinary significance to every aspect of United States participation in world affairs in 1957.

Notes to Chapter I

1. *Department of State Bulletin*, v. 36 (February 11, 1957), pp. 211-213; *Documents on American Foreign Relations, 1957*, no. 5.

2. Paul-Henri Spaak, "The West in Disarray," *Foreign Affairs*, v. 35 (January 1957), pp. 189-190.

3. Excerpts in *Department of State Bulletin*, v. 36 (January 28, 1957), pp. 123-126; *Documents on American Foreign Relations, 1957*, no. 1.

4. See especially the excerpts from Khrushchev's report to the Twentieth Party Congress, February 14, 1956, in *Documents on American Foreign Relations, 1956*, pp. 180-196.

5. *Department of State Bulletin*, v. 36 (January 21, 1957), pp. 83-87; *Documents on American Foreign Relations, 1957*, no. 53. See further section 4, below.

6. Same as note 3.

7. Same as note 1.

8. *New York Times*, January 17, 1957; excerpts in *Documents on American Foreign Relations, 1957*, no. 2.

9. *Department of State Bulletin*, v. 36 (May 6, 1957), pp. 715-719; *Documents on American Foreign Relations, 1957*, no. 6.

10. Dean Acheson, "Foreign Policy and Presidential Moralism," *The Reporter*, v. 16, no. 9 (May 2, 1957), p. 14.

11. *Mutual Security Appropriations for 1957: Hearings before the Subcommittee of the Committee on Appropriations, House of Representatives*, 85th Cong., 1st Sess. (Washington: G.P.O., 1957), p. 120.

12. Joint statement, February 28, in *Department of State Bulletin*, v. 36 (March 18, 1957), pp. 438-439; *Documents on American Foreign Relations, 1957*, no. 24.

13. *Department of State Bulletin*, v. 36 (April 8, 1957), pp. 561-562; *Documents on American Foreign Relations, 1957*, no. 22.

CHAPTER TWO

FOREIGN POLICY IN WASHINGTON

IT HAS already been suggested that the international diplomatic business of early 1957 fell into two broad, overlapping categories, one concerned with the emergency situation created by the events of late 1956, the other with long-range policy adjustments looking to the period ahead. This distinction is especially evident in the foreign policy actions of the United States Government during these months when the international situation was gradually becoming stabilized and settling back into the familiar pattern of "competitive coexistence." On the level of emergency action, the administration found it necessary to propose to Congress with all urgency a special resolution on the Middle East, designed to deter any Communist aggression against that area. Not until congressional action in this matter had been completed in early March did attention focus with any regularity on more routine issues and on forward planning in such fields as national defense, mutual security, and foreign economic policy.

It has also been hinted that there was a considerable difference in the character of Washington's response to these two different types of demands. Despite some grumbling and delay on the part of the Democratic-controlled Eighty-Fifth Congress, the administration's rather drastic proposals for the Middle East were eventually approved in a form that appears to have been reasonably satisfactory to the President and the Secretary of State. The range of positive security commitments undertaken by the United States, already embracing forty-two separate governments over and beyond the general commitment embodied in the Charter of the United Nations, was thus extended into a new and highly vulnerable area whose precise geographical limits no one in authority was willing to define. But this readiness to assume new international responsibilities was wholly confined to the special circumstances existing in the Middle East. The much more modest proposals of the administration in other fields encountered a stubbornness of congressional resistance that went far to blunt their potential impact and in some cases suggested a reluctance to carry out responsibilities already undertaken. The administration itself, moreover, was engaged in a continuing review of its defense and international programs with a view to effecting economies wherever possible. The net result was that many of the existing weaknesses in the national position vis-à-vis the Soviet Union remained substantially unremedied despite the new commitment in the Middle East and despite an unusual volume of official admonitions about the need to maintain a strong over-all posture in the United States and throughout the free world.

4. ENACTING THE MIDDLE EAST RESOLUTION

The explanation of this rather uneven performance lies deep in a national outlook which, though wholeheartedly opposed to the U.S.S.R. and Communism, as a rule was only intermittently concerned about the strength and welfare of the non-Communist world. American opinion had never fully absorbed the notion that the best hope of combating world Communism successfully in the long run lay in strengthening Communism's potential victims abroad. Policies directly aimed at foiling Communist designs—nonrecognition of Communist China, limitation of trade with the Soviet bloc, liberation of the Eastern European satellite countries—were more easily understood and therefore more popular than those aimed merely at building up the power of resistance of allied and neutral states. The "political warning system" or network of security pacts that now ringed the

Communist borders in Europe, the Far East, and Southern Asia had been constructed with general if not always enthusiastic public support, largely because it was presented as a method of frustrating Communist aims. Even more acceptable, since it depended less on the cooperation of other governments, had been the policy embodied in the Joint Congressional Resolution of January 1955 whereby the United States, with the endorsement of an overwhelming congressional majority, had unilaterally announced its determination to fight if necessary to protect Formosa (Taiwan) and the Pescadores Islands against armed attack by the Chinese Communists.[1]

In the light of these preferences, it is not surprising that the similar resolution on the Middle East which was enacted early in 1957 should have turned out to be one of the more successful examples of collaboration between Congress and the executive, described by President Eisenhower (September 3) as an instance of "the legislative process at its best." In making this comment Mr. Eisenhower did not overlook the fact that the eventual acceptance of what had come to be known as the "Eisenhower Doctrine" had been achieved only at the cost of considerable disputation, substantial modification of the administration's original plans, and a series of delays which were at least commensurate with the measure's importance as a new departure in American foreign relations.

The essential purpose behind the draft resolution which the administration had determined to lay before Congress at the beginning of January was succinctly stated by Secretary Dulles: "to deter Communist armed aggression in the Middle East area" by removing any doubt that an armed Communist attack there would be "met, if need be, by the armed forces of the United States." With such an intention, expressed in such clear and unequivocal terms, not many members of Congress would have been inclined to quarrel. Resistance to Communist aggression in practically any part of the world was a settled principle of United States foreign policy, embodied in various unilateral policy pronouncements as well as bilateral and multilateral security pacts.

There was, however, considerable doubt in Congress about the form, substance, and timeliness of the specific measure now proposed to it. Such reservations were particularly strong in the Senate, where the matter remained under consideration for two full months in spite of Secretary Dulles' appeals for speed and his intimations (January 24 and 25) that without prompt action the Middle East might soon be lost "in a great and maximum disaster," involving "the inevitability of a world war" which the free world might or might not be able to win.

The reasons for this congressional hesitation lay partly in domestic politics (House and Senate and their interested committees were controlled by Democratic legislators who acknowledged no automatic obligation to follow the administration's lead) but more importantly in the extreme complexity and uncertainty of the Middle Eastern situation itself. That conditions in that area remained dangerously explosive was apparent to everyone. But that there was an imminent danger of Communist armed aggression, as the administration appeared to suggest, was not so clear, even to those who accepted the administration view that the recent Anglo-French debacle had created a "power vacuum" in the region. To many observers it seemed that the really pressing problems in the Middle East were more localized in character and only indirectly related to Communism. Most of the troubles of the area in recent years could be traced to the unbridled nationalism and xenophobia which had secured such a hold on Egypt and various other Muslim countries. These were the forces that had precipitated the conflicts over the Anglo-Iranian Oil Company and the Suez Canal as well as the perennial strife between Israel and the neighboring Arab states.

Admittedly these conditions had proved highly advantageous to the Soviet Union, whose actions throughout the last two years (and especially during the last two months) had shown a determination fully to exploit the weaknesses of the situation and the credulity of the Arab masses. But did this mean that the Soviet Union, or some other Communist state, was now considering armed aggression in the Middle

East? Outside of the American administration, most observers found it unlikely. Communist governments were not generally in the habit of resorting to armed attack when they saw a chance of gaining their objectives by other methods. Why should they risk an armed showdown when they already had good footholds in Egypt and Syria and when the current trend of events throughout the Arab world seemed so favorable to them? If further Soviet gains were to be forestalled, these observers reasoned, the important thing was to try to remedy the underlying conditions that facilitated Soviet penetration—to ease the bitterness of the Arab-Israeli conflict and to ameliorate the depressed economic conditions so prevalent in many parts of the Middle East.

A consciousness of these wider factors was undoubtedly responsible for the fact that the administration proposal, when formally presented to Congress in a special presidential message of January 5,[2] was not confined to direct safeguards against Communist aggression but was also addressed to at least some aspects of the local situation which were considered specially to invite Communist advances. As anticipated, the heart of the administration's draft resolution [3] involved a congressional authorization to the President "to employ the Armed Forces of the United States as he deems necessary to secure and protect the territorial integrity and political independence of any . . . nation or group of nations [in the general area of the Middle East] requesting such aid against overt armed aggression from any nation controlled by international communism." But beyond this the President also sought authority (1) "to cooperate with and assist any nation or group of nations in the general area of the Middle East in the development of economic strength dedicated to the maintenance of national independence"; (2) "to undertake military assistance programs with any nation or group of nations of that area desiring such assistance"; and (3) to utilize for these purposes up to $200 million in Mutual Security funds already appropriated—the expectation being that further installments of $200 million would be requested for use in each of the next two fiscal years. The authority thus requested was to be exercised with due regard for

United Nations obligations, and was to be surrendered when
the President determined that peace and security in the area
were "reasonably assured."

Despite this somewhat broadened focus, the administration in its attempt to "sell" the program continued to dwell
almost exclusively on the threat of Communist aggression.
After its recent setback in Hungary, the President explained
in his message, "international Communism needs and it seeks
a recognizable success." The greatest risk in the present situation, he felt, was "that ambitious despots may miscalculate."
The United Nations, Mr. Eisenhower declared, "cannot be a
wholly dependable protector of freedom when the ambitions
of the Soviet Union are involved." (Although he made no
mention of the Baghdad Pact, the President apparently took
for granted that it too would be incapable of deterring
Soviet aggression in the Middle East, especially at a time
when its strongest member, the United Kingdom, had been
virtually ostracized by its own allies as a result of the attack
on Egypt.) Under these circumstances, said the President, a
greater responsibility devolved upon the United States "to
make more evident its willingness to support the independence of the freedom-loving nations of the area."

To substantiate the claim that there was a pressing danger
to the area from international Communism, Secretary Dulles
in a series of appearances before the House Foreign Affairs
Committee and the Senate Foreign Relations and Armed
Services committees [4] called special attention to the financial
and economic difficulties besetting some of the Middle Eastern countries as a result of a loss of oil revenues, the inevitable result of Egypt's closure of the Suez Canal and the
sabotage of the oil pipelines across Syria. The result, Mr.
Dulles said (January 14), had been to convince the Communist rulers "that a great victory is almost within their grasp."
We ourselves, he went on, were thus confronted with "the
most serious threat we have faced over the past ten years."
On January 24 Mr. Dulles cited "desperate" appeals from
Iran, Iraq, Turkey, and Pakistan in which those countries
were said not only to have sought assurances of aid in case
of a Soviet attack but to have suggested the possibility that

they might collapse if aid was not forthcoming. Admittedly the reaction of these particular Middle Eastern states, which were already aligned with the West through the Baghdad Pact, was markedly different from that of some other governments of the area. Led by Syria and (at least unofficially) by Egypt, the neutralist elements in the Arab world had denounced the new American "doctrine" no less vehemently than did the U.S.S.R. itself. (See further section 13.)

Under such circumstances, administration representations failed to carry complete conviction to the interested members of Congress. Reporting the administration resolution without amendment on January 26, the House Foreign Affairs Committee expressed the opinion that Secretary Dulles had failed to make his point about the imminence of Communist aggression. In the two Senate committees, the proposal faced a more detailed and critical scrutiny in which its constitutional as well as its substantive aspects were destined to come under severe examination. Several Democratic Senators were plainly incensed at what to them appeared the alarmist tone of administration pronouncements, only two months after Mr. Eisenhower had been reelected on the general understanding that all was well with the national foreign relations. There was considerable criticism of Secretary Dulles' past handling of Middle Eastern affairs, and attempts were made to trace all recent difficulties back to his refusal of funds for the building of Egypt's Aswan High Dam in July 1956. The tone of the exchanges in the committee room occasionally became so sharp that some Republicans expressed fears for the future of bipartisanship in foreign policy. Plainly the Democrats were in no mood to follow the President's leadership in the same measure as they had done in 1955 and 1956, and the battle for the Middle East resolution was not to be won until the administration had submitted to modification of its draft in a number of important respects.

On the constitutional side, the most serious question raised had to do with the President's request that he be "authorized" to take the various steps enumerated in the draft resolution, including the employment of the national armed forces. Although similar language had appeared in the Formosa resolution of 1955, the view was widely held that authority to employ the armed forces under the circumstances in question was already inherent in the powers of the presidency, and that a specific authorization would merely shift to Congress a responsibility that properly belonged to the executive branch. Rather than give the President the "blank check" he was felt to be requesting, various influential Senators favored the substitution of some kind of congressional declaration which would merely affirm the interest of the United States in the safety of the Middle East and its willingness to use its armed forces, if necessary, to preserve the independence and integrity of the states in that area. Eventually the key section of the administration draft was rephrased as follows: [5]

". . . Furthermore, the United States regards as vital to the national interest and world peace the preservation of the independence and integrity of the nations of the Middle East. To this end, if the President determines the necessity thereof, the United States is prepared to use armed forces to assist any such nation or group of nations requesting assistance against armed aggression from any country controlled by international communism: *Provided*, that such employment shall be consonant with the treaty obligations of the United States and with the Constitution of the United States."

In addition, Congress stipulated in its final draft that the resolution as a whole could be terminated at any time by a concurrent resolution of the two houses.

Aside from politics and constitutional qualms, the resistance aroused by Mr. Eisenhower's original formula reflected considerable uncertainty about the administration's concrete intentions in the Middle East and their relation to other aspects of United States foreign policy. What, more specifically, was the real purpose of a plan which had been developed in obvious haste, bore no traces of consultation with allied governments, had apparently not been cleared through the National Security Council, and evidently envisaged the possibility of military action independently of either NATO or the United Nations? What precise countries were included in the vague term "Middle East," and against what nations "controlled by international communism" were they to be protected? (The State Department conceded that no nation within the area was currently so controlled, despite what appeared to be considerable Communist influence in such countries as Egypt, Syria, and Jordan.) Above all, what action would be taken by the United States in case an "overt armed aggression" actually occurred? There were no substantial American ground forces in or near the area—only a battalion of Marines attached to the atomically equipped Sixth Fleet in the Mediterranean. Would this be a case for "massive retaliation" against Moscow, or were we setting out to defend the Middle East with some of the new tactical atomic weapons of which there had been so much talk in recent months? Asked about this latter possibility at his January 23 news conference, the President replied that the question was hypothetical: "I don't know what we would do and I wouldn't guess on it at all."

An equal vagueness surrounded the military and economic assistance features of the administration program. Moved by considerations of economy as well as logic, a good many congressmen reasoned that provisions relating to foreign aid were wholly superfluous in a resolution whose proclaimed purpose was to erect a "stop sign" before the Russians. The simplest procedure, they felt, would be either to omit such provisions entirely or to reserve them for later consideration in connection with the regular Mutual Security enactments. But to this expedient the administration altogether refused to agree. Elimination of the economic and military assistance provisions, wrote the President in a special appeal to Senate minority leader William F. Knowland on March 2, "would gravely impair our ability to help these nations preserve their independence." The resolution, he now emphasized, was "directed against two dangers, direct armed aggression and indirect subversion. To counter one and not the other would destroy both efforts." It was not our intention to create the impression "that our country wants only to wage peace in terms of war." But aside from the fact that most of the $200 million requested immediately would go for economic rather than military assistance, few details were offered as to what kind of aid would be provided, and to whom. Once the resolution was adopted, it was planned to send a special survey mission to the Middle East under the leadership of former Democratic Congressman James P. Richards, whose task it would be to gauge local reactions to the plan and explore the needs of individual countries. "The only way I can find out exactly how to spend the $200 million," said the President on January 23, ". . . would be through the medium of the Richards mission. . . ."

Amid so many uncertainties, even a Republican-controlled Congress might have proceeded with caution. Although the House approved the administration text by a substantial majority on January 30, it was another five weeks before a heavily modified text came to a vote in the Senate. In the meantime new delaying factors had emerged in the controversy over Israel's continued occupation of territory on the Egyptian side of the armistice demarcation line, which had raised a possibility, unpalatable to many Senators, that the United States might join in recommending United Nations economic sanctions against Israel (cf. section 12). By the time this cloud had blown over, most Senators of both parties had concluded that there was no longer any reasonable alternative to accepting the essentials of the administration plan. Some prominent Democrats, led by former President Truman, had urged approval of the resolution from the first; others were reaching the conclusion that even if approval was undesirable, it would probably do less harm than a repudiation of the President before the eyes of the entire world. Besides, the administration had long ago signified its acceptance of the major amendments introduced as a result of discussion in the Senate committees.

On March 5, therefore, two months to the day from the President's original message, the Senate adopted its own text of the resolution by a vote of 72 to 19, the opposition being made up of liberal and Southern Democrats together with three Republicans. Apart from the avoidance of the term "authorize," the principal departures from the administration version lay in the imposition of certain restrictions on the use of the military and economic aid funds and in the addition of a new section calling for continued assistance to the United Nations Emergency Force in the Middle East, "with a view to maintaining the truce in that region." This revised text [5] was promptly approved by the House and on March 9 was signed by the President, with the optimistic comment that it marked "an important forward step in the development of friendly relations between the United States and the Middle East area," offered "a further demonstration of the will of the American people to preserve peace and freedom in the world," and would "increase the administration's capabilities to contribute to reducing the Communist danger in the Middle East and to strengthening the general stability of the area." Ambassador Richards, the President added, would be leaving promptly for the Middle East as the first step in carrying out the policies set forth in the resolution.

The international impact of the "Eisenhower Doctrine" and the achievements of the Richards mission will be examined in a subsequent chapter (see section 13). In domestic terms, and perhaps in broad international terms as well, the resolution was significant more for its general tendency than for the detailed provisions that had been so arduously debated in Washington. The essential point was that the United States was now consciously extending its security commitments into a vast new area of the globe and explicitly affirming its readiness to fight, if necessary, to keep that area from going Communist as the result of military aggression. Whether or not the method had been ideally suited to conditions in the area, this country had deliberately entered whatever "power vacuum" existed there and in so doing had assumed an unequivocal obligation to find ways of helping the Middle Eastern countries to maintain their independence. Not many weeks were to pass before Washington would feel called upon to take decisive action within the framework of the Middle East resolution to counter a clear threat to the independence of Jordan, a country that stood in no immediate danger of Communist aggression but one whose delicate internal situation had occasioned special concern at the time the program was being developed.

Though strictly unilateral in form, the resolution thus ranked in significance with such earlier acts of United States policy as the conclusion of the Rio Pact, the North Atlantic Treaty, and the Southeast Asia Mutual Defense Treaty. As Secretary Dulles remarked on one occasion to the Senate committees, the network of American security commitments was little by little being extended all around the Communist periphery:

"Gradually one part of the world after another is being brought into it, and perhaps we may end up with a, what you might call, universal doctrine reflected by multilateral treaties or multilateral world-wide authority from the Congress."

5. DEFENSE AND THE BATTLE OF THE BUDGET

If the dominant aim of American world policy was to preserve the peace by making it clear that Communist armed aggression would be "met, if need be, by the armed forces of the United States," its effectiveness would naturally depend on the availability of such military forces as would in fact be capable of dealing with any Communist attack that might occur. It is true that armed attack, or the threat of it, was not the only line of action available to the Communist rulers in advancing their program. One of the leading themes of the Twentieth Soviet Party Congress in 1956 had been the alleged possibility that Communism might eventually triumph around the world without the necessity of fighting at all. Such gains as the Communists had secured in recent years had been won mainly by shrewd and unscrupulous diplomacy rather than by the direct use of military force. Recent experience abundantly testified that it was not enough to deter outright attack; other avenues of Communist expansion had to be watched as well. Still, force and the threat of force remained a formidable element in the Communist armory, one that the United States could not safely disregard and to which in practice it had invariably given priority attention.

A certain amount of misgiving about the capacity of the

American armed forces to discharge the comprehensive mission assigned to them was apparent in the debates that preceded the adoption of the Middle East resolution. To be sure, President Eisenhower had given assurance in his State of the Union Message [6] that the United States had "made great strides in assuring a modern defense, so armed in new weapons, so deployed, so equipped, that today our security force is the most powerful in our peacetime history," able both to "punish heavily any enemy who undertakes to attack us" and to serve as "a major deterrent to war." Yet there were times when the President himself appeared to feel that the present situation in the defense establishment left a good deal to be desired. Conceding at his news conference on February 6 that the national territory of the United States itself had "never been more vulnerable to Soviet attack than now," General Eisenhower suggested nevertheless that "relatively" we were "in as good a position as we have ever been in time of peace." "I don't believe," he said, "that that position by any manner of means is deteriorating at the rate that some people would have you think."

Whether well-founded or not, the uneasiness prevailing in some American quarters was a natural reaction to the state of affairs which had developed in the world since the invention of nuclear weapons and more particularly since the development of atomic and hydrogen bombs by the U.S.S.R. However powerful the forces of the United States and its allies, no one could be completely comfortable in the knowledge that the Soviet Union was also in possession of means for visiting atomic destruction on objectives in Europe or even in the United States. Under the best of circumstances, Air Force Secretary Donald A. Quarles pointed out in a speech of January 7, 1957, "the military scheme of things in this air-atomic age" could only be described as one of "balanced terror."

"We must be prepared to stand firm and ready to strike back massively even though we are confronted by atomic weapons delivery systems, such as ballistic missiles, that could in a few short hours wreak vast devastation on our homeland. Our comfort, if it can be called comfort, is that the attacker could not himself escape destruction and so could not profit by pulling the trigger."

In milder language, President Eisenhower voiced a similar thought (February 6):

"The likelihood of any nation possessing these great weapons of massive destruction using them in attack grows less, I think, every year. I believe as their [the Russians'] understanding of them grows, then the less the chance that they would go on an adventure that brought these things into play, because, as I see it, any such operation today is just another way of committing suicide."

Given the appalling character of modern weapons, it was comforting to reflect that perhaps neither side would ever make use of them. Yet there was always the possibility that this assumption of mutual restraint might prove erroneous— that one side or the other might miscalculate its chances of survival and decide to take the risk of using its biggest weapons despite the possibility of retaliation by the enemy. The President's old friend Marshal G. K. Zhukov, the Soviet Defense Minister, went out of his way several times during early 1957 to express his disagreement with "the argument that because these weapons could destroy both sides if used there would be no sense in using them." Actually, said Marshal Zhukov (March 16),[7]

"atomic weapons are being introduced more and more to replace conventional weapons and will be introduced increasingly in the near future (unless they are banned), and in the event of a major armed conflict will inevitably be used as basic means of inflicting defeat. . . . We hold that the Soviet Armed Forces should be perfectly prepared both to defend our homeland and troops against atomic weapons and to make effective use of atomic and hydrogen weapons, and should inflict devastating counterblows on aggressors immediately if necessary. . . ."

Events, in Marshal Zhukov's view, had already outmoded the "naive" belief of "American imperialists . . . that in the event of war in Europe or Asia they will be able, as in the past, to sit it out across the ocean and escape devastating and destructive blows. . . . There is no nook or cranny in the world where an aggressor can hide now. The Soviet Air Force is able to inflict devastating blows against any opponent, no matter where he is or where he may hide."

Such statements, which a few years earlier might have been dismissed as pure bluff, now had to be taken seriously in view of the Russians' known progress in the field of nuclear weapons, military aviation, and particularly the development of guided and ballistic missiles, in which some observers believed the U.S.S.R. had already secured a lead over the United States. (On August 26 Moscow was actually to announce a successful test of the world's first "intercontinental ballistic rocket.") And even if there was an element of bluff in the Soviet contentions, this fact was not without its own significance in estimating the possible course of world events under conditions of "nuclear stalemate." The mere realization of the destructive power of "big" nuclear weapons, as President Eisenhower had pointed out, was itself a powerful deterrent to their use. He himself was plainly determined not to let them be used except in the last extremity. Was it not possible, however, that the Russians might feel somewhat less inhibited, if not in actually using their superweapons, at least in *threatening* to use them? In that case, they might be able to achieve by a mere gesture even more than they could hope to gain by an actual attack. Some hint of what this technique might be expected to accomplish was afforded by the recent Suez crisis, in which a Soviet reference to "rocket technique" had been followed almost immediately by Britain's agreement to a cease-fire. Although London stoutly denied that its decision had been influenced by Moscow's not very subtle threat, there was no doubt that the peoples of Europe were extremely reluctant to become the targets of Soviet missiles and for that reason might in future be even more hesitant to support policies opposed by Moscow. American deterrent power would be of little avail if it left the Soviets free to attain their ends by "atomic blackmail."

At all events, it seemed reasonable to expect that the Russians under presently foreseeable circumstances would take considerable pains to avoid the risk of a head-on military collision with the United States. General Alfred M. Gruenther, until recently NATO's Supreme Allied Commander in Europe, declared on February 28: "I am personally convinced that our deterrent power is now so great that there is never going to be a third world war—assuming we maintain that power." Defense Secretary Charles E. Wilson apparently shared this view. Our nuclear striking power, he suggested (May 8), had been the major factor in restraining Communist aggression in the past; and our armed forces were now equipped with nuclear weapons of such power and in such quantity "as to defy comprehension of the total effect." Admiral Radford likewise described the armed forces (February 25) as "adequate" for any war that might be touched off either by a surprise nuclear attack or by aggression against an ally. The preponderance of official opinion plainly regarded our overwhelming air-atomic capability as an effectual deterrent to Soviet attack for some time to come, no matter how powerful the forces on the other side.

Rather less reassuring was the openly divided state of official opinion on the related question of so-called limited wars, such as might be brought on not by all-out Soviet attack but by localized aggressions of the type that had occurred in past years in such places as Korea, Greece, Vietnam, and Malaya and might conceivably be destined to occur in the Middle East. The problems that could arise in this connection were lucidly expounded on June 30 by General Maxwell D. Taylor, the Army Chief of Staff, a vigorous critic of the alleged tendency to overconcentrate on the deterrence of all-out aggression:

"Because of the suicidal nature of a general nuclear war, it appears . . . increasingly unlikely that any nation will deliberately embark on such a war with its prospect of reciprocal annihilation. However, that does not necessarily mean that communism will renounce aggression as a tool of policy.

"Instead, while avoiding general war, it may incline toward local or limited aggression which thus appears to be an increasingly serious threat to world peace.

"This form of aggression, if not arrested, may lead to the erosion of the free world and to our loss, piecemeal, of that which we are pledged to defend. If resisted, it must be resisted promptly and successfully; otherwise it may spread to that general atomic war which it is our purpose to avoid."

Other critics, carrying their reasoning a step further, demanded that more attention be given to the prospect of "limited nuclear wars"—i.e., wars fought with smaller types of nuclear armament but without resort to the massively destructive weapons that both sides would presumably hesitate to use or have used against them. Noteworthy expositions of this viewpoint were a statement by retiring Atomic Energy Commissioner Thomas E. Murray (June 27) and a book on *Nuclear Weapons and Foreign Policy* prepared for the Council on Foreign Relations by Henry A. Kissinger.[8]

Despite the number of localized or "little wars" that had occurred since 1945, it was generally conceded that the United States had given far less attention to specific preparation for such contingencies than it had to preparation for all-out retaliation against an aggressor. The dominant view with regard to "little" wars had been epitomized in President Eisenhower's comment of December 15, 1954 that "If you could win a big one, you would certainly win a little one." "It seems logical that if we have the strength required for global war we could certainly meet any threat of lesser magnitude," was the more sophisticated formulation of Secretary Quarles (February 2, 1957); while General Nathan F. Twining, on taking over his responsibility as Chairman of the Joint Chiefs of Staff, gave assurance (August 14) that there was "no situation that we haven't got the stuff to handle." What these statements appeared to mean was that if confronted with a limited aggression the United States would not hesitate to draw on its stockpile of nuclear weapons as far as necessary, whether the aggressor had done so or not. United States military policy, Secretary Wilson declared (May 2), was based on "the use of atomic weapons in a major war, and of such atomic weapons as would be militarily feasible and usable in a smaller war, if such a war is forced upon us." "If we must become involved in a 'little war' to meet overt Communist aggression," said Secretary Quarles (February 2), "we should act decisively and with all necessary strength, using our best weapons if required. . . . I cannot believe that any atomic power would accept defeat while withholding its best weapons."

Originally motivated at least in part by economic considerations, this tendency to place maximum reliance on nuclear weapons was still occasionally defended on economic as well as military grounds. According to Secretary of the Army Wilber M. Brucker (May 7), "The comparative cost of atomic fighting power has declined to such an extent that the economics of the situation could force us to use it in our own defense in preference to high explosive weapons in many circumstances." Contrary to the expectations prevailing at the time the "new look" military program was originally formulated, however, the current pattern of American defense had not resulted in any spectacular economies. On the contrary, after a respite of a couple of years, defense expenditure was now once again on the rise. "The new and more powerful weapons which are being delivered into our Armed Forces in increasing quantities and varieties are much more costly to produce, operate, and maintain than the weapons they are replacing," the President explained in his Budget Message on January 16.[9] "Furthermore, we are now engaged in the development of a whole new family of even more advanced weapons for all the services. Large expenditures will be required to bring these weapons into use."

As the direct result of the increased costs of military "hardware," the Budget Message further disclosed, expenditure for military defense was expected to increase from $36 billion in the fiscal year 1957 to $38 billion in fiscal 1958; and an even larger amount ($38.5 billion) would be needed in new obligational authority or appropriations for the latter year. Regrettably, the President pointed out, the effect of these increases would be to reverse the downward trend in recent budgets and raise total budgetary expenditures ($71.8 billion) and new obligational authority ($73.3 billion) close to the levels obtaining when he first took office in 1953.

These increases in the budget for fiscal 1958, the President insisted, did not reflect any weakening in his convictions about the importance of strict economy in the military as well as in other fields:

". . . We must not delude ourselves that safety necessarily increases as expenditures for military research or forces in being go up. Indeed, beyond a wise and reasonable level, . . . money spent on arms may be money wasted on sterile metal or inflated costs, thereby weakening the very security and strength we seek."

In line with this concept, the new defense budget not only provided each of the three services with less than it thought needful, but accentuated still further the trend toward primary reliance on nuclear weapons and particularly on air-atomic retaliatory power. The maintenance of "ready nuclear-air-retaliatory forces so strong that they will deter a potential aggressor from initiating an attack" headed the President's list of basic military responsibilities. Among the innovations contemplated in this field were the gradual replacement of the B-36 bomber with the more powerful B-52, and the enhancement of Navy striking power through the addition of "new and modernized attack carriers, jet aircraft capable of higher speeds and higher altitudes, atomic submarines and guided missile ships." The ground forces were not excluded from the modernization trend. The Army was to be bolstered by the establishment of six "atomic support commands" for deployment abroad, principally in Europe. Armed with Honest John rockets and Corporal guided missiles, their main purpose would be "to furnish atomic firepower necessary to reinforce the defense capacity of ground forces."

In contrast to other recent budgets, the administration blueprint for fiscal 1958 contemplated no further reduction in the numerical strength of the armed forces, which had stood at 3.5 million at the end of 1953, was now down to 2,790,954, but was to be slightly increased to 2.8 million. The Army, with personnel stationed in seventy-three countries overseas, would be stabilized for the time being at one million men, although a reorganization of the divisional structure would reduce the total number of divisions from nineteen to seventeen. The Air Force, though still the favored service in terms of appropriations, had been allotted substantially less money than it had requested and was being cut back from 133 wings to 128, with even further reductions in prospect. But its strength in heavy bombers, the prime instrument of "deterrent-retaliatory power," would not be affected; and the nonstop, round-the-world flight of three of the new B-52 bombers almost at the very time the budget was being submitted was hailed by the Air Force (January 18) as a demonstration of its "capability to drop a hydrogen bomb anywhere in the world."

Although some members of Congress voiced distinct uneasiness over the proposed restrictions on the growth of national air power and the relatively slow progress of the missile development program, a larger number were dismayed that the administration had not more to show for its economy efforts. Military expenditure was, after all, the largest item in the budget; and the submission of a spending budget of such dimensions, with no promise of tax reduction, had provoked loud outcries in every section of the two houses. The President himself had repeatedly cited the need for government economy and described the danger of inflation as "the principal threat to efficient functioning of a free enterprise system." His Secretary of the Treasury, George M. Humphrey, had said flatly on January 16 that the administration budget should be cut and that if the government could not reduce the "terrific" tax burden, "you will have a depression that will curl your hair." Outside the government, demands were heard for a budget cut of anywhere up to $8 billion, the greater part of which would clearly have to come out of defense, Mutual Security, and other international programs.

Though sympathetic in principle to the search for new ways of cutting expenditure, the President repeatedly expressed the opinion that it would be difficult to make substantial cuts in the current budget without impairing national security. He was not much impressed by the argument that large economies could be effected by better planning in the Pentagon and the elimination of competition among the three services. "Good defense is not cheap defense," he emphasized (May 14), adding that he earnestly believed the defense budget he had submitted "represents, in today's world, the proper dividing line between national danger on the one hand and excessive expenditure on the other." No really substantial reduction in defense costs would be attainable, he felt, until a sound agreement on the limitation of armaments was reached; and he several times (e.g., April 3) held out the hope of "some . . . amelioration in the tenseness of the foreign situation" which would permit us to "save some money" in the future even if not this year.

Only moderately impressed by these allusions, the House Appropriations Committee proceeded to trim almost $2.6 billion from the appropriation requested for the Defense Department, ending up with a figure somewhat below the $34.6 billion appropriated the year before. Admitting that the U.S.S.R. was closing the gap in military strength and could conceivably plunge the country into war, the committee nevertheless expressed the view (May 21) that "the nature and extent of a military threat against the United States and its allies appears, in certain respects, to have abated." The administration, unable to share this view, promptly appealed for restoration of about half the reductions, pointing out that the remainder represented only paper savings which would not substantially affect national security in any case. Very little of the money was restored, however. The final appropriation bill as passed by both houses and approved on August 2 carried a total of only $33,759,850,000 to maintain the three services through the new fiscal year already under way.

But even before the appropriation process was completed, the administration on its own initiative had undertaken a far more drastic economy drive which appeared likely to have startling effects on the size and shape of American fighting power in the years ahead. The belated discovery was made at the Pentagon that the current level of expenditure on the armed forces had been seriously underestimated. Instead of $38 billion as predicted in January, expenditure in fiscal 1958 seemed likely to hit $40 billion or even more if present rates were maintained; by fiscal year 1959 it might be of the order of $42 billion. The official explanation of this "unplanned upsurge" stressed such factors as the high cost of the missile development program and the general upward movement of prices and wages. Its effect was to confront the administration with the choice of cutting expenditure drastically or allowing the budget to be thrown out of balance and breaching the statutory limit on the national debt. Apparently without hesitation, the administration vigorously embraced the former alternative. Early in July the word went out to all Federal agencies to try to hold expenditures to the level of the fiscal year just past. Secretary Wilson, who had said in April that "not one dollar" could be safely trimmed from the Defense budget, now announced that expenditure in his department would have to be held strictly to $38 billion, not only in fiscal 1958 but in fiscal 1959 as well. If this ceiling conflicted with current military programs, it was evidently the latter that would have to give way.

A sweeping reduction in manpower was the first requisite. In two directives of July 16 and September 19, Secretary Wilson ordered a reduction of 200,000 men in the active armed forces, the bulk of it to be carried out by mid-1958. The brunt of the reduction would be borne by the Army, as is shown by the following figures giving authorized strength of the individual services before and after the proposed cuts (actual strength being a bit lower):

	Before	After
Army	1,000,000	900,000
Air Force	925,000	875,000
Navy	675,000	645,000
Marine Corps	200,000	180,000
	2,800,000	2,600,000

According to Secretary Wilson, there was a good prospect that it might be necessary to decree a third cut which would reduce the total of men under arms to 2,500,000 by fiscal year 1959. This happened to be the precise figure that had been suggested to the Russians as a target for *mutual*, rather than unilateral, reductions in a first-stage disarmament agreement (see section 11). Thus far, however, the Pentagon had no indication that the U.S.S.R. had made any reductions in its own forces below their estimated 1956 level of 3,600,000 to 4,000,000.

These reductions and the accompanying financial readjustments fell with a crushing impact throughout the military establishment. Contracts for new production were pigeonholed; research on missiles and other new weapons was cut back and various development projects were abandoned, despite lack of progress in the disarmament talks and despite the new Soviet claim to have tested a long-range "ballistic rocket." The Navy, relying more and more on its new supercarriers and atomic-powered submarines, prepared to place ninety-six vessels in "mothballs," among them the last of its active battleships. The Air Force, still clinging to its strategic bomber strength, made plans to eliminate another five tactical wings, reducing the total to 123. But it was in the Army that the most drastic repercussions were felt. From nineteen divisions at the beginning of 1957, the Army would now have to be down to fifteen by the middle of 1958. One and more probably two of the proposed "atomic support commands" (now called "missile commands" because of their capability for either atomic or nonatomic warfare) would have to be eliminated, together with fifteen to twenty antiaircraft battalions and other units at home and abroad.

These reductions were presumably to be carried out "without impairment of our national security" and "without materially affecting our deployments of major combat units abroad." As in the past, an increase in operating efficiency was supposed to compensate for each new reduction in numbers. President Eisenhower said on September 3, a month before Sputnik I, that he had "come to believe that a very fine and adequate defense for the United States can at present prices be sustained . . . with an expenditure program, if it can be planned in advance, at about $38 billion." Above that level, he said, one got into the realm of things that were "unnecessary"; below it, into "an area of unacceptable risk." But even if these retrenchments did not lessen the nation's aggregate fighting power, they plainly tended to tie it down more than ever to certain predetermined lines, among which the capability for massive air-nuclear retaliation remained the most prominent. A capacity to participate in "little" wars, particularly of the nonatomic variety, would certainly not be enhanced by taking 100,000 men from the Army and another 20,000 from the Marine Corps.

These reductions also appeared likely to accentuate the long-term trend toward withdrawing American forces from overseas positions, leaving the job of local defense mainly to allied contingents while concentrating on the maintenance of a central striking force based largely in the United States. Secretary Dulles had revealed as early as May 29 that the whole problem of overseas bases and forces had been under official scrutiny in order to determine whether there were not "excesses" which could be "pared down without in any way injuring and, perhaps in the process increasing, the defensive value of those bases for the free world." In June came an agreement with Japan to reduce substantially the size of the American forces in that country and withdraw promptly all United States ground combat forces (see section 19). Immediately there were rumors that similar withdrawals would be effected in Europe. Secretary Dulles and the President conceded that the American forces assigned to NATO would probably be "streamlined," though not "reduced"; and Secretary Wilson on June 27 predicted "a real hard push all around the world to bring the boys home if they are not too busy where they are." By August 15 Mr. Wilson was talking of a reduction of as much as 10 percent in personnel in Europe, although it appeared that no withdrawal of complete units was contemplated.

The long-range prospect regarding overseas deployments would presumably depend in large measure on the type of strategic doctrine that might eventually be evolved to fit the new $38 billion expenditure ceiling. But Washington in the weeks before the first Soviet Sputnik seemed farther than usual from a coherent, generally accepted strategic doctrine. Some said that the whole problem of "big" versus "little" wars was being reexamined, and that improved preparedness for "limited" atomic war was at last in prospect, thanks partly to the wide range of small atomic weapons now available. "Operation Plumb Bob," the 1957 series of atomic weapons tests in the Nevada desert, had been largely focused on the development of smaller weapons with reduced fallout; and Secretary Dulles now contributed an article to *Foreign Affairs* [10] which seemed to be looking beyond "massive retaliation" to a time when smaller nuclear weapons might have a decisive role to play. But other authorities, including Admiral Radford and Secretary Wilson, denied that any "new look" was in progress at the moment. General Twining, Admiral Radford's successor, reiterated in his first speech as Chairman of the Joint Chiefs of Staff that the United States was determined to use its atomic retaliatory power if necessary. Thanks to this power, he added, "we can devastate their country even if they succeed with a surprise attack."

This capability might offer rather cold comfort to the tens of millions of Americans who, it was authoritatively estimated, might be killed overnight in the event that such a surprise attack occurred. Their chances of survival in such an eventuality would not be greatly improved by congressional cuts in the annual civil defense appropriation, or by the slowdown imposed for economy reasons in the development of up-to-date antiaircraft defense systems for American cities. The main hope appeared to be that General Twining's calculations were right and that the prospect of nuclear retaliation would continue to prevent a Soviet attack from taking place. Rather than venture on a course that might bring the American air-atomic capability into play, the Communists would perhaps find it better to continue searching out ways of advancing their influence short of total war—possibly by limited, local aggressions, certainly by subversion, economic and political penetration, and exploitation of the numerous weaknesses of the free world. For that reason it still seemed reasonable to suppose that the really significant East-West battles of the next few years, like those of the past four, would be fought in the economic and political rather than the military arena.

6. AMERICA AND THE WORLD ECONOMY

Inherent in the approach of the United States Government to world affairs was the view that neither in the military nor in the economic and political fields could the United States be considered as engaged in an individual, single combat with the Soviet Union or the forces of international Communism. American statesmen were constantly pointing out that in resisting Communist expansionism this country was acting as a partner, or at most a trustee, of many other nations which were felt to be equally concerned with the preservation of a free way of life. "So long as collective security depends almost wholly upon the deterrent of retaliatory power and the ability to wreak great destruction upon an aggressor nation," wrote Secretary Dulles in the *Foreign Affairs* article just cited,[10] "there has to be almost sole dependence upon the United States. No other nation can afford the cost of maintaining adequate deterrent power." But this the Secretary evidently regarded as a temporary condition. Though responsibility happened at the moment to rest mainly on the United States, the objective was not merely the defense of the United States but the common defense of the free world in accordance with the principles of collective security. The same was true in all fields of common endeavor, Mr. Dulles pursued. "Nations, like individuals, cannot live to themselves alone. . . . We realize that peace and prosperity for one requires, in the long run, that all should have the opportunity to pursue happiness. We see the need for more vital domestic forces in all free lands, to resist Communist subversion or attack."

In the realm of economics, this common struggle to reverse the Communist tide had two main aspects, one direct and the other indirect, one negative and the other positive. The direct aspect consisted in the attempt to deprive the Communist world of certain material advantages which could be obtained only through trade with non-Communist areas—particularly the opportunity to build up its military potential through the purchase of those materials and industrial goods which were classified in the West as "strategic." The indirect but more positive aspect concerned the attempt to strengthen the economic system of the non-Communist world through a more effectual allocation of resources and a better balanced and expanding exchange of goods and services—one that would both demonstrate the superiority of non-Communist economic methods and develop the necessary economic base for an effective military defense and a flourishing political life.

For some years past the attempt to deny strategic goods to the Communist bloc had been carried on primarily through a system of agreed controls which the Western nations had undertaken to impose on their own exports to Communist destinations. These controls, however, had been growing more difficult to maintain ever since the death of Stalin and the adoption of "peaceful coexistence" as the dominant theme of Communist world policy. As early as 1954, the list of strategic commodities banned for export to the Soviet Union and its European satellites had been materially shortened, although the more extensive list of items denied to Communist China as a result of its participation in the Korean war still remained fully in effect. A pronounced growth in East-West trade had followed; from 1955 to 1956 the increase for the countries most closely associated with the United States was of the order of 25 percent. But trade with the Communist world still represented only a small proportion of total Western trade, and Western businessmen as well as the Communist governments continued to urge that the restrictions be further relaxed. By 1957, advocates of relaxation were concentrating on the "China list" and urging that trade with Communist China (as well as other Communist areas in the Far East) be liberalized to at least the same extent as trade with Eastern Europe.

True to its established role as the leading opponent of Chinese Communist aims, the United States Government looked with marked disfavor on these projects. Nevertheless it agreed early in 1957 to negotiate a partial relaxation of controls in view of the prospect that otherwise Great Britain and probably other allied governments would act unilaterally. Although the fifteen-nation committee concerned with these matters duly assembled in Paris in May 1957, no agreement could be reached on the extent of the relaxation, and on May 30 Great Britain announced that it would act on its own responsibility and eliminate the "China differential" altogether in its own trade with the Communist nations. While France, West Germany, Italy, Japan, and other allies prepared to follow the British example, the State Department declared itself "most disappointed" and stressed that so far as the United States was concerned, there would be no change in the "total embargo" on trade with Communist China which this country had imposed in 1950.[11] Yet even in the United States this policy was being maintained with less assurance than in the past. President Eisenhower himself expressed a belief (June 5) that "trade, in the long run, cannot be stopped." United States trade with Communist Eastern Europe, though confined to nonstrategic items, was meanwhile beginning to increase significantly for the first time in a decade, partly though not entirely as the result of relief shipments to Hungary and liberalized economic relations with the new government in Poland (cf. section 10).

Complex and controversial though it often appeared, the problem of economic relations with the Communist world was simplicity itself compared with the manifold problems of economic relations among the non-Communist nations. So far as the United States was concerned, the underlying objective was plain enough, and President Eisenhower recalled it once again in his State of the Union Message: "With other free nations, we should vigorously prosecute measures that will promote mutual strength, prosperity and welfare within the free world." Yet the possible means to this end were so various, their ramifications and interrelations so complex, and the play of conflicting interests so intense that even those most closely concerned found difficulty in maintaining a comprehensive view of the issues at stake. Only with the aid of drastic simplification can we attempt to summarize them within the limits of this chapter.

The fundamental economic reality about the non-Communist world was the fact that while its aggregate wealth and resources greatly surpassed those of the Communist bloc, the distribution of this wealth was extremely uneven and bore little or no relation to the requirements of the East-West struggle. A very large part of the free world's economic strength was concentrated in North America, principally in the United States; whereas the countries that rimmed the Communist empire in Europe and Asia were on the whole much less favorably situated. Few of them could maintain and equip entirely by their own efforts the armed forces that were thought necessary to guard against the possibility of Communist aggression, even at a time when the main defense of the free world was believed to lie in the deterrent of American retaliatory power. Many of these nations, particularly in Asia, had difficulty in assuring even the minimal living standards and the modest expectations of improvement which were regarded as indispensable if internal stability was to be maintained and opportunities for Communist agitation and subversion kept within safe limits.

These conditions, though inconvenient and even dangerous in some respects, were not susceptible of any drastic revision. Their unfavorable features, for the most part, could be alleviated only gradually under the best of circumstances. The problem confronting the free world in the postwar years (in so far as the individual free world countries recognized that they were confronting a common problem) was not one of effecting a drastic redistribution of wealth and power, but of trying to shape the development of international economic life from year to year in such a way that the more acute contrasts would be softened and the most serious deficiencies remedied before they could cause trouble. Of necessity, the main instruments of this effort were the normal mechanisms of international trade and investment. But since these mechanisms did not always operate with sufficient speed or discrimination, there had been many instances in which governments and international institutions had felt called upon to intervene directly in the interest of obtaining prompter and more favorable results.

As the custodian of the world's most richly developed national economy, the United States stood at the center of these processes and often exerted a decisive influence upon the way they operated. Essentially, the problem was one of mutual adjustment between stronger and weaker economic systems. Everyone needed American products—capital equipment, military equipment, consumer items, foodstuffs, or all four together. America, with some few exceptions, felt much less need of the things they had to offer in return. The task of working out arrangements for satisfying these outside needs, keeping the American economy itself in operation at a high level, and maintaining some kind of compensatory flow of goods and services to the United States was a permanent preoccupation of free world economic statesmanship. One measure of its success was the state of the so-called "dollar gap," the term applied to the over-all deficit frequently incurred by other nations in their current transactions with the United States. On paper, at least, the "dollar gap" had disappeared as long ago as 1954, and foreign countries had been able during the interval to add substantially to their reserves of gold and dollars. But in the troubled winter of 1956–57 the "dollar gap" had reopened, a development which at least one trained economist, Hugh Gaitskell of the British Labor party, described on September 17 as potentially more serious than anything that had been happening in the Middle East.

The nominal closure of the "dollar gap" in 1954–56 did not mean that the United States had suddenly begun buying as much from other countries as it sold or otherwise provided to them. American imports of goods and services, though large and increasing, still paid only a part of the bill for American exports. In 1956 such imports amounted altogether to about $19.8 billion, compared to civilian exports of $23.3 billion plus military exports (mainly financed by grant aid) totaling another $2 billion or more. It was a standing objective of United States foreign economic policy to raise the level of imports still further (to the extent, at any rate, that this could be done without injuring American enterprises) and also to increase the volume of new United States capital invested abroad, which likewise played a part in offsetting the export total and in 1956 was reckoned at perhaps $3.2 billion on a net basis.[12] Thus far, however, there had always been a balance which had to be made up mainly by direct governmental grants and credits. The total of such governmental payments by the United States for 1956 (including military aid) was just short of $4.9 billion.[13] For the twelve years 1945–57 it exceeded $62 billion.

It was this direct governmental assistance, in recent years dispensed mainly through the Mutual Security Program, that provided the indispensable supplement to other items in the American balance of payments and enabled the outside world to balance its accounts with the United States without foregoing the most necessary American goods and services. Furthermore, it was primarily through this program that the United States was able to bring its direct influence to bear in the free world's economic life and assist its allies and friends in meeting their most urgent needs on both the economic and military fronts. Military assistance in the form of weapons, equipment, and training; defense support assistance, enabling selected allies to maintain armed forces larger than they themselves could pay for; development assistance in the form of grants and loans for basic economic projects; technical assistance through bilateral programs and through the United Nations and the Organization of American States—these and a variety of lesser undertakings reflected Washington's conviction that the current state of the free world required a supplemental input of American resources over and beyond what was made available through normal economic processes.

It was President Eisenhower's frequently expressed conviction that although the Mutual Security Program was actually "the most misunderstood of any of the Federal Government's activities," our expenditures on it represented "one of the cheapest ways we have of insuring the position in the world we want to maintain" (March 13); that there were "no dollars today that are being spent more wisely for the future of American peace and prosperity than the dollars we put in foreign aid" (March 27); that the program did "more than any other, dollar for dollar, in securing the safety of our country and the peaceful lives of all of us" (May 21); and that it meant "more to our leadership in holding together the voluntary federation that must combat communism in the world than any other thing" (August 21). This personal evaluation was generally borne out by a number of independent studies of the program which had been commissioned by legislative and executive authorities and were carried out during the winter of 1956–57. Although their conclusions varied considerably in detail, all of them, as the President remarked on May 21 in submitting his formal recommendations for the next fiscal year,[14] agreed on two points: (1) "that both the military and economic elements of our mutual security programs are essential to the security of the American people and to world peace"; and (2) "that these programs will continue for some years to come to be indispensable to the attainment of our country's goals in the world."

However strongly grounded in experience and observation, this opinion proved to be in sharp conflict with the economizing mood of Congress and the country. "Foreign aid" had never been a popular concept. Its unpopularity in 1957 could be guessed from the attention given a current book revealingly entitled *The Great Giveaway*.[15] The submission of the President's budget with its $71.8 billion spending total provoked an immediate and widespread demand for cutbacks in a field which most people considered much less essential to the national security and welfare than an adequate military budget. Mainly for technical reasons, the President had planned to request a considerable increase in the Mutual Security appropriation for the fiscal year 1958—$4.4 billion, compared with less than $3.8 billion appropriated the year before. This proposal occasioned such an outcry that the administration itself reduced its estimates by a full half-billion dollars before submitting its detailed recommendations to Congress. Yet even this reduction was far too small to satisfy the economy advocates, Republican and Democratic. Ignoring a series of strong presidential statements on the unwisdom of further reductions, Congress in passing the annual Mutual Security authorization bill in mid-August cut out another half-billion and thus reduced the total to $3.4 billion. Despite further appeals from the President, Secretary Dulles, Admiral Radford, and others, new amputations occurred in the appropriation process, so that the administration was eventually left with a total of well under $2.8 billion ($2,768,760,000) in new money, plus $667,050,000 in reappropriated funds from prior years. Reductions of any such magnitude, Secretary Dulles had warned (August 19), would "challenge the Mutual Security policy itself" and aggravate the effect of earlier cuts which had already "brought the common defense into an area of serious risk."

Not less significant than the over-all reduction in funds, which struck particularly hard at the "military assistance" and "defense support" sections of the program, was the emasculation of an important new plan brought forward with the aim of adapting the Mutual Security effort more closely to the needs of underdeveloped countries and, incidentally, shifting the emphasis as far as possible from outright grants to repayable loans. Elaborating on an idea first developed in a special Senate committee on the aid problem, the administration had proposed the establishment of a "Development Loan Fund" or revolving credit scheme for the specific purpose of providing capital for meritorious long-term development projects which did not qualify for support from existing financial institutions. For the first year's operations the President had requested an appropriation of $500 million, with the expectation that an additional $750 million would be required in each of the two following years. Congress approved the principle of the Development Loan Fund and authorized an initial appropriation of $500 million, but at the same time established a ceiling of $625 million on the appropriations that might be voted for subsequent years beginning with the fiscal year 1959. Thereafter it proceeded to limit the actual appropriation for fiscal 1958 to $300 million. In signing the appropriation bill on September 3, the President indicated that he might have to call a special session later in the year to consider a supplemental appropriation. (Later it was decided to wait until the next regular congressional session in 1958—see section 27.)

Restrictions on the government's authority to make loans and grants for Mutual Security purposes accentuated the importance of normal trade and investment as the only remaining means of promoting sound economic conditions in the United States and abroad and enabling other countries to satisfy their requirements from this country. As Mr. Dulles somewhat optimistically observed in his *Foreign Affairs* article, "The United States market, which dependably offers so much that others want, and which dependably buys so much that others would sell, is the great economic stabilizer of the free world. It helps to combat Communism and the self-centered nationalisms which are alike in rejecting the concept of interdependence."

In both the trade and investment fields, the past few years had in fact witnessed significant progress. Through 1954, 1955, and 1956 the volume of United States commercial trade had mounted steeply. Civilian exports had grown from $12.9 billion in 1954 to $17.3 billion in 1956; imports had increased from $10.2 billion to $12.7 billion; and there had been comparable increases in the "services" account.[16] Although there was still a wide gap between the export and import figures, the deficiency had been partly made up by a really spectacular increase in the volume of United States capital invested in other countries. In what might represent an important turning point in postwar international finance, American private investors during 1956 had added nearly $4 billion to their holdings abroad, bringing them to the unprecedented total of $33 billion. These were government figures, compiled according to what some observers considered obsolete criteria. Other estimates set the year's total for gross private investment abroad at nearly $5 billion, almost two-fifths of it in Latin American and other underdeveloped countries.[17] Through early 1957 this large outflow of private capital continued on a scale that actually exceeded that of the government's economic aid program and drew favorable comment in various international financial quarters.

Although the United States Government had a small "investment guarantee" program designed to reduce the risks affecting private capital invested abroad, this remarkable upsurge in new investment was attributable less to direct government action than to an improved "investment climate" in many foreign countries. This was a development that American official spokesmen had urged on innumerable occasions. There now seemed to be some reason to hope that the foreign investment problem might be beginning to solve itself, even though such financial authorities as Benjamin F. Fairless (May 10) and John D. Rockefeller, III (May 18) pointed out that the amount of private capital invested abroad thus far was only "a drop in the bucket" compared to the capital requirements of the underdeveloped countries. In submitting his recommendations to Congress, President Eisenhower had asked for no new measures in the investment field except for the establishment of the Development Loan Fund, a forward extension in the lending authority of the Export-Import Bank (which was approved), and a modification of the tax laws affecting overseas business, which was not acted upon by Congress at its 1957 session.

In the trade field, in contrast, the President had laid considerable stress on the importance of new legislative action aimed at stabilizing world trade practices along the liberal and multilateral lines embodied in the Reciprocal Trade Agreements Program and the General Agreement on Tariffs and Trade (GATT). Of preeminent urgency, in his view, was the approval by Congress of United States membership in the proposed Organization for Trade Cooperation, the body which was intended to administer the provisions of the General Agreement under a charter signed at Geneva on March 10, 1955.[18] To President Eisenhower, the O.T.C. possessed outstanding importance not merely as a device for helping to keep open the channels of international commerce but also as a symbol of America's willingness to participate in international cooperative efforts outside the military field. Convinced that membership in the organization could only benefit the United States, he apparently had genuine hopes of bringing Congress around to his point of view and thus getting his second administration off to a favorable start in the whole field of commercial policy.

Repeating his recommendation regarding United States membership in a special message to Congress on April 3, 1957,[19] Mr. Eisenhower laid special stress on the thought that O.T.C. would bring "major benefits for American trade" by helping us to prevent discrimination against our exports and open up new markets abroad. Congress, however, was unimpressed. Matching the economy sentiment which had almost engulfed the Mutual Security Program was a ground swell of protectionist feeling that had begun to threaten not merely the O.T.C. but even the fundamental program of reciprocal trade agreements initiated almost a quarter-century earlier.

Among the most significant developments of this peiod in the United States was a reinforcement of the traditionally protectionist sectors of the economy by new interests, notably the growing textile industry in the Southern states, which were bringing about a realignment of economic forces in the country and, in particular, had greatly diluted the economic liberalism formerly associated with the Democratic party. Southern Democratic spokesmen tended to oppose a liberal import policy out of regard for the competitive position of Southern industry, just as many of them tended to oppose the Mutual Security Program lest it result in increased production of raw cotton, fabrics, and other competing products abroad.

For these and other reasons, the debate on O.T.C. was once again, for the third successive year, put over to a later congressional session. Some thought the chances for favorable action might be better in 1958; others pointed out that renewal of the Trade Agreements Act would also be up for consideration in that year, and predicted a battle royal between liberal and protectionist groups with no certainty that either measure would be approved (section 27). Meanwhile the protectionist tide was surging along a broad front and registering a number of advances as well as a few setbacks. As always, the textile industry was particularly clamorous for protection, and scored two notable successes in persuading the government to obtain a "voluntary" limitation on Japanese cotton textile shipments to this country (section 19) and impose a drastic quota restriction on imports of woolen and worsted fabrics (May 24). Concurrently, the assertion of domestic oil producers that excessive petroleum imports were discouraging their operations and thus jeopardizing national security led to a special investigation and a presidential appeal to the importers to limit their imports voluntarily or face a possibility of mandatory quotas (July 29). (A special exemption for the West Coast was rescinded December 24.)

Faced by a somewhat comparable though rather more serious situation, the languishing lead and zinc mining industries made an attempt to secure special legislative aid, and on the failure of this effort carried a strong appeal to the Tariff Commission (September 27). Although the shipping industry was flourishing at the moment with the aid of Federal subsidies and requested no new benefits, the international airlines were becoming seriously annoyed with the State Department over certain new routes and landing rights accorded to foreign carriers in the process of bringing the country's bilateral aviation agreements up to date. One airline executive protested vehemently against what he termed the practice of administering airline rights "as a part of the foreign aid program." The demands of these and other claimants to a favored position could be supported by impressive arguments. Carried to their logical conclusion, however, they would have gone far to wipe out the foothold gained by other countries in the American market, thus impairing further the ability of the latter to carry on normal economic relations with the United States.

As had been true for some years past, it was the agricultural rather than the industrial sector of the American economy that raised the biggest problems for both domestic and foreign economic policy in 1957. Unlike some of their industrial counterparts, the nation's farmers had not reduced their output as foreign agricultural production recovered and world demand for their products fell off. Maintained at a high level in past years as the direct result of government policy, farm output had failed to decrease significantly despite the Eisenhower administration's recent experiments with flexible price supports and the withdrawal of land from cultivation through the soil bank. Official disappointment was tempered, however, by the fact that the volume of unsold wheat, cotton, and other surplus farm products actually held by the government under its price support program had been at least temporarily reduced through the successful operation of the various surplus disposal schemes worked out in the past two or three years. From a total of almost $8.3 billion in mid-1956, the government investment in unsold farm commodities declined to a bit over $7.3 billion a year later. Particularly gratifying were the results obtained under Public Law 480, the Agricultural Trade Development and Assistance Act of 1954, which had authorized among other things the sale for foreign currencies of surplus agricultural commodities to an aggregate value of $3 billion over a three-year period. By June 30, 1957, disposal programs drawn up under this and other provisions of the act totaled over $5.2 billion,[20] and Congress in renewing the legislation for another year at its 1957 session authorized a further $1 billion in foreign currency sales during the fiscal year 1958.

Although the international impact of this and other disposal programs had been somewhat mixed, the benefits on the whole appeared to outweigh the disadvantages. Many countries in Asia and elsewhere had profited by the opportunity to purchase needed foodstuffs without having to dip into their limited reserves of dollar currency. Conspicuous among the beneficiaries of the program were Yugoslavia and more recently Poland, which contracted to purchase $65 million worth of surplus wheat and cotton under two agreements concluded in June and August 1957 (section 10). The principal opposition arose in other grain-producing countries such as Australia and particularly Canada, which took strong exception to some features of the United States disposal effort and claimed that its own overseas markets were being invaded by techniques which in some instances were difficult to reconcile with the General Agreement on Tariffs and Trade (cf. section 22). A supplementary policy involving the sale of surplus cotton abroad at competitive prices caused fewer adverse repercussions than had been expected, although it apparently gave such countries as Egypt and the Sudan an added incentive to ship their cotton to the U.S.S.R. and thus associate themselves more closely with the Soviet economic orbit.

Despite the marked growth in American agricultural exports, prospects for a lasting solution of the surplus problem appeared remote in view of the unexampled productivity of American farms and the reluctance of the government to invoke more drastic methods of limiting production. A perceptive comment on the international aspects of the problem was offered by Senator Hubert H. Humphrey on his return from a visit to the Middle East and Southern Europe in mid-1957.[21] Our trouble thus far, the Senator from Minnesota asserted, had been a failure to appreciate the positive opportunities afforded by our agricultural abundance:

"The stocks of food and other agricultural commodities which the United States is fortunate enough to possess, over and above its immediate domestic requirements, are a grossly underrated national asset. American food and fiber are vital to the very existence of millions of undernourished people. Utilizing this asset could provide a ray of hope for building stronger economies and greater political stability in most of the countries I visited.

"But the full extent of this asset cannot be realized as long as it is regarded, not as an asset, but as a liability. We have cheapened the spirit behind our humanitarian food contributions abroad, and weakened our own bargaining power in negotiating trade agreements for food and fiber, by continually proclaiming that our food reserves are something for which we have no use, and want to get rid of at any cost.

". . . The principal object in the use of these stocks should not be simple disposal, but the promotion of the foreign trade and foreign policy of the United States."

7. THE LIMITS OF WORLD RESPONSIBILITY

No major nation can consistently please the rest of the world with all the varied aspects of its international activity; and the United States, with its widely ramifying economic relationships, its world-wide troop deployments, its vigorous program of nuclear weapons testing, and its interest in opposing Communism on a global scale, received its full share of ill-tempered criticism from friends as well as foes. Not that all foreign comment on the United States was in any sense unfavorable. In the course of 1957 the Presidents of Vietnam and Bolivia, two countries which had benefited from America's helping hand in times of grave emergency, paid unusually generous tributes to the value of American assistance, the first in an address to the United States Congress in Washington (May 9) and the second in a message to his own Congress in La Paz (August 6). Prime Minister H. S. Suhrawardy of Pakistan voiced exuberant praises of the United States both in Washington and New York and in his home capital of Karachi. Pakistan, he said again and again (July 11, July 23, August 5), was "proud" to be allied with a country which had shown that world peace was safe in its hands, had proved that it did not want to be master of the world, and had "widened the horizon of democracy and saved many from the clutches of totalitarian regimes."

SOMEBODY'S TOES MUST BE STEPPED ON

By Hesse for The McNaught Syndicate, Inc.

Many other statesmen of the free world undoubtedly shared these opinions; yet to hear them uttered in this clear and open fashion was an exceptional experience. Normally it was the shortcomings, rather than the positive contributions, of American policy that bore the weight of official and popular attention in the non-Communist world. This negative emphasis, though psychologically natural, was not entirely healthy in its effects on the American outlook in world affairs. "Americans," wrote the British sociologist Geoffrey Gorer in the London *Daily Telegraph*,[22] ". . . want to be liked, well liked, and in response they will give more and demand less than any other dominant nation recorded in history." To some extent the converse was also true. American leaders had often thought it necessary to point out that the United States was not engaged in a "popularity contest" and therefore should not be unduly disturbed even if its efforts were not fully appreciated. By 1957, however, such warnings were beginning to seem superfluous. Disappointed in our allies, disillusioned with world politics generally, American opinion on the whole seemed relatively indifferent to whether we were liked or not. Seldom had the public and its representatives in Congress displayed a more tepid interest in the various international programs developed in Washington for the mutual benefit of the United States and other countries of the free world.

Although the President and his responsible advisers had refused to succumb to the prevailing disillusionment, its influence had been very evident in the battle over the Mutual Security legislation. Even more unmistakable was the current congressional attitude toward the United States Information Agency and other official activities aimed at getting America's story before the world and acquainting other peoples with the truth about American life and policy aims. In the hope of seizing the opportunity afforded by Communist setbacks and extending the government's informational effort in hitherto neglected areas of the Middle East and Africa, the President at the beginning of the year had sought a modestly increased appropriation of $144 million for the U.S.I.A. together with much smaller amounts for the related activities carried on under State Department and White House auspices. "World

events have magnified both the responsibilities and the opportunities of the United States Information Agency," he said
(January 10). "Just as, in recent months, the voice of Communism has become more shaken and confused, the voice of truth
must be more clearly heard." In one of the year's sharpest
challenges of the President's judgment, Congress nevertheless
reduced the allotment for U.S.I.A. to $96.2 million and de-
creed corresponding reductions in the other programs. Determined to expand its activities in the increasingly important
African field, the Information Agency found itself compelled
to retrench drastically in other areas, particularly in Western
Europe, where sources of information about the United States
were abundant if not always unbiased.

There were other fields in which the urge to reduce expenditure ran counter to the desiderata of an effective world policy.
The State Department's own operating budget was cut down
during the spring from $228 million to $189 million, to the
evident detriment of plans for raising the caliber of the nation's diplomatic representation through improved language
training, more adequate expense allowances, and the like.
Ironically, these reductions came at a time when the administration was being harshly criticized for its practice of staffing
some of the most important diplomatic posts abroad with
wealthy Republicans who lacked diplomatic or other pertinent
training. Although the President sharply denied that campaign
contributions were a factor in his diplomatic appointments, it
was generally conceded that the expense of holding a major
ambassadorship was usually far in excess of the emoluments
and could be sustained only with the aid of substantial private
means.

Even more fundamental than the economy trend of 1957
was the persistence in the nation of certain familiar attitudes
toward international affairs that served as an effective brake on
governmental action and sometimes restricted the possible
benefits of Washington's policy initiatives. The cost of peace,
as President Eisenhower had emphasized in the State of the
Union message, was not measured only in monetary terms.
Beyond money, it involved "changes in attitudes, the renunciation of old prejudices, even the sacrifice of some seeming self-

interest." A number of important foreign policy matters which arose during 1957 hinged on precisely this kind of psychological adaptability and served to illustrate the extreme difficulty of the mental adjustments that were being demanded of the American people under the relentless pressure of world events.

Even the President's official family had not been entirely without problems of this order, although the first year of the new term saw an extensive renovation of the top personnel concerned with foreign affairs which was thought likely to produce an official climate more sympathetic to the President's viewpoint. Frequently cited in this connection were the advent of Christian A. Herter as successor to Herbert Hoover, Jr. in the post of Under-Secretary of State and the designation of former Ambassador C. Douglas Dillon to coordinate foreign economic policy as Deputy Under-Secretary for Economic Affairs. Among the Assistant Secretaries of State, the only holdover from the previous administration was Walter S. Robertson, whose continued responsibility for Far Eastern policy typified the stability of the administration's official attitude toward Communist China. Appointments to the major ambassadorial posts raised no important problems so far as political outlook was concerned. The new Ambassadors to Great Britain (John Hay Whitney), France (Amory Houghton), and Italy (James D. Zellerbach) were known Eisenhower supporters, while the President's appointees to the U.S.S.R. (Llewellyn E. Thompson, Jr.), the German Federal Republic (David K. E. Bruce, a Democrat), India (Ellsworth Bunker, another Democrat), and Japan (Douglas MacArthur, II) were experienced diplomats and thoroughly familiar with basic American policy.

In the field of public attitudes, the administration did not of course regard all changes of outlook as equally helpful in the pursuit of a consistent foreign policy. A gradual erosion of national support for the established policy toward Communist China (section 17) caused official Washington considerable embarrassment and elicited from Secretary Dulles a number of observations about what he referred to on August 17 as the obligation of every citizen "to be responsive to United States foreign policy in so far as that policy is legally and authoritatively expressed." What the President had in mind, rather, was an abandonment of certain ingrained prejudices and suspicions regarding the outside world; the growth of a more cosmopolitan and even comradely spirit; a willingness to accept other peoples on their own merits, to deal with them as true equals, for certain limited purposes even to merge our national destinies with theirs. President Eisenhower was far from enthusiastic over such manifestations as New York City's refusal of an official welcome to the King of Saudi Arabia or the congressional agitation which led President Tito to cancel a projected visit to the United States. "You don't promote the cause of peace by talking only with the people with whom you agree," he said on January 30. He himself deplored "any discourtesy shown to a visitor . . . whose purpose is to see whether he can assist in ameliorating any of these difficulties."

It is to be noted that the somewhat parochial attitudes which the President was evidently trying to combat in the international field were not necessarily confined to the sphere of foreign affairs. On the contrary, they quite often represented the projection of attitudes already familiar on the domestic scene. The problem of race relations which so preoccupied all Americans in 1957 was one of those that had important international as well as domestic aspects. Prejudice and discrimination in this country, as Vice-President Nixon among many others pointed out (April 30), "made the task of those responsible for the conduct of our foreign policy infinitely more difficult" and provided an abundance of material to Communist propagandists, particularly in Asia. President Eisenhower himself declared at the height of the Little Rock school integration crisis (September 24) that

"it would be difficult to exaggerate the harm that is being done to the prestige and influence, and indeed to the safety, of our nation. . . . Our enemies are gloating over this incident and using it everywhere to misrepresent our whole nation. We are portrayed as a violator of those standards of conduct which the peoples of the world united to proclaim in the Charter of the United Nations. . . ."

This generalization was amply borne out by news reports from all parts of the world. "What shocks the public conscience," gloated one newspaper in Singapore at the time, "is that this rotten state of affairs is permitted in a country which, according to Eisenhower, 'has the responsibility of the free world's leadership laid upon it by destiny.' What manner of men inhabit that country?" [23] As the President pointed out a few days later, however, the Little Rock incident at least carried with it the comforting realization that "the great overwhelming mass of America believes that our courts and the respect for our courts must be sustained."

This acceptance of the legal determination of an acutely emotional issue was also not entirely unnoticed abroad; and it is noteworthy that a similar respect for law contributed greatly to the resolution of a somewhat comparable issue in the international field. This was the issue of the status-of-forces agreements which the United States had concluded in recent years with NATO and with numerous individual countries where American armed forces were stationed. These agreements, which the President considered "absolutely essential" to our alliance system (July 17), contained a standard provision whereby American servicemen accused of committing crimes while off duty became liable to trial in the courts of the host country. In practice the host country usually waived jurisdiction, and very few G.I.'s actually languished in foreign jails; but the whole principle of the agreements was acutely objectionable to some American isolationist and patriotic groups, and there were recurrent demands that they be repudiated or drastically revised.

This agitation was brought to a head during 1957 by a series of sensational cases growing out of deaths of foreign civilians caused by American servicemen. Most prominent among them was the Girard case in Japan (section 19), in which the United States Supreme Court ultimately decided that under the agreements in force there was no basis for contesting Japanese jurisdiction. This decision by the highest national tribunal went far to quiet the commotion at home and made it easier for the administration to fight off a series of congressional attacks on the whole complex of status-of-forces agreements. Their repudiation, the President warned (July 20), "would gravely threaten our security, alienate our friends and give aid and comfort to those who want to destroy our way of life." The only practical alternative to the agreements, he seemed to feel, would be to bring our troops home and in effect fall back on the concept of "Fortress America."

The outlook which rebelled so strongly against the idea of Americans being tried in foreign courts had also played an influential role in the shaping of national policy in the field of immigration to the United States. The distinguishing feature of American immigration policy in recent decades had been a marked reluctance to admit outsiders in any numbers and an insistence that those who were admitted should conform to certain specialized criteria of desirability, both ethnic and personal. This broadly restrictive approach had not prevented the United States from taking constructive action in emergency situations such as that caused by the sudden influx of 171,000 Hungarian refugees into Austria in late 1956 and early 1957. Acting with unusual speed and effectiveness, the United States by December 1957 had provided a haven for some 38,000 of this group, thus taking first place among recipient countries in terms of sheer numbers if not in terms of absorptive capacity. But antipathy to heavy immigration and fears of possible subversion prevented Congress from acting in 1957 on the President's recommendation that Hungarians admitted on an emergency basis be granted a permanent haven; nor was any action taken on his twice-repeated proposals for basic changes in the immigration law, including a moderate increase in the annual quota and a revision of the national origins quota system.[24] As a stopgap, Congress did enact near the end of the session a compromise measure facilitating immigration in certain hardship cases and permitting the administration to waive the embarrassing fingerprint requirement for temporary visitors. This last innovation deprived the Russians of an important propaganda point and enabled the State Department to talk more realistically about a possible resumption of East-West cultural and scientific exchanges. (American-Soviet negotiations in this area, discontinued at the time of the Hungarian revolt, were resumed in October 1957 and seemed likely to result in a somewhat broadened exchange of individuals and delegations in various specialized fields.) [25]

Immigration policy affected primarily individuals rather than governments; but a very similar spirit could be seen at work in relation to American participation in various intergovernmental arrangements which might conceivably be expected to affect in some way the domestic pattern of life in the United States. Those Americans who most feared such possibilities were wont to look for salvation to the proposed constitutional amendment which was each year brought forward in slightly revised form by Senator John W. Bricker of Ohio [26]—a device which, in Senator Bricker's own opinion (February 19), offered "the only way to stop the international planners who are determined to drag America down to a common level and socialize American life." Because it contemplated far-reaching encroachments on the power of the executive in the field of foreign affairs, the Bricker Amendment was regularly opposed by the President and Secretary Dulles, and had not been taken up on the Senate floor since 1954. Its partisans, however, kept up an active fight against all of the internationalist tendencies to which the amendment was directed. They were influential in the opposition to the status-of-forces agreements and the proposed Organization for Trade Cooperation, and they succeeded during 1957 in placing important limitations on United States participation in another hopeful new organization, the International Atomic Energy Agency.

Originally suggested in President Eisenhower's 1953 "atoms-for-peace" speech before the United Nations, and finally approved by an international conference in New York on October 26, 1956,[27] the International Atomic Energy Agency could be described as a favorite administration project and one that rather faithfully reflected American official views about the proper scope and functioning of an international institution charged with promoting the peaceful uses of atomic energy. In a message urging early Senate approval of the agency's statute (March 22),[28] the President called it both "a practical approach and a symbol of all that people of good will hope to see accomplished through the use of atomic energy." Senator Bricker and some of his colleagues, however, were less concerned with these prospects than with the possibility that Communist China might gain entrance to the organization or that some of the fissionable material the United States intended to provide it might wind up in Communist hands. Considerable resistance to the project developed in the Senate Foreign Relations Committee, despite a warning from Secretary Dulles (May 10) that a rejection of this "native American product" would have "a very disastrous effect on the prestige and influence of the United States in the world." While Senators pondered, weeks went by and the first general conference of the agency was postponed from August to October. Convinced eventually that the State Department would vigorously oppose any undesirable development within the organization, the Senate on June 18 mustered a 67 to 19 vote in favor of ratification, though only on the express understanding that the United States could withdraw from membership in case the statute was later amended in a manner opposed by the Senate.[29]

Armed with this authority, the President ratified the Statute and the agency officially came into being on July 29 (cf. section 27). In the meantime, however, its domestic opponents had returned to the attack with a proposal to limit the President's authority to make nuclear materials available to the agency. In the preceding autumn Mr. Eisenhower had undertaken to provide the organization with 5,000 kilograms of Uranium 235 and to match any contributions it received from other sources up to July 1, 1960.[30] But under legislation inspired by Senator Bricker and approved in July 1957 by the Joint Congressional Committee on Atomic Energy, any further allocations beyond this level would require prior congressional approval. In opposition to this proposal, the State Department argued that such a restriction would be interpreted as "a reflection of congressional distrust of the new agency" and "raise serious doubts as to the spirit in which the United States was undertaking its participation." The majority of the committee promptly retorted that nuclear materials were becoming "the lifeblood of our country" and must not be distributed "in such quantities as to deprive this country of an element vital to its needs." Rather than risk a showdown, the administration said it would try to "live with" the restrictions; whereupon Congress added to the final bill a further provision imposing similar limitations on contributions of nuclear material to other international agencies such as the new European Atomic Energy Community (Euratom).

It should be added that Congress took a rather more favorable view of the bilateral atomic cooperation agreements that the United States was concluding with many countries of the free world. Nor should it be imagined that the distrust with which some Americans continued to regard the outside world was entirely groundless. Successive revelations of Soviet espionage activities within the United States afforded a powerful argument to the advocates of extreme caution in *all* foreign dealings. At the same time, it would be futile to deny that the hedging and trimming necessitated by domestic resistance, whether of the active or passive variety, imposed a serious check on the over-all effectiveness of American foreign policy, in 1957 as in earlier years. President Eisenhower's vision of "a true time of peace, when men and nations shall share a life that honors the dignity of each, the brotherhood of all," was only fitfully reflected in the day-to-day development of American foreign policy. Yet perhaps the setbacks and the many compromises never quite obscured the fact that, as the President had said in his State of the Union Message, "the great concept of the dignity of all men, alike created in the image of the Almighty, has been the compass by which we have tried and are trying to steer our course."

Notes to Chapter II

1. Public Law 4, 84th Cong., approved January 29, 1955; *Documents on American Foreign Relations, 1955,* pp. 298-299.

2. *Department of State Bulletin,* v. 36 (January 21, 1957), pp. 83-97; *Documents on American Foreign Relations, 1957,* no. 53.

3. H.J. Res. 117 and S.J. Res. 19, 85th Cong., in *Department of State Bulletin,* v. 36 (January 28, 1957), p. 128; *Documents on American Foreign Relations, 1957,* no. 54.

4. See U.S. House, Foreign Affairs Committee, *Economic Cooperation with Nations in the General Area of the Middle East,* 85th Cong., 1st sess. (Washington: G.P.O., 1957) and U.S. Senate, Foreign Relations and Armed Services Committees, *The President's Proposal on the Middle East,* Hearings on S.J. Res. 19 and H.J. Res. 117, 85th Cong., 1st sess. (Washington: G.P.O., 1957, 2 parts).

5. H.J. Res. 117, 85th Cong., in *Department of State Bulletin,* v. 36 (March 25, 1957), p. 481; *Documents on American Foreign Relations, 1957,* no. 55.

6. Excerpts in *Department of State Bulletin,* v. 36 (January 28, 1957), pp. 123-126; *Documents on American Foreign Relations, 1957,* no. 1.

7. *Pravda,* March 20; *Current Digest of the Soviet Press,* v. 9, no. 12 (May 1, 1957), p. 14.

8. Henry A. Kissinger, *Nuclear Weapons and Foreign Policy* (New York: Harper, for the Council on Foreign Relations, 1957); see also Robert Endicott Osgood, *Limited War: The Challenge to American Strategy* (Chicago: University of Chicago Press, 1957).

9. *New York Times,* January 17, 1957; excerpts in *Documents on American Foreign Relations, 1957,* no. 2.

10. John Foster Dulles, "Challenge and Response in United States Policy," *Foreign Affairs,* v. 36 (October 1957), pp. 25-43.

11. *Department of State Bulletin,* v. 36 (June 17, 1957), pp. 967-968; *Documents on American Foreign Relations, 1957,* no. 120.

12. Preliminary figures from Walther Lederer, "Developments in the U.S. Balance of International Payments," *Survey of Current Business,* v. 37, no. 3 (March 1957), pp. 11-18.

13. E. S. Kerber, "Government Foreign Assistance in 1956," *ibid.,* no. 4 (April 1957), pp. 13-17.

14. *Department of State Bulletin,* v. 36 (June 10, 1957), p. 920; *Documents on American Foreign Relations, 1957,* no. 9. Influential among the reports referred to were those of the "President's Citizen Advisers on the Mutual Security Program" headed by Benjamin F. Fairless *(New York Times,* March 6, 1957) and the Special Senate Committee to Study the Foreign Aid Program, chaired by Senator T. F. Green (Senate Report 300, 85th Cong., May 13, 1957).

15. Eugene W. Castle, *The Great Giveaway: The Realities of Foreign Aid* (Chicago: Regnery, 1957). For a contrary view see M. F. Millikan and W. W. Rostow, *A Proposal for a New United States Foreign Economic Policy* (Cambridge: Center for International Studies, Massachusetts Institute of Technology, 1956).

16. "Expansion in Foreign Business," *Survey of Current Business,* v. 37, no. 2 (February 1957), pp. 30-32; *Foreign Commerce Weekly,* v. 57, no. 14 (April 8, 1957), p. 31.

17. Samuel Pizer and Frederick Cutler, "Record Growth of Foreign Investments," *Survey of Current Business,* v. 37, no. 8 (August 1957), pp. 22-30; Emilio G. Collado and Jack F. Bennett, "Private Investment and Economic Development," *Foreign Affairs,* v. 35 (July 1957), pp. 631-645.

18. *Documents on American Foreign Relations, 1955,* pp. 59-68.

19. *Department of State Bulletin,* v. 36 (April 22, 1957), pp. 657-658; *Documents on American Foreign Relations, 1957,* no. 8.

20. "Progress Report on the Agricultural Trade Development and Assistance Act," *Department of State Bulletin,* v. 37 (August 12, 1957), pp. 281-295.

21. U.S. Senate, 85th Cong., 2d sess. *The Middle East and Southern Europe: Report of Senator Hubert H. Humphrey on a Study Mission,* July 1, 1957, printed for the use of the Senate Committee on Foreign Relations (Washington: G.P.O., 1957), pp. 10-11.

22. Quoted in *New York Times,* July 23, 1957.

23. Quoted *ibid.,* September 27, 1957.

24. Message of January 31, in *Department of State Bulletin,* v. 36 (February 18, 1957), pp. 247-250; *Documents on American Foreign Relations, 1957,* no. 10.

25. Cf. *Department of State Bulletin,* v. 37 (July 15, 1957), p. 119; (September 2, 1957), pp. 386-388; (November 18, 1957), pp. 800-803.

26. S.J. Res. 3, 85th Cong.; in *New York Times,* January 8, 1957.

27. *Documents on American Foreign Relations, 1956,* pp. 517-540.

28. *Department of State Bulletin,* v. 36 (April 15, 1957), pp. 615-617; *Documents on American Foreign Relations, 1957,* no. 154.

29. Text of understanding in S. Exec. Rept. 3, 85th Cong., 1st sess., June 15, 1957. For details cf. Demaree Bess, "The Battle Over Atoms-for-Peace," *Saturday Evening Post,* v. 230, no. 20 (November 16, 1957), pp. 31, 119-122.

30. *Documents on American Foreign Relations, 1956,* p. 516.

CHAPTER THREE

EUROPE AND THE EAST-WEST STRUGGLE

"No reasonable man," said President Eisenhower in another section of his 1957 State of the Union Message, "will deny that the freedom and prosperity and security of Western Europe are vital to our own prosperity and security. If the institutions, the skills, the manpower of its peoples were to fall under the domination of an aggressive imperialism, the violent change in the balance of world power and in the pattern of world commerce could not be fully compensated for by any American measures, military or economic." Thus the President reaffirmed, at a moment of unprecedented international confusion, the basic American interest in the survival of independent societies in that extensive portion of Europe which had given birth to so much of what we know as Western civilization.

The denial of this rich prize to the Soviet Union was not, of course, the only objective of American policy in this part of the world. Beyond the preservation of Western Europe, official Washington looked forward to an eventual ebbing of the Communist tide which had overrun the Central and Eastern portions of the European Continent. It yearned for the correction of certain existing conditions which in American eyes were neither politically nor morally defensible—the division and partial Soviet occupation of Germany, the domination by Moscow of the "captive states" of Eastern Europe, even the seventeen-year-old incorporation of Lithuania, Latvia, and Estonia into the Soviet Union. In spite of the disheartening result of Hungary's recent attempt to leave the Soviet bloc, the fact that a "national" Communist regime

had been able to establish itself in Poland suggested to some
Americans that the long-desired retraction of Soviet power
in Eastern Europe might actually have begun. The American
Government remained anxious to do what it could to assist
the forces of "liberalization" or "liberation" in Eastern
Europe and even in the U.S.S.R. (cf. section 2). An even
more fundamental task, however, was the reestablishment of
some kind of moral and psychological "position of strength"
in Western Europe, where the confidence and solidarity of
the NATO allies had been badly shaken in the stress of recent months. Without losing sight of ultimate objectives,
Washington had first to concentrate with its allies on repairing the damage of the Suez crisis and imbuing the
NATO alliance with new vigor and purpose.

As already indicated, a similar order of priorities inevitably
governed Soviet action on the European scene in the winter
of 1956–57. There can be little doubt that Moscow was at
least as hopeful of witnessing the breakup of the Western
alliance and the withdrawal of American power from Europe
as was the United States to see the Eastern European peoples
freed from Soviet domination. But major efforts in this direction had to await the restoration of order within the Communist orbit, a clarification of the relations between the
Soviet and other Communist governments, and, perhaps, a
resolution of the internal conflicts that were apparently still
going forward within the Soviet leadership. In the meantime
Soviet activities in reference to NATO and Western Europe
could amount to little more than a "holding operation,"
although Moscow, as always, was to prove adept at giving
even its delaying actions an effective psychological twist. Its
alarming performance during the recent Middle East-Hun-
garian crisis had left the West with much to ponder upon.
With no clear view of the Kremlin's real intentions, the
Western nations could only feel that the dangers inherent in
the present East-West relationship had become more formidable than ever.

Of particular concern to the Western governments and
peoples was the significance of two of the more demonstra-
tive manifestations of recent Soviet political warfare, one

unequivocally bellicose, the other ambiguously pacific. The first had been the open threat of a "rocket" attack on Britain and France (November 5, 1956), which had brought into sharp focus the whole question of recent changes in the art of war and their effect on the security of Western Europe. The second had been the much publicized Soviet Government declaration of November 17, 1956 "Concerning the Question of Disarmament and Reduction of International Tension." [1] Amid further boasts of Soviet military superiority, this document had contained an unlooked-for hint that Moscow might at last be ready to take a "new look" at some of the great questions composing the East-West deadlock in Europe. Particularly noticed had been its stress on the notion of a mutual withdrawal or "thinning out" of military forces in Central Europe for the purpose of reducing tension, lightening the burdens of military occupation, and creating a more normal situation in Europe as a whole. Coupled with this idea had been a quite unheralded offer to join the West in carrying out mutual aerial inspections in Europe along the lines of President Eisenhower's famous "open skies" proposal—though only in a limited area extending 800 kilometers East and West of the demarcation line between the opposing military forces.

Although the Russians in the past had invariably poured scorn on the "open skies" plan, their advocacy of a mutual reduction or withdrawal of military forces in Europe was by no means new in Soviet political warfare. For years the Kremlin had been proposing some action along these lines as part of its general effort to unpin the Western alliance and secure the removal of American forces from Europe. The motives behind this agitation, indeed, had been so obvious that it had normally provoked a wholly negative response in official Western circles, despite its appeal to an important segment of non-Communist opinion in Germany and elsewhere in Western Europe. Under present circumstances, however, with a major war scare just past and with the possibility that new and even more dangerous explosions might occur in Eastern Europe at any time, such suggestions were assured of a more sympathetic hearing than in the past.

Throughout the West, in fact, there had been growing disillusionment with the accomplishments of official Western policy in recent years, as measured both by the condition of NATO and by the state of relations with the Soviet Union. The Suez crisis had shown the much vaunted solidarity of the Western allies to be a myth; the state of the military "shield" in Western Europe plainly left a great deal to be desired; the incorporation of Western Germany into the Western defense system had not yet strengthened Western defense appreciably and had done less than nothing to cure the division of Germany. On the contrary, this latter condition now seemed more firmly frozen than ever, to the evident discontent of West German political circles. Perhaps it was time, people were saying, to reconsider the old policy of refusing to discuss any modification of Western military or political arrangements in Western Europe. Conceivably the Russians themselves would like to reduce their costly European commitments and genuinely desired some form of accommodation with the West, even if they were not prepared to swallow the annexation of Eastern Germany by the West German Federal Republic or to tolerate the establishment of non-Communist governments in the satellite states. Such prominent nongovernmental figures as Hugh Gaitskell in Great Britain and Chester Bowles in the United States were among those who urged that the possibilities opened up by recent Soviet initiatives should at least be thoroughly explored.[2]

This preoccupation with the idea of East-West accommodation in Europe added an extra dimension to the course of European developments during the greater part of 1957. While the leading powers on both sides struggled to hold together their respective alliance groups, the notion of some kind of "new deal" for Europe as a whole continued to shimmer in the atmosphere and exerted a measurable influence on the character of East-West diplomatic exchanges. To a certain extent, the governments on either side continued to treat the issues at stake primarily as a matter of political warfare, in which the first requirement was to simulate an interest in agreement in order to place one's antagonist at a political disadvantage. But on the Western side, at least, the interest in seeking out areas of agreement was in large part genuine, even though there was no inclination in official quarters to put unwarranted confidence in Soviet good faith. Evidences of President Eisenhower's keen anxiety for a better East-West understanding have already been cited (section 2). This concern for agreement was to be especially evident in the protracted negotiations of the United Nations Disarmament Subcommittee, whose field of interest, though world-wide, was particularly involved with the European problem.

Through the spring and summer, it appeared quite possible that the great powers would actually reach agreement on a "first stage" disarmament program that might in turn serve as a point of departure for wider settlements. To many this prospect appeared to have been further enhanced by Khrushchev's domestic political victory in July and his apparent intention to reinstate "peaceful coexistence" as the main theme of Soviet foreign policy. In reality, however, matters took an opposite course. The laboriously developed Western disarmament proposals were eventually rejected with contumely; Soviet antipathy to the reunification of Germany on any basis acceptable to the West was sharply reaffirmed; a new harshness made itself felt in all aspects of Soviet policy as Moscow once again turned to the Middle East as the scene of a new political offensive. A plausible explanation of this apparent reversal in the Kremlin's line was subsequently discovered in the technological breakthrough which preceded the ascent of the two Soviet earth satellites. But it is not impossible that Moscow was also influenced in part by the growing certainty that the United States, whatever its interest in a better understanding with the Kremlin, had no intention of altering its fundamental policy toward the Communist world.

The successive phases of this broad East-West competition as it developed in the European theater provide the underlying theme of the present chapter. Section 8 examines the military problems confronting the Western alliance in the wake of the year-end crisis and in the light of the projected reorientation of British defense policies. This is followed in section 9 by a discussion of new developments in the relations of the major Western European countries with each other and with their overseas territories, particularly in Africa. The evolution of Soviet policy toward the West, and of Western policy toward the Soviet Union, is portrayed in section 10 in the light of the changes and readjustments taking place within the Communist world. The complicated issues involved in the disarmament talks, though inevitably intertwined with military and political matters on both sides of the Iron Curtain, are reserved for more detailed treatment in section 11.

8. NATO AND THE DEFENSE OF EUROPE

Since the negotiation of the North Atlantic Treaty in 1949, it had been universally recognized by the signatory governments that the overriding purpose of their association was to defend the independence and integrity of its members in face of the possibility of Soviet military attack. After a period of widespread preoccupation with the further potentialities of the alliance in the political and economic fields, the sudden renewal of a warlike atmosphere in the winter of 1956–57 had abruptly recalled the attention of NATO statesmen to NATO's original and basic mission. The situation now confronting the NATO governments was in some ways as baffling as the one that had first called the alliance into being eight years earlier. Though it was doubtless true, as President Eisenhower declared in an anniversary message on April 4, 1957, that the "strong defensive shield" created by the NATO countries had been "a major factor in maintaining the peace in Europe," doubt was being expressed in many quarters as to how effectively it would continue to perform this function in the period ahead. Aside from glaring differences among the NATO governments on policy matters, even their collective military arrangements were increasingly being called in question.

Undoubtedly the total military power of the alliance had grown tremendously in the past eight years. General

Lauris Norstad of the United States, the new Supreme Allied
Commander in Europe, rated the NATO forces at four or
five times as strong as in 1952. But NATO strength in 1952
had admittedly been very far from adequate. That was the
year in which the NATO Council, meeting at Lisbon, had
agreed on the necessity for a vast expansion in the forces de-
fending Western Europe and had determined that sixty to
ninety divisions would be needed to stop a full-fledged Soviet
invasion. Most of these divisions had never come into being.
Like the United States, the European members of NATO
had thought it best to rely on the increasing effectiveness of
American atomic weapons rather than make the sacrifices
needed to keep great numbers of men in uniform. Since
Lisbon, NATO's "force goals" had repeatedly been revised
downward while nuclear weapons had assumed steadily increasing importance in NATO planning.

The question that disturbed some of NATO's military
authorities was whether this process was not going too fast
and too far. Admitting that it was politically easier to base
the strategy of the alliance primarily on nuclear weapons,
did this emphasis provide the best assurance that NATO
would be able to carry out successfully its mission of deterring or repelling a Soviet attack? In the opinion of General
Norstad, there was serious danger in any attempt to reduce
NATO's ground forces in Central Europe below a certain
"irreducible minimum," a figure which he was accustomed
to set at thirty divisions. NATO's strategy of deterrence, the
General pointed out in an important address in New York
on January 29, 1957,[3] rested on two distinct elements. One
was the retaliatory force embodied in the American Strategic
Air Command and the British Bomber Command. It was
common knowledge that this retaliatory force would be
brought into play immediately if the NATO line was violated, and General Norstad assured his audience that it
could "annihilate the enemy," no matter how large the Soviet air or missile fleet.

The other element consisted of the multinational ground,
naval, and air forces under General Norstad's direct command in Europe, which the speaker described as an indis-

pensable "shield" and a vital part of the over-all deterrent. This shield force, the Supreme Commander insisted, was no less essential than the retaliatory forces which constituted the "hard core" of Western military strength. Not only was it needed psychologically to convince the enemy that he could not move forward in Europe without detonating World War III; it had a vital military role to play in holding up an attack during the interval before retaliation could be effective, and in holding the bases from which the retaliatory force would operate. Equally important, in General Norstad's view, was the symbolic function of the shield force in demonstrating to the NATO peoples that all members of the alliance were participating fully in the risks of the association as well as its advantages. "Nothing," he said, "could be more enfeebling to the spirit that so far has animated NATO than a suspicion, however faint, that some of its partners were withdrawing behind their own frontiers, counting upon their long-range weapons to preserve the balance."

To students of NATO affairs it was evident that admonitions of this character, which were often heard in NATO quarters, were addressed primarily to the United States. This country's growing reliance on its long-range deterrent force, its periodic dalliance with the idea of a reduction of forces in Europe, had already occasioned more than a faint suspicion that America would eventually fall back on a "peripheral" strategy based not in Central Europe but on positions in Great Britain, Spain, and other points remote from the threat of invasion. But General Norstad's comments also had a much wider application. Other NATO members had found it even more difficult to keep NATO supplied with the array of fighting strength demanded by the European headquarters of the alliance. Instead of the thirty divisions he regarded as the irreducible minimum, General Norstad at the moment could count on no more than fourteen or fifteen: five American and four British divisions, plus smaller Belgian, Dutch, Canadian, and Danish contingents. Most of the French units originally assigned to NATO were now in North Africa. True, a part of this deficiency would

presently be made up by the progress of rearmament in
Western Germany, which was still nominally pledged to
contribute twelve divisions to the alliance and was actually
preparing to make its first three infantry divisions available
by midsummer. A further mitigating factor was the steady
increase of allied and especially American firepower, which
to a certain extent made up for numerical deficiencies and
which would no doubt be further increased by the formation
of the new American "atomic support commands" (section
5). But these prospective gains were offset by the growing
modernization of the Soviet forces in Eastern Europe and,
perhaps even more serious, by the prospect of a new round
of reductions in the Western "shield" force, a process in which
Great Britain now appeared intent on setting the pace.

When Sir Anthony Eden had promised in 1954 that Great
Britain's effective military strength on the Continent would
not be unilaterally reduced except in the event of an acute
overseas emergency, the British Government had reserved the
right to reopen the question if the discharge of this obligation should at any time throw too heavy a strain on British
finances.[4] In the opinion of the new Conservative cabinet
which took office under Prime Minister Macmillan on January 10, 1957, the moment for a review of Britain's military
commitments had now arrived. Goaded by the exigencies of
its economic position and the growing rivalry for overseas
markets, Great Britain had for some time been gradually reducing its active forces throughout the world and moving in
the direction of a nuclear-deterrent strategy comparable to
that of the United States. The fiasco of the Suez campaign and
the accompanying disillusionment over the attitude of the
United States had increased public pressure for a reexamination of global strategy and for greater independence in foreign
policy generally. The progress of the British nuclear weapons
and missile programs (Britain successfully detonated its first
hydrogen bomb at Christmas Island in the central Pacific on
May 15) encouraged the belief that a more radical shift in
defense planning was both timely and expedient. Barely two
weeks after assuming office, Mr. Macmillan disclosed that Defense Minister Sandys would formulate a new defense policy

"in the light of present strategic needs . . . which will secure a substantial reduction in expenditure and manpower."

The drastic nature of Mr. Sandys' new plan, officially described as "the biggest change in military policy ever made in normal times," was not to be fully evident until its publication in final form as a government White Paper on April 4.[5] Its general trend, however, was foreseen from the first. In many respects it bore a striking resemblance to the "new look" military policy initiated four years earlier in the United States. The combined effect of scientific advances and of financial and economic considerations, Mr. Sandys reasoned, had invalidated the old strategy of maintaining scattered forces at dozens of potentially threatened points throughout the world. The overriding task was "to prevent war rather than to prepare for it"; and the only way to prevent war—or, at any rate, the only existing safeguard against major aggression—was "the power to threaten retaliation with nuclear weapons." Accordingly, it was now decided that Great Britain would henceforth concentrate on the development of a deterrent force emphasizing nuclear weapons suitable for delivery by manned bombers and ballistic rockets, together with nuclear warheads for defensive guided missiles. Admittedly, this British deterrent force would represent only a modest contribution to the total deterrent power available to the West. British spokesmen made it quite plain, however, that they were not prepared to rely entirely on American deterrent power, over which they had no control and which might or might not be available when needed. As Mr. Sandys said on April 16, "We think it is just as well to make certain that an appreciable element of nuclear power shall, in all circumstances, remain on this side of the Atlantic, so that no one shall be tempted to think that a major attack could be made against Western Europe without the risk of nuclear retaliation."

With the aid of these readjustments, the British were confident that they could look forward to substantial economies in expenditure and a very great saving in manpower. The uniformed strength of the three services, already reduced from about 822,000 to 690,000 would be cut by a further 65,000 during the next year and by the end of 1962 would be stabilized if possible at about 375,000—far less than the figures currently under discussion in the United Nations (section 11). Call-ups under the National Service Act would cease after the end of 1960. A considerable part of these reductions would be accomplished by cutting down or withdrawing the garrisons maintained in such overseas areas as Jordan, Libya, and Korea. Their responsibilities would be taken over so far as possible by a central reserve stationed in the British Isles and equipped with a fleet of transport aircraft ready to rush to any danger spot. But NATO's defensive shield in Western Europe would also be quite sharply affected. While emphasizing that the frontiers of the free world in Europe must be firmly defended and that Great Britain must continue to do its fair share, the White Paper said plainly that the United Kingdom had been making a "disproportionately large contribution" and could no longer continue on the same scale. According to the final version of the plan, the four divisions constituting the British Army of the Rhine would be reduced during the next twelve months from a strength of about 77,000 to about 64,000, and the Second Tactical Air Force would lose about half its planes; and there would be consultations with the allies about further reductions to be made subsequently. The firepower of the remaining ground units was to be augmented with atomic rocket artillery, and some of the air force squadrons were to be provided with atomic bombs.

Like the American concept on which it seemed to be modeled (though it outran current American thinking in its stress on substituting guided and ballistic missiles for manned aircraft), the British "new look" appeared acceptable from the standpoint of economics but was seriously questioned on larger strategic and political grounds. Clearly, one of its principal effects would be to commit the United Kingdom, like the United States, to the use of nuclear weapons even against a nonnuclear attack—a further limitation on the free world's flexibility and freedom of action in face of possible Communist provocations. Similarly, the emphasis on the nuclear deterrent, combined with the reduction of manpower in all parts of the world, might provide increased striking power vis-à-vis the Russians but might also lessen the effectiveness of British action in localized situations where the Russians were not directly involved. The nuclear deterrent would hardly be very effective in an Arab tribal war, an African insurrection, or a riot in Singapore or Hong Kong.

In addition, Britain's adoption of an air-nuclear strategy was open to certain specialized objections involving both its position in NATO and the special relationship it still sought to maintain with the United States. One of the evident weaknesses of the British plan was the fact that it could not be carried out without substantial American cooperation in the field of missiles, where the two countries had thus far proceeded more or less independently except for some exchange of inforformation under an agreement negotiated by Mr. Sandys in 1954. A broadening of these arrangements was the principal objective of the new Defense Minister when he undertook his second official pilgrimage to Washington late in January 1957. Certain understandings reached on this occasion were submitted for review by President Eisenhower and Prime Minister Macmillan at their March meeting in Bermuda, at which an "agreement in principle" was reached "that in the interest of mutual defense and mutual economy certain guided missiles will be made available by the United States for use by British forces." [6]

This understanding was presumed to relate principally to "intermediate-range" missiles, suitable for equipment with either atomic or conventional warheads, which could be directed at targets up to 1,500 miles away—roughly the distance from London to Moscow. Although the communiqué had spoken of "guided" missiles, later discussion centered rather on *ballistic* missiles of intermediate range. The general idea appeared to be that the United States would supply Britain with "first-generation" missiles to serve as a stopgap until such time as the British might be able to develop their own missiles of more advanced type. But while Mr. Macmillan was telling the House of Commons that these devices would become available "in the fairly near future," Pentagon authorities were pointing out that the United States itself did not yet have an operational intermediate-range missile and estimating that it would be several years before British orders could be filled.

Subsequently the implementation of the program was rendered even more uncertain by the economy drive in the American Defense Department and the deferment of all but the most urgent research and development projects (section 5). Only after the advent of the two Soviet Sputniks did there appear a prospect of accelerated operations aimed at producing intermediate-range missiles to be based at launching sites in Great Britain and on the Continent as well (section 28).

President Eisenhower's sympathetic understanding of the reasons behind Britain's prospective defense cuts was to prove especially valuable to the British Government in light of the commotion they had aroused in other NATO quarters. However unevenly they had fulfilled their own commitments, the continental members of NATO had regarded the continued presence of British and American troops as essential to the whole scheme of Western defense—essential not only in relation to the U.S.S.R. but also in relation to a rearming Germany. The growing influence of the German Federal Republic in NATO councils, symbolized by the appointment of a German general (Lt. Gen. Hans Speidel) to take over the principal NATO command on the Central European front, was a source of considerable bitterness and apprehension in other Western European countries. Misgivings about the intentions of the new Germany were to be intensified a few weeks later when Chancellor Adenauer in commenting on the British White Paper (April 5) declared that Germany, too, ought to be allowed tactical nuclear weapons for its own defense. (This statement caused considerable outcry within the Federal Republic itself, where there was strong antipathy to nuclear weapons, particularly in Socialist and intellectual quarters.) But with or without nuclear weapons, a "thinning out" of British (and perhaps American) forces on the Continent would leave Germany more than ever the preponderant power in Western Europe, a prospect that remained highly unwelcome to those who remembered the Nazi occupations of 1940–45. Nor was it easy to convince the continental governments that reduction of British forces was a good way to strengthen Western Europe against the threat of Soviet invasion.

There was also a widespread feeling that if the British were

entitled to reduce their forces for economic reasons, other allies
could hardly be denied the same privilege. What General Norstad and his associates had reason to fear was a "chain reaction"
that might end by destroying the defensive shield in Western
Europe altogether and leaving the area denuded of any effective defense apart from the Anglo-American retaliatory bomb-
ing capability. The growing availability of tactical nuclear
weapons and American short-range missiles within his command was no excuse for a reduction in the forces in being, the
General warned, because these developments had been anticipated when the existing force goals were set. Significant reductions by any country, he declared (February 18), "will give us
the greatest concern and could be most serious for all of us."

An additional circumstance that loomed large in the eyes of
some of Britain's European allies was the fact that these cuts
had been decided upon without preliminary consultation
either in NATO or in the seven-power Western European
Union, to which the British pledge of 1954 had been more
especially directed. Two special meetings of the Council of
Western Union, held in February and March to discuss the
British plan, found France, Western Germany, and Belgium
all objecting so strenuously that Britain actually agreed to
defer half of the intended cuts in the Army of the Rhine until
NATO had time to restudy the whole problem of conventional
and atomic forces in their relation to economic and financial
resources. Instead of the immediate reduction of 27,000 which
the British had originally contemplated, the White Paper thus
spoke of an initial reduction of 13,000, although it gave clear
intimation that additional cutbacks were to be expected later.
This limited retreat was facilitated by the agreement of the
West German government to increase its payments toward the
support of British forces in Germany during the coming
year and take certain other steps to ease the British financial
position.

Pending completion of the study by NATO's military authorities, the progressive modernization of the NATO forces
in Europe was still going forward, with emphasis on the introduction of short-range missiles and other modern means of
defense which might offset in some degree the evident trend

toward manpower reductions throughout General Norstad's command. On April 12 it was officially announced at NATO headquarters that the United States within the next few months would begin to provide certain NATO nations—for purely defensive purposes—with Honest John and Matador ground-to-ground missiles and Nike ground-to-air missiles. Though these devices would be delivered without their nuclear warheads, the American forces in Germany were known to have a growing stockpile of nuclear weapons which would presumably be made more widely available in case of war.

These preparations to make maximum use of nuclear weapons in case of an emergency affecting the European theater had not gone unobserved in Moscow, which since the beginning of the year had kept up a steady fire of denunciation against the proposed United States atomic support commands, the proposed supply of intermediate-range missiles to Great Britain, and the prospective introduction of atomic and other new weapons on the territory of NATO countries. In the five weeks that followed the Bermuda conference, at least eight NATO countries and seven outside of NATO were emphatically warned by Moscow in diplomatic notes or radio broadcasts that they would run a direct risk of Soviet atomic retaliation if they permitted their soil to be used for such purposes. Particularly forceful was a warning to Western Germany (April 27) to the effect that in becoming "the main European springboard and chief NATO shock force for atomic warfare in Europe," the Federal Republic was "playing with fire" and initiating a course of action that could lead to Western Germany's becoming "one big cemetery."

These vociferous threats from beyond the Iron Curtain were to share attention with the British defense cuts when the Foreign Ministers of the fifteen NATO governments assembled in Bonn on May 2 and 3 for the regular ministerial meeting of the North Atlantic Council, the first to be held in the West German capital. As had often happened in the past, the belligerent attitude of the U.S.S.R. evoked a more resolute reproof than the Council could ordinarily manage when one of its own members went against majority sentiment. Having agreed as far back as 1954 that NATO must be in a position to make use of nuclear weapons in the defense of Western Europe, the Council—which, of course, afforded only a partial reflection of popular attitudes in the fifteen NATO member countries—now declared that it would not be shaken in this resolve by any outside menaces:

"The Atlantic Alliance must be in a position to use all available means to meet any attack which might be launched against it. It is the availability of the most modern weapons of defense which will discourage attempts to launch any such attack on the Alliance. Pending an acceptable agreement on disarmament, no power can claim the right to deny to the Alliance the possession of the modern arms needed for its defense." [7]

Acknowledging by implication that this rejection of outside interference did not solve NATO's own strategic problems, the Council went on to say that while awaiting the studies to be undertaken by the NATO military authorities, it was already convinced that any future decisions should be taken in common (rather than unilaterally, as the British had done) and should not fail to take account of the need for "a powerful shield of land, sea and air forces, to protect the territory of member states." Secretary Dulles, it was reported, had explained once again that American forces in Europe might be "streamlined" in the coming months but would not be reduced in fighting strength. After reaffirming the traditional NATO views on current international questions and complimenting the alliance on what was described as its growing "maturity and solidarity," the Council concluded with a tribute to Lord Ismay, NATO's Secretary-General, on the conclusion of five years of dedicated service. His successor would be M. Spaak of Belgium.

Returning to Washington after private consultations with Dr. Adenauer and French Premier Mollet, Secretary Dulles described the Council meeting (May 7) as in many respects the best he had ever attended. "There was an informality and a scope of discussion which stemmed from a fresh sense of common purpose," he said. Undoubtedly NATO, despite the British defense cuts, looked much more like a going concern than had been true a few months earlier. Most of the immediate problems arising from the autumn crisis had by this time been settled. Aided by a mild winter and by somewhat increased oil shipments from the United States, Europe had come through its temporary petroleum crisis without serious harm, even if the deeper psychological effects of recent events still defied assessment. For the moment, at least, everything appeared to be on the upgrade. Even the Soviet Union had suddenly assumed a milder tone and was renewing its talk about a relaxation of tensions, improvement of relations, and development of contacts between nations. "The Hungarian situation was a rather sharp affair, sharp like Hungarian paprika," Khrushchev had observed on April 15. "And added to this Hungarian pepper was Egypt. But things now are settling down."

Nevertheless the great questions of Western policy still remained unsettled. Nothing had been done to alleviate the fate of Hungary. The reunification of Germany appeared as far away as ever. The softening of the international climate would probably make it all the more difficult to prevent the gradual dissipation of NATO strength in Europe. A revealing sign of the times was Belgium's announcement in June that the term of compulsory service in its armed forces was to be reduced from eighteen months to fifteen. Squeezed by rising prices and declining exchange reserves, Great Britain was showing every determination to carry out the full program announced in the defense White Paper. General Norstad, proceeding from an opposite starting point, was understood to be at work on a five-year forecast of defense requirements in the European theater which took full account of missiles and other new weapons but still held to the "irreducible minimum" of thirty divisions on the central front. Clearly, the only way this requirement could be met would be for Britain and the United States to avoid major reductions, for Germany to contribute the full twelve divisions it had originally promised, and for France to return to Europe a good part of the 400,000 men now employed in combating the Algerian rebellion. Considering the unlikelihood that all these conditions would be fulfilled, it was no wonder that many persons continued to scan the Eastern skies in hope of some favorable portent that would dispel the dangers of the time and make these extra exertions unnecessary.

9. NEW PERSPECTIVES IN WESTERN EUROPE

Undesirable though it might be from the standpoint of Europe's physical security, the urge to reduce defense burdens and lighten military budgets was certainly not to be wondered at in a world where war had become so terrible and where defense had become so costly that the military expenditure of the fifteen NATO allies in the eight years since their alliance was concluded was reckoned at almost $372 billion. Least of all was it to be wondered at in a year like 1957, when defense costs were at a new peak and strong inflationary pressures were being felt throughout the NATO area. Great Britain, which had just escaped a serious financial crisis and had recently been forced to ask the United States and Canada to revise its repayment obligations on earlier loans, was engaged in a constant race to keep exports growing faster than its internal labor and production costs. France, saddled like Britain with heavy commitments in the field of social welfare expenditure, labored under the additional burden of the war in Algeria, whose cost to the French people could be calculated in various ways but was commonly rated at about $1 billion a year. Among the major European powers, only the German Federal Republic, which had started with a physically ruined country but had been free from overseas commitments and until recently from military obligations, had managed both to complete its economic recovery and to forge rapidly ahead in the race for world markets. And even this brilliant achievement had its dark side in so far as it tended to arouse the jealousy of neighboring states and unbalance the delicate mechanisms of European trade and payments. Western Europe, though momentarily enjoying a measure of general prosperity beyond anything it had known in the past, had clearly not found any pattern that would assure stability and prosperity in the future.

Outside the economic field, the Western European nations were also faced with unsolved problems of great delicacy and complexity which affected their relations both with each other and with the outside world. What place ought Europe really to occupy on a globe that was being increasingly dominated by two "superpowers," moved by opposite ideological principles and rapidly acquiring the capacity to destroy not only each other but everything that lay between them? In the ideological conflict between Communism and freedom, the majority of Europeans had no hesitation in ranging themselves on the side of freedom, which for practical purposes meant the United States. Yet very few of them were at all satisfied with the position of dependence on this country which they had occupied for the past dozen years, and which the United States seemed at least as anxious to terminate as they could be. The experience of the Suez crisis and its aftermath had strengthened the feeling that European views and interests would not always coincide exactly with those of the United States, and that there ought to be more effective ways of ensuring that they were taken into account. Premier Mollet summed up this feeling and suggested a possible answer in a speech before the French National Assembly on January 22:

"Between an America which is now too impulsive and now too slow to understand perils and a Soviet Union which is disquieting and sometimes still menacing, how often we have wished for a united Europe acting as a world force, not neutral, but independent."

Somewhat similar questions arose with respect to the position of Europe in relation to the overseas territories which in former times had contributed so much to European prosperity and presented so large a field for European initiative. The past ten or twelve years had seen Great Britain, France, the Netherlands unceremoniously ousted from one former colonial territory after another, and clinging with rather uncertain prospects to such overseas rights and positions as they still retained. Whatever might be said in criticism of European colonialism in past decades, nothing very satisfactory could be said about the present relationship between Europe and the larger world beyond the seas. In their bitter hostility toward their former European masters, some of the leaders of the "anticolonial" movement had not only refused to cooperate for common ends but in certain instances had drifted perilously close to association with the Communist bloc. Surely there must be ways in which European skills, initiative, and capital could play a more constructive part in the developing life of these countries—especially, perhaps, in Africa, where the independence movement on the whole was younger and the atmosphere less poisoned by mutual distrust than it was in the Middle East and Asia. A fruitful association of European with African enterprise, some Europeans believed, might also equip Europe to play a more constructive role in years to come in relation to the United States and the U.S.S.R.

The months that followed the Suez crisis were a period of intensive thought along these lines and witnessed a number of significant steps toward closer association within Western Europe and also between Europe and Africa. Significantly, these trends were welcomed by the United States almost as heartily as they were condemned by the Soviet Union. Ever since the days of the Marshall Plan, Washington under both Democratic and Republican administrations had regarded itself as the foremost advocate and patron of European "unification." The present revival of interest in intra-European projects was considered a healthy trend and one that offset in some degree the negative impact of the Suez affair. While reserving the right to look closely at any intra-European arrangement that would affect American commercial interests, United States authorities from the President down stressed their readiness to provide practical assistance to such efforts wherever possible.

Concerning the African aspects of European union Washington had less to say, presumably because the French-originated concept of "Eurafrica" was introduced into the discussions at a comparatively late stage and had too many unexplored angles to permit an immediate judgment. Nevertheless the idea of a European-African association helped to smooth the formal reconciliation between the American and French governments which had taken place on the occasion of Premier Mollet's visit to Washington at the end of February. According to the official communiqué of February 28,[8] the President agreed with his guest that the objectives France professed to be seeking in the development of its African territories were "in conformity with the desire of both Governments to improve living conditions of mankind and to assure them, along with a better standard of living, the benefits of essential democratic liberties."

The mechanisms which were intended to carry forward this movement toward closer association in Europe—or "Eurafrica" —had already been worked out in preliminary form by the six continental nations which had formed the European Coal and Steel Community in 1952 and had been expected to compose the abortive European Defense Community, rejected by the French National Assembly in 1954. Inspired largely by the energy of Foreign Minister Spaak of Belgium, representatives of France, Western Germany, Italy, and the three Benelux governments had within the last few months completed the broad outlines of two major treaties: one establishing a European Economic Community or "Common Market," linking the six participating countries in a single customs area without internal tariff barriers; the other setting up a European Atomic Community to pool their efforts in promoting the peaceful uses of atomic energy. These were not the only current projects for closer integration among the six nations of "little Europe." There was also talk of a "green pool" or agricultural union, and of similar unions in the fields of transportation, electric power, and posts and telecommunications. But only the Common Market and the Atomic Community or "Euratom" had reached a stage where they were ready for final consideration at the governmental level. M. Spaak was particularly insistent that the treaties be made ready for signature while sympathetic governments were in power in the principal countries involved and before he himself took over from Lord Ismay as Secretary-General of NATO.

In contrast to the situation in earlier years, there appeared to be a good chance that this new association of six continental European countries would not remain a purely "little European" grouping but would be linked in some way with Great Britain and possibly with other outlying Western European countries such as the Scandinavian states and Austria. As Chancellor of the Exchequer in the Eden government, Mr. Macmillan had put forward during the summer of 1956 the idea of a European "free trade area," broader though less intimate than the Common Market, in which Great Britain might also participate provided it was not required to drop its special economic ties with the Commonwealth countries. Foreign Min-

ister Selwyn Lloyd had an even more far-reaching concept—
a sort of "grand design" for coordinating all of the multifari-
ous European economic, military, and political organizations
under the aegis of an all-European parliamentary assembly. No
one doubted, however, that the task of constructing an institutional framework which would accommodate both British and
continental interests would be long and arduous and would
have to wait at least until the Common Market and the Atomic
Community had taken definite shape.

At the moment, the most critical difficulties concerned not
Britain but France, as an indispensable member of any European association of even limited scope. Despite the warmly
"European" outlook of Premier Mollet, France was still influenced strongly by the nationalist and restrictionist mentality
which had led a majority of French deputies to vote against
the European Defense Community. With a deeply ingrained
tradition of economic protectionism and an instinctive fear of
close association with Germany, France at the beginning of
1957 was putting forward various new conditions designed to
ensure that its membership in the proposed economic and
atomic energy communities would affect it as little as possible.
Yet even France, with its lingering dream of "great power"
status, could not be blind to the necessity of measures for
strengthening the European fabric and recovering for Europe
as a whole some of that influence in world affairs which no
European country could any longer exercise individually. In
the course of an arduous series of negotiations that extended
through the winter, most of the specific points at issue were to
be so far compromised as to enable Premier Mollet to join his
European colleagues in Rome for the formal signature of the
two treaties on March 25, 1957.

Of the various French objections to the preliminary treaty
texts, those relating to Euratom caused comparatively the least
difficulty. From many points of view, the need for Euratom
was much more easily demonstrated than the necessity for the
Common Market. Western Europe was rapidly outgrowing its
conventional energy resources; even if continued access to
Middle Eastern oil was assured, atomic power would soon become a vital necessity if an adequate rate of economic growth

was to be maintained. Individually, no continental country was in a position to produce such power economically; but by combining their efforts and taking advantage of American, British, and Canadian assistance in technology and fissionable materials, it was believed that they could develop an atomic power industry sufficient for foreseeable needs and could thus keep their dependence on imported coal and petroleum within tolerable limits. This reasoning was fully substantiated by the findings of a group of three experts who visited North America and Britain on behalf of the six governments early in 1957 and received assurances of cooperation from the authorities in Washington, Ottawa, and London.[9]

Most of the problems involved in actually setting up Euratom were technical and institutional; there was no question about its basic mission of promoting the formation and rapid growth of nuclear industries by sponsoring research and channeling financial resources, materials, and skills in accordance with an over-all plan. The only provision to which France made serious objection was the stipulation that the members of the proposed community must renounce the right to manufacture nuclear weapons. This stipulation would have consigned France permanently to the ranks of atomic "have-not" powers, widened the gulf that separated it from the other members of the "Big Four," and deprived it of one more element of superiority over Western Germany, which had renounced atomic weapons at the time of its admission to NATO in 1954. Rather than allow the negotiations to break down over this point, a compromise was accepted whereby France would continue doing research on nuclear weapons but for the time being, at any rate, would refrain from carrying out tests.

The proposed European Economic Community raised more difficult questions, and no one could forecast in advance just how it would affect the 160 million inhabitants of the prospective member countries. Here the essential objective was the gradual removal of restrictions on the movement of goods, manpower, and capital within the area of the six countries and the establishment by them of a common tariff vis-à-vis the outside world. The result, it was hoped, would be the creation of a unified internal market big enough to realize the advantages of large-scale production and more effective competition both within Europe and outside. A good many non-European countries entertained substantial reservations about this project, and the United States made clear on several occasions that it, too, would look with disfavor on any arrangement involving discrimination by the community against the trade of non-members. Within the proposed community, there were serious misgivings on the part of various high-cost producers who would lose the protection of national tariff walls. Particularly feared in France was the impact of competition with other countries having lower wage and social security costs. A whole series of mitigating provisions had to be worked out, largely for France's benefit—a transitional period of twelve to fifteen years; the right to maintain special French import taxes and export subsidies for two years; a limited right of veto on tariff reductions; a beginning toward "harmonization" of labor practices and social security costs. Then, just as agreement appeared in sight, France came forward in late January with startling new proposals. In effect, it asked that the Common Market, hitherto thought of as being limited to Europe, be expanded to include not only the metropolitan territories of the participating countries but also their overseas possessions.

This unexpected proposal, which for practical purposes would concern mainly the French and Belgian-administered territories in Africa, was somewhat obscure in its motivations but was obviously related to France's current difficulties in the field of colonial policy. In the midst of its bitter fight to retain control of Algeria, France was making a valiant if belated effort to modernize the administration of its other overseas territories—now mainly confined to Africa—and give them a political and economic status more closely attuned to mid-century requirements. A law enacted in June 1956 had laid the basis for extensive self-government in French West Africa, French Equatorial Africa, and Madagascar, where elections were held with generally satisfactory results on March 31, 1957. Economic development in these territories was also being pressed to the limit of French resources; and France looked forward even more hopefully to the exploitation of the newly discovered oil resources and other mineral wealth of the

French Sahara in southern Algeria, which might, under favoring circumstances, enable it to dispense with the precarious oil supplies of the Middle East.

Two major difficulties loomed at the very threshold of these projects: a lack of development capital, and the continuance of the Algerian nationalist rebellion. For Algeria, France had for many months been seeking a formula which would preserve that territory as French soil but take the steam out of the insurrection and silence France's numerous critics at the United Nations. With a new debate on Algeria just beginning in New York, an application of the "common market" idea had seemed to offer definite forensic advantages. France's objective, Foreign Minister Christian Pineau explained to the General Assembly on February 4, was to help Algeria find its true advantage in "a large France-African whole, based on a community of cultural, economic and strategic interests." A French-African common market, M. Pineau continued, would itself be only a stepping stone toward the ultimate goal of "Eurafrica": "Europe in its entirety, bringing to Africa its capital and its techniques, should enable the immense African continent to become an essential factor in world politics."

What this would mean for the members of the proposed Economic Community had meanwhile been outlined in more detail at a conference of the six Foreign Ministers in Brussels. In addition to throwing open their territories to the products of overseas France, it was suggested that the Common Market countries should join in setting up a billion-dollar colonial development fund for the advancement of French and other overseas territories. A further essential part of the scheme was the establishment of closer trade ties between African areas and the Common Market countries, a feature that might contribute to economic development in Africa but would hardly be welcomed by Great Britain and other outside countries that were interested in African trade, whether as participants or competitors.

Neither in New York nor in Brussels were the French proposals received with great enthusiasm. At the United Nations, advocates of Algerian independence looked on the "Eurafrica" plan as a mere subterfuge and continued to insist that Algeria was entitled to nothing less than "self-determination" (cf. section 16). In Western Europe, countries like the Netherlands which had no African possessions of their own were not much inclined to begin shouldering responsibility for the French empire, either politically or financially. France itself, for that matter, was not eager to see its Algerian citizens availing themselves of all the privileges of the Common Market, such as the free movement of labor from one country to another; nor were Frenchmen over-enthusiastic about inviting German capital to participate in the development of their overseas territories. Yet Western Germany was the only member of the prospective union with important additional capital available for overseas investment. The final arrangement among the six governments provided that during an initial five-year period, France and Germany would participate in the venture to the extent of $200 million each. A total of $181,250,000 would be contributed by the other members of the union. The lion's share of the funds thus assembled would be directed to the French overseas territories, which would receive $511,250,000 while the balance of $70 million was reserved for the Belgian Congo, Ruanda-Urundi, Italian-administered Somaliland, and Netherlands New Guinea.

As signed on March 25, the Rome treaties [10] also provided for the establishment or expansion of certain common institutions which would, it was hoped, eventually become the nucleus of a broader European government. As with the European Coal and Steel Community with its Council and High Authority, the activities of the Economic and Atomic Energy Communities were to be guided by executive bodies (here known as Commissions) supervised to some extent—though less closely—by high-level Councils composed of governmental representatives. Also included in the organizational charts were special advisory committees on technical and economic and social matters. All three European communities, moreover, would have in common the Court of Justice and parliamentary Assembly already functioning in connection with the Coal and Steel Community. With a somewhat increased membership chosen from the parliamentary bodies of the six participating countries, this Assembly would meet once a year to hear the reports of the three executive bodies, and would have the right to require their resignations by passing votes of censure. This was a rather more substantial function than was accorded to Europe's two other parliamentary assemblies, set up in connection with the seven-nation Western European Union and the fifteen-nation Council of Europe. Their authority was mainly confined to budgetary matters and the adoption of resolutions.

The completion of these arrangements was not allowed to occur without a typical manifestation of dissent by the Soviet Union, which on March 16 issued a long official statement [11] asserting that Euratom and the Common Market would heighten the danger of war, play into the hands of American and West German "monopolists," lessen the chances for German reunification, expose France to renewed danger of German domination, and enable economically stronger countries to impose their will on weaker ones. As an alternative, Moscow called attention to certain of its own past proposals dealing with all-European conferences and agreements on economic cooperation and atomic development. This hostile demonstration did not noticeably delay the signature of the treaties, nor did it appear likely to interfere significantly with their ratification by the various national parliaments, which was duly effected in the course of the summer and autumn. "The road to European unification will be long and often difficult," said an official Dutch statement of July 10, "but the acceptance of the treaties means that retreat is impossible and the only question left is how long it will take before the ultimate goal is reached."

The decision to include African and other overseas territories in the Common Market would not facilitate the projected association of Great Britain with its continental neighbors through the medium of a free trade area. Participants in the free trade area, as distinguished from the Common Market, would be expected to eliminate internal tariff barriers as among themselves but would retain whatever tariffs they thought proper in relation to outside countries, subject only to the requirements of the General Agreement on Tariffs and Trade and other international undertakings. In putting forward the idea of a free trade area, moreover, Great Britain had stipulated that it should apply only to manufactured goods and not to foodstuffs. In the agricultural field, the United Kingdom wished to retain the right to protect its own farmers and maintain preferential arrangements affecting the agricultural production of Canada, Australia, and other Commonwealth members. This reservation had not been very popular with such countries as Denmark and the Netherlands, which saw no reason why they should remove their tariffs on British manufactured goods while Britain continued to discriminate against their agricultural products. The inclusion of African territories, which also produced mainly agricultural items, complicated the problem still further and strengthened British reservations about the whole project. Studies and discussions continued, mainly within the seventeen-nation Organization for European Economic Cooperation, but prospects of an agreement did not for the moment grow noticeably closer. British official interest appeared to revive somewhat with the approach of 1958, the inaugural date of the Common Market; but this trend was offset to some degree by growing opposition in France, where it was felt that the free trade scheme failed to demand "equality of sacrifice" on the part of the United Kingdom or to provide for close enough cooperation in such matters as social policy and finance.

Great Britain's invariable concern with its Commonwealth associations was possibly even stronger than usual at this period in consequence of the profound changes that were currently taking place almost from month to month in the basic structure of the Commonwealth and Empire. In spite of Soviet and other accusations of "colonialism," Britain was actually moving with remarkable speed to accord the privileges of independence to those of its subject peoples that seemed most nearly ready to exercise them. Two British colonial territories achieved independence within the Commonwealth in 1957. The African colony of the Gold Coast ceased to exist on March 6, becoming the independent state of Ghana and the ninth member of the Commonwealth of Nations (section 16). Malaya took its place in the Commonwealth on August 31 (section 18), and Singapore, Nigeria, and the British West Indies were expected to follow the same road within the next two or three years. These triumphs for the principle of self-determination offset in some degree the international opprobrium Great Britain had incurred in some quarters in recent years by its opposition to self-determination for the Greek-speaking population of Cyprus.

Even the Cyprus quarrel, however, began to lose some of its acuteness during the spring of 1957 after the EOKA terrorist leaders declared a truce and London released the Greek Cypriote representative, Archbishop Makarios, from his detention in the Seychelles Islands. British sources found it necessary to emphasize that this conciliatory gesture, occurring just four days after the Bermuda conference, had been made spontaneously and not at the suggestion of President Eisenhower. The inability of Greece, Turkey, and Great Britain to agree on the island's future continued to militate against the effectiveness of Western policy in this disturbed part of the world; but at least the shootings and bombings had virtually ceased, and the governments concerned all professed to be seeking a solution compatible with their common interest as NATO members. To the extent that they managed to submerge or mitigate their differences, they would be that much better able to cope with the always dangerous manifestations of Soviet diplomacy and political warfare. (See further section 26).

10. EUROPE THROUGH MOSCOW EYES

Such improvements as might be detected in the situation of the West during these months can have afforded no satisfaction to the men in the Kremlin, whose basic policy had been and apparently was still directed to the breakup of what they called the "aggressive North Atlantic bloc" and the withdrawal of American power to the other side of the Atlantic. Any hopes they might have entertained for the im-

mediate collapse of the Western alliance in the wake of the
disturbances of the last autumn had, however, plainly been
premature, even if it was not yet certain how far the Western
governments had succeeded in permanently repairing their
badly shaken association. To the extent of its ability, Moscow
continued during the first half of 1957 to hinder and oppose
the West's political recovery and particularly the strengthening of NATO's defensive "shield" through the introduction
of short-range missiles and tactical nuclear weapons. Such was
the evident purpose of the threatening letters dispatched by
Premier Bulganin to assorted European heads of governments (which he insisted were not threats at all), as well as
the last-minute attempt to obstruct the conclusion of the
Rome treaties. Through most of this period, however, the
Soviet Government clearly felt itself to be on the political
defensive. Efforts to bring its weight to bear on the outside
world were evidently being subordinated for the most part
to the urgent task of reestablishing order and security behind
the Iron Curtain.

Just how badly the Communist world had been hit by the
disturbances of the autumn and winter was impossible for
any outsider to determine. Indeed, it lay beyond the knowledge of the Communist leaders themselves, whose techniques
for measuring the attitudes of human beings were presumably no more infallible than those of the Western governments. One of the purposes of the innumerable conferences
among Communist dignitaries which took place during the
early months of 1957 was undoubtedly that of gaining a
clearer notion of the state of affairs prevailing both in the
satellite countries and in the U.S.S.R. itself. Even when the
situation had been fairly fully sized up, there would still
be differences of opinion about how best to handle it and
how far Moscow should go toward reinstating the comparatively easy-going policies and free-wheeling diplomacy of the
1955–56 period. A basic difference of approach between
Khrushchev, the man of the Twentieth Party Congress, and
more conservative-minded or "Stalinist" figures such as
Molotov and Kaganovich had been evident to some observers
for months past and was evidently still playing a role beneath

the surface. The political "line" promoted by Khrushchev
through most of 1956 appeared at the moment to have fallen
into serious discredit. Whether it had a chance of revival
would depend in part on how successfully the Soviet Government and party were able to dig themselves out from the
debris of catastrophe in Eastern Europe.

The difficulties Moscow now confronted were basically the
result of developments outside the Soviet frontiers rather
than within the Soviet Union itself. The situation at home
still appeared reasonably sound. Economic progress during
the past year had not attained the exaggerated goals set forth
in the Sixth Five-Year Plan promulgated in February, but
was still proceeding at a substantially faster rate than that
of the more highly developed economies of the United States
or Western Europe. The Soviet military establishment was
certainly no less formidable than it had been in the past:
Defense Secretary Wilson told Congress on May 28 that the
capabilities of the Soviet forces for land, sea, and air warfare,
including the ability to deliver nuclear weapons, had definitely increased in the last year. Nor did Soviet public
opinion appear sufficiently agitated by recent events to warrant great concern. There might be some tendency among
the younger generation to ask embarrassing questions about
Hungary and Poland and to indulge a taste for foreign,
"bourgeois" manners and customs. But basically the Soviet
man in the street seemed to have confidence in his government, reasonable faith in its pronouncements, and a definite
pride in Soviet achievement.

What had broken down was not the internal system of the
U.S.S.R. but the larger system of the "camp of socialism."
Already breached by the independent stand of Tito's Yugoslavia, Moscow's control of developments in the Communist
world had now been further undermined by Poland's insistence on the doctrine of "separate roads to socialism," Hungary's unsuccessful attempt to throw off the Soviet yoke, and
the accompanying political and ideological ferment both in
Eastern Europe and in the Communist parties of the West.
Most outside observers believed that the economic plight of
Poland and Hungary and the resultant collapse of satellite

economic planning had been the primary factors behind the severe cutbacks in the U.S.S.R.'s own Five-Year Plan which had been announced at the end of 1956. If Moscow felt somewhat insecure from a military standpoint and reacted with unusual vehemence to new developments in Western defense planning, its uneasiness was presumably due at least in part to the realization that the armies of its satellites, though perhaps ready enough to fight for the independence of their homelands, might well balk at fighting the West for the greater glory of the Soviet Union. Finally, if Moscow violently resented every expression of outside interest in conditions in Hungary and elsewhere in Eastern Europe, its feelings were at least comprehensible in view of the humiliation it had suffered at the hands of the Hungarian people and the possible danger of fresh revolts against its authority.

A review of international developments in the years of the "cold war" might easily suggest that Moscow had never felt entirely secure in its control of Eastern Europe, which had been imposed on unwilling populations over the protest of the Western powers and had never been acknowledged as permanent by the non-Communist governments, particularly the United States. For well over a decade, Soviet and American aims in this area had remained fundamentally in conflict; the clash of policies, now open, now latent, had been perhaps the most important among the many obstacles to a general East-West settlement. This permanent Soviet-American rivalry over Eastern Europe had entered a new phase at the outset of the disturbances of the preceding autumn, with each side redefining its policy objectives in terms which, though milder in some respects, still appeared mutually incompatible. The United States, disclaiming any intention of intervening militarily in Eastern Europe, had nevertheless invited the Eastern European governments to assert their independence of Moscow and had held out the hope of substantial assistance in making the necessary economic adjustments.[12] The Soviet Union, in a government declaration of October 30, 1956,[13] had put forward the concept of a "great commonwealth of socialist nations," bound together by a common allegiance to "the people's democratic system" (i.e.,

Communism), but based on "the principles of complete equality, of respect for territorial integrity, state independence and sovereignty, and of noninterference in one another's internal affairs."

It was on the basis of these superficially similar but really opposite concepts that Washington and Moscow continued during early 1957 their tenacious contest over the future of Eastern Europe. Their rivalry took different forms in Hungary, in Poland, and in Yugoslavia, the three Communist countries whose orientation appeared most susceptible to outside influence. Involved in the outcome, however, was the future of Communism not only in these countries but also in the other Soviet satellites, in Eastern Germany, and perhaps in the Soviet Union itself. There was, however, a vast difference between the two protagonists both in the character of their aims and in the degree of vigor with which they pursued them. The resoluteness with which the Soviet Union had set out to reassert its control in Eastern Europe was of a quite different order from that of the United States in contesting it. The contrast was epitomized in Mr. Dulles' already quoted comment of April 22: "When Hungary was invaded and freedom crushed, we sponsored a United Nations condemnation of the Soviet Union."

That American interest in the fate of Hungary was not limited to that unhappy country but reflected a wider concern for the issue of freedom from Soviet tyranny was once again made clear by Ambassador Henry Cabot Lodge in replying in the United Nations General Assembly on February 28, 1957 to the already familiar Soviet charge that the United States had fomented the Hungarian revolution. This accusation was wholly untrue, said Mr. Lodge; but it was true that the United States would not "remain silent and unprotesting" in face of the relentless Soviet assault on human dignity and freedom, in Hungary or elsewhere. "We will do what we can, always in conformity with the purposes and principles of the United Nations, to show these hapless victims that they are not forgotten, that they are not lost"— that the "old ties of kinship and friendship have not been broken, that this is but a long night, and that the end of that long night is the dawn."

Whatever the long-range objective, however, there seemed to be little enough that could be done in a practical way to alleviate the sufferings of the Hungarian people. While Soviet tanks stood ready to intervene again if necessary, the Kádár government during these weeks was stamping out the last sparks of revolt, breaking up the revolutionary workers' councils, ferreting out and executing those active in the "counterrevolution," and retracting one item after another in the superficially liberal program with which it had taken office in November. The numerous appeals voiced by the General Assembly had failed to deter the Soviet and Hungarian authorities from their methodical work of repression, and there was little likelihood that further United Nations action would prove more effective.

Thus the principal United States objective as 1957 began had been simply to keep the situation before the eyes of the world public. To this end it had supported the adoption of one more resolution (January 10) establishing a five-nation committee to investigate and observe conditions in Hungary on behalf of the Assembly.[14] Although the Hungarian government refused its cooperation and protested the alleged intrusion into Hungary's internal affairs, numerous sources of information on Hungarian events would be available to the committee in New York and other free world centers. On another front, the United States in common with other nations was active in providing emergency relief through Red Cross and other channels and in finding at least temporary homes for Hungarian refugees in Austria and Yugoslavia. So far as the central problem of Hungary's national status was concerned, however, its efforts remained distressingly ineffectual.

The situation in Poland offered greater possibilities for constructive action. Gomulka's new regime might be thoroughly Communist in outlook, but had already proved that a Communist outlook was not incompatible with a resolute concern for Polish independence. Having managed to avoid the crushing of Poland's national revolution by Soviet armed force, Gomulka now faced the incredibly difficult task of preserving enough elbow room to get the country started on a specifically Polish "road to socialism." To do this he had to be sufficiently "Communist" to avoid Soviet reprisals and ward off trouble from the die-hard Stalinists in his own party organization; at the same time he had to be sufficiently "national" to retain the support of the Polish public and obtain necessary assistance from private and governmental sources in the West.

In this perilous venture Gomulka was apparently assisted in no small degree by the diplomatic endeavors of Chou En-lai, who visited Eastern Europe in January and would seem to have served as an effective mediator between Warsaw and Moscow. At least equally important was the unmistakable endorsement accorded Gomulka by the people of Poland in that country's national election on January 20, in which even the Roman Catholic hierarchy urged support of the Communist-dominated National Front ticket. This popular vote of confidence not only strengthened Gomulka's hand in dealings with the U.S.S.R. but enabled him to offer more determined resistance to those Poles who advocated a return to Stalinism—as well as those who advocated a broader liberalization of the regime.

Gomulka's hope of substantial economic assistance from the United States, on the other hand, was only partially fulfilled. A Polish delegation which went to Washington in February in search of credits totaling $300 million had to content itself in June with $95 million, the bulk of it in surplus agricultural commodities to be paid for in Polish currency. A first agreement signed June 7 [15] provided for an Export-Import Bank loan of $30 million plus the sale for zlotys of $18.9 million worth of cotton, fats, and oils. Once Congress had extended the Agricultural Trade Development and Assistance Act (section 6), a second agreement was concluded on August 14 [16] whereby Poland would purchase, also for zlotys, an additional $46.1 million worth of surplus wheat and cotton.

Whereas Poland still professed to belong to the Soviet bloc, Communist Yugoslavia had long since asserted its complete

independence of the Soviet Union and in so doing had qualified for much more substantial American aid, both economic
and military. Despite a marked amelioration in Yugoslav-
Soviet relations since the death of Stalin and more particularly since Khrushchev's visit to Belgrade in 1955, President
Eisenhower had formally determined as recently as October
1956 that Yugoslavia was still eligible for American assistance. At the same time, he had announced that it was
thought best to hold up any further shipments of major military equipment until Yugoslavia's orientation was more fully
clarified.[17] But subsequent developments had reopened the
latent cleavage between Yugoslavia and the U.S.S.R. Tito,
as the originator of the doctrine of "separate roads to socialism," had been a warm supporter of Khrushchev's policies
and was bitterly critical of the "ingrown Stalinist tendencies"
which he blamed for recent developments in the Soviet bloc,
particularly in Hungary. In consequence, Soviet-Yugoslav relations had again deteriorated; Moscow was showing a tendency to renege on its economic commitments; *Pravda* and
the Yugoslav *Borba* were engaging in wordy ideological
battles.

President Eisenhower, though unable to guarantee President Tito a public welcome on his proposed visit to Washington, thus saw no reason to delay further the shipment
of 200 jet planes and other military items which had long
since been scheduled for Yugoslavia. On May 14, 1957,
the State Department announced that the ban had been
lifted in the conviction that Yugoslavia intended to remain
independent and that it was important for the United States
to adhere to its established policy of "lending support to
those countries seeking to withstand Soviet pressures." [18]
Though glad to receive the promised equipment, Belgrade
betrayed some annoyance over the fact that the delivery had
been directly linked to bad relations with Moscow. Tito's
stand, as expressed on many occasions (e.g., May 27), was
this: "We do not wish to have hostile relations with the
West, but we do not wish to quarrel with the East." In the
nature of the East-West struggle, such a position could not
be fully satisfactory to either side, although it gave both

Washington and Moscow a measure of assurance that Yugoslavia was not going to join the opposite camp while Tito remained in control.

From both the Soviet and Western viewpoints, relations with Yugoslavia were important not only in themselves but because Yugoslavia's experience stood out as a possible model for other Eastern European countries that might succeed in loosening Soviet bonds. There is reason to believe that the question of Soviet-Yugoslav relations played an important part in the quarrel that was apparently going forward within the Soviet party leadership during these very months when the United States was attempting, by various methods and with varying success, to advance the cause of independence in individual Eastern European countries. According to the official account released after Khrushchev's victory over his Soviet opponents at the end of June,[19] Soviet policy at home and abroad had for months been hamstrung by the attitude of a reactionary "antiparty group" which included Malenkov, Molotov, and Kaganovich and was supported by Foreign Minister Dmitri T. Shepilov.

The attitude of this group, if the official account can be believed, had been characterized by "the certain fact that they were and still are shackled by old notions and methods, that they have drifted away from the life of the party and the country, failed to see the new conditions, the new situation, take a conservative attitude, stubbornly cling to obsolete forms and methods of work that are no longer in keeping with the interests of the advance towards communism. . . ." Being without appreciation for "the creative movement of the masses" and unable to see that the Soviet Union was going through "a powerful rise in popular activity and a fresh surge of creative energy," this group was said to have stubbornly resisted Khrushchev's initiatives in the domestic field. In the sphere of foreign policy it had "attempted in effect to oppose the Leninist policy of peaceful coexistence between states with different social systems, of relaxing international tension and establishing friendly relations between the U.S.S.R. and all the peoples of the world." Molotov, in particular, was said to have shown "narrow-mindedness and

hampered in every way the implementation of the new pressing measures intended to ease international tension and promote universal peace." Specifically, he had repeatedly ob-
structed efforts to improve relations with Yugoslavia, had
opposed the conclusion of the treaties with Austria in 1955
and Japan in 1956, had opposed the new ideological formula-
tions on foreign policy put forward by Khrushchev at the
Twentieth Party Congress, and had opposed personal contacts between Soviet leaders and foreign statesmen. In a
word, this group had been in opposition to the whole trend
and spirit of Soviet policy as it had developed under Khrushchev's influence since the beginning of 1955.

Although it was surprising to many observers to find Malenkov and Shepilov accused of these particular shortcomings,
the official indictment corresponded reasonably well to what
had been known of the attitude of such old Stalin associates
as Molotov and Kaganovich. Moreover, the revelation that
the Kremlin had been split by policy differences of this magnitude went far to account for the somewhat uneven quality
of Soviet foreign policy during the spring of 1957. The sudden replacement of Shepilov by Andrei A. Gromyko on February 15 had brought no immediate change in the "hard"
line which had set in at the time of the Hungarian revolt,
and which had remained much in evidence in Moscow's comments on Middle Eastern and NATO affairs. By mid-April,
however, both Khrushchev and Bulganin had begun to talk
in terms of a new "relaxation of tensions" and a possibility
for improved relations between nations, including the establishment of new contacts on both the official and popular
levels. From this time forward there had been renewed expressions of Soviet interest in disarmament, new references
to the importance of cultural exchange, new suggestions
about the timeliness of a meeting of heads of governments
on the Geneva pattern. On June 2, Khrushchev had appeared
on an American television program with a bland appeal for
mutual understanding and "competitive coexistence" along
much the same lines that he had advocated before the Hungarian disaster.[20]

Although this propagandistic invasion of the American

BUT THE WALL'S STILL THERE

By Poinier in *The Detroit News*

home caused some annoyance in official Washington, it did not necessarily mean that the insidious policy of "competitive coexistence" had finally won the day in Moscow. Khrushchev at this period had not yet vanquished his opponents on the Central Committee. The latter, apparently, had objected with particular vehemence to two of his recent projects in the economic field: a plan for a thoroughgoing decentralization of the management of Soviet industry (May 7) and a plan for overtaking the United States within four years in the per capita production of meat, milk, and butter. "We are not going to blast the capitalist world with bombs," the party secretary had said on May 22. "But if we catch [up with] the United States in the level of meat, milk and butter production per capita we shall be releasing a mighty torpedo at the mainstays of capitalism."

Early in June, while Khrushchev, accompanied by Bulganin, attempted to sell his peaceful coexistence thesis to the unreceptive population of Finland, the "antiparty group" in Moscow would seem to have laid plans for nothing less than a *coup d'état*. Shortly after the two leaders' return, on June 17, there was a meeting of the party Presidium. According to the best-informed accounts, Khrushchev suddenly found himself surrounded by enemies and told that he must resign forthwith. Even Bulganin is said to have joined the opposition. With great presence of mind, Khrushchev managed to have the issue transferred to the full party Central Committee, thus gaining time to rally support in the party and, even more important, in the military establishment headed by Marshal Zhukov. A protracted debate is known to have taken place in the Central Committee from June 22 to 29 and to have been followed within a few days by the summary expulsion of Malenkov, Kaganovich, Molotov, and Shepilov from all their party and governmental posts, as well as the downgrading of various other dignitaries who had taken the wrong side. Marshal Zhukov was rewarded by a full membership on the new Presidium, apparently symbolizing the decisive role of the armed forces in maintaining the balance of Soviet politics. His turn would come later (section 23). Khrushchev, breaking with former Soviet patterns, refrained from liquidating his chief opponents but banished them to relatively inconsequential jobs many miles from Moscow. Molotov became ambassador to the nominally independent Mongolian People's Republic. Bulganin remained as Premier, but his diminished prestige was plainly evident when he accompanied Khrushchev on an official visit to Czechoslovakia a few days later. Instead of "B. and K.," it was now "K. and B."

Having got the better of his opponents at home, it might have been expected that Khrushchev would proceed with all haste along the path of "relaxation of tensions" which he had appeared so eager to follow. That this was his intention seemed to be indicated by the promptitude with which he made overtures for a better relationship with Yugoslavia. At a meeting with Tito in Rumania at the beginning of August, he assured the Yugoslav President that their old understanding about "separate roads to socialism" was still in effect and that Soviet-Yugoslav relations would continue to develop on the basis of "equality, mutual assistance and cooperation, the respect of sovereignty, and noninterference in internal affairs."

In relation to the West, on the other hand, Khrushchev's performance can only be described as exceedingly disappointing to all who had hoped for a change in the Soviet position on major issues. At the London disarmament talks, which were widely viewed as the acid test of Moscow's desire for improved relations, the Western delegates waited in vain for some gesture of acceptance or even interest in their proposals (section 11). The people of Western Germany, with elections only a few weeks away, found themselves confronted not with a softening but a hardening of the Soviet stand on German reunification. The Western capitals observed with dismay that the most noticeable sequel to Khrushchev's victory was a marked renewal of tension and instability in the Middle East (section 14).

The reasons for this apparent reversal of Soviet policy cannot be set forth with any precision, despite Khrushchev's unusual freedom in making his views available to the foreign press. We do not know, for example, how far he may have been influenced by the prospect that impending successes in the field of missiles and earth satellites would enable the Soviet Union to talk from a new "position of strength." What we do know is that Khrushchev invariably laid the responsibility for the unsatisfactory state of East-West relations at the door of the United States and took every opportunity to accuse Washington of bad faith and of not really wanting agreements such as it professed to be seeking. In all his public utterances he showed a special antipathy toward American policy in Eastern Europe and toward the personality of Secretary Dulles, whose attitude he professed to regard as much more negative than that of the President or the American people generally. In a typical interview with a *New York Times* correspondent a few weeks before these events,[21] he had declared it to be an "indisputable fact" that the United States and its allies were contemplating aggressive war. With a caustic reference to the "policy of balancing on the brink of war," he had asserted that despite Moscow's desire for talks leading to agreement, "if we are confronted with conditions such as Dulles likes to put forward such as the liberation of East European countries from 'slavery', it might take 200 years before we ever come together. For on these matters we are inflexible."

To a man holding opinions of this order, several developments of the spring and summer might have come as confirmation of his outlook. On June 20 the special United Nations Committee on Hungary released a long, documented report that glaringly illuminated the Soviet role in crushing the Hungarian revolt,[22] and the United States immediately made known its intention to press for the recall of the Assembly to consider the committee's findings (see section 24). American authorities meanwhile continued to express their confidence in the ultimate liberation of the Eastern European countries. The President himself made a moving reference to this theme in a speech at Williamsburg on June 24, and Mr. Dulles in commenting on the upheaval in the Kremlin (July 16) spoke openly and at length of our desire to promote similar trends within the Soviet Union itself.

There was also a misunderstanding about a possible visit

to the United States by Marshal Zhukov. At his news conference on July 17, the President replied to a questioner that
he "couldn't see any harm" if the Soviet Defense Minister
were to exchange visits with Secretary Wilson; but when the
Soviet Embassy attempted to pursue the matter, it was informed on behalf of Secretary Dulles that the President's
comment was only "a hypothetical answer to a hypothetical
question." Mr. Dulles' main concern in the matter had apparently been to avoid giving alarm to allied governments,
and the adverse reaction in Moscow had perhaps not been
fully anticipated. "We evaluated that press conference very
carefully indeed," Khrushchev complained later.[23] ". . . We
felt that this would contribute to an understanding. We
wanted Zhukov to go." But, he added, "We are a proud
nation and we do not want to go down on our knees to
arrange these things."

A further influence that might have moved the Kremlin
in the direction of an intransigent policy was the tendency
of German affairs on the eve of the parliamentary elections
in the Federal Republic. Throughout the spring, as Chancellor Adenauer and his supporters sought to rally the German
electorate behind the established policy of rearmament and association with the West, political observers had looked to Moscow for some gesture aimed at confounding the dominant
Christian Democrats and their allies and encouraging the
Social Democratic opposition. The latter, while thoroughly
opposed to Communism, was advocating a renegotiation of
Germany's commitment to NATO and an attempt to bring
about the reunification of Germany within the framework of
some kind of all-European security system to be set up by
agreement between East and West. This was a program
that the U.S.S.R. had often advocated in the past but for
some reason refrained from pressing just at this period when
it seemingly had an opportunity to unbalance the Western
position in Germany. Instead, Moscow during these months
displayed a quite unusual hostility to the Adenauer government and denounced West Germany's "remilitarization"
with a vehemence that seemed to many to bespeak real fear.
A West German delegation that had gone to Moscow in

the hope of discussing the repatriation of German prisoners of war and other detainees encountered a blank wall of obstruction. Not even a tripartite declaration by the Western powers, renewing their commitment to German reunification in freedom as "an elementary requirement of justice" (Berlin, July 29) [24] could dislodge the Kremlin from its negative stand. Khrushchev, apparently, had given up hope of immediate gains in Western Germany and decided to stake everything on the continuance of Soviet control in Eastern Germany. On a visit to the "German Democratic Republic" on August 7–14, he endorsed a new variant of the Communist program for reunifying Germany (an "equal federation" between the East and West German states) but denounced Chancellor Adenauer in terms that suggested he had no real expectation of an understanding being reached.

Secretary Dulles, on his part, refrained from openly urging Adenauer's cause as he had done four years earlier. Indeed, he had no need to do so. The combination of internal prosperity, modern campaign techniques, and Khrushchev had proved unbeatable. On September 15, the voters gave Dr. Adenauer's party a landslide victory, with 51.8 percent of the popular vote and 270 seats in the 497-seat Bundestag—more seats than the three other parties could command together. The Social Democrats with 169 seats could still deny the government the two-thirds majority needed for constitutional changes. But so long as the eighty-one-year-old Chancellor remained at the head of affairs, there could be little doubt of Germany's attachment to the Western cause or its resistance to Soviet policies in Europe. This prospect was reassuring to the other Western governments but would be unlikely to reduce Soviet intransigence either on the German problem or on other contentious issues.

11. THE DISARMAMENT NEGOTIATIONS

One aspect of Germany's association with the West which appears to have caused the Russians particular irritation was the link maintained by the Western governments between the problem of German reunification and the disarmament questions which had been under discussion in London since the late winter. On a visit to Washington in late May—his fifth since 1949—Chancellor Adenauer had obtained a fresh assurance from President Eisenhower (1) that the United States did not contemplate any action in the field of disarmament "which would prejudice the reunification of Germany," and (2) that any comprehensive disarmament agreement, in the American view, "must necessarily presuppose a prior solution of the problem of German reunification." [25] A similar assurance on behalf of all three major Western powers was included in the Berlin Declaration of July 29.[26]

These statements did not, in reality, signify any important change in Western policy. The United States and its allies had long emphasized that disarmament on any substantial scale would be impracticable until such time as significant progress was made in the solution of East-West political issues. In reiterating this principle with special reference to Germany, their main purpose was to assure the Bonn government that its interests were not being overlooked in the complex discussions at London. From the Soviet point of view, however, this emphasis on the link between disarmament and a German settlement must have come as a disagreeable reminder that the Western governments, though anxious to find a basis of agreement on disarmament, were definitely *not* interested in disarmament "at any price." They wanted disarmament—or, more correctly, a "limitation of armament" under proper safeguards—but they also wanted satisfactory political settlements; and they were perfectly frank in saying that they would not take one without the other. They might take a "first step" toward disarmament without political conditions, but that was all.

Satisfactory political settlements, however, could be obtained only if Moscow radically changed its policy on Germany and other questions which the Kremlin had hitherto regarded as matters of vital interest. To a man of Khrushchev's suspicious temper, it would not be too difficult to conclude that whatever his own attitude toward disarmament, the Western governments were not really interested in the subject and were merely trying to use the talks as an insidi-

ous device for easing the Soviet Union out of its position in
Germany and Eastern Europe. If so, they would only be
applying a technique which the Russians themselves had repeatedly employed in their proposals for a mutual withdrawal of forces from Germany and adjacent areas. Whether
or not Moscow currently viewed the matter in just these
terms, it seems evident that the opposite political purposes
of East and West had a great deal to do with the slow
progress and ultimate failure of the 1957 talks in the United
Nations Disarmament Subcommittee.

The strategy of the American and other Western delegations in these protracted negotiations, undertaken in response
to the usual request from the United Nations Assembly,[27]
was plainly governed by the realization that East-West political differences were still too deep to afford much hope of an
over-all disarmament agreement in the foreseeable future.
Under the leadership of the United States, the Western representatives from the beginning concentrated most of their
attention on proposals for a limited, "first-stage" agreement
which could be put into effect promptly and would at least
reverse the current trend toward constantly increasing armaments and military expenditures. "The essential thing, at
this point of history," Mr. Dulles explained in a radio address
on July 22,[28] "is actually to get started and to move from the
phase of wearisome and unending talk into the phase of
actually doing something." "Time is not unlimited," Mr.
Dulles added. "Each year that passes without agreement adds
to the practical difficulty of achieving adequate limitation
and control." Admittedly every forward step in this difficult
field involved some risk "that hostile forces may gain advantage for themselves." Care must be taken in dealing with
these matters, for they affected the very existence of the free
nations. Nevertheless, Mr. Dulles felt, "The risks of seeking
to move forward are far less than the risks of being frightened
into immobility." Accordingly, he explained, the United
States had developed a set of proposals for a "first-stage" disarmament agreement which "goes as far as can be gone now
without endangering our own safety and that of our allies."

It was a peculiarity of the United Nations disarmament

discussions that the participating Western governments (the United States, the United Kingdom, France, and Canada) did not always operate in such close unison as they customarily did in other forums of East-West negotiation. Other Western delegations independently put forward a number of fresh ideas and proposals in the course of the London talks. For practical purposes, however, the chances of any agreement continued to hinge on the attitudes of the United States and the U.S.S.R., as the two powers that possessed and would continue to possess the greatest potential for either nuclear or conventional warfare. France and Canada had no nuclear weapons, and Great Britain, which had had the atomic bomb since 1952, was just getting around to conduct its first hydrogen bomb tests in the spring of 1957. The United States, on the other hand, had been conducting nuclear test explosions since 1946 and had tested a hydrogen or thermonuclear device as early as 1952; while the U.S.S.R., whose record of nuclear testing went back to 1949, had entered the thermonuclear field in 1953 and by the end of 1956 had carried out at least seventeen atomic and thermonuclear tests and probably a good many more. In 1957 all three powers were continuing their test programs at an accelerated rate, setting off a total of forty-three more recorded explosions—more than twice the number detonated in any previous year. But it was still the United States and the U.S.S.R. who led the field, with twenty-four and thirteen (recorded) explosions respectively in 1957. Great Britain with six explosions remained statistically in the rear even though three of the detonations were of the thermonuclear type.[29]

The steadily mounting emphasis on the nuclear and thermonuclear elements of military power had had two consequences of particular importance in terms of disarmament prospects and also in terms of the East-West political warfare that seemed to be well-nigh inseparable from any disarmament discussion. First, it had greatly reduced the likelihood that nuclear weapons could be totally eliminated from national armaments, as recommended by the General Assembly and devoutly wished by men of good will the world

over. Not only had each of the nuclear "Big Three" become
too dependent on nuclear weapons to be willing to go back
entirely to conventional means of defense. Even had they
agreed to do so, there was no known way of detecting eva-
sions and violations of their agreement. "We have had to
come to the conclusion," said Mr. Dulles (July 16), "that, as
far as existing fissionable material is concerned, we cannot
safely ourselves deny its use for weapons purposes because
we cannot get any assurance that others will do the same."
"Therefore," he added in his radio speech on July 22, "we
must make our plans on the assumption that the nations
which now have nuclear weapons would use them in war."
It was largely for this reason that the United States in the
last couple of years had shifted its attention from the attempt
to control nuclear armaments as such to the attempt to prevent their use in a massive surprise attack. "If you can relieve
the world of the great fear of surprise, devastating attack,"
said President Eisenhower (August 7), "then disarmament,
in my opinion, will follow step by step almost automatically."
This was the reasoning that had inspired the President's
"open skies" proposal at the Geneva conference—a proposal
which still remained a central element in the American disarmament program.

Soviet reaction to these developments had taken a different
course. For the record, Moscow still demanded an absolute
ban on the manufacture and use of nuclear weapons, a demand that still had considerable propaganda value in Asian
and other pacifist circles. But since Marshal Zhukov and
other Soviet military men openly proclaimed their intention
to make full use of these very weapons in case of war (section
5), this point could not be pressed too far. For the most part,
Soviet propaganda now concentrated on the second major
issue raised by current preparations for atomic warfare. This
was the question of possible biological damage to the human
race resulting from nuclear explosions, including weapons
tests. Without in the least curtailing its own test program,
the Soviet Government endeavored in every way to mobilize
the world-wide agitation over radioactive fallout and atmos-
pheric pollution and to turn it against the West in a way

that would embarrass the Western powers and, perhaps, force them to limit or discontinue their own testing activities.

Soviet procedure in this respect was vividly reminiscent of the world-wide Communist campaign against the alleged American use of "germ warfare" in the Korean war. Unfortunately, in this instance Moscow had got hold of a more substantial issue, one that could be exploited without recourse to the towering falsehoods of the Korean war period. Scientific opinion was divided about the extent of the biological dangers resulting from current nuclear tests. But even the scientists connected with the United States Atomic Energy Commission, who tended to minimize them, admitted that any increase in the present level of testing might have dangerous consequences. Many scientists and innumerable laymen took a more alarming view, particularly in such countries as India and Japan, whose government repeatedly remonstrated with all three atomic powers against their testing activities. Though there was no indication that any of the latter were disposed to modify their programs in deference to public uneasiness, all three were at pains to emphasize the precautions they were taking to minimize fallout and other undesirable consequences. At their Bermuda meeting in March, for example, President Eisenhower and Prime Minister Macmillan agreed that future American and British test series would be announced well in advance, and offered to register their tests with the United Nations and open them to "lmited international observation" if the U.S.S.R. would do the same.[30]

Under these circumstances, nuclear testing and the "open skies" plan were bound to emerge as the central issues in the disarmament discussions of 1957. The United States, as the originator of the "open skies" plan, was still determined to press it upon a reluctant U.S.S.R.; the latter, as the power that would presumably gain most from a suspension of nuclear testing, was equally determined to press this item on a reluctant U.S.A. It is true that each government might have been somewhat embarrassed had the other suddenly given in and accepted its maximum proposals. Keen as it was for the principle of mutual aerial inspection, the United

States would not have found it easy to admit Soviet aircraft
to overfly and photograph its own territory; even the establishment of an inspection zone in Europe would be a difficult business, as the ensuing negotiations were to show.
Similarly, the U.S.S.R. would undoubtedly have suffered
some inconvenience had the United States agreed to its
proposals for an unconditional suspension of nuclear tests.
In that case it would either have had to give up its own test
program, which presumably was less advanced than that of
the United States, or to continue its tests clandestinely and
run the risk of detection. Nevertheless, both powers were so
thoroughly committed to their basic positions that they
would have found it difficult to draw back. The essential
question, therefore, was this: How far would the U.S.S.R.
go toward accepting the "open skies" plan, and how far
would the United States go toward accepting a suspension of
nuclear tests?

To discover the answer to this question required a period
of almost six months, during which it is fair to say that the
world was kept in a state of mystification beyond any previous experience. The complications of the subject had become
so great and the accounts of progress were so conflicting that
no one outside of official life and few people in it could hope
to gain any clear idea of what was going on. Although the
Western governments were certainly not unaware of the
"propaganda" importance of the issues under discussion, they
cannot be said to have shown much effectiveness in present-
ing them to the international public. The American delegation in London, headed by Mr. Stassen as the President's
special assistant for disarmament matters, exuded an un-
quenchable optimism which was largely discounted by other
Western delegations and by the press. But both Secretary
Dulles and the President appeared impressed by the relatively
serious behavior of the Soviet delegate, Valerian A. Zorin, and
felt that the Russians were showing an unusual readiness to
subordinate propaganda to serious negotiation. Both the
Secretary of State and the President believed that the
U.S.S.R., like the United States, was subject to strong economic pressures and for that reason might share this country's

interest in finding a safe way to reduce the crushing burden of modern armaments.[31]

Based on this estimate of the Soviet attitude, the President and Secretary Dulles showed a greater than usual readiness to modify the American position on specific aspects of the disarmament problem—though only within the limits stated by Mr. Dulles when he said (May 14) that "We do not intend to weaken the United States militarily merely in reliance on the promises of others which cannot be verified." As already indicated, moreover (section 2), other Washington authorities were considerably more skeptical about the desirability of any agreement with the Russians. Thus a rather intense intragovernmental struggle in Washington was superimposed on the East-West tug of war in London.[32] The picture was further complicated by differences among the Western governments, both those that were participating directly in the negotiations and those that would be involved in any general plan of disarmament or aerial inspection. The State Department was to take considerable pride in the fact that it eventually managed to get all the NATO governments together on a unified air inspection proposal, an achievement that consoled it in some measure for its ultimate inability to reach agreement with the Russians.

The detailed negotiations dealt with a variety of other matters in addition to the central questions of air inspection and nuclear testing. Both the United States and the U.S.S.R. had been in the habit of periodically putting forward "package proposals" dealing with a large number of controversial points, the latest such efforts being the already cited Soviet statement of November 17, 1956 [33] and a general statement of the United States position made by Ambassador Lodge before the General Assembly on January 14, 1957.[34] A new omnibus Soviet proposal was introduced into the London talks on April 30,[35] and the definitive Western proposal was finally submitted on August 29,[36] after Zorin had already rejected its main provisions in detail. From these and related documents the following major issues emerged:

1. *Nuclear Weapons.* Dependent as they had become on the use of nuclear and thermonuclear weapons in their own

defense planning, both power groups agreed for purposes of negotiation that disarmament would be meaningless unless something was done to curb the nuclear threat. In the past, the Russians had repeatedly advocated an outright renunciation of the use of such weapons for military purposes; and they repeated this proposal in their formal submission of April 30. They could do so with the more assurance because it was perfectly clear that the West would not agree to any such measure. "We do not propose to eliminate nuclear weapons or the possibility of their use," said Mr. Dulles on July 22, "for, as we have seen, this cannot be assured." The United States proposal in this field was more complex, more realistic, and, from the Soviet point of view, more insidious. First, the United States proposed *a halt in production of new fissionable material for weapons purposes.* In contrast to the detection of existing stocks of nuclear weapons, such a "freeze" on new production was believed to be susceptible of effective international inspection and control. From the American viewpoint it would have two further advantages: it would prevent any increase in the Soviet nuclear stockpile beyond its present dimensions, and it would prevent new countries from entering the nuclear arms race (an aspect which was not much appreciated by France). Throughout the negotiations, the United States insisted that this feature must be included in any agreed first-stage disarmament plan. In addition, the United States urged that once the freeze was in effect, measures should be taken to reduce existing nuclear weapons stockpiles by gradual transfers of fissionable material to peaceful uses, thus implementing President Eisenhower's hope (December 8, 1953) of a reversal in "the fearful trend of atomic military buildup" and a diminution in "the potential destructive power of the world's atomic stockpiles."

2. *Conventional Armaments and Armed Forces.* Both sides also agreed that it would be desirable to limit by international agreement the size and armament of national military establishments. In view of the current widespread tendency to reduce military manpower even without agreement, this would presumably work no particular hardship on either

side. Mr. Dulles admitted frankly that he attached little importance to manpower ceilings as a measure of potential military strength, especially if they failed to cover paramilitary forces and trained reserves. For a first-stage disarmament agreement, the United States proposed a ceiling of 2.5 million men for the United States and U.S.S.R. (whose nominal strength at the moment could be estimated at about 2.8 million each, if it was assumed that the reductions announced by Moscow in 1955 and 1956 had been carried out), and 750,000 for France and Great Britain (which were already down to about 690,000). The U.S.S.R. accepted these figures for the first stage but sought immediate agreement on a further reduction to 1 or 1.5 million and 650,000 respectively —although it later indicated assent to the Western idea of ceilings of 2.1 million and 700,000 for the second stage and 1.7 million and 650,000 for the third stage. Moscow also urged a 15 percent reduction in conventional armaments and military budgets, in contrast to a 10 percent figure suggested by the United States.

3. *Territorial Limitations.* As in past years, the Soviet Union also advocated a series of readjustments designed to reduce the level of armed forces in particular areas. Specifically, its proposals of April 30 called for (1) a prompt reduction in the number of Western military bases maintained in the territory of other countries; (2) a reduction by one-third in the forces maintained in Germany by each of the great powers; and (3) a reduction in the forces maintained by the great powers in other countries belonging to NATO or the Warsaw treaty organization in Eastern Europe. Since such proposals would tend to weaken the military position of the West in the most crucial theater of the East-West struggle, they were viewed with some reserve by the Western governments despite their interest in encouraging a withdrawal of Soviet forces from the heart of Europe. Dr. Adenauer particularly feared that such arrangements might tend to make the division of Germany permanent.

4. *Outer Space Vehicles.* The most novel feature of the American disarmament proposals of 1957 was a suggestion that timely international controls be instituted in the new

field of earth satellites, intercontinental missiles, long-range unmanned weapons, space platforms, and the like. The reasoning here appeared to be that control of activities in this field was desirable in itself and would be much easier to put into effect now than later. Although the matter was not intensively discussed in London, its timeliness was to be emphasized by the Soviet success in launching a long-range ballistic missile in August and subsequently placing two earth satellites in orbit. (See Chapter VII.)

5. *Inspection and Control.* A perpetual stumbling block to agreement in past years had been the impossibility of reconciling Western and Soviet ideas on the type of inspection and control required to ensure that whatever agreements were made would be faithfully carried out. It was basic to the Western position that no disarmament steps should be taken in the absence of appropriate control measures. The U.S.S.R., while agreed in principle on the necessity for control, had shown great reluctance to accept any control measures involving international inspection—especially air inspection—of activities in its territory. In the last couple of years, however, the positions of the two sides had appeared to move somewhat closer together, and Moscow in its proposals of November 17, 1956 had even accepted in a very limited way the principle of mutual aerial inspection as a safeguard against massive surprise attack (see below). The United States, on its side, had readily accepted Premier Bulganin's idea that ground control posts should also be established at important ports, rail junctions, highways, and airports. But there was still no agreement as to the precise details of an inspection and control system, either for preventing surprise attack or for verifying compliance with other disarmament undertakings.

6. *Aerial Inspection.* In the all-important field of aerial inspection as a safeguard against surprise attack, the first hint of possible agreement had come in Moscow's somewhat grudging offer of November 17 to consider aerial inspection in an area extending 800 kilometers on both sides of the military demarcation line in Europe. This particular zone, which included most of Western Europe and the Soviet satel-

WESTERN INSPECTION PROPOSALS
August 2, 1957—Plan A

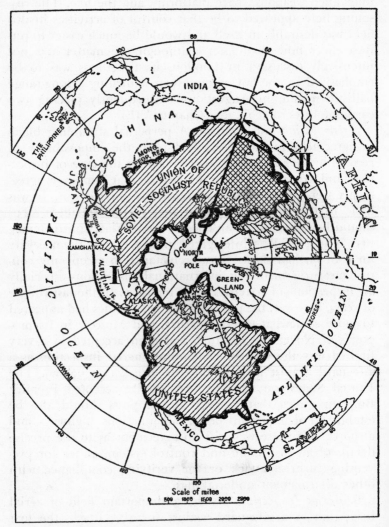

The basic Western proposal called for a system of air and ground inspection covering (I) the continental United States, Alaska with the Aleutian Islands, Canada, and the U.S.S.R.; and (II) a European area extending to the outer limits shown above, *or* a more limited European zone including "a significant part of the territory of the Soviet Union, as well as the other countries of Eastern Europe."

WESTERN INSPECTION PROPOSALS
August 2, 1957—Plan B

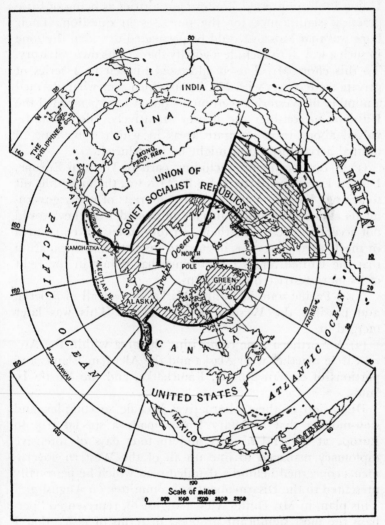

As an alternative, the Western governments proposed a system of air and ground inspection covering (I) the Arctic territory of the U.S.S.R., Canada, the United States, Denmark (Greenland), and Norway; also Alaska and the Aleutians, with a small strip of Canadian territory; also Eastern Siberia, Kamchatka, and the Kurile Islands; and (II) a European zone as in Plan A.

lite countries but virtually none of the territory of the Soviet
Union itself, impressed Western authorities as being of little
practical significance for the purposes in question. Their
hope was that Moscow could be persuaded to widen the zone
in such a way as to include a goodly share of its own territory.
To this effort Mr. Stassen addressed himself in a series of
private conferences with Mr. Zorin which somewhat alarmed
a number of Western governments but at least persuaded the
Russians to consider the matter attentively. Discussion revolved about three separate areas in which some type of
mutual aerial inspection might be introduced:

(1) A European zone including parts of Western Europe,
Eastern Europe, and the U.S.S.R. This was the most difficult
to arrange because it involved the interests of many governments and because the Russians intimated that they would
not accept inspection of their territory unless an equal area
in the United States was opened to inspection—a stipulation
that the United States found somewhat unfair in the light
of its more restricted dimensions.

(2) A Pacific zone including Alaska, part or all of Siberia,
and possibly the Western United States. This was later
merged in

(3) A Northern zone comprising the area within the Arctic Circle together with Alaska and the Aleutian Islands and
portions of eastern Siberia, Kamchatka, and the Kurile Islands.

Discussion of these alternatives became so complex and
slow-moving that Secretary Dulles made a special trip to
Europe at the end of July and in four days of intensive
diplomacy managed to line up all of the Western governments concerned behind a detailed plan which he personally
presented to the Disarmament Subcommittee on August 2. [37]
This plan, in Mr. Dulles' view (August 6), represented "perhaps the most significant proposal in terms of peace that I
think has been made in recent history, perhaps ever...."
Undoubtedly it was one of the most complicated. "Our proposal," Mr. Dulles explained to his news conference, "is
now made in alternative terms; it can be very broad, covering in effect all of the North American continent north of

Mexico, all of Europe, and all of the Soviet Union; or, if it is desired to start on a more experimental basis, it can be done in the northern area, which would include the area north of the Arctic Circle and, in addition, Alaska, the Aleutians, Eastern Siberia, Kamchatka, and the Kurile Islands." President Eisenhower's summary (August 7) was less complete but easier to follow. Our main proposal, he explained, involved "the inspection of all North America, north of Rio Grande, and all of Europe in exchange for the same inspectional privileges of Russia and her satellites."

All that seemingly remained was for Russia to accept one of the two alternatives or suggest modifications. Disappointingly, however, the Russians seemed suddenly to have lost interest in the whole matter. Far from applauding the Western initiative, Zorin when he came to make his formal reply on August 27 raked up all the old Soviet arguments against the basic idea of aerial inspection and aerial photography, which he now characterized in familiar terms as a mere pretext for gathering target intelligence. In the present state of world confidence, he asserted, no country could possibly be expected to expose itself to such hazards. He was particularly bitter because the Western plan, while covering the entire Soviet Union, failed to include various Western bases in Spain, North Africa, and the Middle and Far East. This was indeed a noteworthy omission, although the President had explained (August 7) that it would be difficult to arrange permission of all the countries concerned, that Communist bases in the "Red China area" would be a complicating factor, and that the matter was not critical anyhow because the objective at this stage was only to create "confidence." So far as the Russians were concerned, this objective appears to have been spectacularly missed; nor was it noticeably retrieved by Mr. Dulles' later statement (September 19) that the United States would have no objection to opening its remaining bases to inspection. From the time the Western proposal was submitted, the Russians virtually gave up trying to discuss a general disarmament plan. Instead they concentrated ever more heavily on the matter of a suspension of nuclear tests, a subject that could be relied upon to pay propaganda dividends whether or not an agreement was reached.

7. *Nuclear Testing*. From the beginning of the discussions, the Soviet position on testing of nuclear weapons had been clear and straightforward. What Moscow wanted (or professed to want) was an immediate cessation of atomic and hydrogen weapons tests by all concerned, independently of any agreements or disagreements on other disarmament matters. From the standpoint of political warfare, this line had obvious appeal to the less sophisticated sections of world opinion and gave the Soviet Union a propagandistic advantage which the West was unable to match. In official Western eyes, however, the Soviet proposal was not only politically irresponsible but highly dangerous in a practical sense. The effect of its acceptance would be to freeze the American and British nuclear arsenals at their present level of effectiveness and prevent the development of new and better nuclear weapons. This was a form of self-denial that neither the United States nor Great Britain was anxious to undertake, especially since they could not be sure that the U.S.S.R. might not continue to carry on tests clandestinely somewhere in its vast territory. A cessation of tests, in the Western view, ought to await the conclusion of a general disarmament agreement and the establishment of a foolproof detection and control system. In the meantime, it was suggested, it might be possible to set up a committee to discuss some kind of limitation of tests by mutual agreement.

So great, however, was the desire of Mr. Stassen to keep the negotiations moving and win Soviet assent to an inspection zone that the administration, at President Eisenhower's direction, decided to take a calculated risk of unusual dimensions. At a crucial series of meetings in Washington late in May, Mr. Stassen was apparently authorized to propose that subject to certain important conditions (to be explained below), the tests might actually be suspended for a trial period of as much as one year. This was considered the longest suspension the United States could accept without risking the breakup of the numerous scientific and technical groups concerned in the test program. Before this proposal

could be placed on record, however, the Russians contrived
to recover the propaganda initiative by proposing (June 14)
that the tests be suspended for two or three years and, further, that an international control system be set up to ensure that the suspension was observed. This last point, a
departure from the previous Soviet line, was considered a
most hopeful token of sincerity, and was particularly welcomed by the Western delegations when they finally submitted their proposal on July 2.[38] In its definitive form, the
Western proposal called for a trial suspension for ten months,
rather than a year—not, however, a suspension in a vacuum
as demanded by the Russians, but a suspension which would
be an integral part of a first-stage disarmament agreement
providing, among other things, for reductions in armed
forces and armaments and for a freeze on production of
fissionable material for weapons purposes. If the Russians
wanted a test suspension, in other words, they would have to
buy it by accepting key features of the Western program. Mr.
Dulles indicated on June 25 that they would also have to
accept an air inspection zone.

Even this carefully limited offer had already caused con-
sternation in American circles concerned with the test program. A group of distinguished scientists went to the President and assured him that their main efforts were now
directed to developing "small" hydrogen bombs with minimum fallout, for which purpose a continuation of the tests
was said to be absolutely essential. Already they had reduced
fallout by 96 percent, the President quoted them as saying
(June 26). "Give us four or five years to test each step of
our development and we will produce an absolutely clean
bomb." (Khrushchev, when this news reached him, was deri-
sive. "How can you have a clean bomb to do dirty things?"
he asked. "If one gets under a clean bomb, what difference
does it make if it is clean or dirty?") The President, too,
appeared to feel that in this instance a possible military advantage would have to take second place to larger considerations. ". . . For the moment," he said (June 26), "it would
appear that the psychological factors and the fears of the
world are such that we should go right ahead with the plan,

with the offers that we have made and we have no intention
of pulling back [from] them for a minute."

As the summer went on, "the psychological factors and the
fears of the world" (plus Soviet intransigence) induced the
United States to move even farther from its original position.
On August 21 the White House announced [39] "a significant
change in our proposals" involving "a suspension of testing
of nuclear weapons for a period up to two years under certain conditions and safeguards." In a further deviation from
its normal attitude, the United States had ceased to insist
that a control organization be established before the suspension started. Suspension could come first, control afterward.
Once again, however, the United States emphasized that this
offer was valid only as part of a first-stage disarmament "package" which would have to include a cut-off on fissionable
materials production for weapons purposes as well as other
features of the Western program. The "inseparability" of
the various Western proposals, including air inspection, was
underlined once again in the final Western "working paper"
of August 29.

But the Soviets, repeatedly and just as emphatically, had
rejected the whole idea of linking test suspension to other
issues. "To put the problem in this way," Bulganin had
written to Prime Minister Macmillan (July 20),[40] "means
to condemn the negotiations for the cessation of tests of
nuclear weapons to failure in advance." To the Russians,
the Western position on nuclear tests was no more satisfactory than the Western (or American) position on a nuclear
cut-off, on aerial inspection, or, for that matter, on Germany
or on Eastern Europe. As their new nuclear and missile testing program got under way in the Siberian wastes, Soviet
diplomatic representatives began to denounce the whole
concept of the Disarmament Subcommittee and demand the
inclusion of more Communist and neutral states in the disarmament discussions—another indication of their political
and propagandistic approach to the whole issue.

Non-Soviet sources did not accept the Soviet contention
that nothing had been accomplished by the London talks,
which lamely adjourned on September 6 after it had become

clear that the Soviet stand would not be modified. Secretary-General Dag Hammarskjold of the United Nations suggested (September 5) that "the serious and extensive nature of the negotiations should in itself . . . be a source of encouragement," since it reflected "the ever-increasing weight attached to the problem of disarmament by the peoples, a concern to which Governments are fully responding." Secretary Dulles believed (September 10) "that more progress toward disarmament has been made at these talks than has ever been made before in the long history of efforts toward disarmament." The agreement reached among at least fifteen (Western) nations, representing a very large segment of military power in the world, seemed to Mr. Dulles "really quite monumental." He felt confident, he said, "that over the span of years the measure of agreement which was arrived at at London will prove significant and will advance the cause of limitation of armaments."

In sharp contrast, as always, were the opinions of Khrushchev as expressed a few weeks later in a notable interview with James Reston of the *New York Times*.[41] The President and Mr. Stassen, said the party secretary, apparently wanted "to find a road to agreement," but he was not so sure about Mr. Dulles. In any case, he strongly objected to the general method of American diplomacy, in relation both to disarmament and to other East-West matters:

". . . We are ready even today to sign an agreement with President D. Eisenhower acceptable to both sides and in the interest of world peace. But the U.S.A. is uncooperative, putting forward a number of . . . conditions, which are known to be unacceptable to the U.S.S.R.

"These are conditions of the strong for the weak. They sound something like an ultimatum. . . . Agreements must be sought which would not be politically detrimental to one side or the other. . . . Proposals which place the Soviet Union in a position of inequality cannot be accepted by the Soviet Government."

Possibly Mr. Khrushchev did not stop to reflect that the Soviet Union's own proposals on international matters invariably had this same tendency to place the other side "in a position of inequality." Similarly, when he went on to reproach the United States for basing its policy "on some internal forces of the Socialist states supposedly capable of liquidating the socialist system," he failed to observe that Moscow had consistently based its own policy on the liquidation of what it called the system of "imperialism." But the very one-sidedness of Mr. Khrushchev's view of the East-West struggle helped to explain why agreements with the U.S.S.R. were so difficult to achieve. If the experience of these months had yielded nothing else, it had at least suggested the possibility that the Soviet Union might be just as mistrustful of the West as the West could be of the U.S.S.R. —and, further, that Moscow felt able to cite plausible grounds for its mistrust. Even this insight might prove helpful to the West in the difficult new phase of the East-West struggle which was about to open beneath the shadow of the Soviet Union's first earth satellite. (See Chapter VII.)

Notes to Chapter III

1. *Documents on American Foreign Relations, 1956*, pp. 479-487.

2. Hugh Gaitskell, *The Challenge of Coexistence* (Cambridge: Harvard University Press, 1957); Chester Bowles, "Our Objective in Europe —and Russia's," *New York Times Magazine*, May 12, 1957, pp. 9 ff.

3. *Department of State Bulletin*, v. 36 (February 18, 1957), pp. 251-255.

4. *Documents on American Foreign Relations, 1954*, pp. 113-114 and 152.

5. Text in *New York Times*, April 5, 1957.

6. Joint communiqué, March 24, in *Department of State Bulletin*, v. 36 (April 8, 1957), pp. 561-562; *Documents on American Foreign Relations, 1957*, no. 22.

7. Communiqué, May 3, in *Department of State Bulletin*, v. 36 (May 27, 1957), p. 840; *Documents on American Foreign Relations, 1957*, no. 12.

8. *Department of State Bulletin*, v. 36 (March 18, 1957), pp. 438-439; *Documents on American Foreign Relations, 1957*, no. 24.

9. *Department of State Bulletin*, v. 36 (February 25, 1957), p. 307; *Documents on American Foreign Relations, 1957*, no. 21; see also *New York Times*, May 8, 1957.

10. Texts in *American Journal of International Law*, v. 51 (October 1957), pp. 865-1104; French text and related material in *Chronique de politique étrangère*, v. 10 (July-November 1957), pp. 544-918.

11. *New York Times*, March 17, 1957.

12. Speech by Secretary Dulles, Dallas, October 27, 1956, in *Documents on American Foreign Relations, 1956*, pp. 44-46.

13. *Documents on American Foreign Relations, 1956*, pp. 252-255.

14. General Assembly Resolution 1132 (XI), January 10, 1957; *Documents on American Foreign Relations, 1957*, no. 48.

15. *Department of State Bulletin*, v. 36 (June 24, 1957), pp. 1003-1009; *Documents on American Foreign Relations, 1957*, nos. 39-47.

16. *Department of State Bulletin*, v. 37 (September 9, 1957), p. 444.

17. *Documents on American Foreign Relations, 1956*, pp. 268-270.

18. *Department of State Bulletin*, v. 36 (June 10, 1957), pp. 939-940; *Documents on American Foreign Relations, 1957*, no. 52.

19. Communiqué of the Central Committee of the Soviet Communist party, July 4, in *New York Times,* July 4, 1957.

20. *Ibid.,* June 3, 1957.

21. *Ibid.,* May 11, 1957.

22. *Report of the Special Committee on the Problem of Hungary* (U.N. General Assembly, *Official Records, Eleventh Session,* Supplement No. 18, New York, 1957); excerpts in *Documents on American Foreign Relations, 1957,* no. 49.

23. Interview with James Reston, in *New York Times,* October 9, 1957. See further the record of the President's news conference, October 9, *ibid.,* October 10, 1957.

24. *Department of State Bulletin,* v. 37 (August 17, 1957), pp. 304-306; *Documents on American Foreign Relations, 1957,* no. 27.

25. Joint declaration, May 28, in *Department of State Bulletin,* v. 36 (June 17, 1957), pp. 955-956; *Documents on American Foreign Relations, 1957,* no. 26.

26. Same as note 24.

27. General Assembly Resolution 1011 (XI), February 14, in *Department of State Bulletin,* v. 36 (February 11, 1957), p. 230; *Documents on American Foreign Relations, 1957,* no. 143.

28. *Department of State Bulletin,* v. 37 (August 12, 1957), pp. 267-272; *Documents on American Foreign Relations, 1957,* no. 148.

29. *New York Times,* October 14 and December 29, 1957.

30. Same as note 6.

31. See especially the record of the President's news conference of May 15, 1957.

32. For details cf. especially Chalmers M. Roberts, "The Hopes and Obstinacy of Harold Stassen," *The Reporter,* v. 17, no. 3 (September 5, 1957), pp. 25-29.

33. Same as note 1.

34. *Department of State Bulletin,* v. 36 (February 11, 1957), pp. 225-228. See also the U.S. memorandum dated January 12, *ibid.,* pp. 229-231; *Documents on American Foreign Relations, 1957,* no. 142.

35. *New York Times,* May 14, 1957; *Documents on American Foreign Relations, 1957,* no. 145.

36. *Department of State Bulletin,* v. 37 (September 16, 1957), pp. 451-455; *Documents on American Foreign Relations, 1957,* no. 150.

37. *Department of State Bulletin,* v. 37 (August 17, 1957), pp. 303-304; *Documents on American Foreign Relations, 1957,* no. 149.

38. *New York Times,* July 3, 1957; *Documents on American Foreign Relations, 1957,* no. 147.

39. *Department of State Bulletin,* v. 37 (September 9, 1957), pp. 418-419.

40. *New York Times,* July 25, 1957.

41. Official Soviet text in *New York Times,* October 10, 1957; see further section 23 and section 25.

CHAPTER FOUR

THE "SOUTHERN GAP" AND AFRICA

ALTHOUGH neither Soviet nor Western policy could be accused of overlooking the fundamental importance of Europe in the East-West struggle, it was evident from the demeanor of both sides that for 1957 the critical theater of East-West conflict lay not in Europe but in the regions loosely referred to as the Middle East. Just where the Middle East began and ended was a moot question among geographers and statesmen. Broadly speaking, the term could be applied to the entire area extending southward from the Soviet frontiers, from Turkey at one extremity to Pakistan and the Indian subcontinent at the other. This was substantially the area of which President Eisenhower was speaking when he declared in his special message of January 5, 1957 [1] that "The Middle East has abruptly reached a new and critical stage in its long and important history."

In contrast to Europe, where the demarcation line between Soviet and Western influence was clearly marked and not easily modified by either side, the situation in the Middle Eastern countries had in recent years become extremely fluid and presented a wide field for political competition and "cold war" maneuvers. The stabilizing influence formerly exerted by Great Britain through its network of political and military arrangements in such countries as Egypt, Palestine, Jordan, and Iraq had been waning ever since World War II and had been virtually extinguished, outside of the remote sheikdoms of the Persian Gulf area, by the failure of the Anglo-French expedition against Egypt in the fall of 1956. But the new nations which had so energetically repudiated British (and French) tutelage were in no position to ensure by their own efforts the security of a region which, thanks to its central situation, its vast oil resources, and its unique spiritual associations, could not long escape the attention of powerful outside interests.

Recognizing the danger of Soviet encroachments in the area, the "northern tier" governments of Turkey, Iraq, Iran, and Pakistan had allied themselves with the West through the Baghdad Pact of 1955, which included Great Britain though not the United States. But the Arab countries, with the solitary exception of Iraq, had been too suspicious of the West and too preoccupied with their quarrel with Israel to accept Western help in maintaining their independence against a possible threat from the U.S.S.R. Two of them, Egypt and Syria, had gone so far as to accept Soviet arms and other assistance which seemed to many observers to have opened the door to far-reaching Soviet penetration throughout the Arab world.

The turmoil which had followed the Anglo-French attack on Egypt raised an obvious possibility that the Soviet Union, whose interest in Middle Eastern affairs was well established and certainly not unnatural, would now attempt to expand its foothold in the Arab countries with a view to eventually bringing the entire area under its influence. This prospect, to be sure, was heavily discounted by responsible persons in the Arab countries themselves. Salah al-Bitar, Foreign Minister of Syria, spoke for a large section of Arab opinion when he declared (January 19, 1957) that he was convinced the Soviet Union had "no ambitions" in the Middle East and sought no privileges either in Syria or in other Arab countries. And yet to Western minds familiar with the record of Soviet imperialism and the views that animated the Soviet leaders, it seemed that nothing would be more logical for the Kremlin than to attempt to push home the advantages already gained in the Middle East and eliminate any possible threat from this quarter by taking it under Soviet control.

In Washington, at least, this prospect was regarded as virtually self-evident. The only thing that could prevent such a move, American officials reasoned, would be a realization on Moscow's part that to make it would involve the risk of serious trouble with the United States. Washington hoped and believed that the attitude of men like Salah al-Bitar was not typical, and that if the United States took the responsibility of trying to prevent further Soviet incursions in the Middle East it could count on extensive local support. In any case, it was resolved to make the attempt. Failure to do so, President Eisenhower insisted in his special message to Congress, would invite consequences that the United States could not accept:

"If the nations of that area should lose their independence, if they were dominated by alien forces hostile to freedom, that would be both a tragedy for the area and for many other free nations whose economic life would be subject to near strangulation. Western Europe would be endangered just as though there had been no Marshall Plan, no North Atlantic Treaty Organization. The free nations of Asia and Africa, too, would be placed in serious jeopardy. And the countries of the Middle East would lose the markets upon which their economies depend. All this would have the most adverse, if not disastrous, effect upon our own nation's economic life and political prospects."

Even if the U.S.S.R. had not been planning further incursions in the region below its southern borders (and it had seldom been known to hesitate when it saw an opportunity of expanding its influence), the determination of the United States to challenge its position in the area was all that was needed to ensure that the Middle East in 1957 would in fact become the preeminent battleground of the East-West struggle. Ironically, both parties to the impending struggle were to justify their actions in the name of the same shibboleth, that of national independence for the states of the Middle East. As always, however, there was a vital difference in their approach and objectives. The underlying motives of the United States in attempting to throw its protection over the Middle East were undoubtedly closer to the ideals of the United Nations Charter, and of the Middle Eastern countries themselves, than were those of an antagonist whose true attitude toward national independence had just been demonstrated in the streets of Budapest. Yet these differences appeared to mean relatively little to some of the nations whose destinies were now at stake. While plainly dismayed at finding themselves propelled into the middle of the "cold war," the ordinary people of the Middle East displayed, by and large, a disconcerting indifference to the relative merits of the two contenders.

This was particularly true in those Arab states whose governments had thus far tried to avoid definite conmmitments to either side and had espoused the doctrine of "positive neutrality" upheld by Egyptian President Abdel Nasser. The exponents of this tendency vehemently repudiated the notion of a Middle Eastern "power vacuum" such as the United States claimed to have perceived. "Arab nationalism," they insisted, was quite capable of filling any vacuum that existed, and there was no occasion for interference by outside powers. Given the realities of great power rivalry, however, some of the Arab governments (notably Egypt and Syria) and many among the Arab peoples appeared more inclined to trust the Soviet Union than the United States. Moscow, they felt, had consistently taken their side against Israel, against Britain, and against France, the archdemons of "colonialism" —whereas the record of the United States, in their eyes, was much less satisfactory. They saw no reason to disbelieve the repeated Soviet claim (e.g., January 12, 1957) that Washington's real aim was not to protect their independence but "to implant the former colonial order in the Middle Eastern countries under a new signboard." This lack of popular confidence in American aims was to act as a serious handicap to the United States in discharging the responsibility it had felt bound to undertake in the wake of the Anglo-French fiasco at Suez. To a considerable extent it offset the limited support that Washington was able to obtain from certain of the Arab governments that were more ready to share its distrust of Soviet intentions.

As already noted, the principal American response to the chaotic situation in the Middle East was the enactment on March 9 of a congressional Joint Resolution declaring that the preservation of the independence and integrity of the

Middle Eastern nations was a matter of vital American concern and that the United States was prepared, on request,
to use its armed forces to assist any country in the area that
might be a victim of armed aggression by a state controlled
by international Communism.[2] (See section 4.) Accompanied
by provisions designed to make possible an enlarged and more
effective program of military and economic aid to Middle
Eastern countries, this declaration constituted formal notice
to the world that the United States was picking up the burden reluctantly let fall by Britain and France. As the only
non-Communist power still capable of offering serious resistance to Soviet designs in the area, the United States made
clear that it was assuming this responsibility as a matter of
fundamental policy, irrespective of the ebb and flow of political allegiances either in the Middle East or among the Western allies. Despite its ostensibly temporary character, the
Middle East resolution in reality implied a firm American
commitment of as permanent a nature as anything in contemporary world politics.

The so-called "Eisenhower Doctrine" did not, however,
constitute a policy for the Middle East; it merely supplied
the framework within which such a policy might be developed.[3] Indeed, this public warning to the U.S.S.R. was not
by any means the only action which Washington thought
needful to bring the Middle Eastern situation under control.
In his message of January 5, the President had readily conceded that the proposed resolution, "primarily designed to
deal with the possibility of Communist aggression, direct or
indirect," would "not solve all the problems of the Middle
East" and was very far from representing "the totality of our
policies for the area." There were other difficulties, Mr.
Eisenhower pointed out, which, though undoubtedly aggravated by international Communism, would have existed
quite apart from that threat. The events which culminated
in the Suez war had for practical purposes almost completely
wrecked the network of legal, political, and economic relationships established in the Middle East in past years. Mutual
confidence between Arabs and Europeans was virtually at an
end. Mutual hatred still reigned between Arabs and Israelis.

Defying the United Nations, Israel still held extensive territories it had wrested from Egypt in the preceding autumn. The Suez Canal was blocked; important oil facilities were wrecked or standing idle. The Arab world itself was divided between the radically minded admirers of President Abdel Nasser and the more conservative elements who still held the reins in such countries as Iraq and Saudi Arabia. The Baghdad Pact was hobbled by the refusal of its Asian members to talk to Great Britain. The restoration of some semblance of order in these matters was no less urgent than the warning directed to Moscow through the Eisenhower Doctrine.

To many observers the tangle of local problems that centered in the Arab-Israeli conflict and the status of the Suez Canal actually seemed a good deal more urgent than the threat of overt Communist aggression that had so alarmed official Washington. But as President Eisenhower pointed out in his January 5 message, such matters as these were currently the object of active concern on the part of the United Nations, whose efforts the United States was supporting; whereas the United Nations could not possibly be expected to assume responsibility for protecting the whole Middle East against the ambitions of the Soviet Union. In the eyes of Secretary Dulles and the President, the Eisenhower Doctrine would seem to have represented a kind of shield erected to hold off the Soviet threat while efforts to improve the local situation went forward on other diplomatic levels. Throughout the months that the Middle East resolution was before Congress, the United States was also playing an active part in the efforts of the United Nations Assembly to sort out the debris of the Suez war, secure the withdrawal of Israeli forces from occupied territory, and arrange for the clearance and reopening of the Suez Canal. At the same time it was intensively cultivating certain of the Arab governments, notably those of Saudi Arabia and Iraq, which were least identified with pro-Soviet tendencies and hence seemed most likely to sympathize with the purposes of the Eisenhower Doctrine.

Because none of these efforts—even the enactment of the

Middle East Resolution—could come to fruition until the urgent problems growing out of the Suez war were on the way to settlement, it is logical that we should look first at the methods by which the situation in the region of the Canal and the Egyptian-Israeli armistice lines was restored to something like its former aspect (section 12). A second section will examine in more detail the clash of American and Soviet policies in the Middle East during the spring of 1957, culminating in the defeat of an overt attempt to unseat the government of King Hussein of Jordan (section 13). This in turn will be followed by an account of the critical state of affairs which developed in Syria in the course of the summer, leading ultimately to the renewal of an acute threat of war in the area (section 14). Two final sections will review major developments in the primarily non-Arab countries of the "northern tier" (section 15) and in the increasingly important African theater (section 16).

12. LIQUIDATING THE SUEZ WAR

The military actions which Israel, Great Britain, and France had undertaken against Egypt in the autumn of 1956 have been variously judged from the standpoint of international ethics and political expediency, and will doubtless be subject to differing evaluations for a long time to come. The fundamental outlook of the several parties to the conflict, however, is not in dispute. In seizing control of the Suez Canal, maintaining a warlike posture toward Israel, and lending support to the nationalist revolt in Algeria, Egyptian President Abdel Nasser had plainly been trying to give expression to what President Eisenhower called "the surging and understandable tide of nationalism"—a mission which, in Abdel Nasser's eyes, apparently demanded a maximum assertion of Egyptian or Arab "rights" wherever these conflicted with the rights and interests of non-Arab peoples. In mounting their military operations against Egypt, the Israeli, British, and French governments had just as plainly believed themselves to be adopting the only adequate means of dealing with a government whose attitude they regarded as a permanent threat to their vital interests. Yet in resorting to open war against an antagonist whose actions against them had thus far remained considerably more limited in scope, they had committed the twofold error of disregarding the restraints imposed by the United Nations Charter and of placing themselves in sharp conflict with the nationalistic spirit that animated not only Egypt but a great many others among the world's newer nations. The result had been a tremendous upsurge of sympathy for Egypt and an equally marked revulsion against Israel, France, and Britain, who had found themselves virtually without supporters among the seventy-six (later eighty) members of the United Nations General Assembly. The Egypt of Abdel Nasser, hitherto regarded in a good many countries as a dangerous source of instability and unrest, had emerged almost overnight as an innocent victim whose claims to protection constituted a first charge on the resources of the world community. Any thought of the protection that other parties might need against Egypt had been largely submerged by a world-wide demand that the "aggression" be halted and the "aggressors" compelled to retire.

The effects of this far-reaching political reversal could be read in the series of resolutions by which the General Assembly, from November 2, 1956 onward, had repeatedly demanded that Israel, France, and Britain immediately cease their military operations and withdraw their forces from what had been Egyptian or Egyptian-controlled territory. These actions, the Assembly had made clear, were the indispensable preliminary to such further measures as the re-establishment of the armistice between Egypt and Israel and the reopening of the Suez Canal.[4] In response to this vehement movement of world opinion, powerfully seconded by direct expressions from both Washington and Moscow, Great Britain and France had reluctantly abandoned their venture and in due course removed their forces from Egypt—a step which was made easier by the Assembly's action in establishing a special United Nations Emergency Force (UNEF) to separate the belligerents and take temporary custody of evacuated territory. Israel, whose national future had been even more deeply involved, had been slower to comply; but

by late December it, too, had promised to evacuate most
though not all of the extensive territory it had seized from
Egypt.

The immediate tasks confronting the General Assembly as
it reconvened after the year-end holidays, therefore, were (1)
to secure the completion of Israel's withdrawal behind the
armistice demarcation lines, and (2) to arrange for the reopening of the Suez Canal, which Egypt had thoroughly
sabotaged at the outset of hostilities. Three separate and
conflicting sets of interests were involved, over and above
the interest of the world community as a whole in the restoration of normal conditions in this sensitive area.

The natural desire of Egypt was to secure the complete
evacuation of its territory (including the part of Palestine it
had occupied under the armistice agreement of 1949) and
to make good its claim to sole authority over the Suez Canal,
originally asserted in mid-1956 but never formally recognized by the international community. Having just regained
physical control of the Canal through the evacuation of the
British and French, it was only to be expected that Egypt
should try to use this control as a means of forcing the con-
cession of its wider objectives. Quite simply, its basic policy
was to delay the clearance and reopening of the Canal until
the invading forces had been fully withdrawn and its exclusive rights in the waterway could be asserted without fear
of contradiction.

Arrangements had already been made for the removal of
the wreckage blocking the Canal by a fleet of salvage vessels
assembled under United Nations auspices, but actual operations did not get under way before the beginning of January.
Thereafter Egypt still retained unlimited opportunities for
obstruction and delay, and made effective use of them during the weeks while Israel's evacuation was pending. Egypt's
bargaining position was strengthened by the fact that Britain,
France, and other Western European nations were heavily
dependent on the Middle Eastern petroleum supplies which
normally reached them through the Canal, and which were
being only partially made up from Western Hemisphere and
other sources. Furthermore, Egypt was assured of particularly

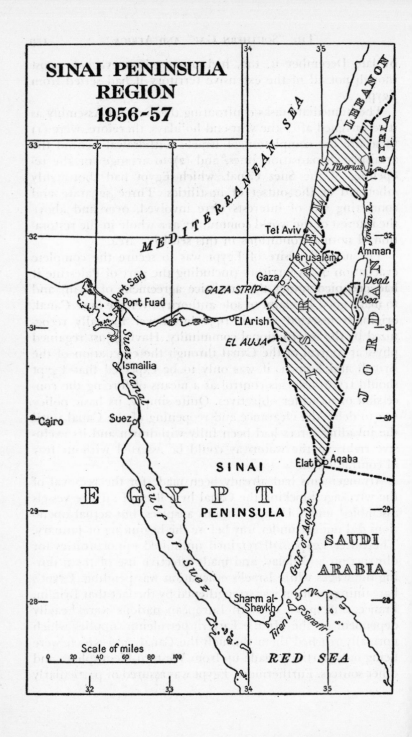

SINAI PENINSULA
REGION
1956~57

MEDITERRANEAN SEA

LEBANON

SYRIA

L. Tiberias

Jordan R.

Tel Aviv

Jerusalem

Amman

Gaza

Dead
Sea

GAZA STRIP

Port Said

Port Fuad

El Arish

EL AUJA

Ismailia

Suez Canal

Cairo

Suez

SINAI

Elat

Aqaba

EGYPT

PENINSULA

SAUDI

ARABIA

Gulf of Suez

Gulf of Aqaba

Sharm al-
Shaykh

Tiran I.

Sanafir I.

Scale of miles
0   20   40   60   80   100

RED SEA

JORDAN

ISRAEL

solicitous treatment by many countries, not excluding the United States, because aside from being a "victim of aggression" it retained a considerable capability for damaging Western interests through propaganda and intrigue in other Middle Eastern and African centers. Should President Abdel Nasser conclude that Egyptian interests were not being sufficiently respected, there was always the danger that he might fall back on closer cooperation with the U.S.S.R.

The aims of Great Britain and France at this period were almost exclusively focused on obtaining a satisfactory solution of the Suez Canal problem. Having failed in their bid to unseat the Abdel Nasser government, they still sought to bring about the early rehabilitation of the Canal and its reopening under conditions which would afford due security to their maritime traffic. Although their decision to withdraw their military forces had been taken on the express understanding (concurred in by the United States) that measures to this end would be taken promptly,[5] the removal of their troops had left them with no effective means of pressure aside from the economic measures which they had invoked without avail half a year earlier. About all they could do was to hope that Egypt would make concessions in the interest of getting rid of the Israeli troops, and that the practical influence of the United States would be exerted in a manner favorable to their interests.

As to Israel, its principal concern—which it plainly regarded as a matter of supreme national importance—was to secure an improvement in its general security position vis-à-vis Egypt, one that would relieve it of the harassment and cramping limitations to which it had been subjected for the past eight years. Premier David Ben-Gurion frankly admitted on March 6 that the quest for security had been the underlying motive of Israel's decision for war in 1956. Unlike its cobelligerents, moreover, Israel had actually won its military campaign and destroyed an Egyptian army, conquered virtually the whole Sinai Peninsula at the head of the Red Sea, and occupied the Egyptian-held Gaza Strip along the Mediterranean. In the wake of the cease-fire, Premier Ben-Gurion had promised that Israeli forces would be withdrawn "from

Egypt," and they had since evacuated all but the easternmost part of the Sinai Peninsula. But the Gaza Strip, in the Israeli view, was not a part of "Egypt"; it was merely a bit of Palestinian territory which had been assigned to Egyptian occupation under the armistice agreement and had been used by Egypt as a base for terrorist raids. The armistice agreement itself, the Israelis further contended, had been made null and void as the result of countless Egyptian violations, and there could be no question of going back to it now as contemplated by the General Assembly.

In addition, Israel wanted reliable assurances that its shipping would in future be able to pass freely through the Gulf of Aqaba, where its port of Elath had been unable to develop because of a long-continued blockade maintained by Egypt on behalf of all the Arab states. The best guarantee, the Israelis reasoned, would be to retain the strategic positions they had seized at the entrance of the gulf—the Egyptian fort at Sharm al-Shaykh (or Sharm el-Sheikh) and the islands of Tiran and Sanafir, Saudi Arabian territory which had been held by Egypt with the consent of King Saud's government. Finally, although not hitherto listed among its formal conditions, Israel was also anxious to vindicate and exercise its right of passage through the Suez Canal. Affirmed by the United Nations Security Council as far back as September 1, 1951, this right had been denied by Egypt on the ground that Israel was in a state of war with it and therefore not entitled to the rights of passage guaranteed to all ships by the Constantinople Convention of 1888.

From the Israeli point of view, this was a well-thought-out and wholly reasonable program which if implemented would place the country in a much safer and better position than in the past. In contrast to France and Britain, moreover, Israel still retained some bargaining power through its occupation of a portion of the conquered territory. Whereas the General Assembly had repeatedly insisted that Israel withdraw behind the armistice lines and "observe scrupulously the provisions of the armistice agreements," the most that Israel had been willing to do thus far was to withdraw its forces from the Sinai Peninsula proper. By January 22, 1957 it had evacuated everything except Sharm al-Shaykh and the Gaza Strip. There, the Israelis intimated, they intended to stay until something was done about their irreducible security needs.

A stand which conflicted so sharply with the expressed will of the General Assembly would, however, be difficult to maintain indefinitely unless Israel could count on more powerful outside backing than had been available to it thus far. As a practical matter, its ability to defy the wishes of the Assembly was directly dependent on the amount of understanding and sympathy it could inspire in the United States. Only with the aid or at least the tacit concurrence of the American Government could it hope to complete its gamble successfully. Official Washington had not been insensitive to the considerations that had prompted the Israeli action, much as it deplored the methods Israel had adopted. "The United States," President Eisenhower declared once again on February 17, 1957, "is aware of the fact that Israel has legitimate grievances and should, in all fairness, see a prospect of remedying them." But when it came to trying to remedy them by open aggression and prolonged resistance to the will of the United Nations, American support had not been and would not be available. "Should a nation which attacks and occupies foreign territory in the face of United Nations disapproval be allowed to impose conditions on its own withdrawal?" the President asked (February 20). ". . . I would, I feel, be untrue to the standards of the high office to which you have chosen me if I were to lend the influence of the United States" to such a proposition.

From the American viewpoint, the situation created by the Israeli-British-French actions in the Middle East had opened up two possible lines of action, both of them fraught with serious dangers and difficulties. Despite the obvious flaws in the procedure of the three attacking governments, Washington might have taken the view that their strength was so important to the United States, and their fundamental interests so similar to this country's, that they must be supported so far as possible even if it required some reinterpretation of international law and ethics. Had this been

its reaction, the United States would presumably have used
its influence in the United Nations, in conjunction with that
of Canada and other "middle" governments, to try to secure
more sympathetic treatment of the basic Anglo-French-
Israeli requirements. Furthermore, it might have tried harder
to encourage a conciliatory attitude on the part of Egypt.
In the light of President Abdel Nasser's obvious determination to exploit the Suez Canal as his principal bargaining
weapon, it might, for example, have displayed more interest
in measures that would tend in the long run to reduce
foreign dependence on the Canal, meet more of Europe's
long-term oil requirements in other ways, and thus give
Egypt an incentive to seek an agreed settlement rather than
simply trying to impose its own terms.

Instead, Washington took the opposite line—partly, no
doubt, in the belief that this was the best way of counter-
acting Soviet influence in the Middle East, but mainly, it
would seem, out of a genuine conviction that only one
morally right course was open to it. The methods of *"Real-
politik"* had been tried and discredited. What remained, in
Washington's view, was the opportunity to try to settle international problems in accord with the dictates of international law and morality as interpreted by the majority in
the United Nations Assembly—a majority which, to be sure,
was heavily weighted with Asian and African "anticolonial"
states possessing decided views on the question. In pursu-
ance of this line of thought, Washington adopted an air of
complete detachment from London and Paris in Middle
Eastern affairs, maintained a variety of economic pressures
against Israel (considerably more severe in their effects than
the corresponding pressures being maintained against Egypt),
and threw its full weight behind the Assembly's majority in
pressing for the unconditional evacuation of occupied territory. Far from prodding Abdel Nasser to guarantee favorable
treatment of Israeli, British, and French interests, Washington in public at least took the view that Egypt, as the party
sinned against by the other three, would naturally conform
to international morality in its own conduct. Admittedly
Egypt in the past had violated both the armistice agreement

and international law, said the President (February 20); but we "should not assume" that it would again do so in the future. "If, unhappily, Egypt does hereafter violate the Armistice Agreement or other international obligations, then this should be dealt with firmly by the society of nations." But no precautions were to be taken in advance. To do so, the President insisted, would be to sanction "the use of force as a means of settling international differences and through this gaining national advantages."

Though obviously rooted in ethical conviction, this rigorous approach was to prove not unhelpful in the pursuit of larger United States diplomatic objectives. To a considerable extent, it offset the unpopularity of the Eisenhower Doctrine in Arab and Asian countries and helped to perpetuate the favorable view of American policy inspired by Washington's firm stand against "aggression" at the very beginning of the crisis. For once the United States had clearly differentiated its attitude from that of the "colonial" powers, and Washington was in no hurry to renounce the comparative popularity this assured it among Asian and African states. Its present concern with blocking a possible Communist aggression in the Middle East, moreover, presupposed a closer understanding with at least some governments in the area. Preliminary contacts had been established with Saudi Arabia, Iraq, and Lebanon simultaneously with the submission of the Middle East resolution to Congress. These governments, though not without serious misgivings about the trend of Egyptian policy in other respects, were solidly aligned with Egypt in its controversy with France and Britain and especially with Israel. Their cooperation under the "Eisenhower Doctrine" was not to be expected unless the present situation was resolved in Egypt's favor and without special advantage to the other parties. Similarly, any hope of preventing a further spread of Communist influence in Syria and in Egypt itself would have to be given up if people in those countries were to get the impression that some kind of "deal" was being made at Egypt's expense. These considerations undoubtedly fortified the determination of the United States to persevere in its original course despite vehement official and public protests in Britain, France, and Israel and some rather sharp criticism within the United States itself.

The objectives of American policy being thus established, there remained the question how Israel's withdrawal behind the armistice lines was actually to be brought about. Force was clearly not available: Egypt was in no condition to undertake the job, the ten-nation United Nations Emergency Force had no authority to undertake military operations, and no one else had the desire to do so. Further Israeli withdrawals, it appeared, could be obtained (if at all) only through intensified pressure, through diplomatic bargaining, or through some combination of the two. Not unnaturally, Egypt and the other Asian and African states favored intensified pressure. The Assembly, in their view, had done what it could by way of admonition. (On January 19 it adopted a new resolution [6] insisting that Israel complete its withdrawal within five days.) The time had now come, they felt, to invoke "sanctions," presumably of an economic character, which would force Israel to heed the Assembly's wishes.

This procedure had little appeal outside the Asian-African bloc. Quite a number of governments felt that the wrong was not all on one side and that Israel's security needs were deserving of some consideration. A group of "middle" powers, headed by Canada and drawn mainly from the Commonwealth and Western Europe, busied itself in seeking a middle ground between unconditional Israeli withdrawal and unconditional acceptance of Israel's security demands. The United States had equally little taste for the idea of sanctions, but was handicapped in looking for compromise solutions by the official feeling that any compromise defined in advance would amount to letting Israel "impose conditions on its own withdrawal."

As on some past occasions, there was a tendency in these circumstances to look to Secretary-General Dag Hammarskjold for the solution that eluded the member governments. The results of Mr. Hammarskjold's studies, however, were not encouraging. The type of assurances demanded by Israel, he pointed out,[7] would involve changes in the armistice

agreement between Israel and Egypt; and the Assembly had
no authority to make such changes even if it wanted to do
so. That could be done only by negotiation between Israel
and Egypt; and Egypt was patently unwilling to revise the
agreement in Israel's favor. Mr. Hammarskjold did feel, however, that even in its present form the armistice agreement
afforded Israel a measure of protection, and that this protection was reinforced to some extent by certain established
principles of international law. Furthermore, although he
was not sympathetic to suggestions that the United Nations
Emergency Force might be used to replace Israeli contingents
as they withdrew from occupied territory, he felt that UNEF
might nevertheless have a legitimate role to play in encouraging "mutual restraint" as between Israel and Egypt—
provided, however, that it was not used to "protect any special position" or "prejudge the solution of the controversial
questions involved." Mr. Hammarskjold's approach, which
the Israelis found intolerably involved and formalistic, was
governed not only by legal considerations but also by the
realization that any protection accorded to Israel, whether
through UNEF or otherwise, depended in the last analysis
on the consent of Egypt. It was in Egypt's power to terminate
UNEF's potential usefulness at any time by simply telling
the 5,700-man force to get out of its territory.

The fact that Egypt had thus far cooperated with UNEF
did, however, suggest the possibility of giving at least tacit
reassurances to Israel which might make it more willing to
heed the Assembly's admonitions. On February 2 the Assembly adopted two more resolutions,[8] one of which repeated
the demand that Israel withdraw "without further delay"
while the other offered some rather tenuous inducements in
the form of suggestions for strengthening the armistice agreement. Among them was listed "the placing of the United
Nations Emergency Force on the Egyptian-Israeli armistice
demarcation line and the implementation of other measures
as proposed in the Secretary-General's report." But no one
could say exactly what this language meant, and it proved
much too vague for Israel, which formally reaffirmed its
demand for definite guarantees as a precondition to with-

drawal. For almost a month the matter hung fire while the Asian and African states clamored for a "sanctions" resolution, the middle powers racked their brains for additional guarantees, and the United States cast about for other means of persuading Israel to withdraw and thus spare it the painful necessity of taking a position on the sanctions issue. Washington was particularly desirous of avoiding a vote on this ticklish question because influential members of Congress were flatly opposed to sanctions and were threatening to withhold their approval of the Middle East resolution if the administration supported them.

In the end a solution was found in a combination of heavy diplomatic pressure with indirect assurances to Israel regarding the security of its frontiers and its rights in the Gulf of Aqaba. The pressure took the form of a series of messages and statements by President Eisenhower [9] adjuring Israel to comply with the Assembly's resolutions and put its trust in "the resoluteness of all friends of justice to bring about a state of affairs which will conform to the principles of justice and of international law." It reached its climax in a presidential broadcast on February 20 [10] in which Mr. Eisenhower declared that we were "approaching a fateful moment when either we must recognize that the United Nations is unable to restore peace in this area or the United Nations must renew with increased vigor its efforts to bring about Israeli withdrawal." "If the United Nations once admits that international disputes can be settled by using force," the President averred, "then we will have destroyed the very foundation of the organization and our best hope of establishing a world order. . . . I believe that—in the interests of peace—the United Nations has no choice but to exert pressure upon Israel to comply with the withdrawal resolutions."

So far as the protection of Israeli interests was concerned, it was by now widely accepted that UNEF would have to be employed at least temporarily as a buffer between the Israeli and Egyptian land forces. What finally persuaded the Israelis to withdraw was a new idea, apparently originated by Mr. Dulles and developed in the course of long and involved diplomatic consultations in which Premier Mollet and Foreign Minister Pineau of France also appear to have played a significant role. Essentially it consisted in an expression of international support for Israel's right of "innocent passage" through the narrow waters of the Gulf of Aqaba. Whereas the Arab states generally took the view that the Gulf of Aqaba, the entrance of which is only 500 to 600 yards wide, comprehended purely national waters which Israel had no right to use, the United States informed the Israelis as early as February 11 that in its opinion these were actually international waters and therefore legally open to the shipping of all nations. Subject to a contrary determination by the International Court of Justice, the United States further declared that it was prepared to exercise the right of "innocent passage" on its own account "and to join with others to secure general recognition of this right." [11] The value of this assurance would naturally depend a good deal on how vigorously the United States was willing to assert its opinion, a point on which the Israelis found Mr. Dulles distressingly vague. In deciding to accept it they were influenced by a suggestion from France (not necessarily concurred in by the United States) that whereas the United States would clearly not encourage its vessels to shoot their way through the Gulf, Israel itself would be entitled to do so, if necessary, as an exercise of its inherent right of self-defense under the United Nations Charter.

By March 1 Israel apparently felt it had picked up enough assurances from the United States and other Western nations to venture on a full withdrawal and thus forestall the passage of a sanctions resolution. Foreign Minister Golda Meir on that day informed the Assembly that Israel would promptly evacuate both the Sharm al-Shaykh area and the Gaza Strip. This decision, she pointed out, was based on a number of "understandings" and "assumptions," the most important of which were (1) that UNEF would move into the Sharm al-Shaykh area and remain there until further notice; (2) that free and innocent passage through the Gulf of Aqaba would be fully maintained; and (3) that UNEF would take over full control of the Gaza Strip, pending a peace settlement or a definitive agreement on the future of that territory. "Can we," Mrs. Meir asked, "from now on—all of us—turn a new leaf, and instead of fighting with each other, can we all, united, fight poverty and disease and illiteracy?" But the matter was not to be so simple. Mrs. Meir's "understandings and assumptions" went far beyond those of the other parties concerned. The most Ambassador Lodge would say was that her "hopes and expectations" seemed "not unreasonable"— though when Israel showed signs of balking, President Eisenhower next day in a message to Premier Ben-Gurion reversed the syntax and described them as "reasonable." Assuring his nation that the President of the United States had thus "assumed a moral responsibility toward Israel," Mr. Ben-Gurion on March 5 reluctantly issued the orders for withdrawal.

Reasonable or not, Israel's hopes and expectations were destined to be disappointed in important respects. UNEF duly moved into the Gaza Strip but found itself quite unable to cope with the local Arab population, stirred up by Egyptian agitators, and within a week had surrendered administrative control to Egypt. Egyptian troops remained outside of the strip, however, and Israel managed to make good its contention that UNEF itself should be confined to the strip rather than being deployed on both sides of the demarcation line as demanded by Egypt and urged by UNEF's own top command. Thanks largely to Mr. Hammarskjold's intercession with President Abdel Nasser, the situation gradually quieted down and Israel at least found itself enjoying more security on its Gaza border than had been true in earlier years. Abdel Nasser also permitted a UNEF contingent to remain at least provisionally at Sharm al-Shaykh despite the fact that its presence there precluded the reestablishment of the former blockade. On March 18 an Israeli freighter sailed down the Gulf without molestation, and on April 6 an American tanker, the *Kern Hills*, exercised the right of "innocent passage" by passing the Strait of Tiran with a cargo of oil for Elath. These developments evoked lively protests from Saudi Arabia and other Arab states and proved quite embarrassing to Washington in its attempts to cultivate good relations in the Arab world. Nevertheless the State Department held fast to its interpretation of the applicable international law, and for practical purposes the Gulf remained open and for the first time gave Israel a broad window to the south.

One objective that Israel had signally failed to achieve was the acknowledgment by Egypt of its right of transit through the Suez Canal. In this disappointment it was not alone, however, since Great Britain and France had been equally unsuccessful in realizing their minimum aims regarding the Canal regime. Egypt, though it fell short of reestablishing its former position on the armistice line and the Gulf of Aqaba, was to be fully successful in vindicating its claim to unrestricted control of the Suez waterway.

While the Assembly had been struggling with the problem of Israeli withdrawal, the United Nations salvage fleet under Lieutenant General Raymond A. Wheeler had been laboriously raising and removing the wreckage of sunken railway spans, concrete-filled canal barges and other obstructions with which the Egyptians had blocked the Canal at the outset of the Anglo-French attack. The physical difficulties of the task were fully matched by the bureaucratic obstructions interposed by Egypt, which showed what Mr. Dulles moderately called "a tendency to drag its feet" in the matter throughout the weeks while the Israeli issue was pending. Not until the Israeli withdrawals had actually begun was General Wheeler permitted to tackle two of the most important obstructions, to which he had for weeks been denied access on the most tenuous pretexts. (Simultaneously, Syria gave permission to the Iraq Petroleum Company to start repairing its damaged oil pipelines in preparation for restarting the flow of oil to the Mediterranean.) By the end of March the Canal was open to all but the largest vessels, and convoys had begun to pass through in both directions; a month later the United Nations announced the successful completion of the entire operation, at a cost which ultimately turned out to have been little more than $8 million. How to apportion this expense, as well as the considerably larger cost of the United Nations Emergency Force, would be a matter for later discussion among United Nations members (see section 25).

Of more urgent importance was the question of how the reopened Canal should be operated, and by whom. This had been an underlying issue in the hostilities of the previous year, and the result of those hostilities had not brought it closer to resolution. Egypt still claimed the full right to manage and operate the waterway within the broad provisions of the basic Constantinople Convention of 1888; the Western powers, including the United States, still presumably believed that the Canal should remain under some measure of international control. These antithetical positions had been only nominally reconciled by the "six principles" accepted by both sides and endorsed by the Security Council on October 13, 1956.[12] The six principles represented general standards to which it was agreed that a settlement ought to conform—e.g., that "the operation of the Canal should be insulated from the politics of any country." But they did not themselves constitute a settlement, nor did they specify by what means the agreed standards were to be enforced.

If the Western nations had been prepared to wait indefinitely for the reopening of the Canal and had been able to make satisfactory arrangements for meeting their petroleum and other commercial requirements in the interval, Egypt might eventually have moved a little closer to their view of what constituted a reasonable settlement. Some effort to bring the Egyptians into a more conciliatory frame of mind was urged in Washington by British and especially French representatives, but with little effect. Having declined to join the British and French in putting pressure on Egypt in 1956, Washington was certainly not going to do so in 1957. Egypt, in any case, was in too strong a position to make it likely that such maneuvers would succeed. Confronted with an informal Western proposal that Canal tolls be provisionally collected by an international agency until the cost of clearing the waterway was paid off, Egypt came back on March 19 with a formal statement of its position [13] in which it insisted on collecting all the tolls itself, reiterated its determination to abide by the 1888 convention, but made no reference to the "six principles" and merely said that disputes arising out of its management of the Canal could be referred to arbitration. Unofficially, President Abdel Nasser was advising all comers that Israeli vessels would continue to be barred in conformity with Egypt's interpretation of the 1888 convention.

From the standpoint of the Western powers, including the United States, the Egyptian document was highly disappointing. Not only did it make no reference to the "six principles," but its unilateral form deprived it of any binding legal character and left open the possibility that it might be revoked whenever Egypt thought fit. For practical purposes, however, it represented very nearly Egypt's last word. For five weeks the United States endeavored through diplomatic channels to persuade Egypt to strengthen its commitments, at the same time making clear that there was no thought in Washington of resorting to military or economic pressure. Egypt in the end issued a slightly revised "Declaration" which it deposited with the United Nations on April 24 with the somewhat unconventional statement that it constituted an "international instrument." [14] Legal authorities remained skeptical, but noted with satisfaction that Egypt at least undertook to be bound by the results of arbitration that might be undertaken in certain contingencies.

At a meeting of the Security Council on April 26, Ambassador Lodge expressed the opinion that although the Egyptian document left a good deal to be desired, the proposed system should nevertheless be given a chance to prove itself in operation. No one dissented, and Great Britain decided a fortnight later to advise its shipowners to use the Canal, reserving their rights with respect to the means of payment. France held out for another two months and made one more fruitless appeal to the Security Council (May 20–21), with the result that the first French vessel did not pass the Canal until June. By July 26, the first anniversary of nationalization, the Canal was operating at full capacity. The only reported instances of discrimination concerned two vessels of Scandinavian registry which had been delayed in transit to and from Israel. Israel itself had apparently postponed indefinitely its proclaimed intention of sending one of its own vessels through the Canal. Abdel Nasser, for all practical purposes, had won his battle.

13. THE EISENHOWER DOCTRINE IN ACTION

However fragile the settlement of the issues growing out of the Suez war, the restoration of a semblance of normal conditions in the Arab-Israel area removed at least some of the grounds for the apprehension that had gripped the American administration at the beginning of the year. By the time this process was completed, moreover, significant progress had been achieved in relation to the larger American aim of blocking further Soviet incursions in the Middle East through the mechanisms associated with the Eisenhower Doctrine. The Joint Resolution had been passed by Congress and signed into law on March 9; Ambassador Richards, the President's special envoy, had spent the ensuing two month in a tour of fifteen countries of the Middle East, Southern Asia, and North Africa and on his return had expressed gratified astonishment "at the confidence of the governments and the people of that area as to the high moral purposes of the United States in what they are trying to do." Reporting to the American public by radio on May 9, Mr. Richards declared that both the peoples and the governments of the Middle East area "have trust in the intentions of the United States, are determined to protect themselves from international communism, and have generally welcomed the American Doctrine." Without blinking the hazards involved, the President's special emissary expressed the hope and belief "that the Middle East nations will sail this course with us." [15]

This optimistic appraisal could be buttressed by a number of concrete facts, among them the signature of several new military and economic aid agreements and, perhaps more important, the failure of an attempted pro-Soviet coup in Jordan (see below). At the same time, it was evident that Mr. Richards' generalizations applied in very unequal measure to the individual countries of the Middle East area. Egypt and Syria, the two countries in which Soviet influence had established itself most strongly, had not been visited at all because of the failure of their governments to extend a suitable invitation. Jordan had also been omitted from Mr. Richards' itinerary. Among the countries he had visited, ranging from Greece and Turkey to Pakistan and Morocco, he had found pronounced variations in the awareness of "the danger of international communism," though all had at least "asserted determination to maintain their national independence against any threat." The truth was that although the Richards mission might have helped to dispel some of the prevailing misapprehensions about American policy, the Eisenhower Doctrine had not by any means succeeded in unifying the Middle East in opposition to Soviet designs. It would be more accurate to say that it had introduced a fresh element of division among Middle Eastern countries, perpetuating and in some cases accentuating the divisions already created by the Baghdad Pact and other manifestations of Western policy in past years.

The tendency of the Middle Eastern governments to divide along preestablished lines in their reaction to the new doctrine had, in fact, been apparent from the very first announcement of the new American policy effort. Generally speaking, the determination of the United States to take a stronger line in opposition to Soviet ambitions was most warmly welcomed by precisely those countries that had already made their decision in favor of the West and had definitely turned their backs on the temptations of "positive neutrality" and pro-Sovietism. These were the Asian members of the Baghdad Pact—Turkey, Iraq, Iran, and Pakistan—together with Lebanon, whose special position had precluded membership in the Baghdad Pact but whose current leaders were strong adherents of the Western viewpoint in all matters involving the Soviet Union. These governments' support of the new American doctrine had been immediate and unequivocal. "A good and timely move," had been the verdict of Foreign Minister Charles Malik of Lebanon (January 10); and the Asian members of the Baghdad Pact, meeting in Ankara on January 21, had hailed Washington's recognition of "the threat posed by Communist aggression and subversion" and declared its proposals "best designed to maintain peace in the area and advance the economic well-being of the people." [16] The only move that would have given these particular governments greater satisfaction would have been a decision by the United States to adhere to the Baghdad Pact itself.

Precisely opposite was the reaction of those governments in the Arab world and elsewhere which had rejected association with the West and identified themselves with the doctrine of "positive neutrality," more or less colored by partiality for the U.S.S.R. True, there was no official blanket repudiation of the Middle East resolution as such, baited as it was with promises of military and economic assistance. But the comments heard in Arab neutralist quarters, particularly in Damascus and Cairo, were caustic in the extreme. Some described the Eisenhower Doctrine as "a plot engineered by the imperialists and fed by Zionism"; others suggested that the source of strife in the Middle East was not Communism but "imperialism, colonialism and Zionism." Particularly resented, even by governments that refused to follow the Egyptian line, was the notion of a Middle Eastern "power vacuum" which seemed to underlie the American plan. Arab governments were quick to echo a comment offered by Indian Prime Minister Nehru, who was just back from the United States and might therefore have been presumed to know what Washington was trying to accomplish. "If there is a power vacuum in West Asia, it has to be filled by countries in that region through their internal strength and unity," Mr. Nehru said on January 6. Tailoring these sentiments to their own situation, the principal leaders of Egypt, Syria, Saudi Arabia, and Jordan, meeting in Cairo on January 19, solemnly "agreed on rejection of the 'vacuum' theory," resolved "never to allow their countries to become a sphere of influence for any foreign power," and determined "that Arab nationalism was the sole basis on which Arab policy could be formulated." This attitude provided an important bond even among governments whose views in other respects differed as widely as, for example, those of Egypt and Saudi Arabia.

It goes without saying that this negative line of thought was sedulously encouraged by the U.S.S.R., whose presumed ambitions had inspired the Eisenhower Doctrine and whose truculent response showed plainly that the resolution had touched it on a sensitive spot. "A vast step of gross interference in the internal affairs of the countries and peoples of the Middle East and their enslavement," Premier Bulganin commented on January 7. (Khrushchev predicted a few days later that the doctrine would end on "the garbage heap of history.") Aside from its alleged "colonial" character, Soviet and other Communist sources said plainly that the Eisenhower Doctrine had aggravated international tension and might result in dangerous consequences. "The voice of war, and not the voice of peace, resounds in Mr. Eisenhower's statement," said an official Soviet declaration of January 12, which further asserted that the United States would bear the entire responsibility for any results that might flow from its employment of armed forces in the area. Chou En-lai of Communist China joined his Soviet colleagues on January 18 in an explicit pledge of assistance to Middle Eastern peoples in preventing aggression and interference in their internal affairs. Thus the Communist governments placed themselves on record in support of goals which nominally at least were the same as those of the Eisenhower Doctrine itself. There were also indications that the Soviet line was being actively implemented by new maneuvers in individual Arab countries. Egypt apparently was receiving new shipments of Soviet arms to replace those it had lost in the autumn fighting; Syria, whose government seemed to be veering farther and farther to the Left, was being awarded five motor torpedo boats and welcoming new species of Communist representatives and technicians.

On February 11 the Soviet Government came forward with a full-fledged diplomatic proposal, obviously intended as a formal answer to the Eisenhower Doctrine, which with minor modifications was to stand throughout 1957 as its preferred remedy for Middle Eastern disorders. In official communications to the United States, Britain and France [17] the Kremlin suggested, not without a hint of menace, that the danger of a further deterioration of international relations in the area be forestalled by joint efforts of the great powers, based on the principles of noninterference in internal affairs and respect for the national independence and sovereignty of the Middle Eastern countries. Specifically, Moscow urged the proclamation by the Big Four of a new set of six principles, including (1) a liquidation of foreign bases and withdrawal of foreign troops from the area, and (2) a joint refusal to supply arms to Middle Eastern countries. Although Prime Minister Nehru appeared to regard this approach as at least preferable to the Eisenhower Doctrine, the Western governments were quick to recognize the old Soviet device of advocating that a given area be denuded of Western military protection and thus left open to Soviet pressure. Replying on March 11,[18] Washington did not trouble to refute the Soviet arguments in detail but contented itself with some sarcastic references to Hungary.

Soviet hostility to the Eisenhower Doctrine had been discounted in advance, and was unlikely to be mitigated by anything the United States would care to do. Much more important, in Washington's view, was the encouragement of a more favorable reaction on the part of the Arab states, particularly those which had thus far avoided direct entanglement with the Soviet Union. In this connection a quite particular significance was attached to the position of King Saud of Saudi Arabia, who had been a strong exponent of Arab neutralism but viewed the radical tendencies now dominant in Egypt and Syria with unconcealed distaste. King Saud had accepted an invitation to visit the United States at the end of January, and authorities in Washington went to unusual lengths to make a favorable impression and if possible win him over to a more sympathetic view of American policy. In addition, the United States was most anxious to make arrangements for continued use of the air base at Dhahran in Saudi Arabia, the formal lease on which had expired some months earlier. Despite some manifestations of public disapproval of Saudi internal policies, particularly

those involving discrimination on religious grounds against
members of the American armed forces, the official objectives were in large measure achieved. The arrangement at
Dhahran was renewed for a five-year period; the United
States promised Saudi Arabia a limited amount of additional
military and economic aid; and Saud manifested a certain
degree of sympathy for the purposes, if not the specific
language, of the Eisenhower Doctrine.[19] He also consented
while in Washington to talk privately with a hereditary
enemy, Crown Prince Abdul Illah of Iraq, and to pass on
his impressions of American policy to other Arab governments.

Returning home by way of Spain and the North African
capitals, Saud arrived in Cairo on February 25 for a continuation of his "summit conference" meetings with the
Egyptian, Syrian, and Jordanian leaders. The American attitude, he told them, seemed to him to reflect a new appreciation of the Arab viewpoint, both on Israel and on the question of neutrality in the East-West struggle. He apparently
made no attempt to put the conference on record in support
of the Eisenhower Doctrine, but did urge that all four
governments make clear their opposition to Communism as
a real threat to Arab interests. In this he was supported by
the young King Hussein of Jordan but strongly resisted by
President Shukri al-Kuwatli of Syria and, passively at least,
by President Abdel Nasser of Egypt. For publication, the
four leaders could agree on nothing better than a renewed
declaration of "positive neutrality" and an expression of
support for the Arab point of view on all current questions.
Unofficially, however, there were signs that a significant realignment of political views was taking place in the Arab
world. Syria and Egypt were coming more and more to occupy the position of an intransigent minority even among
the Arab neutrals—a position which President Abdel Nasser,
at least, appeared to find somewhat uncomfortable. King Saud
and King Hussein, on the other hand, were becoming conscious of a new feeling of solidarity which was destined to
have important consequences in the months to come.

To encourage such a realignment, or at least to associate

as many countries as possible with the objectives of the
Eisenhower Doctrine, was one of the evident purposes of
American diplomacy in the weeks that followed the Cairo
meeting. One reflection of this aim was the itinerary worked
out for Vice-President Nixon's late winter tour of independent African countries, which included among others
Morocco, Tunisia, Libya, Ethiopia, and the Sudan but significantly bypassed Egypt. In all these countries the Vice-
President exerted himself to explain the purposes of the
Eisenhower Doctrine and its importance in safeguarding the
independence of Middle Eastern and African nations. In
most of them he appears to have been heard with attention
and sympathy. Although the Sudanese leaders appeared quite
dubious, in Libya (March 15) Mr. Nixon's party had the
satisfaction of hearing Premier Mustafa Ben Halim pro-
nounce as glowing a tribute to the Eisenhower Doctrine as
any that had been uttered in the Arab world. (See further
section 16.)

Of more immediate interest to most Middle Eastern countries was the official mission of Ambassador Richards, who
was empowered to offer not only explanations but definite
commitments of military and economic aid. This advantage
was somewhat offset, however, by the expectation that each
country benefiting from such assistance would join the roving
ambassador in some kind of statement aligning it with the
purposes of the Eisenhower Doctrine. The prospect of having
to "sign on the dotted line" was a major deterrent to neutral-
ist-minded countries and strengthened the prospect that Mr.
Richards' principal successes would be achieved in countries
already predisposed in favor of American policy. In most instances the exact amount of assistance promised was not
made public, although the President later reported (July 31)
that the Richards mission had concluded "agreements in
principle" for assistance totaling $118.7 million, somewhat
more than half of it ($67.7 million) being for economic
assistance. This was well within the $200 million ceiling for
fiscal 1957 which had been set by congressional resolution.

Mr. Richards' travels were nothing if not wide-ranging.
Joint statements or communiqués,[20] all more or less favorable

to the Eisenhower Doctrine, were issued in Lebanon, Libya, Turkey, Iran, and Pakistan. Neutral Afghanistan expressed itself somewhat equivocally, but in Iraq Mr. Richards encountered a particularly hearty welcome and was able to allocate funds both to the Iraqi Government and to the Baghdad Pact organization. (The Baghdad Pact, which had seemed moribund a few months earlier, was rapidly coming to life again in the wake of a disclosure that the United States, though still declining formal membership, had decided to become a full participant in its Military Committee. See section 15.) In Saudi Arabia, King Saud received the presidential envoy and reaffirmed his promise to oppose Communism. Yemen manifested "a friendly spirt" but would sign no document; Ethiopia, on the other hand, indicated cordial support of the Eisenhower Doctrine. On April 19, the State Department noted with gratification that no fewer than eight out of the ten nations visited thus far had announced "opposition to international Communism."

While Ambassador Richards paused to take breath in Eritrea, the Eisenhower Doctrine was undergoing a harsher test in the streets of Jordan's capital of Amman. We have already noted the emergence of King Hussein as one of those Arab leaders who showed a measure of sensitivity to the Communist danger, with which he combined a clear appreciation of the threat of radical "Nasserism" to the established order in the Arab world and in his own kingdom. If anything, the young monarch's reservations had been fortified by the behavior of Jordan's own constitutional government, a product of precisely those left-wing, ultranationalist, and indiscriminately anti-Western tendencies of which President Abdel Nasser had become the symbol. Similar attitudes were very prevalent among the Jordanian population, particularly in the newer, former Palestinian parts of the kingdom, where the presence of some half-million Arab refugees was a potent influence in a radical direction. The cabinet headed by Sulayman al-Nabulsi was thoroughly penetrated by this outlook and showed no particular attachment to the existing order of things in Jordan.

King and cabinet were at least agreed on the desirability

of terminating Jordan's historic relationship of dependence on the United Kingdom, even if it involved increased dependence on other Arab states. Even before Nabulsi took office in the fall of 1956, Jordan had agreed to place its armed forces under a joint comand established by Egypt, Syria, and Saudi Arabia and headed by an Egyptian general. At Cairo on January 19, 1957 the Nabulsi government mortgaged Jordan's economic future by undertaking to accept an annual subsidy of $35 million from the same three states and in effect pledging itself to receive no more financial assistance from the United Kingdom. On the basis of these promises, the Anglo-Jordanian alliance treaty of 1948 was formally terminated in March and the last British forces left the country early in July.

Although King Hussein had personally taken a leading role in severing Jordan's ties with Britain, he had become increasingly unsympathetic to the tendencies of the Nabulsi government in other respects. Particularly alarming from his point of view was the rapid growth of pro-Soviet influences in the Jordanian civil service and in the armed forces headed by Major General Ali Abu Nuwar, the Chief of Staff. While Premier Nabulsi violently denounced the Eisenhower Doctrine, the King as early as February 2 made bold to issue a personal warning to the nation against the dangers of Communism—dangers which, as we have seen, continued to preoccupy him at the time of the second Cairo conference. As the weeks went by and the issues posed by the Eisenhower Doctrine became more acute, there were indications that a showdown might be impending between the King and the leftist forces who virtually controlled the government. For a time it seemed that the crucial question would be whether or not to invite Ambassador Richards to Amman and give him a chance to explain the American point of view. Premier Nabulsi, however, supplied a different ground for action by announcing on April 3–4 that Jordan intended to establish diplomatic relations with the Soviet Union, would accept Soviet aid if offered, but would refuse American aid as incompatible with the country's independence.

On April 10 King Hussein, acting apparently on his own

initiative, demanded the resignation of Premier Nabulsi and prepared to set up a more congenial government. His aim, apparently, was to shift the center of gravity in Jordanian affairs away from the radical, anti-Western elements which predominated in former Palestinian areas and to rely more heavily on the conservatively minded Bedouin population with its tradition of loyalty to the royal house. The most serious initial resistance to this undertaking developed not from Nabulsi but from General Nuwar, who appears to have interposed directly in the cabinet-making process, attempted to dictate the choice of a new prime minister, and prepared to rally the army in opposition to the will of the sovereign. The crisis occurred on April 13 when the King put in a personal appearance at an army base near Amman, faced down his antagonists, won over the support of loyal Bedouin forces, and compelled General Nuwar to depart in all haste for Syria. As yet the royal victory was far from complete, however. Nabulsi, who remained as Foreign Minister in the new government headed by Hussein Fakhri al-Khalidi, continued his propaganda against the Eisenhower Doctrine and was evidently preparing, with Syrian and Egyptian encouragement, to rouse the mob against its constitutional ruler. The new government was forced to resign on April 25, and the situation was made worse by the fact that the new Chief of Staff, Major General Ali Hayari, had followed General Nuwar to Damascus and was proclaiming the whole affair an "imperialist plot" hatched by unnamed, non-Arab military attachés.

From an international standpoint the danger in all this was not merely that Jordan might be definitively lost to the free world but that it might collapse altogether and start a general scramble for territory which could easily touch off wider hostilities. Some Syrian and Saudi Arabian armed forces had been stationed in the country since the preceding autumn; Iraq was now carrying out a precautionary mobilization on the frontier; Israel had often intimated that it would seize the west bank of the Jordan if its neighbor went to pieces. This seemed hardly the type of situation that could involve the use of American forces under the Middle East resolution, which had been carefully limited to the contingency of "armed agression from any country controlled by international communism." Yet its relevance to the broad purposes of the Eisenhower Doctrine was obvious. The doctrine would not be worth much if it allowed Jordan to succumb to mob violence and externally fomented leftist intrigue.

There was another possible guide to American action in the somewhat shadowy Tripartite Declaration of May 25, 1950, in which the Western Big Three had undertaken to oppose any violation of frontiers or armistice lines in the Arab-Israel area.[21] Although this understanding had completely failed to prevent the Israeli-Egyptian hostilities of the previous autumn and was now regarded in London and Paris as a dead letter, Washington apparently considered it still in force. Asked at his news conference on April 17 about the applicability of the Eisenhower Doctrine to the situation in Jordan, the President stated that our policy in the matter was governed by the Tripartite Declaration *and* the Middle East resolution. Secretary Dulles explained a few days later (April 23) that we had "great confidence in and regard for" King Hussein, and desired "to hold up the hands" of the young monarch "to the extent that he thinks we can be helpful." How far this was the case, he added, would be for the King to judge.

A much more vigorous mark of interest was forthcoming on April 24, as Washington reverberated to the news of the popular disturbances which had meanwhile broken out in Amman. After a telephone call from Secretary Dulles, the President in Augusta, Georgia authorized a statement to the press [22] to the effect that both he and the Secretary of State "regard the independence and integrity of Jordan as vital"— seemingly a direct invitation to Hussein to request American assistance under the Eisenhower Doctrine. Next day, April 25, came even more sensational news: the United States Sixth Fleet, including the carrier *Forrestal* and 1,800 Marines, had been suddenly ordered to the Eastern Mediterranean. Washington officials now spoke openly of the Middle

East resolution and of a "threat to the independence and integrity of Jordan by international Communism."

These moves completed the promotion of the Jordanian crisis from an internal to an international matter and elicited vehement denunciations from the U.S.S.R., which claimed that the "real imperialistic essence" of the Eisenhower Doctrine had now been revealed. But it also provided King Hussein with whatever assurances he needed to assert his own authority and complete the rout of his leftist opponents. On April 25 still another government was installed in Amman, this one under Ibrahim Hashim, a stanch royalist, and the King set vigorously to work to weed out subversive influences and follow up the threads of Egyptian and Syrian intrigue which had almost cost him his throne.

The abortive plot against Hussein represented a major setback for the leftist-neutralist policy of Egypt and Syria and completed the conversion of King Saud from an opponent to a supporter of the Jordanian royal house. From the very beginning of the crisis, the Saudi monarch had ranged his influence on Hussein's side; and the young King's first move after the situation was brought under control was to fly to Riyadh for a conference with the elder ruler and a full discussion of the Egyptian and Syrian "plot." Hussein's return to Amman on April 29 was signalized by the dramatic disclosure that the United States had decided to follow up its military gesture with an emergency grant of $10 million to assist in Jordan's economic development and the maintenance of political stability, and that more might be available if needed. Both in Amman and in Washington it was emphasized that this money would come from regular aid funds and did not involve formal association with the Eisenhower Doctrine, which the King remained anxious to avoid if only to give no handle to his enemies. American assistance would be none the less welcome on that account, especially since Egypt and Syria were plainly in no mood to provide the budgetary assistance they had promised in January. Just before the fiscal year closed on June 30, the United States announced two further grants to Jordan totaling $20 million, half in military and half in economic assistance. Together with Saudi Arabian contributions, this would at least temporarily fill the gap left by the cessation of the British subsidies.

The resolution of the Jordanian crisis virtually completed the political crystallization which had been set in motion by the promulgation of the Eisenhower Doctrine. The position of the individual countries in the Middle East was now fairly clear, and at the beginning of May Ambassador Richards was advised to complete his mission without waiting any longer for the opportunity to visit Jordan, Egypt, or Syria. His winding-up visits to the Sudan, Greece, Israel, Libya, Tunisia, and Morocco produced few surprises: apart from the Sudan, all of these governments were already known to be favorably disposed to the Eisenhower Doctrine. In other respects, meanwhile, the Middle Eastern situation seemed at last to be moving in a more hopeful direction. While King Hussein inveighed against Egypt and Syria and prepared to prosecute his domestic foes, King Saud paid state visits to Iraq and Jordan which seemed to have written *finis* to his old feud with the Hashimi dynasty. So far as possible, Saud avoided displaying open antagonism to the Egyptian and Syrian governments. His preferred role was that of a conciliator of Arab differences and a symbol of Arab unity; but in case of a showdown between conflicting tendencies in the Arab world—which he obviously hoped to avoid—there was no doubt in Washington as to where his sympathies would lie.

In Lebanon, too, the pro-Western trend appeared to be gaining with the success of moderate candidates in a series of parliamentary elections held during June. Great Britain's re-admission to a role in Middle Eastern affairs was signalized by a meeting of the Baghdad Pact Council (Karachi, June 3-6) which also celebrated the beginning of full United States participation in the alliance's military planning activities and recorded "deep gratification" over the Eisenhower Doctrine [23] (see section 15). There was an air of considerable self-confidence in the diplomatic notes in which the Western powers rejected on June 11 a new Soviet proposal (dated April 19) for a mutual renunciation of force in the Middle East area.[24] Apart from an occasional flare-up on the Israeli-Syrian border and the disheartening situation of nearly a million Arab refu-

gees, even the Arab-Israeli situation seemed to be on the upgrade. Reporting to Congress on the first months of activity
under the Middle East doctrine (July 31),[25] President Eisenhower felt that although the situation afforded "no grounds
for complacency," the resolution had helped to bring about a
substantial over-all improvement, had "served as an unmistakable warning to international communism against all forms
of aggression," and would increasingly contribute to Middle
Eastern peace and stability as long as its purposes and principles were maintained.

14. SETBACK IN SYRIA

That these favorable appearances were not entirely trust-
worthy was to become amply evident in the ensuing weeks.
The sequel to Khrushchev's victory over the "anti-party group"
in Moscow at the beginning of July (section 10) was a radical
intensification of Soviet activity in the Middle East, culminating in a virtual "cold coup" in Syria which was to confront
the world with new threats of war and imperil much of the
accomplishment of the past several months. A foretaste of what
was coming occurred in July and August in what looked like
a concerted attack on the positions Great Britain still retained
in the region of the Arabian Peninsula and the Persian Gulf.
A tribal revolt against the authority of Great Britain's ally,
the Sultan of Muscat and Oman, broke out in mid-July in
inaccessible desert country and persisted for nearly a month
before the rebels could be scattered by British aircraft and
armored cars. There was no proof here of Soviet complicity,
but the leaders of the rebellion—ostensibly led by the Sultan's
supposed vassal, the Imam of Oman—were obviously working
hand in glove with the Arab League office in Cairo, and the
Russians lent full support in inflating the affair to international proportions and in seeking a hearing before the United
Nations Security Council. That body met on August 20 but
decided by a 5-4 vote (with the United States abstaining) not
to place the matter on its agenda.

Concurrently, new outbreaks occurred along the border between Yemen and the British Protectorate of Aden, for years
the scene of intermittent warfare which the Communists had

done their best to inflame and which had given some concern earlier in the year. There was accumulating evidence that Yemen, which had refused to associate itself with the Eisenhower Doctrine, might now be emerging as a new outpost of Soviet influence. Substantial quantities of arms had lately been entering the country, presumably from Czechoslovakia, and the British claimed that fifty or more Soviet instructors and advisers had already begun the process of shaping the country to Communist ends. At the moment Yemen as a military threat ranked scarcely higher than the forces of the Imam of Oman. Yet such developments were bound to raise a question about the future of Britain's position both in strategic Aden and in Bahrein, Kuweit, and other parts of the oil-rich Persian Gulf area.

Far more immediate and unequivocal was the intensification of the Soviet threat in Syria. Although that country had already leaned well over to the Soviet side, it had thus far been prevented from losing its balance entirely by the influence of such comparatively moderate nationalists as President al-Kuwatli and Premier Sabri al-Asali, who formed at least a partial counterweight to younger and more radical figures such as those grouped around Colonel Abdel Hamid Sarraj, the Chief of Army Intelligence. Three separate but related developments during August 1957 appeared to spell the final defeat of these more moderate influences, and with it the destruction of the last important barriers to unobstructed Soviet influence.

The first of these developments was a visit to Moscow by a group of Syrian officials, led by Defense Minister Khalid al-Azm, who on August 7 reached an exceptionally broad understanding with the Russians [26] providing for Soviet cooperation in a variety of Syrian economic development projects, for the provision of Soviet credit "without strings," for increased two-way trade, and (according to unofficial reports) for the furnishing of additional military equipment and training assistance. Secondly, the Syrian Government on August 13 announced the discovery of what it described as an "American plot" to overthrow the existing regime in cooperation with ex-President Adib al-Shishakly and other exiled Syrians. Three officials of the United States Embassy were branded as undesirable and required to leave immediately. (The United States, denying and ridiculing the charges, promptly retaliated by announcing that Syria's Ambassador had ceased to be acceptable.) Third, Syria's Chief of Staff, a moderate, resigned on August 15 and was replaced two days later by the young and fiery General Afif Bizri, known as the army's most extreme leftist and presumably a "front" for Communist influences if not a Communist himself. Thus, in the short space of ten days, the groundwork appeared to have been laid for the subjection of Syria's economy, its army, and probably its politics to virtual Soviet control and for the destruction, perhaps irretrievably, of normal relations with the United States.

Although the degree of direct Soviet involvement in these events was by no means clear, they obviously fell into the general pattern of East-West competition which had loomed so large in the Middle East since the promulgation of the Eisenhower Doctrine. Syria's virtual identification with the Soviet bloc, moreover, was not a matter for rejoicing in other Middle Eastern states. Turkey, Iraq, Jordan, Lebanon, Israel all sensed a new threat to their military security; King Saud deplored the new advance of leftist influences in the Arab world; even President Abdel Nasser (who did not tolerate any overt Communist activity in Egypt) appeared rather uneasy about the rapid progress of the forces he had conjured up, and not entirely happy about the way his own services to "Arab nationalism" were being overshadowed by developments in other countries.

In none of the Middle Eastern capitals, however, were the events in Syria greeted with such dismay as in Washington. Here was precisely such a "recognizable success" for "international communism" as the Eisenhower Doctrine had been intended to prevent. Yet the Middle East resolution as enacted by Congress afforded few hints as to what could be done about it. Here again, as in the Jordanian affair, what confronted the United States was not a case of aggression by a state "controlled by international communism" but an internally motivated readjustment of a country's internal politics and international policies; and, as President Eisenhower observed on August 21,

BUSY NEIGHBORHOOD

By Shanks in *The Buffalo Evening News*

there were "very definite limitations on what you can do in the internal affairs of any other country." The only possibly constructive action that Washington was said to be considering was an attempt to "quarantine" Syria, in cooperation with its neighbors, in the hope that right-wing elements within the country might be emboldened to reassert themselves. That the Arab states would lend themselves to such a procedure did not, however, seem probable.

The lively concern displayed in Washington did nothing to damp the exaltation of the men who now seemed to be running Syria's government. Reaffirming the country's policy of "positive neutrality," Khalid al-Azm offered the United States this counsel (August 22): "We are at the outer edge of that policy—do not force us to go beyond it." Particularly irritating to the Syrians was an emergency fact-finding mission to the Near East which was undertaken on behalf of the State Department by Deputy Under-Secretary Loy W. Henderson. In contrast to the procedure of Assistant Secretary George V. Allen on a similar errand following the Soviet-Egyptian arms deal in 1955, Mr. Henderson refrained from visiting the country most directly involved but spent most of his fortnight abroad in Turkey (where he conferred with the Kings of Jordan and Iraq) and in Lebanon. Returning to Washington on September 4, the special envoy reported that Syria's pro-Soviet moves were "extremely serious" and could have "serious effects on the security of the whole free world."

Obviously alarmed by Mr. Henderson's findings, Washington promptly disclosed that deliveries of military equipment to Jordan, Iraq, Lebanon, and Saudi Arabia were being expedited and that a supply of arms would be rushed to Jordan by air. A still higher pitch of concern was registered in a statement issued in the President's name by Secretary Dulles after a White House conference on September 7.[27] After referring to Mr. Henderson's report on "the apparently growing Soviet Communist domination of Syria," the large build-up of Soviet bloc arms, and the prevalence of border incidents and intensive propaganda and subversive activities directed against Syria's Arab neighbors, the statement for the first time directly invoked the Eisenhower Doctrine: "The President affirmed his intention to carry out the national policy, expressed in the congressional Middle East resolution which had been adopted, and exercise as needed the authority thereby conferred on the President." In addition to authorizing accelerated delivery of "economic and other defensive items" to the countries of the area, the President was said to have expressed the hope "that the international Communists would not push Syria into any acts of aggression against her neighbors and that the people of Syria would act to allay the anxiety caused by recent events."

The people of Syria did not act, however, and although the United States admitted that the Sixth Fleet had once again moved into the east central Mediterranean, Washington itself within a few days was working "to allay the anxiety caused by recent events." Tension fell off considerably after Secretary Dulles told his news conference on September 10 that action under the Eisenhower Doctrine seemed to him unlikely and that he believed the situation would be worked out peacefully. There were reports that this change of tone reflected the moderating influence of King Saud, with whom the President had remained in friendly correspondence ever since his winter visit. Although Washington insisted that American policy was not being made in Saudi Arabia, it was widely conceded that the United States in this instance had somewhat overplayed its hand and had notably failed to improve its standing in the Arab world. The other Arab governments, little as they might like Syria's course of action, were even more opposed to policies that divided the Arab world, set one Arab state against another, and threatened to involve the area in hostilities. On this occasion all the initiatives had clearly been taken by the United States. Moscow had on the whole remained passive, except for a new note to the Western powers on September 3 [28] in which it again urged its proposal for a mutual renunciation of force and of interference in internal affairs of Middle Eastern countries.

A hint that trouble might still develop from the Soviet side was the letter dispatched by Premier Bulganin to Turkish Premier Adnan Menderes on September 11 with a serious warning not to heed America's alleged advice to attack Syria. Neither Mr. Dulles nor Mr. Gromyko were notably conciliatory in their comments on the Middle East in the opening debate of the new United Nations Assembly session on September 19-20. None of the parties concerned, however, appeared willing to risk the situation's getting out of hand. King Saud was devoting his talents to bridging the differences between Syria and the other Arab states, and President Eisenhower on October 3 expressed the view that the situation appeared to be "solidifying to some extent." No one would have claimed a triumph for American foreign policy, but neither would anyone have suspected that Khrushchev within a few days would once more fan the crisis to white heat and confront the world with what seemed the most serious threat of war since the dark days of November 1956. (See further section 25.)

15. ANKARA TO NEW DELHI

Developments affecting the Baghdad Pact and the countries of the so-called "northern tier" in 1957 require less detailed notice than the events just recounted. The conclusion of the Baghdad treaty in 1955 had marked an important stage in the progress of the East-West struggle in the countries of the Muslim world and had been a principal factor in the division of the Arab nations into separate political camps behind the rather tenuous façade of Arab unity. Since that time, however, Middle Eastern politics had gone through several further stages and the center of interest had shifted accordingly. Although the Baghdad Pact still formed part of the political landscape, its significance as the shield of the Middle East had been progressively diminished by the refusal of the United States to become a member, the success of Soviet "leapfrog" tactics in Egypt and Syria, the ostracism of Great Britain following its attack on Egypt, the promulgation of the new American doctrine for the "general area of the Middle East," and the growing emphasis of both British and American defense policy on the "nuclear deterrent." Despite valiant efforts to keep alive and active, the Baghdad Pact organization was thoroughly entangled in the uncertainties besetting the Middle East as a whole. At most it represented one among several instruments available for the realization of Western purposes—

purposes which, as the Syrian episode showed, could be defeated despite the multiplicity of means available.

Within the limits of this rather reduced status, believers in the Baghdad Pact could nevertheless boast some genuine progress in 1957. The breach with Great Britain was healed quite early in the year, and although the United States still refused to join the organization in a formal sense, its *de facto* participation was further extended through the decision to join the pact's Military Committee, first announced on March 22 during the Bermuda Conference. This decision was formally implemented at the annual meeting of the pact's Council of Ministers, held in Karachi on June 3-6, with Mr. Henderson representing the United States as an observer.[29] The principal development of this session was the approval of plans to set up a "more comprehensive military planning structure"—apparently a joint planning staff, rather than the joint military command the Middle Eastern members of the pact would have preferred. In addition, the Council laid down programs of intensified activity in the economic and "counter-subversion" areas, in which the United States was already a full participant. On the economic side, major emphasis was placed on a plan for linking the capitals of the member states by telecommunications and roads and railways, an enterprise of some magnitude toward which the Richards mission had recently allocated $12.5 million. Other economic projects of current interest included a nuclear research center which had already begun operation in Baghdad and a plan for closer economic cooperation and possibly a "free trade area" among Turkey, Iraq, Iran, and Pakistan.

In the course of their Karachi meeting the Baghdad Pact representatives also made the customary finding that their area still faced a "threat of direct and indirect aggression backed by massive and growing military potential," and that this created a "need for constant vigilance and for strengthening the ability of the Member Nations to meet and repel this threat." Inspiriting though such words might be, and encouraging as was the presence of a high American authority like General Twining at the deliberations of the Military Committee, it was not easy to see how the Baghdad Pact nations, now or in the future, were to develop sufficient strength to "meet and repel" Moscow's threat to the Middle East. Of the four Middle Eastern members, only Turkey and Pakistan were capable of putting substantial military forces in the field, and these in case of emergency would plainly be needed for home defense. Protection of the gap between Turkey in the west and Pakistan in the east—if it could be protected at all, as some observers seemed to doubt—would evidently depend less on any military forces conjured up by the Baghdad Pact organization than on the "nuclear deterrent" wielded by the United States and to a lesser extent by Great Britain.

But if the defense of the Baghdad Pact area against military aggression still depended ultimately on Anglo-American air-atomic power, its defense against subversion, infiltration, and possible internal breakdown presented quite different problems—problems which might prove considerably more immediate, if recent Soviet tactics were any guide. It would not have been at all desirable for Turkey, Iraq, Iran, or Pakistan to become another Syria, either because its military forces were too weak to protect its internal security or because its domestic economic and political structure was too frail to support real independence. Reassuringly for the West, the domestic difficulties of one kind or another which confronted all of these countries during 1957 did not prove sufficiently grave to nullify their official pro-Western policies or impair their resistance to Soviet political warfare tactics. The unsuccessful attempt of Turkey's Republican People's party to supplant the somewhat authoritarian Democratic party regime of President Celâl Bayar and Premier Menderes in the elections of October 27 was completely divorced from foreign policy issues. Equally so were the retirement in June of Iraq's pro-Western Prime Minister Nuri al-Said, the designation of Dr. Manouchehr Eghbal as successor to Iranian Prime Minister Hussein Ala, and the nomination of Ismail Ibrahim Chundrigar as Prime Minister of Pakistan to replace H. S. Suhrawardy, who was compelled to resign in October following his return from the United States and the collapse of his coalition cabinet. (Mr. Chundrigar in turn gave place in December to Malik Firoz Khan Noon, a strong supporter of the Baghdad Pact and SEATO who had been Foreign Minister in the two preceding governments.) With the possible exception of Turkey, none of these countries could as yet be considered fully versed in the operation of democratic institutions of Western type. There was already speculation about what might happen in Pakistan when its first national elections were held in 1958. In the meantime it was significant that each of the Baghdad Pact members in Asia had thus far managed to surmount the various internal and external crises which had confronted them since making their choice for the West.

Of equal importance, on any comprehensive view of the prospects for the Middle East and Southern Asia, was the situation of two further countries which were geographically associated with the "northern tier" even though politically distinct from it. One of the perennial drawbacks of the Baghdad Pact had been its negative effect on Afghanistan and India, both of which had been repelled from the Western cause in approximately the same measure as Pakistan and the other Baghdad Pact members had shown themselves attracted to it. This reaction, particularly in India's case, could be attributed partly to ideological preoccupations related to "noncommitment" and "positive neutrality"; but it was also bound up with a direct antagonism to Pakistan which was common to both countries. As a result, the conclusion of the Baghdad Pact, while it established a barrier of sorts against Soviet penetration in one area, had in some measure opened a door to it in another. Soviet machinations in Afghanistan in the last year or two, though evidently confined for the most part to the nonmilitary field, had been comparable in scale to those in Egypt. India had played a more cautious game in relation to the Soviet Union, but its constant agitation against the Baghdad Pact and more recently the Eisenhower Doctrine had done much to discredit both those arrangements in the eyes of "uncommitted" countries.

No decisive change in Afghanistan's position as between East and West occurred during 1957, but there were some indications that the government of Premier Muhammad Daud was anxious to avoid total commitment to the Communist camp despite its eagerness to take advantage of any benefits offered by Moscow or Peking. A new agreement concluded in Moscow in July provided for Soviet assistance in oil prospecting in northern Afghanistan and in the training of technical personnel, as well as for the regulation of certain boundary problems; [30] and in October the Prime Minister paid a visit to Communist China. But there was also an increase in American assistance to Afghanistan, with emphasis on developing the country's air and land communications with the non-Communist world. Of considerable importance in this connection was an improvement in the relations between Afghanistan and Pakistan, the fruit of a three-day visit to Kabul by Premier Suhrawardy in June. On this occasion it was decided to resume normal diplomatic relations after a two-year lapse and to try to avoid polemics in the two countries' territorial dispute over "Pushtunistan."

No such promising development could be reported in connection with Pakistan's quarrel with India over the possession of Kashmir, now going into its tenth year with both countries still occupying a part and claiming the whole of the disputed state. If anything, the conflict had been further aggravated at the beginning of 1957 by India's acquiescence in a decision of the Kashmir Constituent Assembly (explicitly disavowed by the United Nations Security Council)[31] which purported to complete Kashmir's irrevocable accession to India as of January 26, 1957. On Pakistan's insistence the matter was discussed several times in the Security Council, which decided in February to send its presiding officer, Gunnar V. Jarring of Sweden, to confer with both parties about possibilities for settling the dispute. No success attended the Jarring mission, primarily because India refused to consider a plebiscite, arbitration, or any other procedure which could result in weakening its own position in Kashmir or strengthening that of Pakistan. While the two governments traded accusations at home and in New York, the Security Council resumed its meetings and eventually, on December 2, authorized a further attempt to bring the parties together by Dr. Frank P. Graham, originally selected as United Nations Representative for that purpose as far back as 1951.[32]

While the Kashmir question remained open, the basic relationship between India and Pakistan could not improve significantly. A three-year commercial agreement looking to a revival of mutual trade was signed early in the year, and the dispute over water rights in the Indus River basin continued under intermittent discussion with representatives of the International Bank. But any progress that might be made in these matters appeared to be offset by the two governments' fundamental political differences, not least of which was their difference on the problem of East-West relations. More than once Prime Minister Nehru said in so many words (e.g., July 22) that the basic obstacle to peaceful settlement of their disputes was Pakistan's membership in military alliances and its consequent tendency to "pursue a wrong path."

There was no denying that Pakistan's participation in the Manila and Baghdad pacts had, in Mr. Nehru's phrase, "brought 'cold war' to India's borders"—and in more ways than one. Like the Arab-Israeli quarrel, though to a lesser degree, the Kashmir dispute had tended increasingly to suck in the various great powers on the side of their local favorites. The Soviet Union, which in the Middle East was unequivocally identified with the Arab and Muslim viewpoint, here tended to take the side of India as against Muslim Pakistan. On February 20, 1957 it actually used its veto in the Security Council to defeat a draft resolution unacceptable to India; this was the eightieth Soviet veto, but the first on Kashmir.

The United States, in contrast, still tried to remain impartial regarding Kashmir, despite the importunities of its Pakistani ally and the insistence of India that its stand was fundamentally prejudiced. When Prime Minister Suhrawardy visited Washington in July, he was unable to obtain any public endorsement of Pakistan's position on either the Kashmir or Indus disputes: President Eisenhower merely "expressed the hope that such regional disputes may be solved speedily, equitably, and permanently, in accordance with the principles of the United Nations." [33] The administration at this period, indeed, was not even in a position to promise definite action on Pakistan's requests for surplus food and other assistance, although a $53,450,000 food surplus agreement was concluded some months later (November 15). In the meantime Mr. Eisenhower "expressed his understanding of the problems facing Pakistan" and called attention to the substantial quantities of economic and military aid already made available. This in itself was sufficient to damn the American-Pakistani relationship in the eyes of India, which strongly condemned the supplying of any American arms to Pakistan despite official assurances that they were intended only for defense.

Of incalculable significance to the interests of the free world was the bearing of this state of affairs on India's own internal economic and political development. That the success of India's struggle to achieve a higher standard of living without sacrificing political democracy was vitally important to all non-Communist nations was generally admitted in the West, even by those who most strongly disapproved New Delhi's fundamental policy of "nonalignment." The measure of economic progress achieved under India's Second Five-Year Plan, which began in April 1956 and aimed at a vast expansion of the country's industrial capacity at an over-all cost of perhaps $11 billion, might in the long run make the difference between freedom and slavery not only for India's 400 million inhabitants but for additional hundreds of millions in other parts of Asia. There was nothing automatic or inevitable about the continuance of the broadly democratic regime thus far provided in India by Mr. Nehru's Congress party, as was clearly demonstrated by the results of that country's second nationwide elections, held in the late winter of 1957. Although Congress retained a safe (if diminished) majority in the national parliament, there were substantial Communist gains on the state level and in one state, Kerala, the Communists actually were able to take over the responsibility of government.

This development could be at least partially attributed to economic factors, and seemed to underline the importance of getting the Five-Year Plan carried out on schedule. But India by this time was claiming with some plausibility that the Five-Year Plan was already endangered by declining foreign exchange reserves, the result in part of unforeseen arms purchases allegedly needed to match Pakistan's acquisitions from the United States. Unlike Egypt and Syria, India made no move to obtain arms from behind the Iron Curtain, although it was receiving substantial economic aid from Communist sources. It did, however, let it be known that the Five-Year Plan faced serious curtailment unless support from abroad was forthcoming in considerably greater measure than could be immediately foreseen. At the time of Prime Minister Nehru's conferences with President Eisenhower in December 1956, it had been widely expected that the United States would step forward to underwrite the plan on a large scale; but such prospects had waned considerably by the autumn of 1957, when Finance Minister T. T. Krishnamachari visited the United States in hopes of raising an American loan of $500 million or more. Yet while India's long-range prospects remained as precarious as they seemed to be through most of 1957, there would always be the danger that international Communism might one day outflank the West's security arrangements at this eastern extremity of the "northern tier" just as it had already done at the other extremity in Egypt, Yemen, and Syria.

16. DEVELOPMENTS IN AFRICA

In the years that followed the Communist conquest of China in 1949, advocates of a forward-looking American policy in the Middle East and Southern Asia had often cited the Chinese experience as a further reason for timely action in areas that might soon emerge as new theaters of East-West conflict. "We mustn't let it happen in India," they said; "we mustn't let it happen in the Middle East." By 1957, with India still secure but with much of the Middle East already lying open to Communist influence, a new slogan was becoming popular: "We mustn't let it happen in Africa." There could be little doubt that Africa's multiple problems would within a very few more years be fully enmeshed in the rivalry of Eastern and Western creeds and systems. Meanwhile that continent had an essential contribution to make to the economic and military security of the West, and posed a unique challenge to Western statesmanship by the breathless rapidity of its current material and human development.

A recognition of the growing importance of Africa in the contest with international Communism provided the principal impetus behind Vice-President Nixon's twenty-two day tour of seven independent African countries in March 1957. We have already noted the significance of the Vice-President's conversations in Morocco, Ethiopia, the Sudan, Libya, and Tunisia in connection with the mobilization of international support for the Eisenhower Doctrine (section 13). Not less significant was his presence on March 6 at the birth of the new British Commonwealth state of Ghana, the former British colony of the Gold Coast, which had emerged as a symbol of peaceful transition from colonial status and whose example many Africans in other areas hoped to emulate. Dr. Kwame Nkrumah, Ghana's Prime Minister and a firm believer in Africa's special mission, asserted both publicly and in private conversation with the Vice-President that although Ghana's policies would be guided by national interest and the cause of national independence, it would not be neutral in the "cold war." (Whether it would be more than superficially democratic in its internal life was to be a matter of lively speculation through most of 1957.) A somewhat similar attitude confronted the Vice-President in Liberia and Ethiopia, two much older independent countries whose leading statesmen stressed their attachment to the American view in world affairs but took occasion to intimate that their special needs and interests deserved considerably more attention than they had yet received in Washington.

Apart from a brief stop in Uganda, Mr. Nixon had no opportunity to examine the tensions asociated with political and economic growth in those African countries that stood lower down on the timetable of independence. (Nigeria, with a tentative target date of 1960, was generally assumed to be next in line.) Nor did his itinerary permit him to see at first hand the burgeoning economic life of the Belgian Congo and the Central African Federation, the novel experiments in controlled self-government going forward in French African territories, or the effects of mounting racial tensions in the Union of South Africa. He did, however, gather opinions and impressions for a comprehensive report, made public by the White House on April 7,[34] which read like a kind of charter of American interest in Africa, in some respects recalling the report on Latin America prepared by Dr. Milton Eisenhower in 1953.[35]

Africa, the Vice-President confirmed, was "the most rapidly changing area in the world today" and might well prove "the decisive factor in the conflict between the forces of freedom and international communism." It was his distinct impression that the leaders of the international Communist movement "consider Africa today to be as important to their designs for world domination as they considered China to be twenty-five years ago." For the moment, Mr. Nixon did not feel that Communist domination in Africa represented a serious danger, despite the vigorous Communist diplomatic, propaganda and economic offensive which had been undertaken in all parts of the continent. All of the African leaders he had consulted had been determined to maintain their countries' independence against Communist or any other form of foreign domination. The main problem, he felt, would be to help the countries in question maintain their independence and alleviate conditions of want and instability that might facilitate a later Communist takeover.

In general, the Vice-President expressed himself as well satisfied with the standing of the United States in the countries he had visited. "There is no area in the world today," he reported, "in which the prestige of the United States is more uniformly high"; and he noted with evident approval that "the welcome sign is out for investment of foreign private capital in Africa." He had a number of specific recommendations to offer—a strengthening of the American diplomatic, consular, and economic missions in Africa, creation of a new Bureau of African Affairs in the State Department, and a considerable expansion of informational activities in African centers. His basic conviction was that "we in the United States must come to know, to understand and to find common ground with the peoples of this great continent." There must, he said, be a "realization throughout the executive branches of the Government, throughout the Congress and throughout the nation, of the growing importance of Africa to the future of the United States and the Free World and the necessity of assigning higher priority to our relations with that area."

In a public report of this kind, Mr. Nixon could naturally not say very much about the one African problem of which he had probably heard most, at least in the Arabic-speaking countries north of the Sahara. This was the problem of the future of Algeria, that vast North African country which, though technically an integral part of France, had for more than two years been gripped by a nationalist insurrection that had cost perhaps 30,000 lives and appeared to many to be still mounting in intensity. Much as France would have preferred to treat this situation as a matter of purely domestic concern, the fact was that the Algerian civil war had long since become a world issue of first-rate importance. Infecting every branch of international relations, to a considerable degree it had undermined the whole Western position in relation both to the U.S.S.R. and to the Asian and African nations, whether pro-Western or uncommitted. So long as France found it necessary to keep an army of 400,000 or more in Algeria to combat an insurgent force that had seldom if ever exceeded 30,000, there would be little prospect of reestablishing an adequate defensive "shield" in Western Europe or of reestablishing trustful relations between the Western and Arab peoples. Few of the latter could see any essential difference between the French repression in Algeria and the Soviet repression in Hungary.

France was fully aware of its unfavorable position in the eyes of world opinion, to say nothing of the heavy financial drain of the war and its unpleasant repercussions at home. For many months the government headed by M. Mollet had sought a political formula which would enable it to end the revolt, satisfy the "legitimate" ambitions of the 8,300,000 Algerian Muslims, and also protect the rights of the 1,200,000 European residents and safeguard the "unbreakable" links that in French eyes must continue to bind Algeria to the mother country. France's basic program, as Foreign Minister Pineau reminded the United Nations Assembly on February 4, 1957, was comprised in three words: "cease-fire, elections, discussion." The insurgents, in other words, must first stop fighting; thereafter new elections would be held (with Muslims and Europeans participating on an equal, man-for-man basis), and a new status worked out for Algeria within the limits of its "indissoluble union" with France. This program, however, had been wholly unacceptable to the insurgent leaders, who seemed quite unimpressed by the fact that it was now accompanied by various economic inducements and presented as part of the rather foggy "Eurafrica" concept (section 9). The hardened revolutionaries of the Algerian National Liberation Front, which was more and more emerging as the controlling force in the insurrection, conceived events in precisely the opposite order. France, they said, must first promise Algeria its complete independence. Then, and only then, would the insurgents be ready to lay down their arms and talk about details.

In this perennial impasse, both sides had come to attach great importance to the attitude of the United Nations Assembly, which had acquired the habit of examining the situation each year despite France's contention that the world organization had no right to intrude in what it considered a "domestic" matter. A formal Assembly endorsement of the nationalist point of view would afford tremendous encouragement to the rebels and spell a further impairment of France's world standing. Hitherto this eventuality had been staved off, partly as a result of moderating efforts by the United States. By early 1957, however, the matter had become particularly acute, not only because of the long continuance and growing violence of the insurrection but also because of the differences among the Western Big Three and the new tendency of the United States to side with the Asian-African bloc even in matters directly affecting its own allies.

With the Asian and African nations (led by Syria as authorized spokesman of the Algerian nationalists) demanding that the General Assembly formally acknowledge the Algerians' right to national self-determination, it was evident that only American influence could prevent the Assembly from adopting a resolution that would be regarded in France as an unforgivable rebuff and might seriously prejudice its whole relationship with the world organization. In the intervals of the Israeli crisis, urgent representations were made to the United States on many levels in the hope of dissuading it from modifying its policy to France's disadvantage. The result, though scarcely satisfactory to Asian and African nations, afforded the clearest indication thus far that there were still matters in which Washington valued its ties with France more highly than the plaudits of the anticolonial bloc. "There must surely be no external interference in Algerian affairs from any quarter," Ambassador Lodge told the Assembly on February 6. "We believe that true progress can only be made on the spot and that if there is no outside interference such progress will take place, and with great advantage to all humanity." To the undisguised relief of France, the General Assembly thereupon limited itself to expressing the hope that "a peaceful, democratic and just solution" of the Algerian problem would be found "through appropriate means." [36]

The anticipated "progress on the spot" did not, however, show many signs of materializing during the weeks that followed. Day after day, month after month the struggle dragged on amid mutual accusations of terrorism and atrocities, continual incidents along the frontiers of pro-nationalist Tunisia and Morocco, and repeated assurances from Robert Lacoste, French Minister Resident in Algeria, that the insurgents were on the run and the rebellion would be liquidated in three months or less. The picture was further complicated by a war of assassination and massacre among the nationalists themselves, with the National Liberation Front apparently winning an increasingly clear-cut predominance over the somewhat more moderate Algerian National Movement. Amid mounting international dismay over this carnage, the United States refrained from taking a public stand on the question in spite of renewed pressure by the Arab states and a warning from Senator John F. Kennedy (July 2) that the problem was no longer "to save a myth of French empire" but "to save the French nation as well as free Africa." The matter was one of great complexity and difficulty, Mr. Dulles retorted (July 2), and he was glad it was not primarily our problem. President Eisenhower implied (July 3) that we were working behind the scenes but had no special objective beyond being "as fair and square and helpful" as possible to all the parties involved.

Even in France it was becoming obvious that the formula of "cease-fire first, negotiations afterward" did not constitute a realistic method of stopping hostilities. Dissatisfaction over Algeria was an important factor in the overthrow of the Mollet government on May 21. The formation of a new cabinet under Maurice Bourgès-Maunoury on June 11 was widely expected to signal a new departure in Algerian policy, despite the retention of Messrs. Pineau and Lacoste in their former positions. M. Bourgès-Maunoury did in fact attempt a new departure, both in Algerian affairs and in the closely related field of French economic and fiscal policy; but the rejection of his Algerian program on September 30 was to indicate that France as a whole had not yet reconciled itself to fundamental changes in Algeria despite the growing economic and political hazards of the existing situation.

Two possible solutions of the Algerian problem had commended themselves to persons alert to find a middle ground between the official French and nationalist positions. One of them involved the association of Algeria with its independent neighbors, Tunisia and Morocco and possibly Libya, in some kind of North African federation which would be more or less closely linked with France by political and economic ties as well as by what was described as a common "Western" heritage. Particularly favored by Tunisian Premier Habib Bourguiba, whose own problems were multiplied by the civil war raging along Tunisia's frontiers, this idea was also supported by Pierre Mendès-France and other French public figures.

The new French government, however, preferred an alternative scheme which had been propounded by Jules Moch and was thought to provide more adequate guarantees for French interests and those of Algeria's European population. As elaborated in a so-called "framework law" which was intended to establish the conditions for future Algerian political development, this plan would have retained Algeria as an integral part of France but afforded some satisfaction to Muslim aspirations by setting up an Algerian federal structure, complete with local assemblies and certain central organs for Algeria as a whole. European interests would be protected by delimiting the individual autonomous regions in such a way that Europeans would retain control in areas of heavy European settlement. Like most such plans, however, this one proved too bold for the French Right, too timid for the Left, and completely unacceptable to the Algerian nationalists. On September 30 it was rejected by the French Assembly by a vote of 279-253.

With a new session of the General Assembly already under way in New York, the National Liberation Front's nine-man Committee of Coordination and Execution assembled in Tunis at the end of October to reaffirm its demand for an outright promise of independence as the necessary preliminary to a cease-fire and political discussions. Even M. Bourguiba, who had undertaken to present the nationalist case before the United Nations, appeared taken aback by their intransigence. He had felt that much might be accomplished through round-table conferences, in which Tunisia and Morocco might mediate between the French and nationalist viewpoints. The nationalist high command, however, at the moment was displaying more confidence than at any previous time. It now claimed to have an army of up to 100,000 men and to be extending operations into the Sahara regions of southern Algeria, where France was just preparing to tap the newly discovered oil deposits so important to its future economic progress. With no negotiated solution in sight, many observers were asking how much longer the United States could continue to treat the problem as a purely French responsibility. Some saw in Algeria the seeds of a conflict which could shake the Western alliance as severely as the conflict with Abdel Nasser's Egypt had done the year before. (See further section 26.)

The turmoil in Algeria inevitably exerted considerable influence on American relations with the new states of Morocco and Tunisia, neither of which could wholeheartedly associate itself with the Western, anti-Communist cause while their sympathies were strained and their relations with France exacerbated by events across their frontiers. M. Bourguiba (who became the first President of the Tunisian Republic following the deposition of the Bey on July 25) appeared practically at his wit's end as a result of repeated French military incursions as well as the continued presence of French garrisons in Tunisian territory. Despite his acceptance of the Eisenhower Doctrine, he periodically reproached the United States with supporting French "imperialism" in North Africa, and in September went so far as to imply that Tunisia might have to join the neutralist bloc if Washington continued to ignore its requests for arms with which to defend its frontiers. The United States in some haste made known that although unwilling to supply arms itself it would help Tunisia obtain them from other Western sources—a decision that was protested by France and was believed by some to have contributed to the downfall of the Bourgès-Maunoury government (cf. section 26).

Morocco was somewhat less affected by the Algerian troubles and enjoyed comparatively stable relations with both France and the United States, although its claims to additional French and Spanish territories in Africa might become a sources of embarrassment at some future time (cf. section 26). Apart from somewhat inconclusive discussions of economic aid, investment, and the still unsettled status of the American air bases in Morocco, the principal development in United States-Moroccan relations in 1957 was the late autumn visit of King Mohammed V to Washington, which served to confirm the impression of American authorities that the former Sultan could be counted among the stanch friends of the West.[37] All in all, both Morocco and Tunisia seemed to have completed the transition to independence in a highly satisfactory manner. Their example offered a measure of reassurance to many in the free world—including at least some in France—who were becoming convinced that Algeria must one day follow the same path.

Notes to Chapter IV

1. *Department of State Bulletin*, v. 36 (January 21, 1957), pp. 83-87; *Documents on American Foreign Relations, 1957*, no. 53. Additional documentation relevant to this chapter will be found in *United States Policy in the Middle East, September 1956-June 1957: Documents* (Department of State Publication 6505, Washington: G.P.O., 1957).

2. Public Law 7, 85th Cong., approved March 9, 1957; text in *Department of State Bulletin*, v. 36 (March 25, 1957), p. 481; *Documents on American Foreign Relations, 1957*, no. 55.

3. Cf. John C. Campbell, *Defense of the Middle East* (New York: Harper, for the Council on Foreign Relations, 1958), p. 128.

4. See especially General Assembly Resolution 997 (ES-I), November 2, 1956, in *Documents on American Foreign Relations, 1956*, pp. 350-351.

5. British note verbale and State Department announcement, December 3, 1956, in *Documents on American Foreign Relations, 1956*, pp. 370-373.

6. General Assembly Resolution 1123 (XI), January 19, 1957, in *Documents on American Foreign Relations, 1957*, no. 77.

7. Reports of the Secretary-General, January 15, 23, and 24 (U.N. Documents A/3500 and Add. 1, A/3511, and A/3512), in *Department of State Bulletin*, v. 36 (February 18, 1957), pp. 271-280.

8. General Assembly Resolutions 1124 (XI) and 1125 (XI), February 2, 1957; *Documents on American Foreign Relations, 1957*, nos. 78 and 79.

9. See especially the White House statement of February 17 in *Department of State Bulletin*, v. 36 (March 11, 1957), pp. 381-392; *Documents on American Foreign Relations, 1957*, no. 81.

10. *Department of State Bulletin*, v. 36 (March 11, 1957), pp. 387-391; *Documents on American Foreign Relations, 1957*, no. 82.

11. U.S. aide memoire, February 11, in *Department of State Bulletin*, v. 36 (March 11, 1957), pp. 392-393; *Documents on American Foreign Relations, 1957*, no. 80.

12. U.N. Document S/3675, October 13, 1956, in *Documents on American Foreign Relations, 1956*, pp. 342-343.

13. *New York Times*, March 29, 1957.

14. U.N. Documents A/3576 and S/3818, April 24, in *Department of State Bulletin*, v. 36 (May 13, 1957), pp. 776-777; *Documents on American Foreign Relations, 1957*, no. 87.

15. Statements of May 8 and 9, in *Department of State Bulletin*, v. 36 (May 27, 1957), pp. 841-844; cf. *Documents on American Foreign Relations, 1957*, no. 56.

16. Communiqué, January 21, in *Department of State Bulletin*, v. 36 (February 11, 1957), pp. 216-217; *Documents on American Foreign Relations, 1957*, no. 75.

17. *Department of State Bulletin*, v. 36 (April 1, 1957), pp. 524-526; *Documents on American Foreign Relations, 1957*, no. 58.

18. *Department of State Bulletin*, v. 36 (April 1, 1957), pp. 523-524; *Documents on American Foreign Relations, 1957*, no. 59.

19. Communiqué, February 8, in *Department of State Bulletin*, v. 36 (February 25, 1957), pp. 308-309; *Documents on American Foreign Relations, 1957*, no. 90. See also the formal agreement dated April 2, in *Department of State Bulletin*, v. 36 (April 29, 1957), pp. 680-681; *Documents on American Foreign Relations, 1957*, nos. 91-92.

20. Collected in *Department of State Bulletin*, v. 36 (May 6, 1957), pp. 725-731; (May 13, 1957), pp. 763-764; (May 27, 1957), pp. 844-845.

21. *Documents on American Foreign Relations, 1950*, pp. 658-659.

22. *New York Times*, April 25, 1957.

23. Communiqué, June 6, in *Department of State Bulletin*, v. 37 (August 12, 1957), pp. 278-280; *Documents on American Foreign Relations, 1957*, no. 76.

24. U.S. note in *Department of State Bulletin*, v. 37 (July 1, 1957), pp. 20-21; *Documents on American Foreign Relations, 1957*, no. 60.

25. *Department of State Bulletin*, v. 37 (August 24, 1957), pp. 338-343; *Documents on American Foreign Relations, 1957*, no. 57.

26. *Current Digest of the Soviet Press*, v. 9, no. 32 (September 18, 1957), pp. 17-18.

27. *Department of State Bulletin*, v. 37 (September 23, 1957), p. 487; *Documents on American Foreign Relations, 1957*, no. 67.

28. Text (with U.S. rejection dated September 24), in *Department of State Bulletin*, v. 37 (October 14, 1957), pp. 602-603; *Documents on American Foreign Relations, 1957*, nos. 61-62.

29. Same as note 23.

30. *Current Digest of the Soviet Press*, v. 9, no. 31 (September 11, 1957), p. 17.

31. U.N. Document S/3779, January 24, 1957, in *Department of State Bulletin*, v. 36 (February 11, 1957), p. 232; *Documents on American Foreign Relations, 1957*, no. 125.

32. U.N. Document S/3922, adopted December 2, in *Department of State Bulletin*, v. 37 (December 23, 1957), pp. 1016-1017; *Documents on American Foreign Relations, 1957*, no. 128.

33. Communiqué, July 13, in *Department of State Bulletin*, v. 37 (July 29, 1957), pp. 186-187; *Documents on American Foreign Relations, 1957*, no. 93.

34. *Department of State Bulletin*, v. 36 (April 22, 1957), pp. 635-640; *Documents on American Foreign Relations, 1957*, no. 94.

35. Excerpts *ibid., 1953*, pp. 382-399.

36. General Assembly Resolution 1012 (XI), February 15, *ibid., 1957*, no. 96.

37. See joint statement of November 27 in *Department of State Bulletin*, v. 37 (December 16, 1957), pp. 956-957; *Documents on American Foreign Relations, 1957*, no. 99.

CHAPTER FIVE

BREATHING SPELL IN THE FAR EAST

IN CONTRAST to the growing intensity of the East-West struggle in the countries of the Middle East, the Far Eastern theater remained comparatively quiet throughout 1957. Here the "relaxation of tensions" so industriously promoted by the international Communist leaders had progressed without major interruption ever since the conclusion of the wars in Korea and Indochina in 1953 and 1954 and the shelving of Communist China's military threat to Taiwan in 1955. The crises of late 1956 had echoed only faintly in this part of the world. Aside from Communist China, whose special relationship with the Soviet Union compelled it to pay close attention to all developments affecting the world-wide Communist cause, most Far Eastern governments took a rather academic interest in the suppression of the Hungarian revolution and did not appear too closely concerned by the fighting around the Suez Canal or the promulgation of the Eisenhower Doctrine. Wherever they perceived a clear issue between "nationalism" and "colonialism," as they had done in the dispute over the Suez waterway, most of them supported the former principle as a matter of course. Their own interests, however, were on the whole more local in character and, in so far as they were affected by the Communist issue, revolved around Communist China much more than the U.S.S.R. Since most of Communist China's overt activities during these months were given a deliberately reassuring appearance, the general atmosphere of the Far East in 1957 was calmer than at any time since the conclusion of the Chinese civil war.

To Americans who had gone through the emotional stress of the conflicts in Korea and Indochina, this state of quiescence was in itself a welcome change from the excitements of earlier years. The political and military alliances forged by the United States in more critical days—the ANZUS treaty, the Southeast Asia Collective Defense Treaty, and the mutual assistance treaties with Japan, Korea, and the Republic of China—appeared in the main to have borne good fruit. For one reason or another the aggressive course of Communist China had been stayed. Under the umbrella of American "striking power," it seemed that our allies were daily consolidating their positions and, it was to be hoped, developing the strength that might be needed to face a renewed outburst of Chinese expansionism at some future time. "I can report that never before within my experience has American prestige in Asia been so high," declared one State Department official early in 1957.[1] "Everywhere we look in the Far East today, although the problems which face us are serious and manifold, nevertheless we find situations which can give us satisfaction when compared with the past."

Yet the optimism prevailing in official quarters at this period was questioned by some observers on a variety of grounds. Was it not based too much on surface appearances, it was asked, and too little on the realities underneath? A mere absence of crisis was not necessarily a sign of health; it might be only the prelude to renewed disturbances of a more dangerous character. Senator Mike Mansfield of Montana hinted at some of these possibilities in a speech of January 29 which was widely hailed as a model of responsible opposition criticism in the style of the late Senator Arthur H. Vandenberg:

"... A calm appears to have settled over [the Far East], and a silence amounting virtually to censorship has characterized the administration's handling of developments in that region. We may well ask ourselves, of what is the calm composed? What is the significance of the silence?

"The calm ... is composed of three tenuous truces: the truce in Korea, the truce in Formosa, and the truce in Indochina. These are the truces which act to maintain an unstable status quo in the Far East, but they settle nothing. . . .

"How long will the calm last? Will the urge to unification in Korea, in Indochina, soon put an end to it? What of the continuing threat to Formosa? What is likely to emerge from the vast and churning maw of the Communist mainland? . . ."

No one knew the answers to these questions, but there was no doubt as to where they would have to be sought. Like virtually every question relating to the Far East, all of them hinged in the last analysis upon the attitude and intentions of the Communist powers and particularly of Communist China. The "three tenuous truces" imposed on that country, primarily by the power of the United States, marked the farthest limits attained by the wave of expansionism that had followed the Communist victory on the China mainland in 1948–49. How long and how effectually they would continue to confine the dynamism of the Chinese revolution depended only partially on the United States, however. No less fundamentally, it also depended on the calculations of Chairman Mao Tse-tung and the other members of Communist China's "collective leadership." The latter had never concealed their determination to complete the work they had undertaken by "liberating" Taiwan (Formosa) and, as a secondary aim, bringing about the reunification of partitioned Korea and Vietnam along "popular" and "democratic" (i.e., Communist) lines. Impressed perhaps by the American "deterrent-retaliatory power" to which Secretary Dulles had frequently directed their attention, they had thus far refrained from renewing their pursuit of these objectives by military means. The possibility remained, however, that they might one day break the truce and resume their career of open aggression, perhaps at some moment of general crisis when they might imagine that America's retaliatory power would be immobilized by that of the Soviet Union. In the meantime they remained free to promote their aims by the non-military techniques of political and economic infiltration and subversion—the same techniques the Russians were now employing with such dramatic results in the Middle East.

The deliberate choice of the Peking regime in favor of this type of "peaceful" expansionism provides the master key to an understanding of Far Eastern developments in 1957, no less than in the years immediately preceding. Just as the U.S.S.R. had outflanked or overleaped the Baghdad Pact by its arms deals and "trade and aid" schemes in the Arab world, Communist China had set out to circumvent the military "truce" and the American-organized mutual security system in the Far East by intensifying its political and economic offensive in every country that seemed to present a favorable target. Signs of this new strategy had been apparent since as early as 1954, the year of the Indochina armistice and the enunciation of the much-vaunted "five principles" of peaceful coexistence. Cultivation of the Asian and African nations had reached a high point at the Bandung Conference in April 1955, months before Bulganin and Khrushchev had set out on their famous "good-will" tour of India, Burma, and Afghanistan. As with the Soviet "trade and aid" offensive, Chinese Communist activities had been limited to at least a minor degree by the paucity of resources available; occasionally the Chinese had promised more than they could perform, with correspondingly bad effects on their standing in some countries of the area. Unlike the Russians, however, they were able to continue their campaign without serious interruption even during the critical months while Moscow was struggling with the political and economic effects of the Hungarian revolt. While the Soviet line wavered between blandness and bellicosity, Peking hardly deviated from the air of smooth self-confidence with which it had set out to allay the fears of its neighbors and gradually draw them into its psychological and political orbit.

The general tone of these efforts could be gauged from the remarks of a Chinese Communist official who told the National People's Congress in Peking on July 15 that the Communist regime had established formal diplomatic relations with twenty-seven countries, informal relations with two more, trade relations with sixty-eight, and friendly contacts with more than a hundred. Within this scheme of practically universal benevolence, a rather definite system of priorities was evident. Taiwan, regarded as an integral part of the Chinese national heritage, stood highest on the list of Communist objectives, but was evidently regarded as a long-range rather than an immediate target in view of the well-advertised determination of the United States to prevent the island from falling to the Communists. South Korea and South Vietnam were likewise under direct American protection, and governed by strongly anti-Communist regimes which offered minimal opportunities for infiltration. Much more promising from the Communist point of view were the other countries of Southeast Asia, three of which were allied with the United States through the Southeast Asia (SEATO) pact, but nearly all of which were attuned in some degree to the appeals of neutralism and economic advantage in which Peking specialized. In a somewhat different category was Japan, the one purely Far Eastern country whose resources and potential power challenged comparison with those of China itself. In the long run, Japan's political orientation might influence the course of Far Eastern history almost as decisively as in the past. Despite its present attachment to the American camp, neither Peking nor Moscow was missing any opportunity to deflect Japan's loyalties and encourage a more relaxed relationship with the "camp of socialism."

Like any other country, Communist China was limited in the pursuit of its foreign objectives by conditions at home as well as by the attitudes of other interested powers, both friendly and hostile. In the present chapter it will be appropriate to look first in section 17 at the general situation of China, both Communist and free. Section 18 will be concerned primarily with salient developments in Southeast Asia, while section 19 will review in somewhat greater detail the major problems affecting Japan's position as between the Eastern and Western camps.

17. FACING THE CHINA PROBLEM

It is to be noted that the rather optimistic views of the Far Eastern situation expressed by authoritative American spokesmen during the early part of 1957 were based entirely on evidences of accomplishment in non-Communist areas of the Far East, not on any indications of weakness in the position of Communist China. At a time when American officials were voicing high satisfaction over the revelation of Soviet weaknesses in Eastern Europe and even within the Soviet Union, they conspicuously refrained from citing parallel trends in Communism's Far Eastern citadel. Our attitude toward the Communist regime in China, Assistant Secretary of State Walter S. Robertson declared in a speech of February 6,[2] was the result of its own repeatedly demonstrated aggressive tendencies and contempt for international law. It was based on a settled conviction that Communist ambitions represented a threat to American and free world security interests, and that any other policy would result in the rapid expansion of Communism in Asia and betray the hopes of the Chinese people themselves. But neither Mr. Robertson nor anyone else was suggesting at this period that the American policy of withholding trade and diplomatic recognition from the Peking regime, opposing its representation in the United Nations, and supporting the rival, anti-Communist Chinese government on Taiwan had materially weakened the Communist grip on the Chinese mainland. "I should be the last to tell you that as a result of our policies the threat of Communism has been met in the Far East," said Mr. Robertson. "On the contrary, the menacing shadow of the international Communists still lies heavily over the area." The most he would say was that "the course we have pursued has had a deterrent effect and has bought some of the time needed for the free nations of Asia to build the strength which they will require to retain their independence."

In an administration which had always attached special importance to the notion of an inherent tendency toward eventual disintegration in Communist despotisms, this lack of reference to internal developments in China was noteworthy because there were already indications that the Peking regime was being forced to grapple with certain difficulties that had not been fully anticipated in its previous political and economic plans. Even if China had not been directly involved in the recent crisis of the Soviet empire, its interests as a leading member of the "camp of socialism" were inevitably affected by the backwash of the Polish and Hungarian developments. In addition, it had encountered some formidable obstacles to its current program for laying the political and material foundations of "socialism" in China. Such difficulties, although their importance should not be exaggerated, might well have contributed to the decision of the Peking leadership to maintain an attitude of comparative quietude in international affairs during 1957. The fundamental ambition of Mao Tse-tung and his associates was to transform China as rapidly as possible from the backward agrarian conditions of 1949 into a modern industrial country, equipped and developed on a scale commensurate with its vast size and population. This was the aim that had inspired both the First Five-Year Plan for 1953–57 and the Second Five-Year Plan already projected for 1958–62. External ambitions, the Communist leaders apparently reasoned, could wait if necessary until this process was further advanced and China's power had become more nearly irresistible than it was at the moment.

But the execution of these far-reaching plans would be possible only if the Chinese leaders could count on the availability of adequate supplies of food and raw materials, on the exertions of a docile and dedicated population, and on considerable help from the U.S.S.R. in the form of capital goods and technical assistance. These necessary presuppositions had now been called in question by developments in China and abroad. Though all accounts of progress under the First Five-Year Plan stressed the imposing scale of China's "socialist transformation" and the tremendous gains in industrial production already achieved (total value of industrial output during the plan period was eventually claimed to have increased from a base of 100 to 223), it had been evident as early as the end of 1956, when the plan reached the four-year mark, that its goals had been over-ambitious in some respects and that the new plan for 1958–62 would have to allow for a rather more moderate rate of progress. As the Soviet Union had been doing for a generation, Communist China had attempted to subordinate everything else to the expansion of its heavy industrial base. The results had been uneven to say the least—on the one hand, excessive capital construction and a drift of population to the cities; on the other, inadequate fuel and raw materials, a lagging food supply (accompanied by localized famine conditions), and widespread discontent over the lack of improvement in popular living standards.

Added to all this was the uncertainty presumably felt in Peking about future Soviet assistance on major industrial projects. Moscow, now deeply immersed in the economic difficulties of Eastern Europe, had already announced a cutback in its own five-year plan, which it would presently be obliged to scrap entirely (section 23). Thus it was not surprising that Peking delayed publishing the details of its Second Five-Year Plan and confined itself for the moment to issuing an interim plan for 1958, details of which were worked out during the summer of 1957. Its salient feature was a 33 percent increase in agricultural investment, aimed at effecting a better balance between industry and agriculture and enabling them to progress in better harmony.

A further consideration, no doubt, was the failure of the Chinese people to respond more favorably to the hardships and deprivations decreed by the regime. Eight years after the civil war, the Communists might boast that the "socialist transformation" of China's economy had been virtually completed and that private ownership was essentially a thing of the past. But they had also to recognize that any revolutionary fervor that might have sustained their efforts in past years was by now pretty thoroughly exhausted. The existence of widespread popular discontent, stimulated in some instances by the Hungarian developments, can be amply documented from Communist sources and was freely admitted by Mao Tse-tung himself in a remarkable speech which he delivered to the Supreme State Conference on February 27 and which was subsequently published in modified form.[3]

Like the Soviet Communists in the period after Stalin's

death, the Chinese Communists were now confronted with the difficult problem of drawing a line between legitimate, "constructive" criticism, which there was some willingness to permit and even encourage, and agitation against fundamental Communist principles. Chairman Mao in his speech appeared to favor a rather broad tolerance of diverse views, summed up in the slogans "Let a hundred flowers blossom" and "Let a hundred schools of thought contend." But the public enunciation of this principle was followed in Chinese intellectual circles by such an outburst of unorthodox opinions, or what Mao called "poisonous weeds," that the Communists soon found themselves devoting most of their attention not to encouraging free speech but to extirpating heresy and curbing "rightists" and "counterrevolutionaries." A broad "rectification campaign" was carried out with the announced aim of eliminating the remnants of "bourgeois" and "capitalist" thinking, and various prominent personalities, including certain non-Communist ministers in the central government, were compelled to retract their "errors" in public. Some observers of these proceedings believed they could detect a difference of emphasis between Mao Tse-tung and some of the other Communist leaders, comparable to the differences between Khrushchev and the Stalinist group in the Kremlin. Others suspected that Mao's speech had been a deliberate ruse aimed at enticing concealed liberals into the open. In any event, the public response made it clear that human nature was still a factor in Communist China and that the Chinese people, despite the disciplined behavior which had impressed all recent visitors to the country, had not been reduced to any condition of mental servitude.

It is not impossible that the experience of the "rectification campaign" may have heightened the sympathy of the Chinese Communist leaders for their Soviet colleagues in the similar difficulties with which the latter were contending in various parts of the Soviet empire. Although our information is decidedly scanty, there is reason to believe that the Peking regime played an important and constructive role in smoothing out the conflicts which had arisen within the Soviet bloc in connection with the Polish and Hungarian developments, and that it used its influence to good effect in promoting an understanding with the Gomulka government on the implications of the doctrine of "separate roads to socialism." As pioneers in the flexible and "creative" application of Marxist doctrine to specific national conditions, the Chinese Communists had a vested interest in the principle of autonomous development for individual Communist countries. Thus it would have been natural for them to favor Khrushchev's attitude in preference to that of his Stalinist critics, and to sympathize with Gomulka's attempt to find a "road to socialism" consistent with Polish conditions.

At the same time, the Chinese leaders had no reason to desire any further weakening of the Communist bloc as a whole, and evidently exerted themselves to convince the Poles and others that in fundamental matters they ought still to defer to Moscow's opinion. The special mission to Eastern Europe which was undertaken by Premier Chou En-lai in the early weeks of 1957 (section 10) appeared to most people to have contributed greatly to the stabilization of affairs in that area and may have assisted Khrushchev in reestablishing his shaken position at home. Although Peking refrained from public comment on Khrushchev's subsequent purges of the Malenkov group and of Marshal Zhukov, it is noteworthy that Mao Tse-tung (unlike Marshal Tito, a supposed Khrushchev supporter) did not allow them to interfere with his plan of visiting Moscow for the fortieth anniversary of the Bolshevik Revolution. Indeed, he stood out on that occasion as one of the firmest opponents of unorthodox or "revisionist" tendencies in Communist affairs. (See section 23.)

But if difficulties at home and differences within the Communist family imposed some check on Communist China's immediate ambitions in the Far East, they did not prevent the Peking regime from carrying forward its effective long-range campaign directed to all the non-Communist countries in the area. Missionary efforts by Chou En-lai in India and Southeast Asia, advocacy of an all-Asian collective security pact to replace the existing Western-oriented security arrangements, enticements to Japan to embark on a broad development of mutual trade, were supplemented by a highly organized system of official hospitality that catered to a constant stream of visiting delegations from other parts of Asia and, indeed, from all over the world.

Nor could it be said that the latent military threat to China's neighbors had diminished, even though Peking's active military forces were being somewhat reduced in conformity with what appeared to be the world-wide trend. A formidable system of jet airfields had been completed opposite Taiwan. In North Vietnam, the local Communist regime had been assisted over the past three years in building up its active forces from seven divisions to twenty. In North Korea, 350,000 Chinese troops still shared the ground with 400,000 North Koreans, and another million uniformed Chinese were stationed just beyond the Yalu River in Manchuria. Especially disconcerting to the United Nations Command in South Korea had been the constant introduction of jet aircraft and other modern weapons and equipment into North Korea, in violation of the armistice agreement and on a scale which by 1957 was officially held to have "seriously upset the relative military balance." (To remedy this inferiority, the United Nations Command on American initiative announced on June 21 that it too would cease to be bound by the relevant provisions of the armistice agreement.[4] While the Communists protested, the Pentagon stated that short-range missiles and presumably atomic warheads would be sent to Korea, although the timetable of this operation was not specified.)

The implications of Chinese Communist diplomatic and military efforts were by no means limited to the particular areas toward which they happened to be directed. In every instance they formed part of a larger pattern—a pattern whose underlying motif was that of total opposition to the world policy of the United States in all its manifestations. For Peking at least as much as for Moscow, the United States was *the* enemy. Chou En-lai summed up the official attitude when he told the Chinese National People's Congress on June 26 that although the world situation had moved toward peace in the last year, these gains were constantly threatened by "the imperialist policy of arms expansion and war preparations under the leadership of the United States."

A sense of special antagonism toward the United States breathed through all of Peking's official pronouncements; and it was evident from the utterances of American authorities that the notion of an inherent incompatibility between the two governments was fully shared in Washington. "A state of unresolved conflict exists between the United States and the United Nations on the one hand and Communist China on the other," declared Deputy Under-Secretary of State Robert Murphy on April 2. "You might say," added Mr. Dulles the same day, ". . . that the United States, despite the Korean armistice, exercises certain aspects of belligerency as regards Communist China." An official State Department document of August 13 [5] spoke of "the existence of a quasi state of war" with Communist China.

"Today the political purposes of Communist China clash everywhere with our own," said Mr. Dulles in a formal address on China policy on June 28; [6] and on this occasion, a few days after the publication of Mao's "hundred flowers" speech, the Secretary of State went on to suggest that our policies should be consciously aimed toward the eventual demise, or at least the transformation, of the Peking regime. In an obvious reference to the current "rectification campaign," Mr. Dulles reverted once again to the phenomenon of internal decay in Communist regimes:

"We can confidently assume that international communism's rule of strict conformity is, in China as elsewhere, a passing and not a perpetual phase. We owe it to ourselves, our allies, and the Chinese people to do all that we can to contribute to that passing."

The notion that we were in a state of permanent, latent, though presumably nonviolent war with Communist China posed difficult issues of practical policy for the United States, especially at a time when many of this country's allies and quite a few Americans, mainly in the opposition party, were visibly growing tired of Washington's inflexible stand and inclined to wish for a more normal relationship with the Peking regime. For the first time in several years, Americans were openly questioning the government's official China policy, hitherto regarded in most quarters as too "controversial" (or too sacrosanct) for public discussion. "It is deplorable," said the Ambassador of Nationalist China, who had no reason to exaggerate this phenomenon, "that we note an increasing trend among some American public opinion leaders to seek some kind of a compromise with Red China and appeasement of its aims." This trend, the Ambassador declared (June 8), extended not only to advocating the relaxation of trade barriers in the Far East but even in some cases to favoring diplomatic recognition of the Peking government and its representation in the United Nations. Senator J. William Fulbright of Arkansas was one of those who were understood to favor a reexamination of official attitudes toward the Peking regime. Another was Senator Hubert H. Humphrey of Minnesota, who publicly called attention on July 8 to "new forces . . . astir" in China that might, in his opinion, foreshadow an evolution toward independence of Moscow. "In my estimation the time has come to take a fresh look at our policy toward Peiping," Mr. Humphrey said. "We should certainly encourage American newsmen to visit Red China. . . . We should consider modifying other barriers, such as the trade embargo, which force China into ever closer relations with the Soviet bloc." [7]

Proposals for a "new look" at policy toward China had been given a sharp impetus at this period by developments on the island of Taiwan, the seat of the exiled Nationalist government which the United States had for years been supporting as the legitimate government of China and the foundation of that country's non-Communist future. But the relationship which this country had maintained with the Chiang Kai-shek regime had not been without its difficulties, and by 1957 was definitely threatening to turn sour. As a political leader, the Generalissimo was obliged to base his entire activity on the ambitious idea of reconquering the China mainland; yet as a practical man he could not fail to see that the United States, whatever its attitude might have been in the past, would not now support any initiative in this direction. Washington had invested large resources in

for a reconsideration of policy toward the two Chinese regimes.

It was apparently in recognition of this demand that Secretary Dulles on June 28 delivered in San Francisco the major speech already referred to [8]—actually the government's first formal pronouncement on China policy in several years. In it the Secretary of State said little of policy toward Taiwan. His main point, delivered apparently with the full approval of the President, was that policy toward Peking was not going to change. Rehearsing once again the manifold shortcomings of the Chinese Communist regime, Mr. Dulles reached the unequivocal conclusion "that, under present conditions, neither recognition, nor trade, nor cultural relations, nor all three would favorably influence the evolution of affairs in China." It would be folly, he said, "for us to establish relations with the Chinese Communists which would enhance their ability to hurt us and our friends." As to representation in the United Nations, he feared that the admission of Communist China to a seat on the Security Council would "implant in the United Nations the seeds of its own destruction." "Nothing," he insisted, "could be more dangerous than for the United States to operate on the theory that, if hostile and evil forces do not quickly or readily change, then it is we who must change to meet them. . . . If Communism is stubborn for the wrong, let us be steadfast for the right."

If this pronouncement failed to shut off all demands for a new look at the administration's China policy as a whole, it at least provided a framework for dealing with subsidiary aspects of the China problem on which the government was compelled to take a position. One of these, the question of international controls on strategic trade with the mainland, had already been settled for the time being by the decision of our principal allies to make their own arrangements directly with Peking rather than be bound entirely by the precautionary attitude of the United States (section 6). Still remaining for Mr. Dulles' consideration was another highly vexatious problem which had been raised by a growing number of journalists and other Americans who wanted to visit Communist China and form their own opinions of the transformations that were taking place there. This issue had arisen both in Washington and in Geneva, where an American representative had been meeting periodically with the Chinese Communist ambassador to discuss, among other things, the fate of certain Americans who were already in Communist China and had been prevented from leaving. (Of ten Americans held in prison or under house arrest in China at the beginning of the year, only four had been released by December 31 despite a Communist undertaking of September 10, 1955 to permit Americans in China to return to the United States if they wished to do so.)

The official dogma regarding visits to China, whether by journalists or by private individuals, was that Americans were not supposed to travel without passports and that their government could not validate a passport for travel to a country whose regime it did not recognize. State Department insistence on this point of view was fortified by the realization that Peking was anxious to encourage American visits for propaganda reasons and was attempting to exploit the Americans already in its hands as bargaining counters. On the other hand, the State Department was under heavy pressure from spokesmen for the press who insisted on the right to gather news and inform the public without regard to political barriers. For months Mr. Dulles was "needled" without mercy on the issue. Ultimately, on August 22, he agreed to a compromise arrangement whereby a limited number of news organizations would be permitted to accredit correspondents to Communist China for an experimental period of seven months—it being understood, however, that basic policy toward China was unchanged and that Chinese Communist journalists would not be granted reciprocal privileges.[9] This last qualification proved quite unacceptable to Peking; indeed, it was generally regarded as a subterfuge until Mr. Dulles explained that although Chinese journalists could not be admitted to the United States *en bloc,* any applications by individual Chinese newsmen would be considered "on their merits."

The Communists, however, showed no particular interest

in such a "deal." For the moment they were quite fully occupied in entertaining a separate group of forty-two young
Americans who had been attending the World Youth Festival in Moscow and while there had accepted an invitation to
visit China at the expense of the Peking government. In
taking advantage of this opportunity they had ignored a
solemn warning from the State Department (August 13) [10]
that they would risk prosecution as well as loss of passport
privileges and would be making themselves willing tools of
a Communist propaganda effort "intended, wherever possible, to subvert the foreign policy and the best interests of
the United States." Reports of the group's activities while
in China left no doubt of the correctness of this judgment;
indeed, they conveyed the impression that many of the
young visitors had been far from backward in displaying
their sympathies for the Peking regime. Although their passports were duly canceled (subject to a hearing in the case
of those who appealed the official ruling), talk of prosecution was quietly dropped.

As time went on, the State Department itself began to
authorize a growing number of exceptions to its "no contact"
policy. It agreed that Chinese Communist athletes might be
admitted to the United States to participate in the 1960
winter Olympic Games. It permitted an American lawyer to
go to China to seek evidence in a pending sedition case. In
December it withdrew its opposition to visits to China by
close relatives of the six Americans still imprisoned there.
Basic policy toward China might still be unchanged. The
seventy-year-old Chiang Kai-shek might still talk of an imminent "final counterattack" on the mainland. The United
States might still resist with success the annual attempt to
debate the problem of Chinese representation in the United
Nations Assembly (section 24). But beneath the official surface, the substance of Chinese-American relations was plainly
altering. Whether the alterations were to the ultimate benefit of the United States and the free world would depend in
large measure on their impact in other areas of the Far East
where Peking had been working night and day to expand
its "peaceful" influence.

18. SOUTHEAST ASIA ON THE TIGHTROPE

One of the well-publicized reasons for Mr. Dulles' antipathy to the idea of cultural and journalist exchanges with Communist China was a conviction that in lowering the barriers against Communist agents and ideas, the United States would be setting a dangerous example to other countries which might be less well equipped to withstand Communist wiles. Our whole policy toward Communist China, the Secretary of State declared in his San Francisco speech (June 28), reflected our deep concern for the safety of the "free Asian governments of the Pacific and Southeast Asia." These countries, he pointed out,

"are not only close to the vast Chinese land mass, but geographically and, to some extent, politically, they are separated as among themselves. The unifying and fortifying influence is, above all, the spirit and resolution of the United States. If we seemed to waver and to compromise with communism in China, that would in turn weaken free Asia resistance to the Chinese Communist regime and assist international communism to score a great success in its program to encircle us."

It was presumably to counteract any tendencies in this direction that Mr. Dulles had found it advisable to present a special recapitulation of United States views on China to the members of the SEATO Council of Ministers at their third annual meeting, held at Canberra, Australia on March 10–13.[11] Here, if anywhere, was the place for a firm collective stand against the threat of Communist expansionism in the Far East. Since its establishment in September 1954, the eight-nation Southeast Asia Treaty Organization with its headquarters in Bangkok had occupied a position in Southeast Asia quite similar to that of the Baghdad Pact in the Middle East. Both alliances were directed nominally against aggression from any quarter, actually (so far as the United States was concerned) against Communist aggression. Both had served to rally those local governments that were willing to "stand up and be counted" on the side of the West, and in the process had antagonized other nearby governments which refused on principle to take a position in the "cold war." Thanks to the military backing of the United States, both pacts had provided a deterrent of sorts against outright military aggression in their respective areas. Neither alliance, however, had proved particularly effective in meeting the new, nonviolent emphasis in Soviet and Chinese world policy.

Unlike the Baghdad Pact, with its four Asian members and its single full Western participant (the United Kingdom), the SEATO alliance was primarily Western in membership. The combination of the United States, Britain, France, Australia, and New Zealand represented a rather substantial aggregation of military power and strategic positions, and inevitably somewhat outweighed the Asian viewpoint as represented by Pakistan, the Philippines, and Thailand. The usefulness of such a grouping in the particular circumstances that had confronted the Far East in the period since the Indochina war had remained a matter of widely differing opinions. Secretary Dulles, as the principal architect of the pact, not unnaturally took the position (e.g., March 6, 1957) that it afforded "an outstanding example of successful cooperation" between eastern and western nations and had made "a positive contribution to peace and stability in Asia." A similar view inspired the official second annual report on the alliance, prepared by the SEATO Council Representatives in Bangkok and made public on March 5.[12] Yet outside observers remained in considerable doubt about the organization's value. "SEATO," wrote one American authority on Southeast Asia,[13]

"was and is an American substitute for Asian neutralism. It immediately suffers from being an import rather than a local product. The trouble with SEATO is that not only did it alienate some of our neutralist friends in Southeast Asia, it has also increasingly disappointed those who originally thought well of it. . . . We would serve our cause better if we forthrightly got rid of it."

One principal complaint among SEATO's pro-Western critics was the fact that despite an impressive array of military planning groups and some experience in combined military exercises, the alliance had no military forces of its own and had to rely almost exclusively on the "striking power" of American forces based mainly outside the SEATO area. At the Canberra meeting, as on previous occasions, Mr. Dulles tried hard to allay these objections by assuring his fellow ministers that American forces in the Pacific were growing stronger all the time and would be used if needed. There was, as he later remarked (November 19), some feeling in SEATO that the United States might be too ready to take military action in other areas of the world but too hesitant to act for the protection of its allies in the Far East.

Important though this consideration remained in the eyes of the SEATO governments, it was generally recognized at Canberra that the nature of the Communist threat to Southeast Asia had distinctly altered in the thirty months since the alliance was concluded. Admitting that a military threat to the area undoubtedly still existed, the assembled ministers agreed that the emphasis in "Communist and Communist-inspired tactics" had shifted "from the open threat of force to more flexible tactics of non-violent penetration and undermining of non-Communist states still accompanied in some cases by armed insurrection." [14] Accordingly, while the Council endorsed the establishment in Bangkok of a permanent military planning office to pool the strategic thinking of all member countries, it laid more emphasis on a directive to its civil organization "to intensify its work of identifying all phases of subversive tactics; to make known its findings amongst member governments; and to expose them to the scrutiny of public opinion." The main responsibility for combating subversion, it was agreed, rested with the individual governments, aided as necessary by their friends, with SEATO playing "an important supplementary role."

In the belief that economic progress and an enlightened public opinion were also essential elements in meeting the Communist challenge, SEATO had always shown at least a nominal interest in economic development schemes, cultural exchanges, and similar long-range endeavors. No great sums of money were involved, since the United States preferred to apply such resources as it had available for these purposes through other channels. At the Canberra meeting, the SEATO Council reviewed the general progress of economic development in the treaty area and made a number of recommendations for cooperative action, as well as urging an expansion of bilateral cultural exchanges and approving a fellowship program and a series of round-table meetings on Asian civilizations. In token of the permanent status of the organization it was decided to establish the new positions of Secretary-General and Deputy Secretary-General; Pote Sarasin of Thailand was subsequently named to the former post. Also approved was a new formula for meeting the costs of the organization, involving some increase in the United States contribution.

In a special statement on the problem of neutralism, the Council pointed out that in spite of the active opposition of some governments, SEATO was not an exclusive organization but remained open to all Southeast Asian countries willing to share its benefits and responsibilities. "It was hoped that as time passed and the value of SEATO became more widely appreciated that those who criticized it today would eventually be willing to welcome it." "As the organization moves into its new and expanded phase of activity," the communiqué concluded, "the Council members are determined that SEATO will work for the enrichment as well as the defense of human life and liberty in accordance with the principles and purposes of the Charter of the United Nations."

Secretary Dulles made no public report on the Canberra meeting on his return to the United States, but told the Senate Foreign Relations Committee (March 18) that it had achieved "solid, though unspectacular, progress." How greatly it would contribute to the future peace and stability of Southeast Asia would naturally depend a good deal on the actions and attitudes of individual member countries— and, possibly to an equal degree, on the behavior of Communist China and of those states which had shied away from SEATO membership. So far as the military aspects of Southeast Asian defense were concerned, the problem did not appear to alter appreciably in its main outlines in the months that followed. Essentially it remained a problem of Communist land power versus allied "mobile striking power." Although the Chinese Communists were putting considerable effort into modernizing their armed forces and claimed to be laying the foundations of "a mighty Air Force and Navy" (equipped at least in part with Chinese-manufactured jet aircraft), the principal threat to Southeast Asia still lay in their huge army, supplemented by North Vietnam's armed forces of 450,000 to 500,000. To immobilize this human tide the SEATO allies, as in the past, would have to rely almost exclusively on the deterrent of American retaliatory power, based in the Philippines, Okinawa, and elsewhere. The never very substantial prospect that a Communist offensive could be met on the ground was further diminished during the year by progressive reductions in the American and British ground forces, although Great Britain still planned to maintain substantial mobile forces in Hong Kong and Singapore.

Most members of SEATO could at least assure themselves that substantial bodies of water lay between them and the Chinese danger. Among SEATO's Asian participants, only Thailand was directly exposed by geographical position to the possibility of an overland attack, which might come either by way of Burma or via the neutral state of Laos. For geographic and cultural reasons, Thailand was also particularly exposed to the weight of Chinese "peaceful" attentions; and not a few observers in the course of 1957 expressed anxiety about the apparent effectiveness of Chinese propaganda in the country, the warm public response to Chinese cultural activities, and the expression of neutralist and anti-American sentiments in some semiofficial newspapers. Public opinion, however, was far from being the controlling force in Thai affairs, which were more directly contingent upon the mutual rivalry of Thailand's three political marshals, Premier Pibul Songgram, Phao Sriyanond, and Sarit Thanarat. The chief event of the year was a coup by Marshal Sarit on September 17 which resulted in the resignation and exile of Marshals Pibul and Phao and the recall of Mr. Pote Sarasin from SEATO headquarters to head a new government. All sources insisted that these events would have no bearing on Thailand's external orientation, and this impression was confirmed by the poor showing of left-wing and neutralist groups in a new parliamentary election held on December 15. Marshal Sarit, the new "strong man," had sponsored journalistic attacks on the West, but was not accused of any subterranean dealings with the Chinese and appeared to stand higher in public estimation than some of the men who had lined their pockets under the Pibul regime.

If Thailand still remained a somewhat uncertain quantity from the standpoint of long-range political orientation, there seemed at the moment to be no particular reason for uneasiness in the case of Pakistan and the Philippines. Pakistan, it is true, was largely immobilized by its quarrel with India (section 15), while the Philippines—and indeed the whole free world—suffered a heavy blow in the death of President Ramón Magsaysay in an airplane crash on March 17. Happily Magsaysay's successor, Carlos P. Garcia, who was elected to a full four-year term on November 12, proved to be a firm friend of the United States and the West even if he lacked some of Magsaysay's dynamic qualities. His abilities would undoubtedly be severely tested during the new presidential term which began December 30 in the midst of a grave crisis in the Philippines' external economic position.

Additional grounds for Western optimism could be found in the increasing maturity and stability exhibited by Great Britain's Asian protégés of Malaya and Singapore, which lay within the SEATO area and closely concerned the alliance even though not formally identified with it. Malaya, indeed, attained its full independence on August 31 as a "Free and United Federation" and the tenth member of the Commonwealth of Nations. Although Prime Minister Tengku (Prince) Abdul Rahman said his country would not join SEATO and would not permit nuclear weapons on its territory, he was equally emphatic in professing the new nation's lasting friendship for Great Britain, which retained responsibility for its external defense under a special alliance treaty and would continue to direct operations against the handful of terrorists who still held out in the Malayan jungles despite repeated amnesty offers. Singapore, too, after a false start in 1956, was back on the road to independence under an agreement negotiated in London by Chief Minister Lim Yew Hock, and a firm date for its elevation to Commonwealth status was expected to be set at the beginning of 1958. These developments helped to substantiate the Western claim that anti-Communism in Asia by no means implied the denial of popular aspirations for an increased measure of national independence.

A similar demonstration was afforded by the heartening progress achieved in recent years in the Republic of Vietnam, which was likewise not a member of SEATO but was included in that organization's defense area, together with Laos and Cambodia, under a special protocol to the Manila Pact. Where Malaya and Singapore still looked to the United Kingdom as their prime sponsor among the big powers, South Vietnam under President Ngo Dinh Diem had turned its back on France, the former colonial power, and now relied almost entirely on the United States for needed economic, diplomatic, and military support. President Ngo's objective, as he explained on a visit to the United States in May 1957, was not merely to save his country from Communism—no small task in itself in view of the continued military and political threat from Communist-controlled North Vietnam—but to build an "open" system which would prove that economic progress in Asia could be brought about by democratic methods. The degree to which Vietnam was actually progressing economically at the moment was a subject of differing opinions, and some members of the American economic aid mission were said to feel that the government's performance in this field scarcely measured up to its proclaimed intentions. Mr. Ngo's great and undeniable achievement was the establishment of a sound and functioning political order in a situation which three years earlier had seemed all but hopeless. Recognition of this accomplishment, which had earned a certain respect even in so skeptical a country as India, could be found in the selection of Vietnam's capital of Saigon as the site of the ninth annual conference of the Colombo Plan (see below).

Not quite so reassuring was the course of events in the

neighboring Indochinese states of Cambodia and Laos. Cambodia, under the leadership of Prince Norodom Sihanouk, still maintained a policy of full-fledged neutralism, though with some waning of the outspoken anti-Americanism which had been much in evidence the year before. Laos, which occupied a more critical strategic position between China, North and South Vietnam, Cambodia, Thailand, and Burma, was the scene of a complex political struggle between the Communist-led Pathet-Lao movement in the northeast and the National Assembly in Vientiane. An agreement providing for the dissolution of the Pathet-Lao forces and the acceptance of their leaders into the government (December 28, 1956) failed to go into effect when the Pathet-Lao sought to impose various extraneous conditions, including the acceptance of Chinese Communist economic aid. The Prime Minister and author of the agreement, Prince Souvanna Phouma, was forced to resign in May but returned to office in August after the Assembly had failed to approve any alternative candidate. This result was generally viewed as a defeat for the United States, which (with Britain and France) had come out openly for resistance to the Pathet-Lao demands.[15] Events moved slowly in Laos, however. The Pathet-Lao forces did not come under even nominal government control until November, and the implications of the deal were to remain hidden for some time afterward. What did seem clear was that the country's long-term prospects of independence were shadowed by the operations of a closely knit, Communist-led group which had received and might again receive support from beyond the national frontiers. That the United States would be able to neutralize this danger by action under the Manila Pact or otherwise seemed not at all certain.

There was another small country adjacent to Communist China which was perhaps even less favorably situated so far as Western attempts to support its independence were concerned. Communist China's military occupation of Tibet in 1950–51 had placed the Himalayan Kingdom of Nepal in the direct path of Communist expansionism, thereby converting this legendary country from a virtual dependency of India into a battleground of competing Chinese and Indian influences. India as well as the United States was concerned over the prospect of Chinese pressure on an area bordering its own frontiers, and New Delhi and Washington had found it possible to cooperate in providing Nepal with development assistance aimed largely at keeping it out of the Chinese orbit. But Nepal had also accepted a promise of Chinese economic aid, and its leading statesmen showed no particular apprehension about the possible designs of their northern neighbor. In mid-1957 a new government was formed by Dr. K. I. Singh, who had been known in the past as a pro-Communist but was believed by some to have had his eyes opened in recent years by prolonged residence in China. Though Dr. Singh was said to accept the necessity for close ties with India, his government lasted only long enough to strengthen the impression that Nepal would remain a sensitive spot in world politics for the foreseeable future. At the year's end King Mahendra was in personal charge of the government and promising that his country, too, would have national elections in early 1959.

Another mutual neighbor of India and China, the Union of Burma, faced the Chinese danger with considerably more experience and with little of the antipathy to the West that was so evident in some Asian neutral countries. One of the significant developments which followed the return of Burma's leading statesman, U Nu, to the premiership early in 1957 was a resumption of economic aid from the United States, discontinued at Burma's request in 1953. The strictly businesslike arrangement announced on March 21 comprised a $25 million development loan and a $17.5 million surplus agricultural commodities agreement. Although Chinese economic and cultural influence in Burma was also growing, the government was kept alert to possible Communist designs by the unsettled state of the frontier with China, a considerable infiltration of illegal Chinese immigrants, and the persistence of half a dozen guerrilla insurrectionary movements of varying political and ethnic complexions. Restoration of full internal order and security was the key item in U Nu's four-year governmental program, in which the United States did not fail to wish him all possible success.

In the island nations of Ceylon and Indonesia, Chinese Communist manipulations were a less immediate threat but still represented a source of apprehension to many outside observers and some indigenous ones. Ceylon's neutralist government, led by Premier S. W. R. D. Bandanaraike, completed the takeover of the former British naval and air bases during 1957 and tightened its relations with both China and the Soviet Union—a country which, in the Prime Minister's optimistic opinion (November 10), did "not want to force its form of government down the throats of other governments," sought only "friendship and peace," and was not "preparing to interfere in the internal affairs of other countries." To Premier Bandanaraike's critics this view of Communist intentions was highly irresponsible even though not untypical of a large section of Ceylonese and Asian opinion.

Indonesia, with nearly ten times Ceylon's population and a commensurate weight in Asian and world affairs, was occupied through most of the year with a most formidable list of internal problems, headed by a series of bloodless revolts or autonomy movements in the islands of the archipelago. A related source of uneasiness for anti-Communists in Indonesia and abroad was President Sukarno's establishment of a new "National Council" or supercabinet to implement the concept of "guided democracy" he had evolved while on a tour of the U.S.S.R. and China in 1956. President Sukarno's insistence that the Communists be given their proportionate share of political representation assured them a significant influence on the national scene; and their progress in the provincial elections held in Java during the summer raised a distinct possibility that they might emerge with a nationwide popular majority when Indonesia held its next parliamentary elections in 1959. Like Communists everywhere, they also stood ready to capitalize wherever possible on the emotional manifestations associated with the anticolonial movement, which in Indonesia's case had focused ever more strongly on a claim of sovereignty over Netherlands New Guinea or "West Irian." (See further section 26.)

Although the United States had found it preferable to

make no response to a request from Indonesia to be allowed to purchase military equipment in this country, both Indonesia and the other neutral states of Southeast Asia were listed among the lesser recipients of American economic assistance. Official Washington thus recognized at least in principle that the area's fundamental economic problems cut across political lines and required attention irrespective of political alignments. If it was true that political instability and susceptibility to Communist maneuvers were directly related to low productivity and inadequate living standards, then the promotion of a well-balanced development of economic resources, both in individual countries and in Southeast Asia as a whole, might be no less important to the area's future independence than the efforts being made in SEATO to counter the direct threats of Communist aggression and subversion. In recent years this aspect of the Southeast Asia problem had if anything taken on increased urgency with the growing resort of both the Soviet Union and Communist China to "trade and aid" schemes such as the $100 million Soviet credit promised to Indonesia in 1956. With or without Communist participation, substantial external assistance was needed if the area as a whole was even to hold its own in the breathless race between living standards and population growth.

These matters had for some years been the special concern of the eighteen-nation Consultative Committee on Cooperative Economic Development in South and Southeast Asia, established under British Commonwealth auspices in 1950 and informally known as the Colombo Plan. The United States had been a full participant in this enterprise since 1951 and reckoned its total assistance to the receiving nations and territories (including India and Pakistan) at approximately $3 billion, most of it provided directly under bilateral arrangements. Aside from technical and development assistance to individual countries in the Colombo Plan area, which embraced about 654 million people or nearly one-fourth of the world's population, the United States was laying considerable stress on a projected Asian Nuclear Research Center which it planned to establish in Manila as a

means toward bringing the benefits of atomic energy to
Asian peoples in line with President Eisenhower's atoms-
for-peace program.

A review of the general status of economic development
in Southeast Asia was the principal business of the Ninth
Colombo Plan Conference, held in Saigon from October 7
to 24. Despite a widening trade gap and a general decline in
foreign exchange assets which threatened to become particularly serious in the case of India, the general impression was
one of modest progress in most countries, combined with a
need for great and sustained effort in the years ahead.[16] One
trend that could not fail to gratify the American delegation
was the apparent readiness of Burma and some other countries to welcome the investment of private capital more
warmly than they had done in the past. In the light of
Washington's firm conviction that private capital must remain the principal instrument of economic development for
the foreseeable future, signs of increased acceptance of this
idea on the part of less developed countries could only be
welcomed. The more the Asian and Western nations succeeded in reconciling their differences on points of economic
doctrine and procedure, the greater would be their chances
of jointly surmounting the challenge posed by the economic
and political totalitarianism of Moscow and Peking.

19. NEW ERA FOR JAPAN

Since 1954, Japan as well as the United States had been
listed as one of the donor nations participating in the Colombo Plan. Although its direct contributions to Southeast Asian
economic development had thus far remained comparatively
modest, many observers both in Japan and in the West believed that intensified Japanese-Southeast Asian economic relations promised considerable advantage to all concerned.
The still relatively undeveloped countries of Southeast Asia
could obviously make good use of Japanese capital goods and
technological skills. Japan, with its dependence on imported
food and raw materials, could find in Southeast Asia the
source of many of its own requirements and a natural outlet

for many of its manufactured products. The Western nations, which did not much welcome Japanese commercial competition, would on the whole be quite willing to see Japanese enterprise directed to an area where it would contribute to the over-all strength of the free world and confer no undesirable advantages on the Communist powers. The most serious obstacle to such a program was the lingering mistrust of many of the countries of Southeast Asia, which had thus far shown little interest in renewing their economic collaboration with the originators of the wartime "Greater East Asia Co-Prosperity Scheme."

The potential role of Southeast Asia as a field for Japanese enterprise, and the necessity of establishing a more confident relationship with individual Southeast Asian governments, was an important element in the thinking of Nobosuke Kishi, the Liberal-Democratic politician who became Foreign Minister of Japan at the end of 1956 and succeeded his ailing party colleague, Tanzan Ishibashi, as Prime Minister in late February 1957. In Mr. Kishi's first statement on assuming the premiership (February 25) he revealed that he would personally undertake an effort to broaden Japan's contacts with other countries in Asia. This, he said, would represent one phase of a more general readjustment of the country's foreign relations suitable to the stage it had now reached in its postwar comeback.

Great changes had occurred in Japan's international position since the signature of the San Francisco Peace Treaty in 1951 and the formal termination of the American military occupation in the following year. Substantial American forces still remained in Japan, but as allies rather than as masters. Their purpose was no longer to keep Japan itself in order, but to assist that country in assuring its defense against outside aggression until such time as Japan's own armed forces could take over the job. That moment now seemed measurably closer than in the past; and in the meantime Japan had taken other important steps to regularize its situation, including a recent interim agreement with the U.S.S.R. (October 19, 1956) which had terminated the state of war and reopened the way for an exchange of diplomatic representa-

tives with the capital of world Communism. Japan now enjoyed normal relations with all of the world's major governments except that of Communist China, which it had thus
far declined to recognize. To crown its new status it had
achieved admission as the eightieth member of the United
Nations on December 18, 1956.

Although they disagreed sharply about Japan's future
course in relation to the East-West struggle, virtually all
Japanese agreed that their country's new position called for
some modification of past foreign policy and, in particular,
for a more independent stand in relation to the United
States. Having been helped by this country to regain something not far short of its pre-1941 standing in the world,
Japan had now to consider how far the continuance of this
special relationship would be useful and how far it might
represent a handicap in the pursuit of specifically Japanese
interests. Valuable though it had been in the past, the American connection could not be called popular in Japan. There
was recurrent friction over the presence and activities of
the American armed forces. Japanese businessmen were dis-
gruntled over the difficulties besetting their sales in the
United States, and resented the American-inspired ban on
"strategic" shipments to Communist countries. The influential Japanese Socialists openly advocated dissociation from
the American alliance system, establishment of "normal"
relations with Communist China, and a neutral position in
the East-West conflict. All Japanese, moreover, were incensed
at the United States (as well as Great Britain and the
U.S.S.R.) for continuing to test nuclear weapons despite
repeated Japanese representations, both official and unofficial,
about fallout and radiation dangers. The essential question
as Mr. Kishi took office, therefore, was how far Japan would
now go in differentiating its stand from that of the United
States, if not in seeking common ground with the Communist powers.

Any notion that Japan under its Liberal-Democratic government would foresake its American alliance and adopt an
outright neutralist policy had been explicitly disavowed even
before Mr. Kishi took over the reins. "The interests of

Japan are in line with those of the free nations," he had said (January 24). "Japan should keep her feet firmly planted on this fact." Yet neither as Foreign Minister nor as Prime Minister did Mr. Kishi attempt to minimize the readjustments he hoped to introduce in Japan's relations with both major political camps. Expanded economic relations with Communist China, including a "rationalization" of strategic trade controls, were a definite part of his program, although he indicated that political recognition of the Peking regime would be "premature." He also favored increased trade with the U.S.S.R. and its European satellites, including Czechoslovakia and Poland, with which Japan was in the process of concluding interim peace agreements on the Soviet model; and he felt that Japan should address itself "realistically" to the task of easing East-West tensions.

With the United States, Mr. Kishi hoped to effect a whole series of new arrangements, including some modification of the basic security treaty of 1951, a voice in the administration of Okinawa and other Japanese possessions currently held by the United States, and improved access for Japanese goods in the American market. Particularly important, in his view, was the kind of frank understanding with American leaders which could be achieved only in face-to-face talks. Preparing to visit the United States in response to an invitation from President Eisenhower, the Prime Minister declared on May 16 that in his conversations in Washington he would emphasize above all else "the imperious need of establishing a genuine relationship of mutual trust."

This was the kind of objective to which the American Government was invariably sympathetic, and Mr. Kishi appears to have had no difficulty in putting over his key point during his few days in Washington. Beginning with a round of golf on June 19, his visit concluded on June 21 with a communiqué [17] setting forth the conviction of both the President and the Prime Minister "that relations between Japan and the United States are entering a new era firmly based on common interests and trust." Secretary Dulles told his news conference on June 25 that he thought the visit had "served a very important purpose and perhaps did more than most of such visits in actually establishing a new basis for future relations." "I feel," Mr. Dulles said, "that it opened up a new era in our relations with Japan, an era which will be much more on a basis of cooperation than of the exercise by the United States of unilateral rights." This prospect, the Secretary explained, flowed more from imponderables than from the actual words of the communiqué. "But there was, I think, introduced into our relationship a new spirit, and I believe that events from now on will confirm the judgment which I now give."

The communiqué itself gave evidence that the talks had not been confined to generalities but had ranged widely over the extensive field of United States-Japanese relations. Inevitably, the concrete decisions reached had fallen short in some instances of the high purposes of the participants, though Premier Kishi had undoubtedly come closer to realizing a portion of his announced objectives than had such previous Japanese visitors to Washington as Premiers Shigeru Yoshida and Ichiro Hatoyama. This in itself was testimony to Japan's increased weight within the free world coalition, as well as its continued responsiveness to the basic American view on relations with the Communist powers. "The President and the Prime Minister," said the communiqué, "agreed that, although the dangers of general war had somewhat receded, international communism remains a major threat. Accordingly, they agreed that the free nations should continue to preserve their strength and their unity." This was the keynote of their understanding and the fundamental theme of all their deliberations.

Within the framework of this broad understanding, the most notable result of the Washington conversations was a decision to review existing security arrangements between the two countries and speed up the transfer of defense responsibilities from American to Japanese hands. The Japanese "Self-Defense Force" had now attained the respectable total of 197,730 men and was building toward a 1960 target of 250,000, including small naval and air forces. Under the United States-Japanese Mutual Security Treaty of 1951, it was understood that the American forces being maintained in and about Japan to deter armed attack on that country would be progressively reduced as Japan itself achieved the capability of providing for its own defense. Up to the time of Premier Kishi's departure for Washington, this date had seemed by no means imminent. But the United States, as we have seen, was engaged in a broad review of its manpower commitments overseas in the light of political and economic factors as well as growing reliance on nuclear weapons. Japan had its own compelling reasons for desiring a reduction in American military personnel, currently numbering about 100,000, and it was therefore agreed in Washington that the United States, "in consonance with the letter and spirit of the Security Treaty, will substantially reduce the numbers of United States forces in Japan within the next year, including a prompt withdrawal of all United States ground combat forces." "The United States," the communiqué added, "plans still further reductions as the Japanese defense forces grow."

The withdrawal of some 35,000 ground combat troops, while it might reduce the prospects of disagreeable incidents involving American personnel, would also affect the Japanese economic position to the extent of $60 million to $100 million in annual dollar revenue. The effect on the Far Eastern military balance was somewhat uncertain. Japanese troops, unlike the G.I.'s they were replacing, would not be available for service in Korea or other overseas areas; but we have already observed that American military authorities no longer appeared to think seriously in terms of major ground operations of the Korean type. For the moment, no plans were announced to reduce American air or naval forces in Japan, although their effectiveness in deterring Communist aggression might in future be somewhat limited by Premier Kishi's insistence that he would not allow atomic weapons to be kept in Japan.

An important element in the decision to speed the reduction in American forces in Japan was the international furor that was raging just at this time over the case of William S. Girard, an American Army specialist (third class) who had shot and killed a Japanese woman trespasser on a military firing range on January 30. In conformity with procedures laid down in the applicable "status-of-forces" agreement, the United States had originally waived jurisdiction in the case to the Japanese Government, but had subsequently tried to withdraw its waiver in deference to objections by some groups at home (section 7). This move was sharply resented in Japan, where popular feeling against the United States was fanned to unusual heights by Socialist and other agitators. In order to preserve "the good faith of the United States" and the integrity of its pledges, the Secretaries of State and Defense jointly decided on June 4 that the case should after all be tried by the Japanese.[18] This decision was subsequently upheld by the United States Supreme Court (July 11),[19] and a Japanese tribunal eventually found Girard guilty of manslaughter and imposed a suspended sentence (November 18).

In the meantime, the President and Mr. Kishi had moved to attack the underlying causes of such frictions by establishing a high-level committee—the "Japanese-American Committee on Security"—to study problems arising under the security treaty and to consult whenever practicable on the "disposition and employment" of United States forces in Japan. This arrangement, Secretary Dulles explained, was aimed primarily at "putting our relations more on a bilateral basis" than in the past without going to the length of formally amending the security treaty. The first business of the committee when it met in Tokyo later in the year was to try to establish the timetable for the promised withdrawal of American ground combat troops, which was not completed until early 1958.

Prime Minister Kishi was not fully successful in his efforts at modifying other concrete aspects of the existing United States-Japanese relationship. To his representations about "the strong desire of the Japanese people" for the return to Japan of administrative control over the American-occupied Ryukyu and Bonin Islands, the President replied that although Japan admittedly possessed "residual sovereignty" over these island groups, the United States would be compelled to maintain the present status "as long as the conditions of threat and tension exist in the Far East." This it was clearly entitled to do under the San Francisco Peace Treaty, but the Japanese had hoped that the difficulties of governing the local inhabitants, particularly the not always docile population of Okinawa, would make Washington more amenable to the idea of turning over administrative responsibility to Japan while retaining the use of the Okinawa base. The President did state that the United States would "continue its policy of improving the welfare and well-being of the inhabitants of the Islands and of promoting their economic and cultural advancement."

Two other matters growing out of Japan's defeat in World War II were discussed but did not figure in the final communiqué. Japan had sought the release of sixty-six convicted war criminals still held by the United States in Tokyo's Sugamo prison. Although no formal agreement was made public, individual pardons and paroles during the following months reduced the number to forty-five as of mid-December, when it was announced that all remaining cases would be reviewed by Japanese parole boards with a view to making recommendations for clemency. Also desired by the Japanese was the recovery of some $60 million in Japanese-owned assets which had been seized by the United States after Pearl Harbor. Action on this request (and on the considerably larger claims filed by the German Federal Republic) would have to await the passage of legislation which the administration proposed to recommend to Congress in 1958.

The Eisenhower-Kishi talks also afforded an opportunity for a review of Japan's efforts to strengthen its relations with other Asian countries. Describing a recent tour which had taken him to Burma, India, Ceylon, Pakistan, Thailand, and Taiwan, Premier Kishi said he had been deeply impressed with the serious efforts these countries were making in the field of economic development and was convinced that further progress in that direction would greatly contribute to stability and freedom in Asia. The President fully agreed, and undertook to study Japanese views about "ways in which free Asian countries might be further assisted in developing their economies." He did not, however, make the hoped-for commitment to underwrite a Japanese-sponsored Asian development program. This would hardly have been possible at a time when the Mutual Security appropriation for the next fiscal year was still under debate. Nor did the President appear entirely sympathetic to Japanese views on trade with the Communist world. While recognizing "that Japan must trade to live," Mr. Eisenhower laid special emphasis on the continuing need for limitation of strategic exports to the Communist countries. Mr. Kishi agreed, but at the same time "pointed out the necessity for Japan to increase its trade." Soon after the Prime Minister's return to Tokyo, on July 16, Japan followed the lead of Great Britain and other Western countries in placing its trade with Communist China on the same basis as trade with the European Soviet bloc (cf. section 6).

The problem of Japan's trade relations, though perhaps the most important single issue discussed in Washington, was also the one on which Mr. Eisenhower was least in a position to provide his guest with the kind of assurances he sought. A flourishing Japanese trade with other free world countries was clearly essential if Japan was to remain a healthy member of the non-Communist community; yet few indeed were the countries that looked without anxiety at the prospect of intensified Japanese competition in their own domestic and foreign markets. It was primarily the difficulty encountered in trading with the free world that so whetted the Japanese appetite for trade with China. As President Eisenhower himself had observed (April 10), ". . . I do say if we are going to keep Japan our friend, on our side of the Iron Curtain, we can't . . . just . . . say, 'you mustn't do that and you mustn't do that.' Finally, you just block them, and they have no place to go except in the arms of somebody where we don't want them to go." Japan's two-way trade with Communist China, at $150 million in 1956, was still on a small scale but the trend has been strongly upward.

Since the earliest days of Japan's postwar economic recovery, the United States had acknowledged a special responsibility for helping that country to regain a footing in the free world's economic life. As Japan became more nearly independent in economic matters, the United States continued to wield a decisive influence as Japan's leading trade partner—the source of one-third of its 1956 imports and the destination of one-fifth to one-fourth of its 1956 exports. Despite a generally favorable year in which both imports and exports had reached new records for the postwar period, Japan in 1956 had incurred a deficit of over $500 million in its trade with the United States and had bought from this country almost twice what it was able to sell it. "In all candor," Foreign Minister Aiichiro Fujiyama remarked on September 20 in the course of a follow-up visit to the United States, "the maintenance and development of the American market is a matter of life and death to the Japanese economy. The very livelihood of entire Japanese towns and cities is at stake."

Particularly disturbing to the Japanese were the efforts being made in some American quarters to raise additional obstacles to the entry of Japanese goods as Japanese competition became sharper. Tokyo had protested more than once against the requirement of certain Southern states that Japanese textiles be specially identified in a manner calculated to reduce their sales. Early in 1957 it accepted, under strong persuasion from the State Department, a "voluntary" limitation on the export of cotton manufactures to this country, which was supposed to remain in effect for five years and was described in Washington as "a major step forward in the development of orderly and mutually beneficial trade between the United States and Japan." [20] But Japan in accepting this arrangement had apparently assumed that the United States would act to secure the suspension of state laws which discriminated against Japanese products; and this the Federal Government professed itself unable to do because of basic constitutional limitations.

Premier Kishi's visit to the United States did not greatly advance the solution of this problem. The Japanese statesman expressed his "deep concern over certain movements in the United States for import restrictions." President Eisenhower reaffirmed the traditional American policy of "a high level of trade without unnecessary and arbitrary restrictions," and "expressed his hopes for the removal of local restrictions on the sale of Japanese products." Secretary Dulles commented a few days later (June 25) that his department considered the laws in question to be quite definitely in conflict with the most-favored-nation principle, that it had not given up hope of securing their repeal, and that it had been quite successful in heading off the enactment of similar laws in certain other states. When Foreign Minister Fujiyama subsequently reopened the whole question of Japan's adverse trade balance with the United States (September 23), Secretary Dulles expressed his understanding and once again pointed out that the United States regarded the economic viability of Japan as "one of the essential elements of stability in the Far East."

More valuable to the Japanese than these reiterated verbal assurances were two Export-Import Bank loans, agreed upon during the Kishi visit and announced June 28 and September 27, to finance the purchase by Japan of raw cotton and other agricultural commodities to a value of $175 million. This limited assistance had become doubly important because Japan had meanwhile run into increased difficulty with its over-all trade balance and was having to restrict its imports severely in order to conserve foreign exchange. Rising prices for the raw materials that fed the Japanese industrial machine had pushed the import bill for the first half of 1957 to a figure 67 percent above the corresponding period of 1956; exports meanwhile had increased by only 12 percent in value terms, and foreign exchange holdings had plummeted from $1,430 million on January 1 to $870 million on June 30. A series of austerity measures was decreed even before Premier Kishi's return to Tokyo, and arrangements were made to withdraw one-half the country's $250 million quota on deposit with the International Monetary Fund. Despite the impending loss of American troop revenue, it was hoped that these measures would suffice to stabilize the situation by early 1958. Yet reduction of imports, and of production in the industries that depended on them, seemed a very roundabout way toward the Eisenhower-Kishi objective of "a high level of world trade beneficial to free nations." Nor

could the deflationary policies that seemed essential to
Japan's financial managers be expected to increase the popularity of Japan's American-oriented government, which
would before long be facing a prospect of general elections.

Thus it was not to be wondered at that Japanese statesmen continued to keep an eye on any prospects for increased
trade with the East as well as with Southeast Asia. Japanese
exports to Communist China in the period from April to
October 1957 actually fell below the figure attained in the
previous year; but it was hoped in Tokyo that with the recent
relaxation of strategic trade controls, exports to the China
mainland might be raised at least to an annual level of $100
million without compromising major security objectives.
Somewhat disconcertingly for the Japanese, Chou En-lai reacted to their initial feelers with a violent attack on Japan's
alleged subservience to the United States, and conveyed the
impression that serious negotiations would have to await a
change of heart on the political aspects of Japanese-Chinese
relations. It would not have been surprising if Peking had
determined to use the trade issue as a lever with which to try
to obtain Japanese political recognition. Negotiations for a
trade pact with the U.S.S.R., originally scheduled at the time
of the peace agreement in 1956, were equally slow in getting
under way, although a five-year treaty of trade and navigation
was eventually signed in Tokyo on December 6. By its terms,
Japan's right to maintain strategic export controls was explicitly recognized.

While awaiting developments on the Chinese and Soviet
fronts, Mr. Kishi in late November undertook a second visit
to Southeast Asia in the hope of reducing some of the antag-
onisms his first tour of that area had failed to dissipate. This
time he concentrated on Australia and New Zealand, Malaya
and Singapore, the Indochinese states, and Indonesia and
the Philippines. In each country he publicly expressed regret for Japan's wartime misdeeds, displaying a courage
that was deemed the more remarkable in view of the approach of an election at home. The most tangible result of
his journey was a preliminary agreement on an $800 million
reparation settlement with Indonesia, one of the few non-

Communist countries with which Japan still lacked formal relations. Some progress was also made toward a settlement with Vietnam, and shortly after the Premier's return it was revealed that a new attempt was being made to resolve outstanding issues with the Republic of Korea.

Although it was too early to evaluate the long-run effectiveness of Mr. Kishi's "economic diplomacy," the benefits of Japan's "new era" thus far appeared to lie mainly in the realm of prestige—in such distinctions as had been conferred, for example, by the newly gained opportunity to play a role in the United Nations. The possibility of playing a constructive part on the international scene would be magnified in the future by Japan's election to a two-year term on the Security Council, which was effected on October 1 by a 55-25 vote of the General Assembly. Japan thus became the first former Axis country to achieve a position on the body charged with primary responsibility for the maintenance of international peace and security. Like many other arrangements affecting Japan, this one was sponsored by the United States but opposed by the Soviet bloc, which still retained the power to inhibit Japan's future development in important respects.

Aside from prestige matters, the Japanese future as 1957 closed was still beclouded by a number of uncertainties in the psychological as well as the material realm. The political attitude of the Japanese nation had not yet crystallized in any definitive way. Shortly after the signature of the San Francisco treaty, Mr. Dulles had pointed out in *Foreign Affairs* that the question whether Japan would eventually emerge as a "sustaining member of the free world" would depend very largely on the extent to which it was genuinely accepted as an equal by other free countries, including the United States. Our own Japanese policy, he had written, was crucial to our entire position in the Far East; its failure would entail the risk of our "being expelled from Japan and seeing all Asia consolidated against us." [21] This warning was not without pertinence even under the altered circumstances of 1957, a year that would be remembered for the emotional storms of the Girard case no less than for the positive evidences of Japan's recovery. The expulsion of the United States from Japan, and the consolidation of all Asia against us, were still the avowed objectives of the Communist powers. Whether they would one day be realized would still depend in large measure on our success in effecting what Mr. Dulles had called the transition "from the rôle of conquerors to one of cooperation in friendly association with the Japanese as sovereign equals."

Notes to Chapter V

1. Howard P. Jones, "America's Responsibilities and Opportunities in Asia," *Department of State Bulletin,* v. 36 (February 18, 1957), pp. 263-268.

2. *Ibid.* (February 25, 1957), pp. 295-299.

3. *New York Times,* June 19, 1957.

4. *Department of State Bulletin,* v. 37 (July 8, 1957), pp. 58-59; *Documents on American Foreign Relations, 1957,* no. 116.

5. *Department of State Bulletin,* v. 37 (September 2, 1957), p. 393.

6. *Ibid.* (July 15, 1957), pp. 91-95; *Documents on American Foreign Relations, 1957,* no. 118.

7. U.S. Senate, Committee on Foreign Relations, Subcommittee on Disarmament, 85th Cong., 1st sess., Staff Study No. 9: *Control and Reduction of Armaments—Disarmament and Security in Eastern and Southern Asia* (Washington: G.P.O., 1957), pp. v-vi.

8. Same as note 6.

9. *Department of State Bulletin,* v. 37 (September 9, 1957), pp. 420-421; *Documents on American Foreign Relations, 1957,* no. 122.

10. *Department of State Bulletin,* v. 37 (September 2, 1957), pp. 392-393.

11. *Ibid.,* v. 36 (April 1, 1957), pp. 531-532; *Documents on American Foreign Relations, 1957,* no. 117.

12. *Department of State Bulletin,* v. 36 (March 25, 1957), pp. 496-503.

13. Frank N. Trager, "Red Shadows in Southeast Asia," *New York Times Magazine,* July 7, 1957, p. 36.

14. Communiqué, March 13, in *Department of State Bulletin,* v. 36 (April 1, 1957), pp. 527-529; *Documents on American Foreign Relations, 1957,* no. 108.

15. U.S. note, April 16, in *Department of State Bulletin,* v. 36 (May 13, 1957), pp. 771-772.

16. Colombo Plan communiqué, October 24, *ibid.,* v. 37 (December 2, 1957), pp. 899-901; *Documents on American Foreign Relations, 1957,* no. 132.

17. *Department of State Bulletin,* v. 37 (July 8, 1957), pp. 51-53; *Documents on American Foreign Relations, 1957,* no. 110.

18. *Department of State Bulletin*, v. 36 (June 24, 1957), pp. 1000-1002.

19. *Ibid.*, v. 37 (July 29, 1957), pp. 196-198; *Documents on American Foreign Relations, 1957*, no. 111.

20. State Department announcement, January 16, in *Department of State Bulletin*, v. 36 (February 11, 1957), pp. 218-219.

21. John Foster Dulles, "Security in the Pacific," *Foreign Affairs*, v. 30 (January 1952), pp. 185-186.

CHAPTER SIX

GROWING PAINS IN THE AMERICAS

THAT the region conventionally known as the Western Hemisphere must always be a central concern of United States foreign policy has long been recognized as one of the commonplaces of international affairs. "No reasonable man," President Eisenhower remarked in his 1957 State of the Union message, "will question the absolute need for our American neighbors to be prosperous and secure. Their security and prosperity are inextricably bound to our own. And we are, of course, already joined with these neighbors by historic pledges."

The far-reaching responsibilities regarding the safety of "the American continents" which the United States had assumed under the Monroe Doctrine antedated by more than a century and a quarter those it had lately undertaken in regard to Europe, the Far East, and most recently the Middle East. Now, at a time when the strategic frontiers of the United States were commonly held to lie in such places as Central Europe and Taiwan, continued dependence upon the Panama Canal was but one among many grounds for an undiminished concern with the Americas. The other countries of North and South America were currently furnishing this country with well over half its import requirements and absorbing more than half of its commercial exports. Nearly two-thirds of the United States private capital invested abroad had been placed in Canada and the Latin American republics. A single resource, oil, alone represented a United States investment of upward of $4 billion in other countries of the hemisphere and vividly illustrated the essential role of Western Hemisphere resources in the economic life of the free world, especially now when access to Middle Eastern petroleum supplies had become precarious. In the political field, the fraternal relationship between the United States and Canada on one side, the ideology and institutions of the Organization of American States on the other, offered examples of harmonious international living which had done much to inspire, and which continued to give meaning to, the pledge of all United Nations members "to practice tolerance and live together in peace with one another as good neighbors."

The importance of the Western Hemisphere countries to each other and to the rest of the free world did not, of course, protect them from the influence of mutual discontent or eliminate grounds for criticism—criticism which affected many aspects of intra-hemisphere relationships. The unique position of the United States, as the strongest, richest, and internationally most active member of the hemisphere family, gave rise to a particularly large crop of jealousies, suspicions, and charges of interference in its neighbors' concerns, neglect of their interests, or both at once. Occasionally the assertion was even made that the United States actually preferred to keep its neighbors in an inferior position. "Almost every time we show any signs of gaining a larger market in any direction which seems unfavorably to affect even a giant industry in the United States, we find tariff action taken against us," said a Canadian steel executive. "It seems to us, indeed, that Americans resent any effort on our part to make our prosperity match their own. . . . You seem to want us to remain hewers of wood and drawers of water." [1] Typical of much Latin American opinion was a statement by former President Galo Plaza Lasso of Ecuador: [2]

". . . The man in the street has been led to believe that the United States, if not opposed, at least views with indifference any plan for industrialization in Latin America, because such plans run counterwise to its own industrial interests. . . . We in Latin America continue to believe that the people of the Western Hemisphere stand in so close a relationship to one another, that it sets us apart from the rest of the world, but we fail to accept that since the close of World War II, the Western World concept has replaced Latin America as the key of United States foreign policy. . . . We hope that the people of the United States realize that continued economic development of the Western Hemisphere is vital to the winning of the 'cold war,' that no matter how strong our bastions are at the 'Iron Curtain,' they will not provide sufficient protection from the dangers we are guarding against if the great masses in Latin America continue to live in poverty and disease."

The emphasis on economic questions in these statements is significant because it shows that the principal issues in Western Hemisphere affairs at this period were rather different from those we have encountered in Europe, the Middle East, and the Far East. The international political questions that so agitated the "old world" still seemed comparatively remote to many of the inhabitants of the new. "Colonialism," in its Asian or African form, was not an important problem in the Western Hemisphere; what "anti-colonial" feeling there was tended to find its outlet less in agitation against the European colonial powers than in hostility to what was described as United States "imperialism," economic and cultural. As to the possibility of Soviet military attack, this was a matter of lively concern to the United States and Canada, but much less so to the twenty countries situated below the Rio Grande. The threat of Communism operating within the Americas had caused a momentary sensation during the short-lived government of President Jacobo Arbenz Guzmán in Guatemala, but had not been regarded very seriously in most quarters since the movement had lost its territorial base with the overthrow of the Arbenz regime in 1954. The activities of local Communist groups in such countries as Brazil and Chile left most Latin Americans comparatively undisturbed, and even Secretary Dulles viewed the situation with equanimity in a press conference statement of November 5, 1957:

". . . While, of course, there are Communist efforts in every one of the American Republics, including our own, we do not take a grave view of the situation. I think the situation on the whole is very much better than it was prior to the Caracas declaration [of 1954] and the overthrow of the government in Guatamala. . . . And, while the Communist Parties are certainly making trouble and attempting to embarrass the governments in many of the Republics, we do not think that the situation is in any degree alarming, and we see no likelihood at the present time of communism getting into control of the political institutions of any of the American Republics."

Mr. Dulles would not have suggested that the absence of an overt Communist threat from within the hemisphere meant that the Western Hemisphere countries were permanently immune to Communist penetration. The map of Latin America was blotched with situations of economic strain and social discontent that seemed made to order for Communist exploitation and, unless carefully watched, might easily invite a repetition of the Guatemalan experience. Even the threat of a Communist attack originating outside the hemisphere was something that no American government could afford to overlook entirely in an age of long-range aircraft and missiles. A matter of daily concern to United States and Canadian military authorities, it received at least intermittent attention from the other American governments in connection with their participation in the Inter-American Defense Board. All of the American governments, moreover, were involved in the East-West struggle to some extent through their membership in the United Nations, although only the United States and Canada could be described as playing a leading role in opposition to Communist designs on the world scene. Through NATO and otherwise, both of the North American powers had contributed heavily, in proportion to their population and resources, to the effort to strengthen the free world and hold back the Communist tide in overseas theaters. With some significant exceptions, such as Colombia's dispatch of troops to Korea in 1950, the Latin American states had been content to stress their detestation of world Communism without attempting to oppose it actively outside their immediate neighborhood. This was perhaps to be expected in view of their much more limited capabilities for international action.

Comparative freedom from "cold war" perils gave the Western Hemisphere countries a unique opportunity to devote their main energy to developing the great material and human potentialities of the two American continents. This without doubt was the main theme of life in the Americas in the 1950's. Expansion and growth were the keynotes, from the top of the hemisphere to the bottom—growth of population, of resources under development, of capital investment, and of output; growth, too, in maturity of outlook and in the adjustment of time-honored social and political relationships to the exigencies of the modern world.

It was this process, much more than the East-West conflict, that gave rise to the dominant issues of contemporary hemisphere affairs. How were these impetuous energies to be kept in harmony and balance with each other, and directed to the ultimate benefit of all concerned? How far must they find their outlet within a national framework, and how far were they a matter of common concern to larger or smaller groups of neighboring states? In particular, what responsibilities did they lay upon the United States, which was itself deeply immersed in this hemisphere experience, even while so much of its own attention and resources was being directed elsewhere? How great was this country's obligation to assist the progress of its neighbors, and how far *could* it participate in their development without arousing antagonism and reviving old fears of "Yankee imperialism" and United States domination? How far must it be prepared to adjust its own national policies, particularly in the economic field, to accord with the needs and preferences of Canada and the Latin American states? Equally important, how far was it obligated to support the cause of political democracy in Latin America, and how far was it justified in cooperating with nondemocratic governments that happened to hold power and, perhaps, to be sympathetic to foreign private capital? How, in one word, was the United States to apply the humane principles of its declared foreign policy in the one area of the world that was comparatively sheltered from the storms of the "cold war" and thus presented a unique opportunity for long-term rather than emergency action?

These were the broad questions that repeatedly arose through 1957 as Washington endeavored to meet the specialized issues that developed from month to month in its relations with the individual Latin American countries, with the inter-American organization, and with Canada. By their very nature, few of them were susceptible of a complete and final answer. Yet most observers would have agreed that they set the framework within which the record of United States policy in the Western Hemisphere would some day come up for assessment.

20. DEFENSE AND DEMOCRACY IN LATIN AMERICA

So far as the twenty republics of Latin America were concerned, it was widely recognized that despite the indisputable value of the "inter-American system," the United States had not succeeded in recent years in developing the kind of policy that could claim the full sympathy and support of Latin American public opinion. Burdened as it was with extra-hemispheric obligations, it had found neither the time, the material resources, nor the diplomatic insights that might have kept its Latin American relations on a fully satisfactory plane. In spite of its announced determination to remedy the "neglect" of our southern neighbors, the Eisenhower administration had not greatly altered the tone or content of United States policy in this area. Its positive intitiatives had been mainly confined to the mobilizing of opposition to the Arbenz government in Guatemala and to a few ground-breaking ventures in the field of personal diplomacy, notably the visit of Dr. Milton Eisenhower to certain South American states in 1953 and the President's own journey to Panama for a ceremonial meeting of American chiefs of state in July 1956. Neither these gestures nor the steadily increasing scale of economic interchange with Latin America had sufficed to establish a durable climate of mutual contentment. Commenting on this situation, the *New York Times* wrote on August 28, 1957:

"In general, and taking a hard-headed, practical point of view, both sides are doing what needs to be done. Yet neither side is quite satisfied with the other. The fault lies partly in a field that may be called public relations. If Latin America would display less of the traditional anti-Yankeeism and self-pity, and if the United States would pay more direct and sympathetic attention to Latin America in the highest spheres of our Government than has been displayed in recent years, the hemispheric atmosphere would clear up considerably. The public discussion is less satisfactory than the facts warrant."

The frequent charge that the United States had continued to "neglect" its friends below the Rio Grande was one that Secretary Dulles, at least, was not prepared to leave unchallenged. "I believe," he said on March 26,

"that never before in history has the United States paid as much attention to its relations with the other Republics of the Organization of American States as has been the case during recent years, and I think that there is an appreciation of that fact by these governments. Just to illustrate: For the first time now we meet regularly with the representatives of the Organization of American States to discuss with them world problems in which they are interested—and I have met with them before the summit conference, after the summit conference, the subsequent Meeting of Foreign Ministers, the Suez Canal crisis—things which they are vitally interested in, because they know that, if a war occurs, a general war occurs, they are going to be in it. Then, of course, there was the Panama meeting and the outgrowths of that meeting. I believe that we are giving very great attention, in fact, an unusual amount of attention, to our relations with all the Latin American States."

Closer consultation with other American governments on questions of world policy undoubtedly represented a step forward as compared with earlier years, and may well have been serviceable at times in developing something like a common American "line" on world problems. A certain coherence of outlook among the states of North and South America, particularly in matters involving the United Nations, would be doubly useful now that their proportionate influence within the world organization was being reduced by the admission of so many new Asian and African states. Generally speaking, however, criticism of United States policy toward Latin America was less concerned with these broader matters than with the specific issues of Latin American affairs, particularly the issue of democracy versus dictatorship and the issues of trade, aid, and economic development. It was the attitude of the United States toward these questions, rather than any failure to take the American governments into its confidence on matters of world policy, that was equated in some quarters with an insufficient concern for Latin American interests.

One common criticism of United States world policy that was *not* much heard in connection with Latin America was that of overemphasizing the issue of military defense against Communist aggression. At a time when budgetary and tactical considerations had brought reductions in local defense forces even in areas like Korea, which might be the immediate targets of any Communist attack, the United States could hardly have been expected to devote much attention to the local defenses of an area that seemed as remote from attack under current circumstances as did Latin America. Washington did not, indeed, go so far as a Costa Rican diplomat who suggested that the Latin American countries might just as well disarm entirely, since the Organization of American States prevented them from fighting each other and their conventional armies would be ineffective against the nuclear weapons and rockets that would be used by any outside aggressor.[3] Washington did, however, quite naturally assign a rather low priority to most phases of inter-American defense cooperation, and to a considerable extent was ready to leave the initiative to its American partners. As Admiral Radford remarked at the conclusion of a tour of South America (May 19), the main problem in this area was not so much one of military defense as of "internal security, primarily economic security, to prevent Communism from seizing any opportunity to penetrate local situations."

This evaluation did not deter the United States from mounting some imposing displays of military strength for the edification of the Latin American audience. "Operation Carib-Ex," a mammoth demonstration of paratroop and naval assault techniques which took place in April in the neighborhood of the Panama Canal, was openly designed as a bid for Latin American "good will." A similar purpose inspired the record-breaking long-distance flights of United States military aircraft in November in connection with an aeronautical celebration that was being held in Argentina at a time when the United States Air Force was particularly anxious to offset the psychological effects of Soviet missile achievements. (Cf. Chapter VII.)

On the inter-American level, the United States observed with interest the discussions carried on during the spring by certain South American countries with a view to concerting their wartime naval and other defense measures, in line with a proposal initially put forward by Argentina and endorsed by the Inter-American Defense Board, the body officially charged with military planning on behalf of all the American republics. A conference of the chiefs of staff of Argentina, Brazil, Paraguay, and Uruguay, held in Buenos Aires in May, emerged with a finding that no separate defense organization for the South Atlantic area was required and that existing inter-American treaties provided a sufficient framework for all necessary military planning. In July the Inter-American Defense Board met in Washington and approved what was described as a new joint military defense plan, one that was said to take account of such diverse factors as the undiminished threat of Soviet aggression, the capabilities of new weapons, the problems of weapons standardization and raw material supplies, and the need to curtail armament costs.[4]

To a good many Latin Americans and to some persons in the United States, this rather abstract military planning activity was less significant than the flow of actual military "hardware" from the United States to other Latin American countries under the Mutual Defense Assistance Program. Most of this material was sold rather than given away; the Mutual Security Act of 1957, for example, authorized only $13 million in grant military aid for the entire Western Hemisphere during the fiscal year 1958. From Washington's point of view, the furnishing of moderate quantities of armaments and military equipment to allied governments in

Latin America was justified not only in terms of strengthening the common defense but also in terms of friendly relations with the governments in question. It did, however, give rise to substantial objection on two separate counts, both in Latin America and in the United States.

As in the Middle East, arms shipments to nationalist-minded governments inevitably entailed a certain danger of stimulating arms races and possibly even leading to overt hostilities among the countries concerned. There were always a certain number of relatively small-scale international conflicts simmering in Latin America, especially in the Central American and Caribbean region. Nicaragua, for instance, at different periods of 1957 found itself at odds with all three of its close neighbors, El Salvador, Honduras, and Costa Rica. The most serious of these conflicts, growing out of a half-century-old boundary dispute between Nicaragua and Honduras, actually led to scattered military actions in the disputed area in the first days of spring, although the Organization of American States, acting with its habitual promptitude, was able to persuade the parties to stop fighting and ultimately (July 21) to refer their dispute to the International Court of Justice. While in no way related to the fact that both countries had received military shipments from the United States, the incident illustrated the inflammable nature of Central American politics as well as the remarkable efficiency of the O.A.S. fire brigade.

Another objection which was rather frequently heard during 1957 stemmed from the refusal of the United States to subordinate its arms supply policies to political criteria and withhold arms shipments from nondemocratic governments, especially those that were actively combating domestic opposition movements. This issue arose with particular force in 1957 in connection with the virtual civil war which was raging in Cuba between the government of President (General) Fulgencio Batista and the forces of the so-called 26th of July movement led by Fidel Castro (see below). In a larger sense, however, it was intimately bound up with the general question of Washington's attitude toward a whole series of nondemocratic regimes, both past and present, among which those functioning in the Dominican Republic, in Venezuela, and until recently in Argentina and Nicaragua were perhaps the most prominent.

Some elements in Latin America, together with their sympathizers in this country, took the view that the United States, as a champion of democratic freedoms in the struggle with world Communism, had an obligation to uphold the same values when they were threatened from other quarters, and, consequently, should deny all support to any right-wing, dictatorial governments in Latin America. Washington, which was inclined to pride itself on the good relations it had enjoyed with many of the governments in question, had normally taken the stand that the internal politics of the other American republics—so long as Communism was not involved —were not a proper concern of United States foreign policy. To discriminate against Latin American dictatorships, in the official United States view, would have violated the inter-American principle of nonintervention and would also have been inexpedient from a practical point of view. This was a matter on which the American republics were much divided among themselves, Mr. Dulles had observed (October 2, 1956). Whatever our own views might be, he did not think it "wise or profitable to carry those views into the current conduct of our relations with those countries."

It was not infrequently alleged that the official attitude of the United States in recent years had sometimes gone even beyond strict neutrality and displayed a certain partiality for authoritarian governments. It was not only the American Communist party that accused the administration of supporting "reactionary" regimes in Cuba and elsewhere. So temperate an organ as the *New York Times* could assert in its issue of August 1, 1957 that American diplomatic representatives had been "bosom friends" and "warm supporters" of such Latin American dictators as Generalissimo Rafael L. Trujillo of the Dominican Republic, General Batista of Cuba, General Marcos Pérez Jiménez of Venezuela, former President Juan D. Perón of Argentina and the late President Anastasio Somoza of Nicaragua. Although the private sentiments of United States ambassadors may not always have been susceptible of such exact definition, it was a matter of record that the United States in recent years had been perfectly ready to work with these dictatorships for common ends and had certainly shown no interest in working against them. Nor did its basic attitude appear to change in any essential way during 1957.

Quite apart from the position of the United States, however, there was some reason to believe that the scope of this particular problem might be gradually narrowing. To say there were evidences of a long-term trend toward expansion of the area of democracy in Latin America might be an overstatement; yet it was indisputable that certain conspicuous military dictatorships had been eliminated in the recent past and that some of the remaining ones were resting on quite insecure foundations. The Perón regime in Argentina had been overthrown in 1955 and replaced by a provisional military government which was pledged to the full restoration of democratic processes as soon as the necessary internal readjustments could be completed. President (General) Manuel A. Odría of Peru had voluntarily relinquished his authority to an elected chief of state in July 1956. Two months later, President (General) Somoza of Nicaragua had been assassinated; his son and successor, President Luis Somoza de Bayle, whose tenure was confirmed by the electorate in February 1957, had embarked on a policy of farreaching internal liberalization. As of early 1957, only five of the twenty republics were governed by old-style military dictatorships: Colombia, Paraguay, and Venezuela in South America, and Cuba and the Dominican Republic in the Caribbean. Although the Paraguayan regime of President (General) Alfredo Stroessner and the Dominican government dominated by Generalissimo Trujillo appeared likely to retain power for some time to come, the situation in the other three republics gave evidence of considerably more fluidity.

Colombia, whose democratic tradition had once seemed among the most firmly established in Latin America, actually moved out of the dictatorship column on May 10, 1957 when President (General) Gustavo Rojas Pinilla bowed to widespread and violent popular protest and abandoned his attempt to prolong the authority he had exercised since June 1953. A five-man military junta, backed by civilian leaders, took over with a promise of free elections and the installation of a civilian president on August 7, 1958. But the road back to democratic government was beset with numerous pitfalls, partly economic (devaluation followed by inflation) and partly political. The historical rivalry between Colombia's Liberal and Conservative parties, whose quarrels had first opened the door to General Rojas' assumption of power, broke out anew and repeatedly threatened the arrangements for an orderly resumption of democratic processes. Largely through the efforts of the Liberal leader, Alberto Lleras Camargo, a twelve-year political truce was worked out and ratified by a popular plebiscite on December 1, and it was hoped that no untoward event would interfere with the choice of a president in the following spring. Meanwhile the United States, which had concluded an agricultural surplus agreement with the Rojas government in April, stepped forward in July with a $60 million Export-Import Bank loan designed to help the new provisional government in its efforts to keep commercial life on an even keel.

A significant feature of the Colombian overturn was the influence exerted against General Rojas by the powerful hierarchy of the Roman Catholic Church, which appeared in several countries to be moving away from its traditional association with Latin America's political and social upper crust and cautiously reaching out toward a closer identification with popular aspirations. Widely remarked upon in this connection was the attitude of the Archbishop of Caracas and Primate of Venezuela, Mgr. Rafael Arias, who issued a pastoral letter on May 1 which took a decidedly critical view of the material prosperity for which President Pérez Jiménez claimed much of the credit. Actually, he said, "an immense mass of our people are living in conditions that cannot be qualified as human." But President Pérez Jiménez, who had promised his country a popular election in 1957, had thus far had no such articulate public opposition to contend with as had shown itself in Colombia. However unevenly its wealth was distributed, Venezuela with its large investment of United States capital and its abundant and growing oil production had the highest per capita income in Latin America. That and an efficient secret police had sufficed to keep political agitation to a minimum, and most observers were convinced that the outwardly unassuming dictator-president would be reelected without difficulty. To make matters certain, he had the most likely opposition candidate (Rafael Caldera) arrested in August, and in November he decided to forego the election entirely, contenting himself with a "yes or no" plebiscite on the continuance of his regime for another five years. Despite some unorganized protest demonstrations, his overwhelming victory at the polls on December 15 was a foregone conclusion. The final official claim of an 81 percent "Yes" vote surprised no one, although it undoubtedly contributed to the disgust of certain officers in the armed forces who were planning an early attempt to upset the regime by force.

Though none of the other South American republics underwent a change of regime in 1957, several of them were contending with internal problems on a scale that would test the efficacy of democratic methods in bringing them through these critical transition years. Possibly of widest significance was the effort of Argentina's provisional president, General Pedro Eugenio Aramburu, to guide his country out of the economic and political wilderness in which Perón had left it and to set it once more on the highroad of democratic life. The timetable for this process had been firmly set: election of a constituent assembly on July 28, 1957; congressional elections February 23, 1958; transfer of authority to a constitutional government May 1, 1958. But the constituent assembly elections, although they produced a nominal majority for the more moderate political groups, confirmed the impression that the experience of Peronism had left the country too deeply divided to face the future with complete assurance. Labor was increasingly restive; Peronist elements were still strong and active; the ultra-nationalist "Intransigent Radicals" led by Arturo Frondizi were using similar demagogic appeals. Perón himself, now living in exile in Venezuela, was boasting the friendship of

President Pérez Jiménez and offering to return whenever the Argentine people should call for him. That they would do so seemed unlikely, although the future trend of Argentine affairs would be difficult to predict with entire assurance before General Aramburu's program was carried through to completion.

Brazil, under the elected leadership of President Juscelino Kubitschek, was currently enjoying a respite from political quarrels as the various party groups, including the nominally outlawed Communists, laid their plans for the next presidential election in 1960. Meanwhile the country's industrial development was proceeding at a prodigious rate, and its foreign exchange reserves, depleted by heavy imports of many kinds, were constantly on the verge of exhaustion. Kept afloat partly by the largest total of Export-Import Bank loans of any country in the world, the Brazilian Government made no secret of its feeling that it had a special claim to United States assistance in view of its cooperation on certain hemisphere defense projects which were strongly opposed by local Communists and ultranationalists. Most noticed among these at the moment was an agreement initialed on January 21 under which the United States, subject to a number of important restrictions, was authorized to set up a guided missile tracking station on Brazil's Atlantic island of Fernando de Noronha.[5]

Chile, the third member of South America's trio of "big" powers, was less intimately linked with the United States in the defense field but was benefiting from United States advice and credits in its efforts to control the rocketing inflation which, along with a sharp decline in the export price of copper, had been its chief problem for some years past. Some improvement in this respect was noted in 1957, and although there was serious rioting in Santiago in April, the poor showing of extremist candidates in the congressional elections held March 3 had been generally felt to attest the growing political maturity of the Chilean electorate. At all events, there had been no lapse from democratic processes such as some observers had feared when President Carlos Ibañez was elected to office in 1952.

An even more vital economic stabilization effort was going forward with United States support in Bolivia, where a situation made perilous by rising prices and labor unrest had been given a definitely subversive turn by radical elements within the governing National Revolutionary Movement. President Hernán Siles Zuazo, who successfully asserted his authority and, in his own words, brought the country back from "the brink of civil war" at the beginning of July, subsequently paid high tribute to the United States for its steadfast support in what he described as one of the most critical hours of Bolivian history.

Many of the political difficulties being encountered in each of these countries stemmed from the low prices being fetched by their principal export products—tin in Bolivia's case, coffee in Brazil's, copper in that of Chile. These foreign exchange difficulties, accentuated by a general drop in the export price of Latin American commodities, were at the root of the widespread demand for some kind of hemispheric or world-wide price support scheme for Latin American primary products. As we shall see in the next section, however, the United States remained opposed to projects of this nature even though willing to lend assistance in cases where local economic difficulties threatened to upset political stability.

In the traditionally unstable countries of the Caribbean area and Central America, the role of economic factors was less clearly distinguishable during most of 1957. Particularly was this true in Cuba, whose booming sugar exports and general prosperity could scarcely be held responsible for the growth of active, countrywide opposition to President Batista's dictatorial regime. While the small force which had landed under Fidel Castro's leadership on December 2, 1956 held out in the remote fastnesses of the Sierra Maestra, acts of sabotage were of daily occurrence and the principal opposition parties, most of whose leaders were in exile, showed an unwonted degree of unity in anticipation of the elections General Batista had promised to hold in June 1958. With ex-President Carlos Prío Socarrás and other opposition figures making their headquarters in Florida, it was difficult

traffic between the two oceans and provide a safeguard against possible expropriation moves.

Internal affairs in Panama and the Central American republics likewise appeared to be progressing satisfactorily, although some tense moments occurred in Honduras in connection with the selection of Dr. Ramón Villeda Morales to head the new civilian government which was inaugurated December 21 after an interval of administration by military junta. Only in Guatemala did the current of events threaten to take an ugly turn. President Carlos Castillo Armas, leader of the anti-Communist revolution of 1954, was assassinated on July 26 by a member of his palace guard who was officially described as a Communist, though not, apparently, one acting under party orders. Like the death of President Magsaysay of the Philippines, this event was sincerely mourned in Washington as a loss to the whole free world. New elections held throughout Guatemala on October 20 produced an apparent majority for the moderate candidate backed by the provisional government, but were subsequently invalidated as the result of a show of force by partisans of General Miguel Ydígoras Fuentes, the favorite of Guatemala's ultraconservative elements. While a new provisional government prepared to hold new elections on January 19, 1958, non-Communist adherents of the exiled Arbenz regime were once more flocking into the country. Perhaps too pessimistically, some observers by late autumn were beginning to predict a second act in the drama of Communism in Guatemala and the Americas.

No comparable danger signals were audible at the moment from British Guiana, whose principal local political leader, Dr. Cheddi Jagan, had been accused in 1953 of trying to turn this British colonial possession into a Communist state. Although Dr. Jagan's party won a major electoral victory on August 12, 1957, the popular dentist seemed content for the time being to cooperate with the colonial government and avoid any gestures that might frighten away badly needed foreign investment. British Guiana, Dr. Jagan said, had no immediate intention of joining the new West Indies Federation that was currently being formed by British possessions in the Caribbean with a view to eventual membership in the Commonwealth of Nations. (British Honduras, whose territory was still officially claimed by Guatemala, was also expected to stay out for the time being.) The new federation, when it took form, would modify the political complexion of the hemisphere by introducing a second major British-oriented unit side by side with Canada. Though basically well disposed toward this development, the United States was somewhat embarrassed by the fact that the prospective members of the federation wished to establish their capital at Chaguaramas, Trinidad, site of a United States-leased base which the Navy was particularly anxious to retain.

21. THE ECONOMICS OF INTER-AMERICANISM

In hailing the overthrow of Guatemala's leftist regime in 1954, Secretary Dulles had gone out of his way to emphasize that the sympathies and aims of the United States extended beyond the defeat of Communism in Guatemala and envisaged active support of Latin American aspirations toward prosperity and progress. "The United States," he said, "pledges itself not merely to political opposition to Communism, but to help to alleviate conditions in Guatemala and elsewhere which might afford Communism an opportunity to spread its tentacles throughout the hemisphere. Thus we shall seek in positive ways to make our Americas an example which will inspire men everywhere." [7] In all of the American republics, the improvement of economic and social conditions in the Americas was accepted as one of the basic goals of inter-American endeavor. As authoritatively restated in the formal declaration of the American Presidents at Panama (July 22, 1956): [8]

"The full realization of the destiny of America is inseparable from the economic and social development of its peoples and therefore makes necessary the intensification of national and inter-American cooperative efforts to seek the solution of economic problems and to raise the standards of living of the Continent."

Not surprisingly, these considerations were taken even more seriously in Latin America than in the United States. For many Latin Americans, indeed, they represented a matter of life-and-death importance. A practiced observer like Galo Plaza, noting the tremendous rapidity of population growth in Latin America, the gross disparities in levels of development and standards of living, the wide diversity of ethnic and cultural traditions, the inhibiting effect of outmoded social arrangements, the crying need for basic education, for modernization and expansion of manufacturing, for better utilization of agricultural resources, could talk in terms of a clear-cut choice: [9]

"We in Latin America must insist on asking you, our friends and neighbors, to understand the reason for our impatience and our urgency: if we are unable to put our physical resources at the service of a vast program of social and economic reform for the majority of our people, and do it now, in the near future we will not be facing reform but revolution in this Hemisphere."

Without contesting the validity of these generalizations, the United States had been decidedly reluctant to endorse some of the conclusions that Latin Americans were accustomed to draw from them. With its world-wide military and fiscal responsibilities and its commitment to the free enterprise philosophy, the United States had consistently maintained that economic and social improvement in Latin America was essentially a field for private endeavor, though one that unquestionably merited some assistance from governments and appropriate international institutions. Latin Americans, by and large, did not dispute the importance of private enterprise, even if the attitude of some ultranationalists and leftists was less than hospitable to United States and other foreign private capital. What distinguished the characteristic Latin American attitude was a much broader view of the responsibilities of government in general and the United States in particular. With the best will in the world, Latin Americans argued, private capital and local enterprise could not begin to accomplish what needed to be done in their countries. Only greatly intensified action by the United States, whether undertaken directly or through the inter-American organization, could provide the resources and bring about the adjustments which to them seemed indispensable if the continent as a whole was to move forward in an orderly manner into the modern age.

This basic difference of opinion was the subject of a continuing dialogue between the United States and the Latin American governments, and provided the main subject of discussion at such inter-American economic gatherings as the Conference of American Ministers of Finance or Economy, held at Rio de Janeiro in 1954, and the Economic Conference of the Organization of American States, which took place in Buenos Aires from August 15 to September 4, 1957. Under a variety of institutional disguises, Latin American governments had for years been urging the United States to undertake for their benefit two basic modifications in its foreign economic policy. First, they wanted the United States to provide greatly increased sums for economic development, preferably not through private channels but through governmental loans or, best of all, through some kind of inter-American investment fund or bank. Second, they wanted the United States to cooperate in providing a more favorable return for their main export products by granting them a preferred status in the United States market, refraining from competition with them in other overseas markets, and setting up stabilization funds, buffer stocks, or other devices aimed at stabilizing Latin American export prices at an advantageous level.

In resisting proposals of this nature, United States representatives were able to point out not only that they were sometimes marred by a lack of realism but also that the existing system of mixed private and governmental endeavor had, after all, produced some very striking results. When all was said and done, Latin America was developing economically at a breathtaking rate, however uneven the pace and however subject it might be to temporary setbacks. For much of this growth, moreover, the United States could claim direct or indirect credit. Even in the short time since the Rio conference in 1954, the level of its imports from Latin

America had risen from $3.3 billion to $3.6 billion a year; its exports to Latin America, consisting in large part of capital goods for further economic development, had grown from $3.2 billion to $3.7 billion in the same period. Total United States private investment in Latin America, which had stood at $7.7 billion at the beginning of 1955, was estimated by mid-1957 at $9 billion; outstanding Export-Import Bank loans in the other American republics came to roughly $3 billion more. A recent study of the operations of United States companies in Latin America [10] had offered some impressive data about their contribution to the prosperity of the host countries as taxpayers, as employers of labor, and as producers of goods for domestic consumption and for export. Added to all this were the highly successful technical co-operation programs in which the United States was participating throughout Latin America, its assistance in economic stabilization efforts in such countries as Bolivia and Chile, its surplus agricultural commodity programs, its assistance on the Inter-American Highway, and its emergency aid to countries like Guatemala and Bolivia which for one reason or another had found themselves in special economic difficulties.

Critics of this record did not question the total magnitude of current United States economic activities affecting Latin America, but contended that their impact was quite unevenly distributed and not always uniformly beneficial. Forty-five percent of the direct United States private investment in the twenty republics, they pointed out, was concentrated in Venezuela and Brazil; 30 percent of it was concentrated in the petroleum industry alone. The United States might be absorbing an increasing volume of Latin American exports, but it was still not buying enough to assure its southern partners of a stable balance-of-payments situation or relieve them of the necessity of periodically clamping down on imports or dipping into their gold and dollar reserves to pay for imports already received. Most Latin American countries were vexed to a greater or lesser degree by the vagaries and uncertainties of United States trade policy: Mexico and Brazil, by Washington's determination to unload surplus

cotton on world markets below the domestic support price;
Venezuela, by the "voluntary" restrictions on petroleum imports; Mexico, Bolivia, and Peru, by the possibility of increased tariff protection for United States lead and zinc
mines. (Cf. section 6.) Countries that produced coffee, copper,
and other primary products were often acutely embarrassed
by the fluctuations of United States demand and prices—and
seldom more so than in 1957. As one experienced United
States businessman observed: [11]

"... A slight change either way in the price of their major exports can spell the difference between prosperity and depression.
. . . While ready generally to accept the normal risk of price
fluctuations, what Latin America needs most of all is a stable
trade under a stable tariff policy on the part of the United
States. Only under such a policy can it schedule its economic
development with reasonable assurance that its plan won't be
upset by sudden shifts in our tariffs for the mere sake of protecting the few even if it hurts the many."

Concerning the importance for Latin America of a stable,
and liberal, United States trade policy, there was no difference between the United States Government and those of
the Latin American republics. Washington was all the more
ready to concede this point because it saw so little prospect
of agreeing to the more specialized type of remedies which
the Latin Americans were constantly urging. Anxious not
to appear unnecessarily obdurate, Washington had also endeavored periodically to enlist Latin American interest in
approaching the economic problem from new angles which
could be profitably explored without the necessity for fundamental policy changes.

The latest important move of this kind had been President
Eisenhower's 1956 proposal to set up an Inter-American
Committee of Presidential Representatives to suggest new
activities for the Organization of American States in the
economic, financial, social, and technical fields, including
particularly "ways in which we could hasten the beneficial
use of nuclear forces throughout the hemisphere, both in
industry and in combating disease." Meeting under the chair-

manship of Dr. Milton S. Eisenhower, the President's brother, this committee in May 1957 made public a set of twenty-seven recommendations for inter-American action in the fields of economics and finance, public health and social security, education and technical cooperation, and public relations.[12] Its most striking proposals concerned a proposed five-year program for the eradication of malaria in the Americas and the establishment of an Inter-American Nuclear Energy Commission to act as a clearinghouse and coordinating center for atoms-for-peace efforts. Such a body, when and if established, would have a good deal to coordinate, since the United States was already working out bilateral atoms-for-peace arangements with fourteen Latin American countries that wanted to set up research reactors and, in addition, was planning to supply fuel for power reactors to be established in Peru and Brazil.

Like most such efforts, the work of the Committee of Presidential Representatives was subject to varying evaluations. Secretary Dulles described it (June 11) as "constructive, not when measured by the yardstick of dollars, which I think is a very fallible measuring rod for these matters, but in terms of getting new concepts under way." Most of the Latin American members of the group would nevertheless have liked to see more emphasis on the dollar angle. During the committee's sessions they had repeatedly brought up the old plea for an inter-American institution to finance economic and social development throughout the hemisphere. Faced with the customary assurance from the United States representative "that the resources still uncommitted by existing public lending institutions are adequate to meet effective demand," they had not altered their views but had agreed to postpone further discussion until the major inter-American Economic Conference which was to be held in Buenos Aires in August. Few of them can have imagined, however, that United States policy as set forth in Buenos Aires would be more favorable to their hopes than the ideas that Dr. Eisenhower had put forward in Washington.

Through a peculiarity of the inter-American organization, the representation of the United States at inter-American

economic conferences was vested not in the Department of
State but in that of the Treasury. At the Rio Conference in
1954, the task of deflating Latin American expectations had
fallen to Secretary of the Treasury George M. Humphrey; at
Buenos Aires, it was one of the first assignments to be undertaken by Mr. Humphrey's successor, Robert B. Anderson.
Pressing obligations in Washington prevented Mr. Anderson
from devoting much time to the conference, but his formal
speech at the first plenary session on August 19 [13] made it
sufficiently clear that United States policy had not changed
on the point of most interest to Latin American delegates.
"As far as we can see ahead," he declared, "we believe that
the adequacy of capital to meet the needs of sound development is not a question of additional institutions but the
fuller utilization of those in being." Foreign capital at best,
Mr. Anderson pointed out, could make but a partial contribution to the total investment requirements of an expanding economy. Domestic savings were also an essential factor.
In a passage that even Khrushchev would have found the reverse of militaristic, the Secretary of the Treasury pointed
to the undesirable economic effects of large military expenditures and suggested that "all of us" should "continue to
scrutinize our military budgets in an effort to accomplish savings that would make resources available in each of our
economies for the kind of constructive development that advances economic well-being."

Discussion subsequent to Mr. Anderson's departure from
Beunos Aires brought out the fact that the United States
remained equally opposed to the second key Latin American
objective, the establishment of international price stabilization machinery designed to ensure a favorable price level or
monetary return for Latin American export products. Experience with agricultural price supports in the United
States was hardly calculated to arouse enthusiasm for the
application of similar techniques on the international level.
Two proposed resolutions along these lines proved particularly objectionable to the United States delegation. One
would have set up a special organization to advance credits
to raw material producing nations when world prices fell,

obtaining repayment when prices rose; the other would simply have called for a "just and equitable relationship between the prices of export and import products." Both, in the words of Assistant Secretary of State Roy R. Rubottom, ran counter to the general United States policy of opposing "government intervention and the regulation of international prices." Likewise unacceptable to the United States delegation were a number of other Latin American proposals which were either directed against well-established United States practices, such as those relating to agricultural surplus disposal, or were thought likely to discourage private capital investment by sanctioning undesirable restrictions or insufficient legal protection.

These differences of opinion assumed such magnitude that the conference of Buenos Aires was unable to accomplish its main task of working out a general inter-American economic agreement to parallel the Inter-American Treaty of Reciprocal Assistance of 1947 and the American Treaty on Pacific Settlement of 1948. (The Economic Agreement of Bogotá, concluded in 1948, had remained a dead letter for lack of ratifications.) On a draft agreement of forty-five articles, the United States was compelled to make nineteen separate reservations. Other reservations were offered by Mexico, Uruguay, and Chile.

Anxious to avoid a complete debacle, the Argentine president of the conference exerted himself with other delegation heads to draft a statement of broad economic principles to which all delegations could subscribe. The resultant "Economic Declaration of Buenos Aires," adopted unanimously on September 2,[14] compromised the major doctrinal differences by calling among other things for "consultations" or other cooperative arrangements on raw material prices and surplus disposal, and for intensified efforts to expand both public and private investment. The matter of a general economic agreement was unanimously handed on to the Council of the Organization of American States, and the conference concluded by adopting forty-three other economic resolutions, of which the United States found it necessary to oppose only the one envisaging compensatory credits for raw material producers.[15]

Although a Uruguayan statesman suggested that these transactions had produced nothing better than a 10 percent increase in the anthology of inter-American resolutions, United States authorities took a much more favorable view. Deputy Under-Secretary of State C. Douglas Dillon, the acting chairman of the United States delegation, declared that the conference had reached an "unprecedented" measure of agreement, marked "a new high point in hemispheric unity," and "added . . . another important block to the great Pan American edifice." President Eisenhower hailed the Declaration of Buenos Aires (September 4) as "an outstanding statement of the principles and objectives of inter-American economic cooperation." Secretary Dulles admitted at his September 10 news conference that not all the participants at Buenos Aires had obtained everything they wanted, but felt that the net effect of the conference would be "to orient our economic policies in this hemisphere along lines which will be in the general interests of us all." Without joining any exclusive grouping, he predicted, Washington would in future display "a greater concern for the interests of these countries in maintaining a reasonable and fair market in the United States," together with "a greater effort than ever before to try to maintain good neighborly trade relations with the countries of this hemisphere."

One other noteworthy development at Buenos Aires had been a tentative decision in favor of establishing a regional Latin American market analogous to the prospective European Common Market, a project which had intrigued and to some extent alarmed those Latin American countries that were interested in European trade or feared "Eurafrican" competition. Like the plans for regional integration in Central America, this decision could be interpreted as a sign that Latin American governments were beginning to think more in terms of self-help and less in terms of waiting for United States actions that Washington was plainly unwilling to take. A similar indication was the decision of seven Latin American coffee-producing countries (Mexico

City, October 21) to make a fresh attempt at price stabilization independently of the United States; still another, the announcement that Venezuela was planning to employ some of its oil revenues in undertaking its own financial and technical assistance program in Latin America. Various Latin American governments, meanwhile, were showing increased interest in forming closer economic and even political ties with Western European countries. Concurrently, some United States observers reported an increased readiness to welcome private capital in lieu of the public loans which were clearly not to be forthcoming on the desired scale.

One way or another, economic development and growth in Latin America were plainly destined to go forward with increasing momentum. For those engaged in it, it was an exhilarating process. "We look forward with a sense of real excitement to the next decade in Latin American business and to the years which will follow," declared the United States business executive already quoted: [16]

"Naturally we want to earn more and more for our stockholders every year, but at the same time I must say there is a special thrill in working with the men who are building the new Latin America. . . . We are welding together a community in the Western Hemisphere which can stand unafraid before the world as proof that individual enterprise, common decency and a sense of the dignity of man can prevail against all comers. . . . We have an opportunity in this hemisphere of proving to the rest of the politically agitated world that individual initiative working in a free society can reap a happier and more prosperous life for all of us. If we meet this challenge successfully—and I am sure that we will—we will have made a decisive contribution not only to the welfare and security of the peoples of the Americas but to the cause of world peace as well."

22. THE UNITED STATES AND CANADA

What was said so eloquently of Latin America could be said with at least equal emphasis of the developing relationship between the United States and Canada, a country with less than one-tenth of Latin America's aggregate population but with an area, a strategic situation, a natural endowment, a level of individual achievement, and a role in hemisphere and world affairs which challenged comparison with and in some respects overshadowed that of the twenty Latin American republics. The unique importance of Canada to the United States, and of the United States to Canada, was so self-evident that statesmen on both sides must occasionally have grown tired of calling attention to it. "When they differ and are divided, the whole free world is in trouble," said Canada's long-time Secretary of State for External Affairs, Lester B. Pearson, on March 11 "—and Canada, I assure you, is in special trouble." President Eisenhower sounded the same note in his press conference of April 10:

"Canada and ourselves are linked so closely, not only geographically, but by friendship and philosophy and beliefs and convictions and, indeed, by common facing of common problems of the most serious nature, that I think it is a particularly unfortunate thing when any occurrence tends to break down the closeness of our relations. . . . I think all of us should do our very best to restore . . . the fine, firm character of our relationships with Canada just as rapidly as we can."

The emphasis of both these statements on the element of disagreement that sometimes intruded upon the historic friendship of the North American powers was significant and by no means accidental. In the midst of a collaboration as intimate as that between members of a private family, Canada and the United States were going through a period of mutual tension not unlike those that sometimes arise in family life—and which are often the more disturbing because, despite their mutual dissatisfaction, the parties remain fully conscious of their permanent need for each other. It is true that in this instance the dissatisfaction could not be considered entirely mutual. Most Americans who thought about the matter felt nothing but good will for Canada—good will plus a kind of vicarious pride in Canada's rapid material development and its increasing, if superficial, resemblance to the United States. Canadians were rather more sensitive. They were inclined to resent the easy assumption that being a Canadian was the next best thing to being an American.

In addition, they had a whole string of practical grievances of which most Americans were blissfully unconscious but which, in Canadian eyes, detracted substantially from the value of the relationship.

One result of this feeling, as Mr. Pearson pointed out in the address just quoted, was a popular tendency in some Canadian quarters "to pull at the tail-feathers of the American [eagle]—a pastime which has replaced that of twisting the lion's tail." In the opinion of most political observers, dissatisfaction over the state of Canadian-American relations was a factor of some importance in the unexpected result of Canada's general election on June 10, which brought twenty-two years of Liberal party government to a sudden close and paved the way for a Conservative administration headed by John Diefenbaker, the newly designated Conservative party leader. Although Mr. Pearson and his colleagues in the outgoing administration of Prime Minister Louis St. Laurent could certainly not have been accused of subservience to the United States, the Conservatives had given the impression that they would put rather less emphasis on Canada's North American ties and proportionately more on its relationship with Great Britain and the Commonwealth. The actions of the Diefenbaker government during the second half of the year were plainly motivated by this intention, although for practical purposes the changes in Canada's orientation did not appear particularly far-reaching. Mr. Diefenbaker and Sidney E. Smith, the new Secretary of State for External Affairs, were too well aware of the many common interests uniting the two North American countries to think in terms of any radical shift, despite their unconcealed hope that the United States could be persuaded to modify its behavior in important respects.

For many Canadians, the episode which had crystallized their dissatisfaction with current United States attitudes and provided an outlet for accumulated grievances was the publication by the Internal Security Subcommittee of the United States Senate of certain testimony charging that a Canadian diplomat, E. Herbert Norman, currently Canadian Ambassador to Egypt, was a Communist. Similar allegations which had come to the attention of the Canadian Government in the past had been officially investigated and found to be without foundation, although it was subsequently admitted that the Ambassador had associated with Communists and other questionable persons in his student days. But the renewed currency given the charges by the Senate committee in its release of March 14 was widely regarded as an intrusion into Canadian internal affairs, and the smoldering anger of Canadians burst into flames when Norman committed suicide in Cairo on April 4. An official note of protest to the United States, dispatched under strong public pressure on April 10, described the Senate committee's procedures as "difficult to understand, unfair and indeed intolerable." Canada, it said, might have to discontinue its long-standing exchange of security information with the United States unless the latter could give assurances that it would not fall into the hands of "persons who might use it without any sense of responsibility or fairness, or regard for the rights of Canadian citizens." The State Department, being without control over the actions of congressional committees, could only assure the Canadians after a long delay that their views were taken seriously by the executive branch.[17] Such an answer could not undo the effects of an explosion of adverse Canadian sentiment which had been hardly if at all less intense than that provoked by the Girard case in Japan.

But it was in the economic field that Canadian dissatisfaction with the United States habitually centered, naturally enough in view of the extraordinarily close interrelationship of the two economies. Many Canadian grievances were the direct result of an economic interdependence which had few parallels in the contemporary world and none on any comparable scale. Almost three-fourths of Canada's imports came from the United States; sixty percent of its exports went to this country. Of a total foreign investment in Canada which was estimated in mid-1957 at $15.4 billion, no less than $11.7 billion represented American capital, compared to $2.7 billion of British and $1.1 billion of other foreign investment. Canada, in turn, had an investment in the United States which was valued at some $7 billion. During the past decade,

United States capital had been flowing into Canada at the rate of approximately $1 billion a year or nearly $3 million a day.

This tide of new investment from across the frontier had played an important part in the steady growth of Canada's national product, which by 1956 had attained a total just short of $30 billion. But it was also a source of uneasiness to many Canadians who noted that most of it took the form of American enterprise, staffed by American personnel and managed by American executives. Prime Minister Diefenbaker, in a speech at Dartmouth College on September 7,[18] noted that 60 percent of Canada's main manufacturing industries and a still larger proportion of its mine and oil production were owned and controlled by United States interests, and that only one in four of the American-controlled concerns operating in Canada offered stock to Canadian shareholders. There was, he said, "an intangible sense of disquiet in Canada over the political implications of large-scale and continuing external ownership and control of Canadian industries."

Even more disturbing to Canada in some respects was the serious and growing imbalance that characterized its yearly trade with its southern neighbor. Year after year, Canada had been unable to sell to the United States as much as it bought from this country; and, since so large a proportion of its trade was with the United States, it faced a chronic deficit in its over-all balance of payments as well. In 1956 it incurred a record deficit of $1,290 million in trade with the United States and an over-all deficit of $849 million; in the first six months of 1957 its deficit with the United States reached $1,003 million, compared with $941 million in the first half of 1956. Though much of this import surplus represented capital goods which would add to Canada's export capacity in future years, Canadians felt that they would prefer a more equal relationship now. They were especially sensitive to any moves by the United States which tended further to restrict their export trade, either by limiting their access to the United States market through tariff or quota restrictions or by cutting into their markets overseas. Canada deserved a fairer share of world trade, said Mr. Diefenbaker in his Dartmouth speech; at present its economy was "altogether too vulnerable to sudden changes in trading policy at Washington."

Agricultural products represented approximately one-fourth of Canada's total exports, and it was here above all that Canadian objectives clashed head-on with those of the United States. Canadian farmers, like their American counterparts, had been producing considerably more grain and other agricultural products than could readily be sold; indeed, production of wheat and other grains in Canada exceeded domestic requirements by a much greater margin than in the United States. Unlike the United States, however, Canada had not thus far resorted to unorthodox disposal methods aimed at checking the growth of its agricultural surpluses, and it viewed with a particularly unfavorable eye the various expedients by which the United States in the past two or three years had managed to boost its agricultural exports and even effect some reduction in the national surplus. During the fiscal year 1957, while American wheat exports were increasing by 60 percent, Canada's were declining by 15 percent. Many were the scathing references made by Canadian officials to American "fire sales" and "giveaway" techniques. In Ottawa's eyes, American surplus deals such as the one with Poland (section 10) were cutting directly into Canadian markets and depriving Canada of legitimate export opportunities. True, many of the American sales were made for local currencies in lieu of dollars; but the long-term purchase agreements which were often a feature of such transactions were regarded by the Canadians as a direct violation of the General Agreement on Tariffs and Trade. Their complaints, moreover, were not directed only to Washington but were heard at all international gatherings concerned with agricultural and trade matters.

These were among the reasons why Premier Diefenbaker soon after assuming office voiced a strong determination to establish closer economic ties with the countries of the British Commonwealth. In London for a meeting of Commonwealth Prime Ministers at the beginning of July, he indicated that he would like to see about 15 percent of Canada's imports from the United States coming from Great Britain instead—a shift which, he felt, would strengthen the British market for Canadian goods without damaging Canadian trade with the United States. Anxious to promote trade with other Commonwealth countries as well, Mr. Diefenbaker urged his fellow Prime Ministers to schedule a full Commonwealth Economic Conference to be held sometime in 1959. In the meantime it was agreed that the next regular annual meeting of Commonwealth Finance Ministers would be held in Canada rather than in London. Mr. Diefenbaker's proposals were the main subject of discussion when the Finance Ministers assembled at Mont Tremblant, Quebec, at the end of September, but no action was taken upon them beyond deciding that they should be further considered by the heads of the Commonwealth governments in 1958.

While Canada prepared to underline its Commonwealth allegiance in connection with the ceremonial opening of Parliament by Queen Elizabeth II on October 14, economic and financial relations with the United States were also brought under review at one of the infrequent sessions of the Joint United States-Canadian Committee on Trade and Economic Affairs. Held in Washington on October 7-8, this confrontation of the new Canadian Ministers of Finance, External Affairs, Agriculture, and Trade and Commerce with their American opposites afforded a useful opportunity to get acquainted in what the official communiqué [19] described as "an atmosphere of cordiality and neighborliness." Aside from an informal assurance that the Canadians were not contemplating any drastic reorientation of their foreign commerce, the meeting produced little beyond a restatement of official positions on both sides and an agreement that both countries had "a deep and continuing interest in each other's economic stability and strength." In reply to Canadian complaints about the effects of some United States commercial policies, the American representatives cited "the dependability of the U.S. economy both as a market and as a supply source." They also pointed out that "the great confidence

A NEW BORDER

By Scott for NEA Service, Inc.

which United States business feels toward Canada is the result of many years of experience and association."

Platitudinous though they might seem, these considerations were by no means without significance in the over-all picture. As in the case of Latin America, there were certain matters on which the governments concerned did not and perhaps never would see eye to eye. The essential point was, however, that their citizens were engaged together on a great enterprise of continental development and, in spite of some friction and mutual dissatisfaction, were producing results that might well endure for generations.

The only serious reason for questioning their permanence, indeed, was Khrushchev's frequent reminder that the Soviet Union had (or would soon have) "rocket weapons" with thermonuclear warheads capable of hitting any target in the world. If the East-West tension should one day seek release in major hostilities, Canada's cities and industries would be no less exposed than those of the United States. The growing vulnerability of the North American continent as a whole had been a subject of mounting preoccupation in both Ottawa and Washington, and was largely responsible for a decision, long in preparation and finally announced August 1,[20] to set up "a system of integrated operational control of the air defense forces in the Continental United States, Alaska and Canada" under an integrated command, to be established in Colorado Springs with an American chief of staff and a Canadian deputy. In the meantime the continental warning system on whose construction the two governments had been cooperating for several years became essentially complete as both the Mid-Canada radar line and the Distant Early Warning (DEW) Line were placed in full operation.

Somewhat ironically, this elaborate continental defense setup, described by President Eisenhower (November 7) as "a complex system of early-warning radars, communication lines, electronic computers, supersonic aircraft, and ground-to-air missiles, some with atomic warheads," had been designed for protection against relatively slow-moving manned bombers rather than against the high-speed ballistic missiles which the U.S.S.R. now claimed to have available. Even against the manned bomber the system had its limitations, as President Eisenhower frankly admitted. "No defensive system today," he said, "can possibly be airtight in preventing all breakthroughs of planes and weapons."

Canadians, like most Americans, naturally found this situation somewhat alarming, particularly after the launching of the two Sputniks in October and November provided concrete evidence of Soviet advances in rocketry. Preoccupation with the Soviet missile threat undoubtedly stimulated Canadian interest in the possibility of new East-West negotiations, an interest voiced on several occasions both by Mr. Pearson and by his successor at the External Affairs Department. Canada, Secretary Smith intimated on December 3, did not entirely share the negative view of the United States regarding the possibilities of fruitful negotiation with the U.S.S.R. "It is not the view of the Canadian Government that we should always say 'no or nyet' to a Russian proposal." This statement, and similar ones made in connection with the NATO heads-of-government conference in Paris (section 28), did not denote any weakening in Canada's steadfast attitude on the essentials of East-West relations. It did suggest a measure of restiveness which the United States would increasingly have to take into account in its international relations, not only in Canada but in all countries within range of Soviet missile attack.

The more routine aspects of Canadian-American relations —questions of boundary waters, river development, energy sources, fisheries, and the like—raised their share of problems during 1957 and seemed likely to claim increased attention in years to come. For the moment, public interest was largely focused on the progress of the St. Lawrence Seaway, construction of which was now in full swing, with every prospect that a navigable waterway from the Great Lakes to the Atlantic would be in use in 1959. Although Congress in authorizing United States participation in the seaway project had stipulated that the tolls on shipping must be set high enough to amortize the cost over a fifty-year period, many Canadians and some Americans were now urging that tolls be reduced or eliminated altogether in order to encourage traffic. However this question might be resolved, few doubted that a growing proportion of the trade of the American Middle West would henceforth be following a new all-water route, a part of which ran entirely through Canadian territory and hence would not be under direct American control.[21] This was a striking example of the way in which the United States, in common with most other Western nations, was gradually adjusting itself to the realities of interdependence as it strove to confront the varied challenges of the nuclear age. With no nation could it more readily and more confidently have acknowledged its interdependence than with Canada.

Notes to Chapter VI

1. Quoted in *New York Times,* November 19, 1957.

2. Galo Plaza, "Latin American Development and United States Industry," *Vital Speeches of the Day,* v. 24, no. 1 (October 15, 1957), p. 20.

3. *New York Times,* November 21, 1957.

4. *Ibid.,* July 9, 1957.

5. *Department of State Bulletin,* v. 36 (February 25, 1957), pp. 316-317; *Documents on American Foreign Relations, 1957,* no. 141.

6. *Department of State Bulletin,* v. 36 (February 11, 1957), p. 221; (April 15, 1957), pp. 610-611; (June 24, 1957), pp. 1025-1028; v. 37 (July 22, 1957), p. 144.

7. Broadcast address, June 30, 1954, in *Documents on American Foreign Relations, 1954,* p. 419.

8. *Ibid., 1956,* pp. 429-430.

9. Galo Plaza, *loc. cit.,* p. 21.

10. Samuel Pizer and Frederick Cutler, "The Role of U.S. Investments in the Latin American Economy," *Survey of Current Business,* v. 37, no. 1 (January 1957), pp. 6-15, 24. For further details see *U.S. Investments in the Latin American Economy* (Washington: G.P.O., 1957).

11. J. Peter Grace, "Latin America: A Challenge to American Business," *Vital Speeches of the Day,* v. 24, no. 1 (October 15, 1957), p. 23.

12. *Report to the Chiefs of State of the American Republics* (Washington: Inter-American Committee of Presidential Representatives, 1957); official summary in *Department of State Bulletin,* v. 36 (June 24, 1957), pp. 1014-1016; *Documents on American Foreign Relations, 1957,* no. 135.

13. *Department of State Bulletin,* v. 37 (September 16, 1957), pp. 463-469; *Documents on American Foreign Relations, 1957,* no. 136.

14. *Ibid.,* no. 137.

15. *Economic Conference of the Organization of American States, Buenos Aires, Argentina, August 15-September 4, 1957: Final Act* (Washington: Pan American Union, 1957).

16. Grace, *loc. cit.,* pp. 23-24.

17. For the diplomatic exchanges between Ottawa and Washington see *Department of State Bulletin*, v. 36 (April 29, 1957), pp. 694-695; v. 37 (September 2, 1957), pp. 384-386.

18. *External Affairs*, v. 9, no. 9 (September 1957), pp. 274-276.

19. *Department of State Bulletin*, v. 37 (October 28, 1957), pp. 683-684; *Documents on American Foreign Relations, 1957*, no. 134.

20. *Department of State Bulletin*, v. 37 (August 17, 1957), p. 306; *Documents on American Foreign Relations, 1957*, no. 133.

21. Cf. Marvin J. Barloon, "The Coming Battle of the St. Lawrence," *Harper's Magazine*, v. 215 (September 1957), p. 35.

CHAPTER SEVEN

THE SPACE AGE BEGINS

WORLD HISTORY in the period since World War II may some day be visualized in rather different terms from those traditionally employed in such volumes as this. In our time-honored preoccupation with the actions of the hundred or so national communities that have come to occupy the surface of our planet, we may today exaggerate the importance of conventional international political and military developments and give insufficient weight to those trends that are so rapidly expanding man's intellectual and physical horizons and altering some of the most fundamental presuppositions that have governed his earthly existence during the past 500,000 years. For us the great political movements of the past generation—the rise and fall of fascist totalitarianism, the reawakening of former subject peoples, the clash of Soviet Communism with the traditional principles of free society—still represent the essential content of our era; and from many points of view we are undoubtedly right. The nature of man, the needs and aberrations of the human personality, still constitute the stuff of history and will continue to do so even if the scene of man's activities should cease to be limited essentially by the earth's atmosphere. Yet even the man-made earth satellites which began to flash around the planet during the latter part of 1957 inevitably threw the political relationships of the nations below into a new perspective. Like the Asian influenza which also circled the globe in 1957 with minimal respect for political boundaries, the two Soviet "Sputniks" offered a striking reminder that the 2.75 billion people who constitute present-day humanity were after all living in the same world even if their family quarrels had sometimes caused them to lose sight of the fact.

For the moment there was no indication that this first step into outer space would bring with it any tempering of political rivalries back on earth. On the contrary, the behavior of the governments most directly concerned indicated that the rivalry between East and West would if anything be intensified and projected outward into space as rapidly as means of doing so could be devised. This startling achievement of Soviet science—for it was the U.S.S.R. that first conquered the scientific and technological problems involved—was treated on both sides essentially as a "cold war" development, as something to be evaluated primarily in terms of its effect on the ideological and power struggle already going on between them.

Nominally undertaken in connection with the Soviet Union's participation in the International Geophysical Year 1957–1958 (an epoch-making series of world-wide scientific observations which involved the participation of sixty-four nations and had been hailed by President Eisenhower as a "demonstration of the ability of peoples of all nations to work together harmoniously for the common good"), the launching of Sputnik I on October 4 was seized upon by Soviet propaganda as proof of the superiority of the Soviet system—a typical product of "the freed and conscious labor of the people of the new socialist society." Had the United States been the first country to launch earth satellites, as it had publicly undertaken to do as far back as 1955, it is probable that the Voice of America would have made similar use of so exceptional an opportunity. As things stood, American spokesmen could offer only a denial that this country had been engaged in any kind of "race" with the U.S.S.R. Their explantations of the budgetary and administrative considerations which had prevented more rapid progress on the American satellite program were reasonable but not wholly satisfactory either to the American or to the foreign audience. They could not obscure the fact that the Soviet Union had "stolen a march" on the world's hitherto acknowledged technological leader and in so doing had won an important psychological victory in the eyes of the international public.

The advantages accruing to the U.S.S.R. from the launching of Sputnik I, followed on November 3 by the half-ton, dog-bearing Sputnik II, were not confined to the psychological arena. These two "stars of peace," as Khrushchev called them, could only have been placed in orbit by some kind of powerful rocket with a thrust comparable to that of an intercontinental ballistic missile. Indeed, the U.S.S.R. had claimed as early as August 26 that it had actually carried out a successful test of a "super-long distance intercontinental ballistic rocket"—and despite expressions of official skepticism in Washington, there were unofficial reports that several such tests had been carried out in recent months under the observation of United States monitors stationed in Turkey. On October 19 the Soviet magazine *New Times* asserted as a fact that Sputnik I had been launched by an intercontinental ballistic missile, the forward compartment of which, it said, could also be used to accommodate an atomic or thermonuclear warhead. The successful test of "a mighty hydrogen warhead of a new design" had already been announced in Moscow on October 7; and on November 4 it was asserted in connection with the launching of Sputnik II that the U.S.S.R. had developed "new and improved instruments and sources of power" representing a "solid mastering of a new branch of science and engineering." Whatever the truth of these assertions, they were made at a time when the United States had not yet perfected either a long-range ballistic missile or an intermediate-range one such as it had already undertaken to supply to the United Kingdom (section 8).

Despite the evidence of the Sputniks, United States authorities were not prepared to accept all Soviet claims at face value or to leap to the conclusion that the military balance of power had been upset. They were not sure the Russians had solved the critical problem of preventing a ballistic missile from burning up or exploding on reentering the earth's atmosphere after its flight through space. They vigorously disputed Soviet assertions that manned aircraft and strategic air forces had become obsolete because of their slowness and vulnerability. Secretary Dulles on October 16 expressed the unchanged opinion that "we have in terms of actual military power, and potential military power, for some years to come, a very marked superiority . . ., particularly in terms of heavy bombers, which are now, and for some years to come will be, the preferred and most effective means for the delivery of missiles." One B-52 bomber, President Eisenhower pointed out on November 7, "can carry as much destructive capacity as was delivered by all the bombers in all the years of World War II combined." Revealing that the United States had already solved the "reentry problem" for ballistic missiles, the President voiced his conviction "that, although the Soviets are quite likely ahead in some missile and special areas and are obviously ahead of us in satellite development, as of today the overall military strength of the free world is distinctly greater than that of the Communist countries." Yet Khrushchev persisted in taking a contrary view. "We have already won over you," he told William Randolph Hearst, Jr. on November 24. "We have the absolute weapon."

Whether or not the Russians by their new achievements had impaired the balance of military power in the world, they had undoubtedly contrived to introduce important new elements into the international situation and had thereby modified the international atmosphere decidedly to their advantage. Throughout the remainder of 1957 the Kremlin unmistakably felt itself to be on the offensive both politically and diplomatically. Moreover, it gave the impression of being willing to take considerably increased risks in pursuit of its objectives, despite Khrushchev's repeated admission that war would be a disaster for everyone concerned. Although the party secretary was still deeply engaged in the attempt to solidify his power at home, the exigencies of Communist internal politics seem if anything to have accentuated the intransigence of Soviet policy internationally. A new obstinacy made itself felt in the resumed debate on disarmament at the United Nations General Assembly, where the Soviet Union flatly refused to continue the discussion on the terms it had appeared to find reasonable a few month earlier. In the Middle East, Khrushchev seems to have deliberately fo-

mented a new international crisis, centering around the relations between Syria and Turkey, which remained at a
point of dangerous intensity for several weeks—though after
the sudden ouster of Marshal Zhukov from the Soviet leadership at the beginning of November, Moscow appeared content to continue its attempts to penetrate the Arab countries
by more conventional means. Khrushchev's confidence in the
possibility of bringing about the victory of "socialism"
through "peaceful competition," rather than through war,
was to be strongly reemphasized at the Moscow celebrations
of the fortieth anniversary of the Bolshevik Revolution, at
which "peace" and "peaceful coexistence" were formally reestablished as the keynote of Communist efforts throughout
the world.

If the U.S.S.R. considered itself to be on the offensive during these weeks, the behavior of the Western nations left
no doubt that they had suffered a grievous shock and viewed
their present and prospective situation with grave misgivings.
Not only had popular confidence in America's military and
technological preeminence been badly shaken. The Western
community was also beset by a host of more familiar problems which had been building up through the spring and
summer and now began to look more formidable than ever.
A leveling off in the economic upsurge of recent years had
created widespread budgetary and balance-of-payments difficulties and confronted the free world nations with a prospect of economic recession. The renewal of United Nations
debate on Algeria and on "non-self-governing" territories
signaled an intensification of the "anticolonial" movement
in many parts of the world, accompanied by new differences
among the Western powers and particularly between France
and its closest allies. With the status of the NATO "shield
force" becoming more problematical than ever, there developed a considerable reluctance to antagonize the Soviet
Union by installing missile bases in continental Western
Europe as urged by the United States. Measures approved by
the NATO heads of government at their extraordinary meeting in Paris in December might help to remedy some of the

most obvious defects in NATO's competitive position vis-à-vis
the Communist world, but would leave in doubt the capacity
and willingness of the Western community as a whole to meet
the combined military, technological, political, and economic
challenge posed by the Communist bloc. Deeply though the
latter might still be rent by concealed weaknesses, the weaknesses of the West had been placed on view before the entire
world and were not unobserved by those "uncommitted"
nations which were still waiting to see which of the two
groups would dominate the future.

This chapter attempts to survey the manifold developments of the opening "space age" in six main subdivisions.
Section 23 is concerned with major events and trends in the
Soviet Union and the world Communist movement. Their
repercussions in the diplomacy of the East-West struggle
are examined in section 24, with particular reference to developments in the General Assembly of the United Nations.
The General Assembly is also the main focus of sections 25,
26, and 27, dealing respectively with the problems of the
Middle East, with the ups and downs of the independence
movement in non-self-governing territories, and with economic and social matters of international concern. Section
28 chronicles the American and Western response to these
developments, primarily in terms of prospects for recovery
of the initiative which the Western nations had at least
temporarily lost to the Soviet Union.

23. COMMUNISM IN NEW DIMENSIONS

There can be no doubt that the successful launching of
history's first artificial earth satellite on October 4 was one
of the most significant triumphs achieved by the Soviet
Union and international Communism since the seizure of
power in Russia by the Bolsheviks in 1917. Moscow's boasts
of scientific and technical accomplishment had so often been
exaggerated or downright mendacious that the West had
become accustomed to discount such evidence as might have
shown it that Soviet technology and engineering were not

without independent merit. All the more devastating was this sudden and indisputable success in a field in which the United States, for whatever reasons, had not yet even begun active operations, and in which its immediate plans fell far short of what the U.S.S.R. had already accomplished. Subsequent developments, including the launching of Sputnik II on November 3 and the failure of the American attempt to send up a much smaller experimental satellite on December 6 (Project Vanguard), deepened the world-wide impression that the United States and the West had suffered a major technological and psychological defeat. But even Sputnik I had sufficed to call in question the Western contention that regimented, totalitarian societies were incapable of matching the scientific and technological achievements of free nations. Such a demonstration could hardly fail to influence the thinking of a world public which for years had been encouraged to judge the rival systems by their material accomplishments rather than by their ethical qualities. Whatever international disrepute Moscow still suffered as the result of its performance in Hungary the year before was amply compensated by the awed respect with which people in every country now bent their ears to the "beep-beep" of man's first emissary to outer space.

Accompanied as it was by other discosures implying significant advances in the field of nuclear weapons and delivery systems, this psychological triumph considerably strengthened the Soviet Union's over-all diplomatic position and opened up tempting prospects for further exploitation of the major foreign policy lines it had employed during the past year or more. Taking advantage of what seemed to be a clear-cut, though possibly temporary, superiority in the field of military missiles, Moscow was now in a position to espouse a "tough" foreign policy and, if it chose, to renew and intensify the "ballistic blackmail" tactics it had employed against Britain and France during the Suez crisis. On future occasions it might not omit to threaten the United States itself, whose territory was now explicity claimed to lie within range of Soviet rocket weapons. As an alternative, the Kremlin could emphasize the "peaceful" character of the latest Soviet achievements and accentuate the propaganda of "peaceful coexistence" and popular aspirations, thus perhaps gaining new converts in Asian and African countries and possibly among disaffected elements in the West as well. To many observers a glimpse of Sputnik I or its accompanying rocket would offer powerful substantiation of the Soviet claim that humanity's future lay with the "camp of socialism."

As matters turned out, Soviet foreign policy—embodied in these weeks to an unprecedented degree in the person of party secretary Khrushchev—made effective use of both methods. "Peaceful coexistence, or else"—such was the burden of Khrushchev's song, repeated in almost daily interviews, speeches, and informal comments at diplomatic receptions. His interview with James Reston of the *New York Times* on October 7 [1] established the pattern and illustrated the technique. Communism, Khrushchev declared, was "the most humane ideology in the world." The Soviet Union continued, as always, to support peaceful coexistence between states with different social systems—not because it was weak or fearful, but because it preferred to spare humanity the horrors of a nuclear war and because, moreover, it was confident of its own ultimate success in the peaceful competition between the two systems.

". . . We proceed from the premise that wars are not necessary for the victory of socialism. We are convinced that in the present competition of socialism and capitalism, victory will be on the side of socialism, while capitalism will inevitably vanish from the historical arena. . . ."

In substantiation of Moscow's peaceful intentions, Khrushchev declared that the Soviet Union was prepared immediately to sign with President Eisenhower "an agreement . . . acceptable to both sides and in the interests of world peace." "Let us create conditions in which people can really sleep peacefully," he urged.

But Khrushchev on this and other occasions also con-

MOSCOW'S NEW FOREIGN POLICY MAKER?

By Carmack in *The Christian Science Monitor*

tended with some emphasis that if the United States desired
to improve relations with the U.S.S.R., it would have to
change its international policy in various fundamental respects. It would have to stop confronting Moscow with proposals that it knew in advance were unacceptable. It would
have to give up the idea that the "socialist system" was going
to disintegrate as the result of internal revolutionary forces.
It would have to recognize the "historical fact" that the
Soviet Union, China, and other countries existed as "socialist states" which would not tolerate any interference in
their affairs. Furthermore—and here Khrushchev's observations took on an unmistakably menacing tone—it would
have to modify its current policies in such areas as the
Middle East; in particular, it would have to desist from what
he chose to describe as a deliberate attempt to organize a
military attack on Syria by Turkey. "We would not be justified in ignoring the fact that of late the world has once
again become overshadowed by the danger of a new war," he
said ominously. ". . . If Turkey starts hostilities against
Syria this can lead to very grave consequences. . . . This spark
can set off a great war conflagration." In such an event,
Khrushchev implied, the U.S.S.R. would not lack adequate
means of defense. "I think I will not be revealing any military secret if I tell you that we now have all the rockets we
need: long-range rockets, intermediate-range rockets and close-
range rockets." According to Mr. Reston's recollection he
further declared that "if war broke out, we are near Turkey
and you are not. When the guns begin to fire, the rockets
can begin flying and then it will be too late to think about
it."

Although Khrushchev insisted that he was only stating
facts and in no way seeking "to intimidate anyone or exert
political pressure on the public," intimidation and pressure
seemed in reality to be an essential constituent of his new
strategy. On the one hand, he continued to support the fundamental policy of "peaceful coexistence" as the most promising route to Moscow's long-term objective of universal Communism. On the other hand, he not only invoked the Soviet
Union's recent military gains as a broad new argument for

"peaceful coexistence" on terms favorable to the U.S.S.R.; he also appeared quite ready to use the threat of rocket attacks as a means of pursuing specific foreign policy objectives. These threats were not confined to the Reston interview but were to be repeated on a number of formal and informal occasions, notably in a series of letters on the Middle Eastern crisis addressed to socialist party organizations in Western Europe. (See further section 25.) Mr. Reston gained the impression that Khrushchev, being dependent on Soviet intelligence sources, might actually believe his seemingly irresponsible charges about American machinations against Syria. Whether he believed them or not, it was disquieting to see him falling back once again on the same kind of threats that had been used against Britain and France in the Suez crisis. The disagreeable impression made by his remarks was not greatly mitigated by the fact that Soviet diplomacy and propaganda on other levels continued to push the cause of "peaceful coexistence" just as if no war cries were resounding at the top.

To most experienced observers it seemed probable that the extraordinary war scare which Moscow thus fomented (and managed to keep alive through most of the interval between Sputnik I and Sputnik II) must somehow be related to Soviet internal developments. Plainly, this first-round victory in the space race had not cured all the internal problems of the Soviet Union or the Soviet bloc. There were some, including Secretary Dulles, who believed the technological effort involved might even have aggravated them by further unbalancing the Soviet economy and intensifying the internal strains which had been so evident a few months earlier. Despite the readjustments effected by Khrushchev, it was by now quite evident that the Soviet Union would not be in a position to carry out the grandiose five-year plan for 1956–60 which had been announced with such fanfare at the Twentieth Party Congress. On September 25, nine days before Sputnik I went into orbit, the party and government had announced that the Sixth Five-Year Plan would be scrapped at the end of 1958 and replaced by a Seven-Year Plan for the period 1959–65. Ostensibly necessitated by the recent decentralization of industrial management, the discovery of new raw material and electric power sources, and a new program for the development of plastics and synthetic fibers, this radical shift was viewed by Western analysts as a confirmation of their suspicion that the Five-Year Plan goals had proved unattainable. While preserving the traditional priority accorded to heavy industry, the new plan also promised "a further rise in the material and cultural standards of the people," with emphasis on Khrushchev's aim of overtaking the United States "in the next few years" in per capita production of meat, butter, and milk.

It was only a little over four months since Khrushchev in his speech of May 22 had first elevated milk, butter, and meat to the status of a new front in the East-West competition. At that time he himself had been fighting a sharp internal battle against the Malenkov-Molotov-Kaganovich group within the Soviet leadership. Now, thanks largely to the support provided by Marshal Zhukov at the critical moment, his foes were routed and Khrushchev was firmly in command of the party and governmental apparatus. Or so it seemed. Perhaps, however, he had only been brought face to face with the fatal dilemma of all dictators: as each group of opponents was eliminated, others loomed as potential sources of opposition. In addition, Khrushchev had still to contend with the special problems inherent in the policy of "destalinization" and internal liberalization in Soviet affairs, a process that was perpetually threatening to get out of control and lead to consequences that would undermine the basis of his authority. During the spring and summer the party secretary had moved strongly to reassert party control in the arts and intellectual life. But there were other problems still unsolved —among them, apparently, the question of party authority over the armed forces. This was an issue as old as the Soviet Union itself, one that had normally found Marshal Zhukov, the dyed-in-the-wool professional soldier, holding out for the autonomy of the defense establishment and strongly resisting interference by party representatives.

Whether this was a basic issue between Zhukov and Khrushchev or merely a cover for rivalries of a more fundamental kind, the Soviet Union's chief military hero was now compelled to vacate the high position into which he had been gradually working himself ever since the death of Stalin. Returning on October 26 from a visit to Yugoslavia and Albania (in the course of which he had delivered a number of highly bellicose talks on the Middle Eastern crisis), Zhukov was informed that he was being relieved forthwith as Minister of Defense and replaced by Marshal Rodion Y. Malinovsky. Amid widespread speculation that Zhukov would be elevated to some high honorific post, there followed a plenary meeting of the party Central Committee and, on November 2, the terse announcement that the Marshal had also been removed from his party positions and would be assigned to other work of an undisclosed but apparently undistinguished nature. Zhukov himself, it was stated, had admitted the truth of the main charges brought against him: attempted curtailment of the work of party organs and abolition of party control of the armed forces; encouragement of his own "cult of personality," carried on with the help of sycophants and flatterers; and a tendency to "adventurism" in both foreign policy and defense matters. Presumably Zhukov did *not* concur in the assertion of some of his military colleagues that he was also a bad general.

Three days after Zhukov's dismissal as Defense Minister, on October 29, Khrushchev unexpectedly turned up at a Turkish Embassy reception with the welcome news that chances for peace in the Middle East had improved. The coincidence was too remarkable to be overlooked, though it failed to settle the question whether the late war scare had been partly of Zhukov's making (as Khrushchev apparently sought to suggest) or had been deliberately contrived as part of the move against him. In either case, the notion that a major international crisis could develop as an adjunct to a power struggle in Moscow was not particularly reassuring to the West, especially since there was no assurance that the power struggle had come to an end. On a superficial view, Khrushchev had now successfully eliminated the last independently powerful figure who could conceivably challenge his authority. Yet Malinovsky and his military associates might in the long run prove no more tractable that Zhukov— who, moreover, was still alive, though not in the public eye. There were also certain members of the party inner circle who might have to be watched more carefully now that Zhukov was not there to protect the party secretary in a crisis. One version had it that Khrushchev had not really intended to demolish the Marshal completely but had acted under pressure from such Stalinist elements as M.A. Suslov, the Marxist theoretician who was one of the secretaries of the Central Committee. "One cell dies and another takes its place," was Khrushchev's cheerful verdict on the affair. To Secretary Dulles it offered fresh grounds for his belief that the next decade—or generation—would witness much more fundamental changes in Russia's internal regime.

That there had been a measure of urgency in Zhukov's final removal from the political scene was strongly suggested by the fact that it not only coincided with the launching of Sputnik II but preceded by only four days the special gala session of the Supreme Soviet which had been called for November 6 to celebrate the fortieth anniversary of the Bolshevik Revolution. Attended by no less a figure than Chairman Mao Tse-tung, as well as by most other principal leaders of world Communism (a conspicuous exception being Marshal Tito, who had pleaded acute lumbago on learning of Zhukov's dismissal), this was more than an occasion for the celebration of past and anticipated Communist triumphs. It also provided an opportunity for a fresh attempt at clarifying the intricate and still unsettled question of Moscow's relationship to the Communist parties in Eastern Europe, in China, and in "capitalist" countries.

The explosive question of "separate roads to socialism"—a phrase that covered a whole complex of problems relating to Soviet leadership and national party autonomy—was still a live issue throughout the Communist bloc and to some extent within individual Communist countries. In Poland, Gomulka was still fighting a two-front war against the party "dogmatists" who wanted to go back to Stalinist ways and the party "revisionists" who favored liberalism at home and maximum independence of the Soviet Union. Such men as Gomulka might well have an interest in the survival of Khrushchev as the exponent of a comparatively liberal and flexible line in Communist affairs. Khrushchev, in turn, presumably had every reason to covet the support of the leaders of Communism outside the U.S.S.R. as a means of strengthening his position at home. In addition, he evidently hoped to secure an agreement on the reestablishment of some central directing and coordinating organ for the world Communist movement to replace the Communist Information Bureau, abolished the year before out of complaisance to the now absent Marshal Tito.

Although this last project appears to have encountered insurmountable objections from some of the more nationally minded Communist leaders (notably Gomulka and Palmiro Togliatti of Italy), it was generally agreed at Moscow that there should be more frequent bilateral meetings as well as broader conferences among party representatives to exchange views and concert strategy. At least some of the parties represented were said to have agreed on the establishment of a new international Communist publication, and renewed stress was apparently laid on coordinated economic planning in Eastern Europe through the Council for Economic Mutual Assistance. But on the basic doctrinal questions no complete agreement could be reached, in spite of Mao Tse-tung's unexpectedly strong endorsement of Soviet views on the leading position of the Soviet Union. A lengthy document was drawn up which purported to define both the principles of "socialist internationalism" and the limits within which national peculiarities might be taken into account in applying Soviet experience in other countries.[2] But the Yugoslav delegates refused to sign it; the Western European party representatives were also omitted from the list of signatories, possibly to make Yugoslavia's abstention less noticeable; and in the end it was issued in the name of the twelve European and Far Eastern parties (other than Yugoslavia) that actually held governmental authority. Although Gomulka did not withhold his signature, his remarks on returning to Warsaw indicated that considerable differences of opinion still persisted and that despite his general support of Khrushchev's position he did not consider the battle to maintain Poland's independent status within the Communist bloc by any means ended. A series of attacks on Poland in the Communist press of other countries confirmed this impression.

In the broad field of world politics, the party representatives assembled in Moscow found it easier to agree. Khrushchev's keynote address on November 6 [3] laid heavy stress on the themes of peaceful coexistence and competition, with new predictions of economic victory over the United States and a broad hint that Moscow, having gained a lead in the missile race, would be favorably inclined to further discussion with the West:

"We should like a summit conference between representatives of the capitalist and socialist countries for the purpose of reaching agreement, with due regard to reality and on a basis of mutual understanding, on ruling war out as a method of dealing with international issues, ending the 'cold war' and the arms drive, establishing international relations based on coexistence and settling controversial issues, not by means of war, but through negotiations, through peaceful competition in promoting economy and culture and in meeting man's requirements as fully as possible."

These ideas were further elaborated both in the twelve-party declaration already cited and in a further manifesto or peace appeal which was endorsed by the representatives of sixty-four Communist parties, including that of Yugoslavia.[4] The tenor of these pronouncements, with their references to the inevitable victory of "socialism," the possibility of a non-violent transformation of the existing order, "the struggle for national independence against colonial aggression and feudal oppression," and the desirability of a united front of "socialist" and "progressive" forces, was strongly reminiscent of the Twentieth Party Congress, at which the idea of "peaceful competition" had first come into its own. Whatever advantages the Soviet Union might have gained in the military field, there was plainly to be no relaxation in the drive to outflank the West by political means. This was a prospect which would have to be given serious consideration in the Western capitals if their response to Sputnik was to take a realistic form.

Washington at the moment was too deeply immersed in examining the shortcomings of its own missile and satellite programs to concern itself to any great extent with the other new portents coming out of Moscow. Its only current diplomatic initiative in relation to the Communist world was concerned with the special question of Yugoslavia. The refusal of that country's emissaries to sign the twelve-party declaration had caught the United States in the midst of one of its periodic reappraisals of policy toward Belgrade, the result of several recent Yugoslav actions which had seemed to reflect a closer alignment with Moscow. Yugoslavia had lately recognized the Soviet puppet government in Eastern Germany, and had voted with the U.S.S.R. on key issues in the United Nations. With a new session of Congress in the offing, the State Department had been impelled to take another look at the policy of supplying Yugoslavia with economic and limited military aid which President Eisenhower had endorsed as recently as May 14 (section 10). After some rather unhappy publicity on both sides, Ambassador James W. Riddleberger had a frank discussion with Tito in early December and gained fresh assurance that the Yugoslav Government had no intention of surrendering its freedom of action. Apparently at Tito's own suggestion, it was decided that the dwindling military aid operation might as well be wound up, although economic aid, to which Congress was less antipathetic in Yugoslavia's case, would continue.

Whether the United States would have any other plans for "lending support to those countries seeking to withstand Soviet pressures" would perhaps not be apparent until the general outlines of Western policy had been further clarified at the Paris meeting of NATO heads of government, which had been scheduled to begin December 16 (section 28). Meanwhile a Polish delegation was visiting Washington in search of further credits to supplement the economic aid agreements concluded earlier in the year; but it had found that official enthusiasm for the Gomulka experiment had cooled considerably in the interval. Gomulka, it now appeared, was not the man to deviate very far from the Soviet line in matters affect-

ing relations with the non-Communist world, and it was uncertain how much importance Washington would attach to
helping him preserve the relative freedom that still prevailed
in Polish internal life. As to the Hungarian problem, this was
a source of continuing preoccupation in Washington, but one
about which the United States had found that it could do little
directly and which it had consistently preferred to approach
by way of the United Nations. It was there, if anywhere, the
State Department calculated, that the moral force of world
opinion might be mobilized in a way that could perhaps
alleviate in some degree the unhappy lot of the Hungarian
people. (See section 24.)

So far as the broader problem of possible negotiations with
the Soviet Union was concerned, it was assumed in Washington that Moscow in raising this issue was merely inaugurating
a new phase in its permanent campaign to weaken and divide
the West. Any new East-West conference, Soviet sources intimated, would naturally take into account the recent "change
in the relationship of forces on the international arena." In
effect, it would be an opportunity for the United States to
abandon its established policy in East-West affairs and permit
world problems to be settled in a manner more favorable to
Soviet aims than Washington had hitherto been willing to
consider. Because the motives behind this agitation appeared
so obvious, the State Department wasted few words in letting
it be known that it contemplated no conference with the Russians under presently foreseeable circumstances. Such meetings had little purpose, said Mr. Dulles in an interview recorded for the British Broadcasting Corporation (December 3),
since there were only a few areas in which worth-while, en-
forceable agreements with the Russians could be reached.

Nevertheless the idea of a fresh start toward negotiation of
East-West differences proved to have considerable appeal
in Europe and to some degree within the United States as
well. As on past occasions, Western reaction to the latest Soviet developments tended to take two distinct and somewhat
contradictory forms. For some people, Sputnik with its accompanying political manifestations proved the necessity for an
extraordinary effort to regain the scientific and military lead

the West appeared to be losing. This in general was the position officially adopted by the Western governments, led by the United States and Great Britain. But there were other Western observers to whom Sputnik offered final proof of the impracticability of past Western policies, the impossibility of getting the Soviets to agree to the kind of programs that the West had been pressing upon them in the past, and the urgent necessity for some form of East-West accommodation before nuclear-armed missiles actually began flying in both directions. Needless to say, this was also the predominant reaction in India and most other non-Western countries. It was a reaction on which Soviet diplomacy and propaganda continued to play while the Western governments attempted to assess the trend of public opinion in preparation for their own "summit meeting" at the annual NATO conference in Paris. (See further section 28.)

24. COLD WAR IN NEW YORK

In agitating for new diplomatic contacts among the major powers, the Kremlin as usual ignored the fact that there was already available in the United Nations an instrumentality expressly designed for such purposes as the prevention and removal of threats to the peace and the adjustment or settlement of international disputes and other threatening situations. Though it habitually made use of the United Nations as a sounding board for propaganda and a vehicle of political warfare, the Soviet Union seldom took to the world organization any matter on which it desired really serious discussion with other governments. Moscow had never reconciled itself to the way in which the Western nations had contrived to increase the authority and prestige of the General Assembly as compared with that of the Security Council, thereby circumventing in some measure the effect of the Soviet veto. Even with the admission of Albania, Bulgaria, Hungary and Rumania to United Nations membership, the Soviet bloc in the Assembly had only nine sure votes out of more than eighty. This minority position may help to account for the fact that the most meaningful Soviet gestures regarding coexistence and East-West relations at this period were made outside the United

Nations framework. If anything, Soviet behavior during the 1957 Assembly session, particularly during its first weeks, laid less emphasis on the "coexistence" theme than it did on the "tough" side of Soviet post-Sputnik policy, notably in relation to the two outstanding topics of disarmament and the Middle East.

From the Soviet point of view, developments at the United Nations in the weeks that preceded the opening of the Assembly's Twelfth Regular Session on September 17 had been of a character to place the world organization in a more unfavorable light than usual. We have already referred to the indictment of Soviet actions released on June 20 by the Assembly's Special Committee on the Problem of Hungary (section 10). Under strong encouragement from the United States, arrangements were made to reconvene the Assembly on September 10 to consider the committee's report and discuss a further resolution on Hungary which had been drawn up on the initiative of the American delegation. Essentially an endorsement of the committee report and a reaffirmation of the Assembly's known views on Hungary, this thirty-six-power draft again called on the U.S.S.R. and the Kádár regime in Hungary

"to desist from repressive measures against the Hungarian people; to respect the liberty and political independence of Hungary and the Hungarian people's enjoyment of fundamental human rights and freedoms; and to ensure the return to Hungary of those Hungarian citizens who have been deported to the Union of Soviet Socialist Republics."

It also requested Prince Wan Waithayakon of Thailand, the president of the Eleventh Regular Session, to serve as the Assembly's special representative on the Hungarian problem and "take such steps as he deems appropriate" to achieve United Nations objectives in the matter. By this it was generally understood that Prince Wan would try to visit Hungary and the U.S.S.R. in the hope of persuading their governments to heed the Assembly's wishes.

In the course of the preliminary debate, Ambassador Lodge assured the Assembly that the United States had no thought of pursuing the Hungarian issue "in a spirit of cold war," and sought only to do whatever was possible to relieve the situation of the Hungarian people. Not unexpectedly, however, the Soviet and Hungarian delegates countered by branding the proposed action as an illegal and arbitrary attempt to interfere in Hungary's internal affairs. Despite some uneasiness among the neutral delegations, the resolution [5] was nevertheless adopted on September 14 by an even larger majority than the one that had established the committee in January. Sixty governments voted affirmatively, and ten more abstained; voting against the resolution were only the nine Soviet bloc delegations and Yugoslavia. In the judgment of the State Department, with the adoption of this resolution the United Nations had taken "every measure possible short of force." Yet there was no indication that the authorities in Budapest and Moscow would be more ready to heed the Assembly's opinion than they had been in the past; indeed, Prince Wan was to report on December 9 that his overtures had been rebuffed in both capitals on the ground that the matters in question did not lie within the competence of the United Nations. Meanwhile, as Moscow girded itself for new parliamentary battles at the United Nations headquarters in New York, the Kádár government continued its methodical reprisals against persons who had taken an active part in Hungary's ill-fated popular revolt.

The adoption of this last resolution on Hungary was the final action of the General Assembly's memorable Eleventh Regular Session, which had begun in the midst of the Hungarian-Middle Eastern crisis in November 1956. Three days later, on September 17, 1957, the Assembly began its Twelfth Regular Session, the agenda of which already included sixty-five separate items ranging from disarmament to Algeria and from the admission of new members to the status of the Joint Staff Pension Fund. Two of the first actions of the new Assembly were the election of Sir Leslie Munro of New Zealand as president of the session and the election of the seventeen-day-old Federation of Malaya as the eighty-second member of the United Nations, a step which the Security Council had already recommended by unanimous vote at a special meeting on September 5.[5a]

The Assembly's annual battle over the representation of China began two days later in the seventeen-man General (Steering) Committee, with India making its customary plea for a full-dress debate on Communist China's claim to supplant the Nationalist delegation, and the United States as usual urging that the matter not be considered during the current session. With gratification and some surprise the United States delegation saw its position upheld by a substantial margin, not only in the committee but in the full Assembly, where the vote taken on its motion on September 24 was ultimately tabulated at 48 in favor, 27 opposed, and 6 abstentions. In 1956 the vote on the same issue had been 47-24-8.

With these preliminaries out of the way, the Assembly could begin to concentrate on some of the larger issues that were coming into focus as one after another of the eighty-two participating delegations offered its contribution to the annual General Debate. Secretary Dulles had led off on September 19 with a speech that dwelt mainly on disarmament and the Middle East, plainly the two most urgent and serious matters with which the Assembly would have to concern itself. Foreign Minister Gromyko had told the Assembly next day that although it was meeting in a somewhat more relaxed atmosphere than the year before, the international situation still remained "altogether abnormal and alarming" as a result of the Western "positions of strength" policy. The Assembly, he suggested, would be well advised to show its disapprobation of Western maneuvers by adopting a special declaration "On the Principles of Peaceful Coexistence Between States." (This plan was ultimately shelved, with Soviet concurrence, in favor of a more innocuous text drawn up by India, Sweden, and Yugoslavia.) Gromyko also had some new proposals, or variations on old proposals, in the disarmament field (see below); and he urged the Assembly to "raise its powerful voice" in defense of the independence of those Near and Middle Eastern countries whose independence, he claimed, was being menaced by the Western powers and particularly by the United States.

Thus the main battlefield of the impending struggle was defined; but there were subsidiary skirmishes in other quarters while the two chief contenders mobilized their forces for the coming debates in committee and plenary sessions. There was even one issue of great practical importance on which both sides found it convenient to agree. The five-year term of Secretary-General Hammarskjold was due to expire in August 1958, and the distinction with which he had filled the position (not to mention the difficulty that would certainly be encountered in finding a suitable replacement) suggested to all parties that it would be advantageous to retain his services for a second term. A recommendation to this effect was unanimously approved by the Security Council on September 26 and endorsed the same day by a virtually unanimous vote of the Assembly. Also approved by unanimous vote on October 14 (with the Soviet bloc abstaining) was a decision to postpone for as much as two years the question of a conference to review the United Nations Charter. As usual, the process of choosing three nonpermanent members of the Security Council proved less harmonious. Panama and Canada were elected without difficulty on October 1, but a real battle took place over the selection of Japan, whose candidacy was favored by the United States, in preference to Czechoslovakia, the Soviet-supported candidate. The U.S.S.R. and various other delegations also opposed a resolution of October 14 which authorized a gradual reduction in the United States financial assessment from 33.33 to 30 percent of the annual United Nations budget. For the 1958 budget of $55,062,850, the United States share was set at 32.51 percent or a little over $17.9 million.

One traditional area of East-West disagreement had been markedly reduced over the past three years by the admission of twenty-two new members to the United Nations; but the two camps still remained at odds over the aspirations to membership of North and South Korea, North and South Vietnam, and the Soviet-sponsored Mongolian People's Republic. Although nothing could be done about this impasse without an agreement among the great powers in the Security Council, the Assembly on October 25 adopted two United States-supported resolutions, both opposed by the Soviet bloc, which expressed regret at the continued exclusion of the non-Communist Korean and Vietnamese republics. Similar resolutions had been passed in January.

Toward the Republic of Korea, as a state that had been born and come to maturity under United Nations auspices, the Assembly acknowledged a wider obligation. In January, at the Eleventh Session, it had adopted the usual annual resolution reaffirming the long-standing United Nations objectives of "a unified, independent and democratic Korea" and "the full restoration of international peace and security in the [Korean] area." In November a further resolution along the same lines was adopted by a wide margin, together with a commendation of the United Nations Korean Reconstruction Agency on the approaching completion of its mission. Several speakers called attention to the threatening concentrations of armed forces and modern armaments in Communist-controlled North Korea; and the Australian delegate voiced a serious warning against the danger of "treating Korea as a dead duck and surrendering to the so-called realities of the situation." "The United Nations," he said (November 15), "dare not sweep freedom under the carpet. It must never permit the fruits of aggression to be plucked at last as the prize of a determined policy of attrition."

But it was universally recognized that the most reliable guide to the prospective trend of East-West relations would be furnished by the debate on disarmament. If the great powers were prepared to move forward in this field, the prospect for solutions in Korea and other areas of East-West deadlock would improve immensely; if not, existing disagreements would in all probability be perpetuated and the danger of universal nuclear catastrophe would continue to mount. With the five-power discussions in the Disarmament Subcommittee (section 11) just over, the prospects for constructive action on disarmament could not be called encouraging. The latest Western proposals, Gromyko had asserted on September 10, had "slammed the door on any possibility of settling the disarmament problem in whole or in part." But Mr. Dulles in addressing the Assembly refused to take this as Russia's last word. Never before, he pointed out, had so many nations with so much military power joined to make proposals of so far-reaching a character; any government that summarily rejected them would "accept a frightful responsibility before all the world."

"Humanity faces a tragic future if the war threat is not brought under control," Mr. Dulles emphasized. "It would mean that men, in order to survive, must learn to live as burrowers within the earth's surface to find protection from death. It would mean that man would be a slave to the rapidly mounting costs of an arms race. It would mean that individual freedom would give way to the requirements of bare survival."

Having already worked out a program of interlocking measures aimed at forestalling this dread eventuality, the Western governments represented on the Disarmament Subcommittee now hoped to get the essence of their plan endorsed by the General Assembly. Even though unacceptable to the Russians, the plan would presumably gain in public estimation if supported by a larger number of non-Communist governments. It was true that other non-Communist governments had thus far shown no great enthusiasm for this highly complex plan, which appeared to take it for granted that nuclear weapons would be used in any future war, and which, moreover, made even the suspension of nuclear testing dependent on a variety of seemingly extraneous conditions. Several of the non-Communist governments had rather different ideas about how the problem should be attacked. Japan, for example, had been actively soliciting the major atomic powers to stop testing nuclear weapons without further delay. India, which had been advocating a "standstill' in the arms race ever since 1954, wanted to see nuclear weapons tests suspended for an indefinite period, and had also proposed the addition of new countries with fresh viewpoints to the Disarmament Commission and its Subcommittee. Even such a thoroughly Western figure as Canada's Prime Minister Diefenbaker was quoted as saying he thought the disarmament discussions would benefit by the infusion of "new blood."

The prevalence of such attitudes undoubtedly had a considerable influence on the formulation of the new Soviet disarmament proposals which Mr. Gromyko first laid before the Assembly in his speech of September 20. Whether because of Sputnik or for other reasons, the U.S.S.R. had apparently lost any interest it might previously have had in negotiating about disarmament on a basis acceptable to the West. As at most times in the past decade, it now chose to put forward not proposals which might lead to agreement, but proposals which would create maximum embarrassment for the United States and its partners. Gromyko's main suggestions were three in number: (1) a mutual renunciation of the use of nuclear weapons for a temporary period of, say, five years; (2) cessation of nuclear weapons tests for two to three years starting January 1, 1958; and (3) enlargement of the eleven-nation Disarmament Commission and its five-nation Subcommittee by the inclusion of countries that opposed the "cold war" and pursued a policy of "peaceful coexistence"—in other words, countries from which the U.S.S.R. could expect more or less uncritical support in any stand it might take.

This plan was put forward approximately a fortnight before the ascent of Sputnik I. As the debate proceeded and the Western powers gradually lined up those delegations that could be persuaded to support their own position, the Soviet tone became progressively harsher. On October 28 the U.S.S.R. proposed that the Disarmament Commission and Subcommittee be dissolved altogether and their responsibilities turned over to a new commission including all eighty-two members of the United Nations. On November 4, one day after Sputnik II, Soviet representative V. V. Kuznetsov astounded his fellow delegates by announcing that the U.S.S.R. would no longer participate in either the Commission or the Subcommittee as presently constituted. All the other members of the Subcommittee, he pointed out, were spokesmen for the "aggressive North Atlantic bloc"; as a result, he said, any possibility of its doing anything constructive had been completely exhausted. Possibly he had forgotten that the Subcommittee when established in 1953–54 had been intentionally limited to "the Powers principally involved" in the development of atomic energy.

Moscow's plain threat to boycott further disarmament discussions altered the whole character of the debate. Thus far the basic problem had been that of lining up a two-thirds majority in support of the Western negotiating position; now, suddenly, it became a question of how to induce the U.S.S.R. to continue the negotiations at all. Although a twenty-four power resolution endorsing the main outlines of the Western position was approved by a handsome majority in the Political Committee on November 6, the Western powers found themselves threatened with a prospect of massive defections before the matter could come to a final vote in the plenary session. There followed a week of intense behind-the-scenes negotiation during which the Western powers agreed to add five, and later ten, new members to the Disarmament Commission in the interests of holding their majority together and if possible preventing a Soviet walkout.

These concessions, though they failed to win the endorsement of the U.S.S.R., at least sufficed to ensure the final passage of the twenty-four-power resolution, which was adopted on November 14 by a vote of 56 to 9, with the Soviet bloc opposed and 15 nations, mostly Asian and African states, abstaining.[6] By its terms the Assembly urged the states particularly concerned to give priority to reaching an agreement on partial measures of disarmament along the general lines which the West had proposed in London, and asked the Subcommittee to submit a progress report by April 30, 1958. Likewise approved was a Belgian resolution calling for a world-wide publicity campaign on the issues involved.[7]

Five days more were required to reach a decision on the enlargement of the Disarmament Commission. In fixing the number and identity of the countries to be added, India was anxious to go as far as possible toward meeting the views of the U.S.S.R.; the Western powers, on the contrary, insisted that if the Commission was to be enlarged, it must be done in a manner that would not place them at a disadvantage. After protracted bickering over the relative merits of such countries as Austria and Belgium, agreement was reached among the non-Communist powers on the designation of fourteen countries to be added to the Commission for the year beginning January 1, 1958, thus bringing its total membership to twenty-five. Among those chosen were seven Western states (Argentina, Australia, Belgium, Brazil, Italy, Mexico, and Norway), together with Tunisia and six neutral or Communist states (Burma, Czechoslovakia, Egypt, India, Poland, and Yugoslavia).[8] Approving this arrangement on November 19 by a vote of 60 to 9, with 11 abstentions, the Assembly also rejected by smaller margins the Soviet plan for an eighty-two member commission as well as an Albanian amendment which would have added seven more neutral and Communist countries to the list already approved. The resolution as adopted would preserve the four-to-one Western majority in the Subcommittee, *if* that body was able to hold further meetings at all. Soviet sources, however, continued to insist that the U.S.S.R. would not participate in such a politically unbalanced group. If there was to be further progress toward disarmament, they intimated, it would have to be sought elsewhere—perhaps at a high-level meeting such as Khrushchev had already suggested and Premier Bulganin was soon to propose afresh. (See section 28.)

25. THE U.N. FACES THE MIDDLE EAST

The debate on disarmament revealed the full measure of Moscow's post-Sputnik intransigence and offered a discouraging prospect for all those who shared the feeling (expressed by Philippine delegate Carlos P. Romulo) that it was imperative to make a beginning toward disarmament lest there "be awesomely an end—the dreadful end of disaster for all of us." Even while the debate was in progress, a lively indication of how such an end might come about had been afforded by Khrushchev's sudden adoption of an extremely bellicose tone with reference to the Middle East, a development that almost exactly coincided with the ascent of Sputnik I (section 23). We are already familiar with the background of this latest Middle Eastern crisis, which had originated as early as August in the pro-Soviet, anti-American shift in Syria and the resultant sharp increase in tension along the Syrian frontiers (section 14). That the threat to peace in the area should now have come under the direct notice of the United Nations, of which President Eisenhower had said in January that "it cannot be a wholly dependable protector of freedom when the ambitions of the Soviet Union are involved," was largely due to the accident that the Assembly happened to be in session and afforded the various interested governments an exceptional opportunity to dramatize and seek international support for their positions.

In his contribution to the general debate on September 19, Secretary Dulles had pinpointed the area of acute peril in stating that as a result of the political overturn in Syria, "Turkey now faces growing military dangers from the major buildup of Soviet arms in Syria on its southern border, a buildup concerted with Soviet military power on Turkey's northern border." Referring to Premier Bulganin's recent message to the Turkish Premier, which he described as an attempt "to intimidate Turkey from making internal dispositions of its own security forces," the Secretary of State suggested that the Soviet Union was not only playing a dangerous game but was manifesting an attitude toward "certain Near East nations" that was in direct conflict with the "Essentials of Peace" resolution adopted by the General Assembly in 1949. (This document had called upon all nations "To refrain from any threats or acts, direct or indirect, aimed at impairing the freedom, independence, or integrity of any State.")[9] The United States, said Mr. Dulles, believed that such a situation should at least be considered and discussed by the Assembly, and would therefore reserve the right to introduce concrete proposals in the matter.

But the idea of a draft resolution along these lines encountered considerable opposition on the part of some of the other Arab states, which, though quite uneasy about developments in and around Syria, objected strongly to seeing that country held up to opprobrium by outside powers. Syria itself, in company with Egypt, was outspokenly hostile to the American approach and seemed more inclined to the viewpoint of Foreign Minister Gromyko, who had insisted on September 20 that whatever trouble there was in the Middle East was the fault of the United States, and that the proper remedy was for the four big powers to follow Moscow's long-standing advice to renounce the use of force and "interference in the internal affairs" of Middle Eastern countries.

No one appeared to view the situation with any special alarm until Khrushchev on October 7 suddenly began to talk about "the danger of a new war" in the Middle East, proclaim the imminence of a Turkish attack on Syria, assert that the Soviet Union could not "remain passive" in such an eventuality, and warn the Turks that "when cannons start to shoot and rockets to fly it may be too late." At the same time Khrushchev in his interview with James Reston (published October 9) advanced the astounding charge that the recent mission of Loy Henderson to the Middle East had been undertaken for the specific purpose of inciting an attack on Syria by its Arab neighbors— and that when this plan had missed fire, Mr. Henderson had turned his attention to pushing Turkey into "an aggressive attack against Syria." This improbable charge the State Department saw fit to deny in a special statement of October 10,[10] in which, however, it went out of its way to warn the Kremlin against underestimating the determination of the United States to stand by its friends. Once again there was a calculated reference to the Eisenhower Doctrine:

"Mr. Khrushchev . . . should be under no illusion that the United States, Turkey's friend and ally, takes lightly its obligations under the North Atlantic Treaty or is not determined to carry out the national policy expressed in the joint congressional resolution on the Middle East.

"Mr. Khrushchev is himself reported to have observed that it is dangerous in these times to assume that hostilities, once begun, will remain confined to a particular locality. That truth should be prayerfully and constantly contemplated by every responsible official of every country."

While Syria complained of daily clashes on its Turkish border and violations of its air space by Turkish and American planes, the United States decided to delay the departure of certain naval units which had joined the Sixth Fleet for training exercises. Turkey itself, immersed in preparations for its October 27 election, remained conspicuously calm, insisting that it was not going to attack Syria and that the forces concentrated near its southern border were there only for routine maneuvers. Some of the Arab states, notably Saudi Arabia and Lebanon, displayed acute concern over the renewed danger that the Arab world might become an East-West battlefield. Egypt, however, showed no hesitation in playing the Soviet-Syrian game. Tension reached a still higher pitch with the disclosure on October 13 that Egypt had for almost a month been transferring "basic elements" of its armed forces to Syria—pre-

sumably to a strength of approximately one battalion—under
the solidarity pact which the two countries had concluded in
1955. Next day it was announced that Egyptian troops were
deploying near the Turkish frontier, a move that seemed
likely to heighten the war fever in Syria but which also increased the uneasiness and irritation of King Saud, who had
not been consulted despite his country's supposed military
partnership with Egypt and Syria.

The stage was now set for one of those major psychological
maneuvers by which the Soviet Union apparently believed it
might be possible to duplicate its diplomatic success in the
Middle Eastern crisis of the previous year. On October 15
Moscow released the texts of a series of letters addressed by
Khrushchev to the principal socialist and labor parties of
Western Europe, in which he warned them that the situation
had become "so dangerous that it cannot be treated with complacency or procrastination" and urged their help in rescuing
the world's peoples from "the brink of a new devastating world
war." Next day Syria, in a move that would hardly have been
made without Soviet advice, carried its case directly to the
United Nations Assembly. The situation had become "intolerably dangerous," said the Syrian representative, who called for
the appointment of a special United Nations commission to investigate conditions in the border area and report back to the
Assembly. This demand was immediately endorsed by Foreign
Minister Gromyko, who now claimed to have information that
Turkey with its American military advisers was planning an
attack on Syria immediately after the October 27 election. In
language that recalled the Soviet threat of direct intervention
in the crisis of November 1956, Gromyko declared that if the
peace was broken it would be the duty of all United Nations
members to "immediately render Syria the armed assistance
necessary to put a stop to aggression." The U.S.S.R., he vowed,
was "prepared to take part with its forces in suppressing aggression and punishing the violators of peace."

Although the crisis was to rage with scarcely diminished
intensity for another fortnight, it cannot be doubted that its
formal submission to the United Nations introduced an important safeguard against its getting out of control. Secretary

Dulles appeared to anticipate a nonviolent outcome when he told his news conference on October 16 that, while a Soviet attack on Turkey would undoubtedly be met by something other than "a purely defensive operation by the United States," he did not think such an attack would occur.

"I believe that the eyes of the world are sufficiently focused on what's going on there so that it is unlikely there will be an outbreak of war. I think that is one of the great advantages of the United Nations, the fact that it is in session, that it is a means of assuring that there will be the eyes of the world focusing on the area, a quick knowledge of what takes place. I believe in that respect there is a great measure of insurance."

While it would be particularly hazardous to speculate about the motivations of Soviet conduct at this period, it seems probable from what is known of the main lines of Soviet foreign policy that Moscow was also opposed to letting a major war develop out of the situation. Although its publicity apparatus continued to sound the alarm and some detached observers gained the impression that the Kremlin actually believed the United States was trying to foment a conflict in the area, it is reasonable to assume that the main Soviet purpose—apart from creating a diversion to cover the move against Marshal Zhukov —was to advance its political warfare aims in the Middle East rather than to create a pretext for military intervention.

If the Soviet Union failed to reap even the full propaganda benefit of its warlike gestures, the fault lay largely with King Saud and his anxiety to avert a crisis that might finally destroy the unity of the Arab world. On October 20 the Saudi Arabian Government announced that the King, who had been watching events from Lebanon, had formally offered to mediate the quarrel between Syria and Turkey and that both parties had accepted. Turkey confirmed this statement; Syria, however, whose civilian government was apparently under heavy pressure from the military, denied agreeing to mediation and unconvincingly pretended that no such offer had been made. While the General Assembly hopefully waited (wondering meanwhile what kind of investigating commission it could possibly set up that would be acceptable to both Syria and

Turkey), a new alarm occurred in connection with a NATO exercise called "Red Epoch," originally scheduled to take place off the Turkish coast beginning October 31 but later restricted in such a way as to keep it out of the danger area.

Ultimately, on October 30, Syria insisted on introducing a draft Assembly resolution calling for an investigating commission. The Western powers, acting in close concert with Turkey, immediately countered with an alternative text referring indirectly to the Saudi mediation offer and suggesting the possibility of a peace mission by Secretary-General Hammarskjold. But by this time the date of the supposed Turkish attack had already passed and Khrushchev had already announced that the situation was improving. There was doubt at the General Assembly that either of the two resolutions could win a two-thirds majority, and on October 31 it was informally agreed that neither resolution would be brought to a vote. Complimenting the Assembly on its "sober and responsible" handling of the issue, Ambassador Lodge observed that an important precedent had been established in thus disposing of a major issue without the adoption of a resolution.

Amid loud rejoicing over what it called the frustration of the "aggressors," the Soviet Union took good care that the tension between Syria and Turkey should not abate too rapidly. Nor did it emerge from the crisis with empty hands. On October 28 its emissaries in Damascus had initialed a twelve-year economic and technical assistance agreement with Syria—the fulfillment of the preliminary arrangement made in August (section 14)—whereby the Soviet Union undertook to provide that country with plans, equipment, technical aid, and credit "without strings" covering most or all of the major development projects which Syria had previously discussed with the International Bank.[11] Unofficially there was talk of as much as $170 million in Soviet economic assistance—even more than the $100 million credits promised in the past to Afghanistan and to Indonesia.

Whatever its economic difficulties at home, the U.S.S.R. was not neglecting any opportunity to undercut the Eisenhower Doctrine by binding individual Arab countries to its economic orbit. Three weeks later, on November 19, Egypt's Minister of War, Major General Abdel Hakim Amer, concluded a cordial visit to Moscow (during which he praised the Russians as "our sincere friends, the friends of freedom") with a new agreement on political and economic collaboration "as well as military questions." Egyptian sources spoke of a line of credit of 700 million rubles (officially $175 million), but insisted—as did the Syrians, for that matter—that they were still anxious to improve relations with the West if the West would show a little more understanding and sympathy for their viewpoint.

Not content with consolidating its ties to Syria and Egypt, the Soviet Union had apparently remained unreconciled to Jordan's new position as a kind of protégé of the United States under the Eisenhower Doctrine. At any rate, it lent considerable support during the first weeks of November to a vicious Egyptian-Syrian propaganda campaign against King Hussein which for a time threatened to develop into another first-rate international crisis. There could be no doubt of the desire of the Egyptian and Syrian Governments to get rid of the young ruler. Accusing him of the unpardonable sin of negotiating with Israel, their press and radio openly proposed his assassination and luridly recalled the death of his grandfather, King Abdullah, at the hands of a Palestinian Arab refugee in 1951. Although Hussein minced no words in saying that Egypt and Syria were being used as instruments of international Communist aggression against Jordan, most observers felt that his standing in the Arab world was not unimpaired by so much adverse publicity, aggravating the handicap of association with the United States.

One easily foreseeable result of the campaign against King Hussein was an intensification of Jordan's public antipathy to Israel, the most obvious way of displaying loyalty to "Arab nationalism." For the first time since Israel had withdrawn its forces from the Gaza Strip in March, conditions along the armistice demarcation lines were now beginning to deteriorate to a degree that aroused general anxiety and had required renewed consideration by the United Nations. As recently as September 4, Mr. Hammarskjold in the introduction to his annual report had noted "the comparative quiet" prevailing in this area as "a welcome symptom," and had expressed the hope that the governments in question, with United Nations support, would "decide to lead their peoples step by step on [the] road toward a more secure and promising future for them all." With the U.N. Emergency Force still deployed along the Egyptian side of the armistice demarcation line, conditions in that quarter remained comparatively calm. But Jordan had been complaining for some time about Israeli tree-planting activities in the neutral zone near Jerusalem, which were discussed by the Security Council on September 6 and again on November 22; an Israeli fighter plane had fired on a Jordanian airliner on October 20; on November 21 a military clash occurred in the Jerusalem area. Renewed tension had also developed in connection with Israeli reclamation work in the demilitarized zone adjoining Syria; Saudi Arabia had complained that Israel had violated its air space; Israel had protested to the Security Council over the seizure of one of its fishing vessels by Egypt.

In the midst of a new dispute relating to Israel's right of access to the Mount Scopus enclave in Jordanian territory, Jordan suddenly announced on November 24 that it would cease to cooperate with the acting head of the U.N. Truce Supervision Organization, Colonel Byron E. Leary, on the ground that he was openly partial to Israel. Just as suddenly, Mr. Hammarskjold announced next day that he would immediately proceed in person to look into the matter. While the other Arab states proclaimed their complete solidarity with Jordan (against Israel, at any rate), the Secretary-General forsook the General Assembly to fly to the Middle East and spend several days in consultation with the governments of Jordan, Israel, Syria, and Lebanon. As the result of his endeavors the Mount Scopus difficulty was provisionally straightened out and Israel was persuaded to cease its fourteen-month-old boycott of the Israeli-Jordanian Mixed Armistice Commission, a step which had also been urged by Mr. Dulles in communications to the Israeli Premier.

In the meantime the General Assembly had been faced once again with the by no means inconsiderable pecuniary cost of Middle East tensions. In addition to the annual problem of what to do about the 933,500 Arab refugees outside of Israel

who were subsisting under the care of the United Nations
Relief and Works Agency for Arab Refugees in the Near East
(UNRWA), it was now confronted with two special financial
issues left over from the Suez war of the previous winter. The
recent reopening of the Suez Canal, regarded on all hands as
one of the United Nations' most creditable achievements, had
cost the world organization a total of $8,376,042.87 which
had now to be reimbursed to the United States and nine
other countries which had advanced funds for the purpose.
Mr. Hammarskjold had suggested that this indebtedness be
repaid over the next three years or so through a voluntary
surcharge of 3 percent on the tolls paid by shipping through
the Canal. This plan was approved by a heavy vote on the
last day of the Assembly's session (December 14), although
the U.S.S.R. and several of its satellites insisted that they
would not pay the surcharge and felt that the entire cost
should be assessed against Israel, France, and Great Britain.
The settlement of this issue did not affect the still pending
question of Egypt's obligation to compensate the shareholders
of the expropriated Suez Canal Company for their financial
loss. Indications were that Abdel Nasser would like to get
this matter settled in order to mitigate his still serious financial difficulties with Britain and the United States, which
were further complicated by the expropriation or "Egyptiani-
zation" of other foreign commercial interests in Egypt.

    A potentially touchier question for the Assembly concerned
the future of the 5,500-man U.N. Emergency Force, still the
only substantial guarantee of the cease-fire prevailing between Israel and Egypt. Although Indonesia had already
withdrawn its contingent and Finland had indicated a desire
to do likewise, UNEF's value was generally recognized and
not even Egypt suggested its abolition. The problem was
that of meeting its expenses of roughly $2 million a month,
for which the Assembly had thus far made very inadequate
provision, while most member governments had been slow
to pay over even the modest sums assessed against them.
Spurred by a warning from the Secretary-General that successful completion of UNEF's mission might be seriously
jeopardized, the Assembly on November 22 authorized Mr.

Hammarskjold to expend up to $38.5 million to keep the force in existence through 1958, and to recover this amount by assessments against the member states in proportion to their assessments under the regular United Nations budget. The expected deficit, it was hoped, would be made up by voluntary contributions from the United States and some other governments. Again the Soviet bloc states indicated that they would pay nothing.

On the perennial problem of the Arab refugees, the Assembly was forced to recognize that not only had no progress been made toward their resettlement in Israel or the Arab states, but that funds for their support were on the point of exhaustion. Henry R. Labouisse, UNRWA's American Director, warned the Assembly that relief services were already down to a minimum of seven cents a day for each individual refugee, and that any further reduction would sink them to "subhuman levels." Of an estimated $40.7 million required for relief and rehabilitation through 1958 (together with $8 million needed for a working capital fund), pledges by the United States and thirty-one other governments had come to less than $29 million, and there were strong indications that some reduction in UNRWA's program would soon be inescapable. To avoid offense to the Arab states, which would do nothing for the refugees themselves but advocated an assessment on the entire membership similar to that contemplated for UNEF, references to possible retrenchment were tactfully played down in the resolution which the Assembly adopted on December 12. Without going into details, this document merely urged governments to help meet the critical need for funds and commissioned the Secretary-General to make special efforts to secure additional financial aid.

Hopes for any real improvement in the condition of the refugees stood or fell with the prospect of an amelioration in Arab-Israeli political relations, and of this there were no detectable signs either at the General Assembly or in the Middle Eastern capitals. As the NATO powers prepared for their heads-of-government conference in Paris, both Arabs and Israelis showed some uneasiness lest the occasion be used by the West to try to impose a peace on unacceptable conditions. They were quite right in thinking that the West would have liked to see a settlement of the Arab-Israeli quarrel, which provided a permanent opening for Soviet political warfare maneuvers and ruled out any restoration of really confident relations with Arab countries. The United States, Britain, and other Western governments were well aware that nothing they could hope to accomplish either through mutual defense arrangements or through economic assistance schemes and the like would produce its full effect so long as this central problem of Middle Eastern politics remained unsolved. There were some indications at the moment that Turkey, Great Britain, and perhaps the United States might again be thinking in terms of territorial sacrifices by Israel as the only conceivable basis for a lasting settlement—though it was not easy to see how such a settlement could be brought about in practice, or to be sure that it would bring peace to the Middle East even if the practical obstacles could be overcome.

Nothing along these lines was to develop from the NATO discussions in Paris (section 28), where it was merely agreed that all members of NATO favored national independence, sovereignty, and economic well-being in this area whose stability was regarded by all of them as "vital to world peace." No consideration appears to have been given the Soviet proposals for a "hands-off" agreement on the Middle East. The most likely prospect seemed to be that the existing unsatisfactory situation would remain substantially unchanged for a while longer, and that so far as the Arab-Israeli relationship was concerned, the West would continue to pay the penalties of a state of affairs that to a considerable extent vitiated its efforts to protect the Middle East through such devices as the Baghdad Pact and the Eisenhower Doctrine.

26. CONFRONTING THE INDEPENDENCE MOVEMENT

If the political condition of the Middle East represented a more or less permanent handicap to the Western nations in their attempt to confront the many-sided challenge of

Soviet Communism, the same was true of their situation vis-à-vis the movement for political and economic independence in those areas of Asia and Africa that had been gradually emerging from European control. In this field, history had confronted the European colonial powers (and, through its association with them, the United States) with an essentially unhappy choice: either to renounce their former control and the important political, military, and economic advantages that had accompanied it, or to cling to their historic positions and thereby incur the opprobrium of a large and increasingly influential segment of the world's population, egged on and encouraged by the Soviet Union and its Communist allies as the self-constituted leaders of the fight against Western "colonialism." In the main, the colonial powers had found it preferable to embrace the first alternative and gradually yield up the essentials of sovereignty to their former subject peoples. Devotion to the principle of freedom in former colonial areas had, in fact, become one of the standard ingredients in the official Western ideology. "We have demonstrated a will for the spreading of the blessings of liberty," President Eisenhower declared at the opening of the NATO "summit conference" in Paris on December 16. "Within the last 15 years our nations have freely granted political independence to 20 countries with populations totaling 800,000,-000 peoples."

Monumental as this transfer of political authority had been by any standards, it had not sufficed to free the Western nations from the stigma of "colonialism" in the eyes of the "anticolonial" world. The United Nations still listed some 170 million people who had not yet attained self-government or independence—20 million in the territories composing the international trusteeship system, and another 150 million living in fifty-eight different non-self-governing territories. As long as this situation continued, and as long as civil war continued to rage in Algeria, whose nearly 10 million inhabitants were "self-governing" only in a very technical sense, the Western powers could not expect the full sympathy or support of Asian and African countries in their attempts to mobilize world opinion against the new-style imperialism of the Communist nations. The Soviet Union and its international apparatus would have everything to gain by continuing to proclaim "the struggle for national independence against colonial aggression and feudal oppression."

To professional anticolonialists, the merits of the particular case, the readiness of the peoples in question for self-government or independence, were more or less irrelevant. People who had themselves emerged from colonial status found it intolerable that men of one race should anywhere continue to exercise political authority over those of another. Communists everywhere regarded the dissolution of the "imperialist system" as an inherent part of the process that in their view was destined to bring about the world-wide victory of "socialism." "While socialism is on the upgrade, imperialism is heading toward decline"—such was the view of contemporary history underlying the twelve-party declaration released in Moscow on November 21. A parallel interest in the liquidation of Western "colonialism" created an important bond between the Communist and the predominantly anticolonial and uncommitted nations of Asia and Africa. On the issue that in Asian and African eyes ranked second in importance only to that of peace, it tended to place the Communist governments in a more favorable light than those of the West.

In the course of 1957, the conflicting tendencies inherent in this situation appeared to many to be gathering momentum as though in anticipation of some imminent crisis. On one side, important new advances were being made in the peaceful transition to independent nationhood: the birth of the new African state of Ghana, the independence of Malaya, constitutional progress in Nigeria, Singapore, and the British West Indies. The incorporation into Ghana of the former United Nations trust territory of Togoland under British administration, effected on March 6 pursuant to a plebiscite held under United Nations auspices, marked the first instance in which a trust territory had successfully traveled the road to independence as envisaged in the United Nations Charter. Similar if less spectacular progress could be observed in some of the ten remaining trust territories, notably in Togoland under French administration, where France had established an autonomous republic that was scheduled to achieve independence within the French Union in 1958. Plans for a United Nations-supervised election to ensure that this process was carried out in accordance with the desires of the local population were approved by the General Assembly at its Twelfth Session (November 29). There were also important developments looking toward wider self-government, if not independence, in other British, French, and Belgian territories, principally in Africa.

On the other hand, 1957 also witnessed a sharpening of the "anticolonial" drive, both within and outside the United Nations, which showed clearly that the "anticolonial" nations as a group were not content to await the slow-moving processes of political education and gradual emancipation which seemed to be the most the colonial powers were ready to contemplate. An indication of the prevailing impatience was the adoption at both the Eleventh and Twelfth Assemblies of resolutions urging the administering powers to speed up the evolution of trust territories toward self-government or independence in accordance with a definite timetable. Another and perhaps more dangerous symptom was the increased acuteness of the three major problems of Algeria, Cyprus, and Netherlands New Guinea or West Irian, each of which found one of the NATO powers in some danger of losing its footing in a swirling tide of anticolonial sentiment. Thanks in part to the refusal of the United States to join the lineup being formed against its allies—and thanks also to the sense of balance displayed by various Latin American and European states which had no ax of their own to grind— in none of these cases did the complaining governments achieve their objectives in the Assembly. In the case of Algeria and Cyprus, the outcome of the Assembly's debate even seemed to hold out some increased hope of negotiated solutions. In that of West Irian, on the other hand, the failure of the Assembly to associate itself with Indonesia's claims led to direct reprisals against Dutch interests in Indonesia, creating a situation that threatened further to undermine the stability of that large but none too solidly based republic.

Undoubtedly the most important of these colonial or quasi-colonial issues from the standpoint of its broad international implications was that of Algeria, which was technically not a colonial problem at all but was regarded by all enemies of "colonialism" as the key test of the attitude of France and of the Western world generally. We have seen how deeply the three-year-old civil war in Algeria had affected not only the position of France but that of the entire North Atlantic community. We have also noted its direct and vital bearing on the attitude of Tunisia and Morocco, two newly independent countries that evidently wanted to stand with the West but had found it extremely difficult to do so in any consistent way while the Algerian struggle continued (section 16). The inability of the French National Assembly to settle on a positive line of action in Algeria had brought down the Bourgès-Maunoury government at the end of September. Developments during the interval of more than five weeks that preceded the formation of a new coalition government under Félix Gaillard on November 6 were to accentuate the complexity of the problem and add to the difficulties of inter-allied relations at the very time when the Western powers were most concerned to reaffirm their unity in face of the new challenge from Moscow.

It was a rather subsidiary aspect of the North African problem that particularly upset the French Government and was to send Premier Gaillard to the NATO "heads-of-government" conference in a mood of unconcealed discontent with France's principal allies. As the result of a series of misunderstandings, the United States and Great Britain announced on November 14 that they were shipping a consignment of small arms to Tunisia in response to urgent appeals from President Bourguiba, who had been intimating that if his needs could not be supplied from Western sources he would try to satisfy them in the East as Egypt and Syria were doing. Washington, which would have much preferred to leave to France the responsibility for satisfying the Tunisian demands, considered the transaction justified in terms of keeping Tunisia aligned with the West. France, however, was seriously upset by what it apparently regarded as an invasion of its own sphere of influence in Africa, and expressed grave apprehensions lest the arms in question find their way into the hands of the Algerian rebels.

Whether or not these fears were justified, the possible effect on the military situation in Algeria was a matter of obvious importance from the French point of view. French military operations during these autumn weeks had been going rather more satisfactorily than usual. A major guerrilla offensive which was supposed to have begun on October 20 had failed to materialize. A French paratroop unit was engaged in wiping out a rebel detachment that had penetrated into the Sahara region. In Algiers, the terrorist apparatus had been shattered and public security reestablished. Elsewhere, the number of terrorist attacks had waned. All this, the French felt, provided a favorable augury for putting into effect their long-standing political program: a cease-fire, elections, and negotiations for a new status for Algeria within the framework of its "indissoluble" union with France.

As an essential step in this direction, Premier Gaillard immediately on assuming office introduced a modified version of the "framework law" providing for the establishment of autonomous Algerian regions. This plan was now approved by a solid majority of the National Assembly on November 30. But the program thus espoused by the French Government was full of loopholes and fell far short of meeting the demand for outright independence which was still being maintained by the National Liberation Front, the principal insurgent organization.

Anxious to open up an alternative road to settlement, President Bourguiba flew to Morocco on November 20 and next day joined with King Mohammed V in an offer to assist in getting negotiations started between the French and the Algerian nationalists. Despite their close ties with the National Liberation Front, the Moroccan and Tunisian leaders endeavored to phrase their proposal in terms that France could accept. The object of negotiations, they said, should be to achieve "a just solution, leading to recognition of the sovereignty [rather than independence] of the Algerian people in conformity with the principles of the United Nations" while safeguarding "the interests of France and French nationals." But the negotiations, they implied, would have to take place between France and the National Liberation Front, whose authority to speak for the Algerian people the French had never recognized. M. Pineau, who had stayed on as Foreign Minister in the new government, was already in New York for the impending General Assembly debate. The Moroccan-Tunisian offer could not be accepted, he said, because the two powers making it were not "neutral" and because it excluded other rebel elements.

Nevertheless the idea of negotiations under Moroccan-Tunisian sponsorship was not without supporters in France, and the possibility that France might be brought around to accept the plan did much to moderate the tone of the debate at United Nations headquarters. Asian and African supporters of the Algerian nationalists did not want to prejudice the chance of negotiations, still less to bring in a resolution that would fail to get a two-thirds majority. Ambassador Lodge gave a carefully balanced exposition of the United States view (December 3) in which he managed to avoid any flat statement except that "it is desirable to avoid any action in the United Nations that might hamper progress toward a peaceful and equitable solution." All kinds of face-saving compromises and temporizing resolutions were discussed and in the end (December 6) the Political Committee found itself unable to approve any resolution at all, having split 37-37 on an Asian-African draft watered down by Western amendments.

A fresh attempt in the plenary session was more successful, and on December 10 the Assembly found itself agreeing 80-0 (with France not participating) on a compromise text [12] that expressed concern over the Algerian situation, took note of the Moroccan-Tunisian offer of good offices, and voiced the decidedly moderate "wish that, in a spirit of effective cooperation, pourparlers will be entered into, and other appropriate means utilized, with a view to a solution, in conformity with the purposes and principles of the Charter of the United Nations." "Pourparlers," it was explained, was a less formal term than "negotiations," although its import was similar.

What kind of pourparlers France would be prepared to enter into, if any, would doubtless depend on the measure of its military success in the coming months. In France and presumably in Algeria itself, many people were coming to share the widespread feeling of the outside world that almost any solution would be preferable to the continuation of a state of affairs that had already entailed so much suffering and loss of life.

Sharply as this mild resolution contrasted with the fervor of some advocates of Algerian independence, it went considerably farther than the Assembly proved willing to go in regard to either West Irian or Cyprus. Though both questions gave rise to some intense and in part embittered debate, in neither was it possible to obtain a formal expression of Assembly views. The issues, indeed, were not precisely identical to those in the Algerian case, aside from the fact that all three were concerned with attempts to supplant the authority of one of the European colonial powers. In Algeria, the nationalist objective was complete independence from France. In Cyprus, it was "self-determination"—not, however, as a step toward independence but as a preliminary to union with Greece. In Dutch-ruled Western New Guinea, or West Irian, there was no nationalist movement at all; here the agitation came entirely from Indonesia, and was directed toward neither independence nor "self-determination" but simply toward substituting Indonesian rule for that of the Netherlands. On both Cyprus and West Irian, critics of the existing status were able to muster a technical majority in the Assembly's Political Committee but fell short of the two-thirds vote required for the final enactment of important Assembly resolutions. The United Nations, in other words, was prevented from taking an official stand by the attitude of a substantial element within its membership (including the United States) which either voted "no" or abstained.

This was already an old experience for Indonesia, which had been trying since 1954 to secure some kind of United Nations endorsement of the claim to sovereignty over Netherlands New Guinea which it based on the Netherlands-Indonesian treaty of 1949. A precisely similar fate had befallen a proposal advanced in February, during the Eleventh Regular Session, to set up a Good Offices Committee to assist in negotiations with the Dutch Government. The new development in the autumn was the increased vehemence of the Indonesian regime, which had begun to intimate that if Indonesia failed to get its "sovereign rights" through the United Nations it would resort to "other methods"—methods which, in President Sukarno's phrase (November 7), would "startle the world." The refusal of the Netherlands to negotiate, Foreign Minister Subandrio assured the Political Committee (November 20), was "very dangerous" and might lead to "unforeseen and undesirable—even explosive—events in the international field." These threats, supplemented by typical anti-Western charges from Soviet quarters, nevertheless failed to upset the Assembly's traditional voting pattern on the issue. An Asian-African resolution, calling for new negotiations between the Netherlands and Indonesia with the assistance of Secretary-General Hammarskjold, was approved by the Political Committee, but lost out in the Assembly on November 29 by a vote of 41 in favor, 29 opposed, and 11 abstentions. The United States, which wanted to offend neither Indonesia nor the Netherlands and took the position that the arguments on both sides were "closely balanced," adhered to its now usual policy of abstention despite the inevitable criticism of this stand by both parties.

The Indonesians had not been talking idly when they spoke of a determination to resort to "other measures." Their reaction to the vote in New York not only "startled the world" but threatened to break down whatever remained of political coherence in Indonesia itself. The target of Indonesian reprisals, spearheaded by the ultranationalist and left-wing groups around President Sukarno, was the remaining Dutch interest in Indonesia, comprising a Dutch colony of some 46,000 persons and a $1.5 billion economic investment whose preservation would have seemed to be of sufficiently obvious importance to both countries. In an atmosphere recalling that of Abdel Nasser's nationalization of the Suez Canal Company, Dutch banks, shipping companies, plantations and other enterprises were taken over, partly by official

and partly by unofficial action, and preparations were made
to expel or repatriate the entire Dutch population, most of
which was of Asian or Eurasian blood. Meanwhile internal
political tensions were sharpening, accentuated by an unsuccessful attempt on President Sukarno's life on November
30. The autonomy movement in the outer islands continued
to gain in strength and was becoming increasingly identified
with opposition to Communism and to the line of policy
identified with President Sukarno. The latter, it was announced, would go abroad for a "rest" early in the new year.
Foiled in its ambition to take over Netherlands New Guinea,
Indonesia's central government seemed to be running into
more and more trouble in trying to manage affairs at home.

The United Nations debate on Cyprus, though similar in
form, seemed unlikely to provoke such untoward consequences. Since February, when the Assembly had unanimously expressed its "earnest desire" for "a peaceful, democratic and just solution" of the Cyprus problem, the local atmosphere in Cyprus had improved considerably thanks to
the release of Archbishop Makarios and the suspension of
the EOKA terrorist campaign (section 9). Although Greece
had declined to entrust the mediation of its differences with
Great Britain and Turkey to NATO, as had been urged by
Secretary-General Spaak, there had been quiet diplomatic
discussions and some rather vague indications that an agreed
settlement might be in the offing.

Discussion at the United Nations did not get under way
until the last week of the Assembly session. In a draft resolution introduced by Greece and amended by the efforts of
Canada and other powers, the Assembly was asked to express
its concern that no progress toward a solution had been made
and to voice its "earnest hope that further negotiations and
discussions will be undertaken in a spirit of co-operation
with a view to having the right of self-determination applied
in the case of the people of Cyprus." This, however, was a
larger order than the Assembly as a whole was willing to sign.
It gained only thirty-three votes in the Political Committee
and only thirty-one in the plenary session, where the final
tally on December 14 brought out twenty-three opposing

votes and twenty-four abstentions, including that of the
United States. "Cyprus," said Ambassador Lodge (December
12), "is not the kind of problem which can be solved by
United Nations deliberations in the absence of agreement
among the parties." Even the Asian and African states showed
no particular interest in this quarrel among NATO members.
The Greek Cypriote nationalists, though heartened by the
fact that the resolution had at least won a "moral" victory
in the committee stage, would evidently have to put their
trust for the immediate future in the conciliatory disposition
of the new colonial governor, Sir Hugh Foot. From a long-
run point of view, the best hope of accommodation appeared
to lie in the possibility—admittedly still tenuous—that Greece,
Turkey, and Great Britain would be more ready to resolve
their dispute now that NATO as a whole faced problems of
such gravity.

That the force of the anticolonial movement was far from
having spent itself was to be further evidenced by a series
of developments in the closing weeks of the year which found
Communist, uncommitted, and even Western-oriented countries attacking one or another of the remaining footholds retained by the colonial powers in overseas territories. Iran
reasserted its claim to sovereignty over the British-protected
sheikdom of Bahrein; Guatemala formally renewed its long-
standing claim to British Honduras; a sudden offensive by
the so-called "Moroccan Liberation Army" all but conquered
the small Spanish colony of Ifni on the African west coast,
prompting Spain to divert important elements of its armed
forces to West Africa and the Canary Islands. In the last days
of December, a powerful instrument for unifying and
manipulating these sporadic anticolonial tendencies in the
Soviet interest was forged in Cairo at an "Asian-African
People's Solidarity Conference," attended by unofficial representatives from forty countries and colonial territories,
which was virtually dominated by the Communists, heard
lavish promises of Soviet support for anticolonial movements
everywhere, and established a permanent "Asia-African
People's Solidarity Council" to coordinate anticolonial activities throughout the Asian-African world. Such develop-

ments testified to the fact that the Western powers, no less than the Soviet Union, faced problems that were likely to continue with them for a decade if not for a generation.

27. OUTLOOK ON THE ECONOMIC AND SOCIAL FRONT

The founders of the United Nations had been well aware that a mechanism for dealing with international disputes and acts of aggression, no matter how perfectly constituted, was not enough to ensure the defense of peace and the growth of a tolerable world order. Threats to the peace, breaches of the peace, and demands for the redress of grievances were merely the acute symptoms of disorder in the international body politic. The responsibility of the United Nations, as defined in Article 1 of the Charter, was not limited to the symptoms but extended to the deeper sources of international friction and instability—to the development of "friendly relations among nations based on the principle of equal rights and self-determination of peoples," to "other appropriate measures to strengthen international peace," and, significantly, to the achievement of "international cooperation in solving international problems of an economic, cultural, or humanitarian character, and in promoting and encouraging respect for human rights and for fundamental freedoms for all without distinction as to race, sex, language, or religion."

In the twelve years since the adoption of the Charter, the importance of these broader areas of international policy had become increasingly evident as new nations joined the international chorus and as the Communist states disclosed their intention to exploit the imperious demand of the world's "underprivileged" populations for better living conditions and a more dignified status as human beings. This was the essential meaning of Khrushchev's insistence on the idea of "peaceful competition" between the "socialist" and "capitalist" systems. The "socialist" system, so he claimed, was in a better position than its rival to satisfy the aspirations of great masses of people in the economically underdeveloped countries—and even within the "capitalist" world—who were no longer content with the meager existence they and their forebears had known. "We believe that our Socialist system will be victorious," he had told the American television audience on June 2, "but that does not mean . . . that we want to impose that system on anyone. We simply believe that the people of each country themselves will come to realize that that system is best for them."

Although few Americans had taken seriously Khrushchev's further assertion that their own grandchildren would live under "socialism," there were responsible observers in the United States (as well as elsewhere in the West) who appreciated the far-reaching implications of Soviet interest in the economic, social, and psychological fields. Vice-President Nixon was one of those who felt that the advent of Sputnik had if anything accentuated the importance of this area of East-West competition. The fearful nature of modern weapons, the Vice-President suggested in a speech of October 15, might still be a deterrent to all-out atomic war, but it was just as certainly a stimulant to "cold war":

"It does mean that we must be prepared for an all-out Communist economic offensive to win the allegiance of hundreds of millions of people in the uncommitted world, as well as even some of those in the free world. . . . If it succeeds in extending Communist rule throughout Africa and Asia, the Kremlin will have assured its victory in the battle for the world. . . . The Western world will be forced to surrender without the firing of a shot. . . . This is a real threat—not so dramatic or spectacular as sputnik and the I.C.B.M.—but in my opinion potentially more dangerous in the long run."

"The greatest danger of all," said Adlai E. Stevenson in similar terms in an address of December 9,

". . . is not the weapons revolution but what I [have] referred to as the nationalist revolution of rising expectations. Here also the Soviet is making a massive effort to win the uncommitted peoples and tip the scale of power by subversion, propaganda and political and economic penetration. This is the hot war now. . . . Any Western response to the Communist challenge that ignores this struggle is no response in my judgment."

There were other factors beside Sputnik that seemed to justify a more attentive regard for these somewhat neglected aspects of the East-West struggle. While world attention focused on the Soviet penetration of outer space, there had been a number of signs that all was not going well with the economic life of the non-Communist nations. The various expedients by which the United States had managed to push its exports to unprecedented levels while continuing to restrict its imports from other free world countries were no longer producing quite satisfactory results. By the middle of 1957, substantial losses of gold and dollar reserves had occurred in a number of countries involved in trade with the United States, thus setting the stage for a new round of uncoordinated remedial measures. France devalued the franc from 350 to 420 to the dollar in a two-stage operation on August 10 and October 27, preliminary to seeking extraordinary credits from American and international sources. Great Britain increased the bank rate and took other deflationary steps designed to "save the pound" while preparing to draw half of the $500 million credit arranged by the Export-Import Bank the winter before. West Germany resisted considerable pressure to revalue its currency upward as an aid to its European competitors. Latin America was suffering from a general decline in the prices of coffee and other typical export products. In the Far East, Japan had begun to cut its imports as the first step in a new austerity program (section 19); the Philippines were about to embark on similar action. India, its foreign exchange reserves nearing exhaustion, was desperately seeking $1 billion or more to carry out at least the "central core" of its Second Five-Year Plan. Increasingly, the whole free world seemed to be going into a downward spiral. By November the American economic indexes were revealing significant declines in production, income, and employment, and apprehension over the possible international repercussions was mounting in Europe and elsewhere.

The possibility of a new economic recession like that of 1948–1949 or even the milder one of 1953–1954 was a topic of lively, if still unofficial, interest at such international economic gatherings as the annual meetings of the International Bank and Fund, the Commonwealth Finance Ministers, the Colombo Plan Consultative Committee, and the Contracting Parties to the General Agreement on Tariffs and Trade. In conjunction with the prospect of an intensified Soviet economic challenge, it lent added significance to such experiments as the proposed European Economic Community, now scheduled to go into operation at the beginning of 1958, and the European free trade area which was under renewed discussion among the seventeen nations of the Organization for European Economic Cooperation. The Economic Community or Common Market, despite the enthusiasm of some of its proponents and a perfunctory endorsement by the NATO heads of government at their December meeting, could not be said to enjoy unqualified popularity in the free world. The notion of an exclusive trading organization in Europe was felt by many outsiders to harbor threats to their trade. Whether the common tariff the new market would present to the outside world would be in harmony with the principles of the General Agreement on Tariffs and Trade, which would have to authorize this departure from multilateral practice, was a subject of searching inquiry and debate. Indeed, the Common Market shared the limelight with American agricultural policies as an object of unfavorable attention at the annual GATT session in Geneva late in the year.[13]

The current economic outlook also lent unusual significance to the economic intentions of the United States, always the most important single influence on world economic trends. The view was frequently expressed in American quarters during these early weeks of the post-Sputnik period that the role of the United States in economic affairs in recent years had been less than distinguished. "The United States has fallen short of its obvious and reasonable responsibilities," declared Henry R. Luce (October 18). "It has failed to do what could reasonably have been expected of it as the greatest economic power in history." Clarence B. Randall expressed the opinion (December 9) that United States businessmen had been "stone deaf and sight blind" regarding the significance of Soviet penetration in underdeveloped countries, even when it meant the seizure of their own markets.

Yet it remained quite uncertain how far the nation's foreign economic policy could or would be adjusted to the new situation that now seemed to be developing. The Reciprocal Trade Agreements legislation, last renewed for a three-year period in 1955, was due to expire on June 30, 1958, and the administration now made known [14] that it would seek a five-year renewal with authority to reduce tariffs by as much as 25 to 30 percent of prevailing levels. Also on the administration program was a fourth attempt to obtain congressional consent to American membership in the Organization for Trade Cooperation. But many observers predicted that these efforts would meet even more determined opposition than in the past; and in the eyes of those who supported a bold approach, the administration program itself was vitiated by certain proposed modifications of the Trade Agreements Act which were felt to open the door to increased protection for threatened American industries.

In the crucial field of economic assistance to underdeveloped countries, official Washington was now beginning to lay increased stress on the importance of countering the Soviet economic offensive. Its principal concern, however, seemed to be to ward off further reductions in the Mutual Security Program rather than trying to expand it. Whereas in May the administration had estimated the needs of the new Development Loan Fund in the fiscal years 1959 and 1960 at $750 million annually, in December it talked only of securing the appropriation of the $625 million which Congress had authorized but not appropriated for fiscal 1959. It did, however, propose a significant $2 billion increase in the lending authority of the Export-Import Bank, which was somewhat limited in its freedom to make loans for general development purposes but was favorably regarded by Congress and for that reason might prove a more suitable long-term instrument for such development assistance as the administration found essential. As always, Washington adhered to the fundamental position (restated by Vice-President Nixon in an address to the National Association of Manufacturers on December 6) that "the primary and the preferred source of capital for newly developing countries must, and it should, be private investment rather than Government loans and grants."

This insistence on the primary role of private capital had long been the keynote of United States participation in the economic work of the United Nations, always largely concerned with the problem of investment capital for the less developed countries. On the one hand, the United States had supported both the United Nations Technical Assistance Program and the establishment of the new International Finance Corporation, which had been set up in 1956 and by September 1957 was able to report five loans totaling $6 million to private industries in four countries. (About twenty additional investments were said to be under active consideration.) On the other hand, the United States had consistently opposed the popular idea of a Special United Nations Fund for Economic Development (SUNFED), to be set up with a capital of perhaps $250 million to make long-term, low-interest loans to underdeveloped countries.

American opposition to SUNFED, which was based on the contention that no funds would be available for such purposes until there had been substantial disarmament, was unwaveringly maintained throughout the Twelfth Session of the General Assembly. The United States did, however, take the initiative in the establishment at the Twelfth Session of a Special Fund, with an anticipated annual budget of perhaps $100 million, which was to begin operations in 1959 and was designed to expand the scope of the existing United Nations technical assistance programs with special emphasis on resource surveys, training institutes, and agricultural and industrial research centers.[15] Such undertakings could be viewed as laying the groundwork for a future development fund, and were so regarded by spokesmen for less developed countries. Representative Walter H. Judd of the United States delegation undertook to try to persuade Congress that the United States ought to contribute not less than 40 percent of the amounts in question.

The adoption of this plan, essentially a compromise between the United States position and that of SUNFED advocates, failed to dissipate the widespread interest in the latter project or to bridge the larger differences of opinion that still prevailed between developed and less developed countries. These differences were aired in several international meetings during the latter part of 1957—perhaps most fully at the annual session of the International Bank and Fund, which opened with a reminder from President Eisenhower (September 23) that economic development was "a homespun product, the result of a people's work and determination, . . . not a product that can be imported from some other country." Eugene R. Black, the President of the International Bank, referred on a number of occasions to the tendency of less developed countries to indulge in wasteful and overambitious projects while evading the sometimes disagreeable steps necessary to control inflation and attract private capital.

Undaunted by these reminders, spokesmen for the less developed countries invariably countered that private capital had not been forthcoming in the requisite amounts, that institutions like the World Bank had been overcautious (in eleven years of operation up to mid-1957, the Bank had committed a total of $3.1 billion in 170 loans in forty-five countries), and that many of their difficulties were directly traceable to the economic policies of the industrialized countries, the sharply increased costs of needed machinery and finished goods, and the low prices paid for their primary products. Two developments of the autumn of 1957 showed that considerably more was at stake in this argument than mere questions of economic theory. Indonesia's seizure of the principal Dutch properties in its territory (section 26) indicated that here, as in Egypt, there had been considerations more important to the underdeveloped nation in question than the maintenance of a favorable investment climate. India's agreement with the Soviet Union on methods of utilizing the 500 million ruble ($125 million) development credit granted in 1956 [16] served as a reminder that countries in need of capital assistance were no longer obliged to limit themselves to Western sources if the West found itself unable or unwilling to meet their requirements.

In fairness to the point of view of the less developed countries, it should be said'that most of them would have preferred so far as possible to obtain necessary external assistance through the United Nations and its specialized agencies rather than assuming the risks and obligations involved in aid received directly from any one of the great powers. The ideal arrangement, from their point of view, would have followed some such pattern as that of the United Nations Children's Fund (UNICEF), an agency dedicated wholly to the welfare of the coming generation and relatively undisturbed by current political considerations. But even UNICEF, though it escaped the direct impact of great-power rivalries, was limited by the comparatively modest scale on which most United Nations members felt able to support its activities. For 1957, total contributions and pledges came to slightly over $17 million, with the United States contributing 55 percent.

Such limitations were even more noticeable in connection with those United Nations activities that were concerned with the relief of distressed groups whose troubles had a political origin. The future of the Arab refugees, for instance, was imperiled not only by inadequate financial resources but also by the long-continued refusal of the Arab states and Israel to provide them with permanent homes. Similar though less publicized difficulties beset other groups of refugees in Europe and the Far East. In contrast to the relatively prompt resettlement of most of the 195,000 refugees from the recent revolution in Hungary, some 40,000 World War II refugees still lived in camps in Europe, with perhaps 250,000 others living outside camps but not yet permanently resettled. Resettlement for these persons could be accomplished only on an individual basis and only with the consent of individual national governments, few of which displayed much eagerness to assist. Collectively, through the General Assembly, they decided on November 26 to continue the office of United Nations High Commissioner for Refugees for another five years starting in 1959; to set up new financial arrangements in the hope that the remaining camps in Europe could be closed out by the end of 1960; and to appeal for assistance to some 700,000 Chinese refugees who had entered Hong Kong since the Communist victory in China.

The plight of the refugee in this "century of the homeless man," as one authority called it, was perhaps the most poignant illustration of the more general problem of human dignity and fundamental human rights with which the United Nations had been concerned for over a decade. Here, too, however, there were definite limitations on what the United Nations as such could hope to accomplish. It could proclaim standards, could recommend and exhort, but actual observance of human rights would continue to depend on the attitude of individual national governments, of their political subdivisions, and of the mass of their population. An example of the unavoidable weakness of the United Nations in this field was afforded by the Assembly's repeated condemnation of the racial segregation (Apartheid) policies of the Union of South Africa, which had not only failed to bring about a modification of the policies in question but had led the South African Government to reduce its participation in the United Nations almost to the vanishing point. At both the Eleventh and Twelfth Sessions, the Assembly gave renewed expression to its views on Apartheid and again urged South Africa to negotiate with India and Pakistan with a view to tempering its official discrimination against persons of Indian origin; but the government of South African Prime Minister J. G. Strijdom seemed as unlikely to heed these appeals as it was to negotiate with the United Nations about the international status of South West Africa, another subject of Assembly concern at each successive session.

On a broader if more abstract plane, the United Nations was still struggling with the attempt to draw up general international covenants on political rights and economic and social rights, as well as a draft convention on freedom of information which after years of effort was now ready for circulation to member states. More promising in some respects was a new emphasis in the work of the Human Rights Commission, originally suggested by the United States, whereby attention had been shifted from matters of theory to concrete human rights problems and the exchange of experience gained through practical work in the human rights field.

Many of the economic, social, and cultural problems that thus engaged the attention of the General Assembly (usually after intensive discussion in the Economic and Social Council and its subordinate commissions) were also of concern to one or more of the eleven United Nations specialized agencies. But whereas in the United Nations proper the Soviet Union and the governments of the Soviet bloc played a role that was invariably obstreperous and usually obstructive, Communist participation in the specialized agencies was much more limited and the opportunities for constructive work were correspondingly increased. The Soviet Union itself was a nonmember of four of the most important of these agencies, the Food and Agriculture Organization, the International Civil Aviation Association, and the International Bank and International Monetary Fund. These organizations were normally spared such embarrassments as the standard (and invariably unsuccessful) Soviet demand for the seating of Communist China in all international bodies in which it participated.

In the case of one of the specialized agencies, the International Labor Organization, the participation of the Soviet Union raised an important political issue unrelated to the China problem. Many Western businessmen, particularly some of those associated with the United States employers' delegation, were unsympathetic to the arrangement whereby Moscow was represented by three nominally independent delegations representing government, employers, and labor. There was also considerable opposition in the United States on constitutional grounds to a draft treaty outlawing forced labor which was approved by the International Labor Conference at its fortieth session in the summer of 1957. Although a committee of distinguished Americans headed by Joseph E. Johnson had recently made a special study of the I.L.O. and urged that the United States make more effective use of its potentialities for promoting improved labor standards and democratic labor practices, some spokesmen for the

American business community continued to question the value of participating at all.

The ideological issues that loomed so large in the work of I.L.O. and in that of the United Nations Educational, Scientific and Cultural Organization (UNESCO) were less in evidence in the Food and Agriculture Organization, in which only Poland participated from the Soviet bloc, and in the World Health Organization, which confined itself to such essentially nonpolitical fields as malaria control. Moreover, there seemed a fair chance that ideological quarrels would be soft-pedaled if not completely banished from the youngest of all the international agencies associated with the United Nations, the sixty-two nation International Atomic Energy Agency (section 7). When this organization opened its First General Conference in Vienna on October 1, the Soviet Union refrained from opposing the selection of former Representative W. Sterling Cole of the United States as Director-General, despite its expressed preference for a more "neutral" figure. Furthermore, it offered to provide the agency with fifty kilograms of fissionable Uranium 235, which might not be much (it was equivalent to 1 percent of the amount already pledged by the United States) but considering the source was not without significance. The statute of this new agency, as President Eisenhower pointed out in a message to the conference on its opening day, represented "the will and the aspirations of more nations than ever before subscribed to an international treaty." If Soviet participation continued in the spirit that marked the agency's opening days, the occasion might indeed by remembered some day, in Mr. Eisenhower's phrase, "as marking the turning point where man's fears of the atom yielded to hope, and to the wider cooperation necessary to establish that peace which is desired of all men."

28. DILEMMA FOR THE WEST

Everyone in the West could understand that it would take considerably more than the establishment of a new international agency to assure peace and avert nuclear destruction in the years ahead. Soviet technological and military prowess, in conjunction with Soviet belligerency in the Middle East and intransigence in the disarmament discussion, was almost universally felt to call for urgent new initiatives on a scale that would involve a major readjustment of past Western policy. Merely to persist in the old attitudes and lines of action (or inaction) associated with NATO and its member governments would be to risk a steady deterioration in the over-all position of the Western world relative to that of the Communist bloc—a deterioration that might well culminate in either a war of desperation or a series of bloodless surrenders that would destroy the essence of all that the West had appeared to stand for.

It was equally evident that these new Western initiatives which all felt to be necessary would have to be taken for the most part outside of the United Nations. Useful as that organization might be for the handling of specific issues and for communication among governments belonging to different political camps, it possessed no qualifications for dealing with the kind of problems by which the West was now confronted. The issues posed by the latest Soviet developments had first to be examined on the level of the individual Western governments, then clarified so far as possible by intergovernmental consultation in a purely Western setting. Only when the Western nations as a group had achieved something like a unity of viewpoint and resolve would it be possible to impart a new impetus to Western policy on a broader international front.

Mainly for this reason, Western action at the Twelfth Session of the General Assembly had been largely in the nature of a holding operation, aimed primarily at maintaining established positions while this work of clarification was going forward in the various Western capitals. From October onward, Western attention had focused less on the United Nations than on the annual December meeting of the NATO Council, generally regarded as the natural point of origin for a new and improved Western policy. In recognition of the unique circumstances of the occasion, the NATO governments had promptly endorsed a suggestion from Secretary-General Spaak that this particular meeting be held at the "heads-of-government" level rather than being limited as usual to the ministers of foreign affairs, defense, and finance of the fifteen NATO countries. President Eisenhower, who had often deplored the difficulty of absenting himself from Washington for visits to other NATO capitals, made plans for his first trip outside the Western Hemisphere since the Geneva "summit" conference of 1955. Even the slight stroke which the President suffered on November 25 was not allowed to interfere with this intention. As the General Assembly completed its session in New York on Saturday, December 14, Mr. Eisenhower was already arriving in Paris in readiness for the NATO meeting opening on Monday morning.

The tremendous publicity buildup which preceded this extraordinary conference made it almost certain that the results would prove somewhat disappointing to the Western peoples, if not to their governments. After the psychological shocks of the preceding months, the Western public badly needed a little encouragement. One of the most serious dangers confronting the alliance, as Prime Minister Macmillan commented at the opening session, was "what I would call, not the breaking of the spirit of our peoples—I do not fear that that will happen—but a kind of wearying of the spirit, because the struggle goes on so long, year after year, and the peoples do not see the end of it." Yet only a substantial unity of outlook among the Western governments would have made possible the impressive manifestation of Western purposes that the occasion seemed to demand. In reality, the unity of the Western governments ten weeks after Sputnik I was still very far from complete. Everyone agreed that there was need for a new Western policy. But there was still no real agreement as to what the policy should be.

Up to the moment of the Soviet Union's triumphant penetration of outer space, Western diplomacy and defense arrangements had reflected a more or less clear-cut assumption that the inherent strength of the Western community was sufficient to assure it of a permanent and, in the long run, decisive margin of superiority over the Communist bloc. The latter, by concentrating its resources, could undoubtedly threaten the West at numerous critical points; but the West, with its tremendous material potential and, above all, its superior intellectual and spiritual endowment, could always keep sufficiently ahead to ensure the survival and ultimate triumph of its own values. Not only could it protect the existing area of freedom in the world with the aid of such devices as NATO, SEATO, the Baghdad Pact, and "the deterrent of retaliatory power." In the official American view, at least, it could expect to witness sooner or later a far-reaching change of heart in Moscow, the transformation of the existing Communist dictatorships, and the righting of such historic wrongs as the division of Germany and the imposition of totalitarian rule in Eastern Europe.

For many in the West, however, this assumption of superiority—always more fully accepted in the United States than in Europe—was fundamentally discredited by the evidence of the two Sputniks. Secretary Dulles himself conceded on November 5 that in the light of the Russians' proved technological skills and power to mobilize them, there was little chance of restoring the "preponderance of power" which the West, particularly the United States, had enjoyed a decade earlier. Other reactions were more categorical. A typical European comment was that of the newspaper *Paris-Presse*, which wrote on October 7 that the free world had at last been awakened from its soothing belief in "the indisputable and invulnerable superiority of America." Prime Minister Macmillan, who had hastened to Washington for conferences with the President soon after Sputnik I, told the House of Commons on November 5 that he would say "without hesitation and without excuse that I believe this to be a real turning point in history, for I believe that never has the threat of Russian and Soviet Communism been so great, or the need for the countries to organise themselves against it to be so urgent." Americans, Mr. Macmillan reported, "are no longer confident that even their great country can do everything itself without allies to secure its own survival and still less to secure the survival of the ideals for which they stand."

If the United States and the West were indeed in danger of

falling behind their main opponent in terms of weapons systems and general scientific and technological advance, one obvious recourse was to intensify and coordinate their efforts in the hope of regaining a safe lead. This was the principal theme of the Eisenhower-Macmillan consultations on October 23–25, the fruit of which was a "Declaration of Common Purpose" [17] affirming that "the concept of national self-sufficiency is now out of date" and that the countries of the free world could find progress and safety "only in genuine partnership, by combining their resources and sharing tasks in many fields." Specifically, the two governments decided to propose to NATO "an enlarged Atlantic effort in scientific research and development," and the President further undertook to ask Congress to amend the Atomic Energy Act "to permit of close and fruitful collaboration of scientists and engineers of Great Britain, the United States, and other friendly countries." Underlying the entire discussion was the notion of a broad pooling of skills, resources, weapons, and production facilities, on either an Anglo-American or a NATO basis, as the only way of drawing the full benefit of each country's special capabilities.

Following immediately on the welcome extended to Queen Elizabeth II and the Duke of Edinburgh on their brief visit to the United States, the Macmillan mission dispelled most of the remaining shadows of the Suez crisis and restored the Anglo-American partnership to something like its old status. From now on, "interdependence" was to be the watchword. To this extent, at least, the free world had reason to be grateful to Khrushchev, even though France, which was immersed in the prolonged cabinet crisis that preceded the formation of the Gaillard government, was not yet a party to this new-found harmony and, indeed, looked with grave suspicion on the separate arrangements being made by its two partners.

In the United States itself there was much to be done if the national setback advertised by Sputnik was to be repaired. "Sputnik has come; American complacency has gone," wrote Senator Kennedy in an article distributed by the North American Newspaper Alliance. [18] "Not since the Korean war

has the general public been jarred with such an acute consciousness of international peril." Concepts which had prevailed as recently as a month or two before were now being
subjected to drastic reexamination, among them the $38 bil-
lion ceiling imposed on the Defense Department during the
summer (section 5). "Our people . . . will not sacrifice security to worship a balanced budget," declared the President on
November 13, although he added that a balanced budget
was still an indispensable long-term aid to a sound economy
and total security. Amid public and congressional clamor for
a greatly intensified missile program, an additional $600
million was made available to the new Secretary of Defense,
Neil H. McElroy, and there was talk of a spending total
of perhaps $39.5 billion for fiscal year 1959. Repeatedly the
President, Secretary Dulles, and Vice-President Nixon min-
gled reassurances about the present position with warnings
of the need for more effort and sacrifice in the period ahead.
Unprecedented attention was given to the need for improvements in the educational system, particularly in the physical
sciences. In recognition of the gravity of the hour, Adlai
Stevenson was brought into the State Department to advise
on preparations for the Paris meeting, and very nearly attended as an American delegate.

But if the first and most obvious response to Sputnik was
to try to safeguard the Western military lead, there were
many in the West who felt that this was not enough. "The
strongest military establishment in the world will not save
America's freedom if we fail to meet the threat which the
Communists present in the nonmilitary areas where they
have been so successful in the past," said Vice-President
Nixon on December 6.

"And if we in the United States take a worm's-eye view of the
world conflict and if we cut foreign aid and hamstring reciprocal
trade and emasculate our information program, I can tell you
that the billions we spend for missiles, submarines and aircraft
will be going right down a rathole."

Aside from the important problem of meeting the Soviet
challenge outside the military arena, Moscow's forward spurt

in the missile field had sharply recalled public attention to the supreme issue of the direct relations between East and West. For even if the Soviet lead were overcome—even if the United States succeeded, for example, in producing intermediate-range ballistic missiles by 1958 and intercontinental ones by the early 1960's—this in itself would afford no absolute guarantee of Western safety. The sole purpose of all our armaments, as American leaders had repeatedly emphasized, was to secure "peace with justice"; and since peace, at any rate, was obviously a two-sided proposition, there was a widespread feeling in the Western world that something would now have to be done about relations with Russia. Mr. Stevenson's greatest concern, he said shortly after completing his assignment at the State Department (December 9), was that a response to Sputnik "in terms just of greater military strength will serve to harden the division between East and West," instead of helping us to learn to live, as we must, with our adversaries as well as our allies.

Other Western authorities went beyond Mr. Stevenson's insistence that the United States lay renewed emphasis on its basic peaceful purposes. Both in the United States and abroad, the demand was heard that a fresh attempt be made to establish contact with the Soviet leaders and lay the political foundations for a peace that would rest on something better than the existing balance of terror. Rather typical in this respect was the attitude of Lester B. Pearson of Canada, recipient of the Nobel Peace Prize for 1957, who declared on November 3 that he saw no prospect of easing the tensions of the cold war if the West continued to insist on "a rigid, unconditional-surrender type of diplomacy" based on "inflexible hostility to Soviet Russia and every move she makes." The proper course for the West, according to Mr. Pearson, was to "go on seeking, patiently and persistently, a basis for negotiation and agreement. . . . When Russia has a legitimate interest in some area or development, we would be foolish to act as if that interest can either be ignored or destroyed." Possibly even more influential in promoting this line of thought in Europe was a series of radio talks given in

Britain by former Ambassador George F. Kennan, the originator of the doctrine of "containment." [19]

Discussion of these possibilities was greatly stimulated by
Khrushchev's proposal of November 6 for a new high-level
meeting of "capitalist" and "socialist" representatives. Long
before the NATO heads of government were ready to con-
vene, the problem of relations with Russia had begun to
overshadow the original concern with retrieving the Western
military position. In a good many instances, however, the
advocates of a new departure in East-West relations appeared
to underestimate the fundamental differences still prevailing
between the two groups. In cold reality, as Mr. Dulles more
than once pointed out,[20] there was no indication whatever
that contact with the Russians now would produce more
favorable results than it had done in the past. The Soviet
leaders themselves had made it sufficiently clear that their
objectives had not changed. They still aimed at breaking up
NATO, getting the United States out of Europe and the
Middle East, and in general securing for themselves a position of undisputed predominance in the world. Their current attitude on disarmament was sufficient evidence that
they had no real interest in seeking agreements of a mutually
advantageous character. If they had now resumed their agitation for East-West talks, presumably it was partly to embarrass and divide the West and partly because they now felt
themselves to be in a stronger bargaining position than
before. This, indeed, was the essence of the Western dilemma.
Lacking a more reliable margin of military superiority, the
Western peoples could find release from present anxieties only
through a settlement with Russia; yet the only kind of settlement that Russia seemed at all likely to consider was one that
would place the West at a permanent disadvantage and increase its vulnerability to future Soviet pressure.

A determination to capitalize on this situation, and if possible forestall Western attempts to redress the military balance, appeared to be the principal motive behind a new
Soviet diplomatic offensive which opened a week before the
NATO conference. By this time Moscow, like the rest of
the world, was well aware that the principal aim of the

United States at the Paris meetings would be to obtain an agreement on the deployment of intermediate-range ballistic missiles and nuclear warheads on the Continent of Western Europe, much as they were to be deployed in the United Kingdom under the Anglo-American agreement reached in Bermuda (section 8). Although it would be at least a year and probably more before such missiles were actually available, the United States attached great importance to the completion of preliminary arrangements in order to keep the Western position intact during the coming months and leave the Soviet Union in no doubt of its intentions. According to some authorities, Washington was counting on these 1,500-mile missiles, situated within easy range of the Soviet Union, to neutralize the *long-range* missiles Russia would soon have available, thus affording some protection to the United States itself until such time as this country was able to perfect its own intercontinental missile. In the interests of prompt agreement, the United States was prepared to give its European allies a considerable voice in determining the circumstances in which the missiles might be fitted with nuclear warheads and actually fired. But the prospect of seeing these devices added to the NATO armory in Europe was obviously not one the Russians could be expected to welcome. From the Soviet point of view, this in itself was sufficient reason to try to frustrate the intentions of the United States and encourage the misgivings which were already being voiced in many European quarters.

In this instance the Kremlin's sabotage effort took the form of a new series of letters from Premier Bulganin to the heads of the Western and various other interested governments, buttressed by a Soviet Government communication to all members of the United Nations.[21] With minor variations of detail, all these epistles told the same story: current Western policies were increasing the danger of a new and frightful war, the only alternative to which was a shift to "peaceful coexistence and cooperation," recognition of the existence of both capitalist and socialist countries in the world, renunciation of the use of force, an ending of hostile propaganda and of the arms race, etc., etc. Aside from a renewed suggestion relative to a "top-level meeting of representatives of the capitalist and socialist countries," the principal novelty was a proposal (already advanced by Poland in the United Nations) to exclude nuclear weapons from the territory of Eastern and Western Germany, Poland, and Czechoslovakia. This idea went back at least as far as the Geneva summit conference, and its successive reincarnations never failed to arouse a sympathetic interest in some sections of Western opinion despite the adverse effect it would presumably have had on Western defense arrangements.

The speeches at the opening session of the NATO leaders on December 16 showed that the latest Soviet move had had a considerable impact. There was, it appeared, an unexpectedly wide official as well as popular interest in the idea of a new negotiation with Moscow—and a corresponding hesitation to accept the American offer of intermediate-range ballistic missiles. Chancellor Adenauer, who pointed out that the acceptance of missiles was a political question that would have to be left to the Bundestag, commented on the moderate language of Bulganin's proposals and voiced the opinion that there could be no objection to inquiring more specifically what the Soviet chief had in mind. Premier Einar Gerhardsen of Norway noted that his country's policy precluded the establishment of missile launching sites or nuclear stockpiles, and suggested that since the missiles were not ready to be installed anyway the whole matter might be put off until Moscow had an opportunity to prove its willingness to enter serious negotiations. Denmark's Premier H. C. Hansen took a similar line. Even Secretary-General Spaak, than whom there was no more steady advocate of an adequate NATO military posture, called on NATO to "assume the offensive" in the diplomatic sphere and make a concrete offer that would prove its eagerness to seize any opportunity of relaxing tensions.

With the NATO chiefs in this mood, even General Eisenhower was in no position to win unconditional acceptance of the American program, although its subsidiary features, dealing with such matters as coordinated research and production, were generally welcomed. The conference had to be prolonged for an extra day to allow time to devise a formula that would reconcile the American interest in a stronger nuclear-missile posture with the European interest in a new try at negotiations. The result, as embodied in the lengthy communiqué that closed the meeting on December 19,[22] was not particularly inspiriting from either standpoint. On the military side, there was no final decision. Details with respect to the deployment and use of intermediate-range missiles and nuclear warheads were to be worked out with the individual governments on the basis of recommendations by the NATO military authorities, whose proposals would be considered at a military conference to be held at ministerial level in the early months of 1958. On the political side, the fifteen governments restated their belief in the Western disarmament proposals already rejected by the Soviet Union, but said they were also willing to examine "any proposal, from whatever source, for general or partial disarmament" or controlled reduction of armaments. Without referring to Bulganin's proposal for a summit conference, they declared that if the Soviet Union persisted in its refusal to negotiate in the United Nations Disarmament Commission, they "would welcome a meeting at Foreign Ministers' level to resolve the deadlock." Such a meeting, if it occurred, would be the first since the ill-fated Geneva Foreign Ministers' conference in the fall of 1955.

Although the thirty-six-paragraph communiqué and an accompanying declaration of principles reaffirmed the standard NATO outlook in all its elements and laid heavy emphasis on the principles of interdependence, improved political consultation, economic cooperation, and the like, it was plain that for many of the participants—and for a large part of the European public—this small feeler extended in the direction of Moscow represented the principal achievement of the session. This was the more true because those countries that had come to the conference with special political objectives— France, for example, had hoped in vain for an acknowledgment of its "preeminent position" in North Africa, and the Netherlands had sought an expression of support in its quarrel with Indonesia—had generally failed to realize them.

Everything now depended on Moscow's answer. Had the diplomatic scales, upset by Sputnik, been evened by the somewhat indefinite prospect of missile launching sites in Western Europe?

To judge by the speeches which Gromyko and Khrushchev delivered before the Supreme Soviet in Moscow on December 21,[23] they had not. "The situation in the world today is different from what it was even a few months ago," said Gromyko. "The Soviet earth satellites have improved the political climate on our planet. They are doing a big job for peace and, not least, for disarmament." But neither Gromyko nor Khrushchev had any use for the NATO formula. The Soviet Union, they said, would negotiate neither in the Disarmament Commission nor at the Foreign Ministers' level. It did not choose to be a minority of one. By way of alternatives, Gromyko suggested a special session of the United Nations Assembly, an international disarmament conference, or a "summit conference" of capitalist and socialist countries. Khrushchev threw in the thought that a preliminary conference might take place between Soviet and American representatives. But both stressed that the only way to bring about fruitful negotiations was for the West to discard its "positions of strength" and "brink of war" policies and open its arms to "peaceful coexistence" on Soviet terms.

This was not the tone of men in a hurry for agreement with the West. In Moscow, apparently, negotiation and talk of negotiation were still viewed essentially as techniques of political warfare, not as a means to the settlement of differences. In the Soviet view, the real differences between the two camps were perhaps not susceptible of being settled at all. The fundamental Soviet aim, as Khrushchev had repeatedly boasted, was not merely to "coexist" with enemies (on Soviet terms) but eventually to supplant them. "We will bury you," he was supposed to have said. This aim the Kremlin would doubtless continue to pursue, whether or not negotiations with the West proved feasible at any particular moment. From its point of view, the main purpose of negotiation would be to improve its over-all political and military position relative to its opponents' and to advance the date when the "imperialist camp" would break up altogether.

Nor did the United States appear even now to view negotiation as a particularly promising way of working out the East-West difficulty. On the last day of the NATO meeting, Secretary Dulles delivered a speech in Paris [24] in which he reaffirmed his own view that fundamental changes would have to occur in the Soviet Union before there could be any hope of genuine peace. "We have got to be able to look forward to an ending of this menace," he said. He himself remained "absolutely confident" that if the free nations held together and preserved their freedom, the time would come when the Soviet rulers would "have to change their attitude toward their own people, toward the rest of the world."

After a brief stopover in Madrid to acquaint Generalissimo Franco with the results of the Paris meeting, Secretary Dulles joined the President at the White House on December 23 for a television report to the American people.[25] Unity, strength, and flexibility had been the themes of the conference, he said, and although Soviet rejection of the Western disarmament plan had compelled the NATO nations to proceed with new arrangements for nuclear weapons and missiles, there was every intention on the part of the West "to continue probing to find some evidence that there is within the Soviet Union the good will to resume serious efforts to achieve nuclear peace and to put behind us the horrible prospect of nuclear war." (All that was required to ease world tensions, the President commented at the end of the program, was "clear evidence of Communist integrity and sincerity in negotiation and in action.") Mr. Dulles in the course of his remarks also laid unusual stress on the importance of meeting the Soviet economic challenge in underdeveloped countries, and did not deny that the implementation of NATO's various decisions would require "sustained effort and sacrifice, perhaps a good deal of sacrifice, on the part of all of us." Alluding indirectly to the widespread view that NATO was suffering from a collapse of morale or a "crisis of confidence," the Secretary of State concluded on a note of reassurance:

"Oftentimes, the dominant mood seems to be one of dissension and perplexity and discouragement. But that impression may well be superficial. Beneath the ruffled surface there can be a great body of good will, confidence, and resolution. It is particularly appropriate that at this time of the year we should recognize and pay tribute to those sentiments, for they are the stuff out of which a better future can be built."

Notes to Chapter VII

Notes to Chapter VII

1. Official Soviet text in *New York Times,* October 10, 1957; see further Reston's comments, *ibid.,* October 8, 9, 10, and 11.

2. Text *ibid.,* November 22, 1957; excerpts in *Documents on American Foreign Relations, 1957,* no. 31.

3. Text in *New Times,* no. 46 (November 14, 1957), supplement.

4. *Ibid.,* no. 48 (November 28, 1957), pp. 1-3.

5. General Assembly Resolution 1133 (XI), September 14, 1957; *Documents on American Foreign Relations, 1957,* no. 50.

5a. The principal decisions of the Assembly are listed in chronological order, with resolution numbers, in the "Chronology of World Events," pp. 391-392.

6. Resolution 1148 (XII), November 14, 1957; *ibid.,* no. 151.

7. Resolution 1149 (XII), November 14, 1957; *ibid.,* no. 152.

8. Resolution 1150 (XII), November 19, 1957; *ibid.,* no. 153.

9. Resolution 290 (IV), December 1, 1949; *ibid., 1949,* pp. 306-307.

10. *Department of State Bulletin,* v. 37 (October 28, 1957), p. 674; *Documents on American Foreign Relations, 1957,* no. 70.

11. *Pravda,* October 30; *Current Digest of the Soviet Press,* v. 9, no. 44 (December 11, 1957), p. 20.

12. Resolution 1184 (XII), December 10, 1957; *Documents on American Foreign Relations, 1957,* no. 98.

13. For details cf. *Department of State Bulletin,* v. 37 (December 23, 1957), pp. 1004-1009.

14. Announcement of December 9, *ibid.* (December 30, 1957), pp. 1042-1043.

15. Resolution 1219 (XII), December 14, 1957; *ibid.,* v. 38 (January 13, 1958), pp. 71-72.

16. *Pravda* and *Izvestia,* November 11; *Current Digest of the Soviet Press,* v. 9, no. 45 (December 18, 1957), pp. 21-22.

17. *Department of State Bulletin,* v. 37 (November 11, 1957), pp. 739-741; *Documents on American Foreign Relations, 1957,* no. 23.

18. *New York Times,* December 8, 1957.

19. George F. Kennan, *Russia, the Atom and the West* (New York: Harper, 1958).

20. See especially John Foster Dulles, "Our Cause Will Prevail," *Department of State Bulletin*, v. 38 (January 6, 1958), pp. 19-22.

21. Letter to President Eisenhower, December 10, *ibid.* (January 27, 1958), pp. 127-130; *Documents on American Foreign Relations, 1957,* no. 14.

22. Declaration and communiqué in *Department of State Bulletin,* v. 38 (January 6, 1957), pp. 12-15; *Documents on American Foreign Relations, 1957,* no. 18.

23. *New York Times,* December 22, 1957.

24. *Department of State Bulletin,* v. 38 (January 13, 1958), pp. 53-55.

25. *Ibid.,* pp. 47-52; *Documents on American Foreign Relations, 1957,* no. 19.

CHRONOLOGY OF WORLD EVENTS

JANUARY 1–DECEMBER 31, 1957

THE UNITED STATES

Major Treaties

Entered into Force:

June 16—Treaty of Amity, Economic Relations, and Consular Rights with Iran (signed Tehran, Aug. 15, 1955; ratifications exchanged May 16, 1957).

July 29—Statute of the International Atomic Energy Agency (signed New York, Oct. 26, 1956; approved by Senate June 18, 1957).

Oct.   3—Convention for the Promotion of Inter-American Cultural Relations (signed Caracas, Mar. 28, 1954; in force Feb. 18, 1955; approved by Senate Aug. 8, 1957; ratification deposited Oct. 3, 1957).

Nov.   7—Treaty of Friendship, Commerce and Navigation with the Republic of Korea (signed Seoul, Nov. 28, 1956; approved by Senate Aug. 8, 1957; ratifications exchanged Oct. 7, 1957).

Dec.   5—Treaty of Friendship, Commerce and Navigation with the Netherlands (signed The Hague, Mar. 27, 1956; ratifications exchanged Nov. 5, 1957).

Congress

Jan. 3-Aug. 30. The 85th Congress holds its First Session and adopts the following major legislation relating to foreign affairs (with Public Law numbers and dates of presidential approval):

P.L. 85-7,   Mar. 9. Authorizing economic and military cooperation with nations of the Middle East. (See text, sec. 4.)

P.L. 85-49,   June 11. Fiscal year 1958 appropriations for State and Justice departments and related agencies.

P.L. 85-117, Aug. 2, Fiscal Year 1958 appropriations for Defense Department. (See text, sec. 5.)

P.L. 85-128, Aug. 13. Extending the Agricultural Trade Development and Assistance Act of 1954. (See text, sec. 6.)

P.L. 85-141, Aug. 14. Mutual Security Act of 1957. (See text, sec. 6.)

P.L. 85-177, Aug. 28. International Atomic Energy Agency Participation Act. (See text, sec. 7.)

P.L. 85-279, Sept. 3. Mutual Security appropriations for fiscal year 1958. (See text, sec. 6.)

P.L. 85-316, Sept. 11. Amending the Immigration and Nationality Act of 1952. (See text, sec. 7.)

Other Developments

Jan. 5. The President in a message to Congress presents a program for defense of the Middle East against Communist aggression. (See text, sec. 4.)

Jan. 20. President Eisenhower and Vice-President Richard M. Nixon begin their second term. Formal inauguration ceremonies are held Jan. 21.

Feb. 21. Christian A. Herter becomes Under-Secretary of State, replacing Herbert Hoover, Jr.

May 28-Oct. 7. A series of nuclear tests (Operation Blumb Bob) is held at the Nevada proving ground.

Aug. 15. Gen. Nathan F. Twining, U.S.A.F., succeeds Adm. Arthur W. Radford as Chairman of the Joint Chiefs of Staff.

Oct. 9. Neil H. McElroy succeeds Charles E. Wilson as Secretary of Defense.

Oct. 18. James B. Smith, Jr., succeeds John B. Hollister as Director of the State Department's International Cooperation Administration.

Nov. 15. Dr. James R. Killian, Jr., is sworn in as Special Assistant to the President for Science and Technology.

Nov. 15. George V. Allen succeeds Roy Larson as Director of the U.S. Information Agency.

Nov. 25. President Eisenhower suffers a cerebral arterial occlusion.

Dec. 16-19. The President attends the NATO heads-of-government conference in Paris. (See below.)

(For official visits, see country names.)

THE WESTERN COMMUNITY

(See also "The Commonwealth of Nations.")

Strategic Trade Controls

May 21-28. The 15-nation China Committee meets in Paris.

May 30. Great Britain announces that its strategic controls on trade with Communist China will be assimilated to those in effect for the European Soviet bloc. Similar announcements are made by Norway (June 1), Belgium (June 14), the Netherlands (June 14), France (June 19), the German Federal Republic (June 19), Italy (June 21), and Japan (July 16). (See text, sec. 6.)

North Atlantic Treaty Organization

Apr. 1. Lt. Gen. Hans Speidel (Germany) becomes Commander of NATO Ground Forces in Central Europe.

May 2-3. The NATO Council holds its regular ministerial meeting in Bonn and reiterates the determination to resist any attack by all available means. (See text, sec. 8.)

May 16. Paul-Henri Spaak (Belgium) succeeds Lord Ismay (U.K.) as NATO Secretary-General.

July 1. Three German divisions are placed under NATO command in Europe.

Dec. 16-19. The North Atlantic Council holds its 20th Ministerial Session at the heads-of-government level in Paris. (See text, sec. 28.)

European Integration

Mar. 25. The Treaty for the European Economic Community and the Treaty Creating a European Atomic Energy Community are signed in Rome by France, the German Federal Republic, Italy, Belgium, the Netherlands, and Luxembourg. Deposit of ratifications is completed Dec. 13. (See text, sec. 9.)

May 10. Renewal of the European Payments Union for one year from July 1 is authorized by the Council of the Organization for European Economic Cooperation (O.E.E.C.).

Nov. 14. Ministerial negotiations on the establishment of a European free trade area begin in Paris pursuant to a decision of the O.E.E.C. Council. (See text, sec. 9.)

Dec. 20. A 17-nation European Nuclear Energy Agency is established through the O.E.E.C. Council.

United Kingdom

Jan. 9. Sir Anthony Eden (Conservative) resigns as Prime Minister and is succeeded Jan. 10 by Harold Macmillan (Conservative). Selwyn Lloyd remains as Foreign Secretary.

Mar. 21-24. Prime Minister Macmillan and Foreign Secretary Lloyd confer in Bermuda with President Eisenhower and Secretary of State Dulles. (See text, secs. 3, 8.)

Apr. 5. A White Paper on Defense outlines radical changes in British military policy. (See text, sec. 8.)

May 15. Great Britain's first hydrogen bomb test is held at Christmas Island in the Pacific. Further tests occur May 31 and June 19. A new series of nuclear tests is held in Australia Sept. 14-Oct. 9.

Oct. 17-20. Queen Elizabeth II and the Duke of Edinburgh make a state visit to Washington.

Oct. 23-25. Messrs. Macmillan and Lloyd confer with the President and Secretary Dulles in Washington. (See text, sec. 28.)

France

Feb. 25-28. Premier Guy Mollet and Foreign Minister Christian Pineau confer with the President and Secretary of State in Washington.

May 21. The Mollet coalition government (installed Jan. 31, 1956) resigns following loss of a confidence vote.

June 11. Maurice Bourgès-Maunoury (Radical) forms France's 22nd Postwar cabinet, a coalition of Radicals and Socialists with M. Pineau as Foreign Minister.

Aug. 10. A dual exchange rate for the franc is established to protect the French balance-of-payments position. A full 20 percent devaluation is completed Oct. 27.

Sept. 30. Premier Bourgès-Maunoury submits his resignation after losing a confidence vote on Algeria.

Nov. 6. Félix Gaillard (Radical) is approved as head of France's 23rd postwar government, a seven-party coalition excluding the extreme Left and Right. M. Pineau remains as Foreign Minister.

The Federal Republic of Germany

Jan. 1. The Saar becomes the tenth state of the German Federal Republic.

Mar. 3-5. Foreign Minister Heinrich von Brentano confers with U.S. authorities in Washington.

Apr. 1. The first conscripts are inducted into the Federal armed forces.

May 26-28. Chancellor Konrad Adenauer confers with President Eisenhower in Gettysburg and Washington. (See text, sec. 11.)

Sept. 15. Elections to the Bundestag give the Christian Democratic party and Christian Social Union 270 seats; Social Democrats, 169 seats; Free Democrats, 41; German party, 17. (See text, sec. 10.)

Oct. 22. The Bundestag elects Dr. Adenauer to a third term as Chancellor beginning Oct. 29. Ludwig Erhard is Vice-Chancellor and Dr. von Brentano remains as Foreign Minister.

Italy

May 6. The coalition government of Antonio Segni (Christian Democrat, appointed July 6, 1955) resigns.

May 20. An all-Christian Democratic government is formed by Adone Zoli but resigns June 10.

June 27. A new all-Christian Democratic government is confirmed with Sig. Zoli as Prime Minister and Giuseppe Pella as Vice-Premier and Foreign Minister.

San Marino

Oct. 13. Installation of a non-Communist provisional government terminates twelve years of Communist rule. A new government formally takes office Oct. 23.

The Netherlands

Apr. 3. An air transport agreement with the U.S. is signed in Washington.

(See also "Indonesia.")

Denmark

May 14. The Social Democrats lose four seats in parliamentary elections. Premier H. C. Hansen (Socialist) forms a new government May 27.

Norway

Sept. 21. King Haakon VII (acceded 1905) dies and is succeeded by his son, Olav V.

Portugal

Nov. 3. National Union candidates are uniformly successful in elections to the National Assembly.

Nov. 15. The Defense Agreement of 1951 with the U.S. is extended to Dec. 31, 1962.

Turkey

Oct. 27. National elections reduce the Democratic party representation in the Grand National Assembly to 424 seats. Opposition parties win 186 seats.

Nov. 1. President Celâl Bayar (Democrat) is elected to a second four-year term by the Grand National Assembly. Premier Adnan Menderes (Democrat) is reappointed Nov. 2.

Austria

Jan. 4. President Theodor Koerner (Socialist, elected 1951) dies. Chancellor Julius Raab becomes acting Chief of State.

May 5. Vice-Chancellor Adolf Schaerf (Socialist) is elected President and inaugurated May 22.

Finland

Apr. 25. The Agrarian-Socialist coalition government of Premier Karl August Fagerholm (Socialist, appointed Mar. 3, 1956) resigns. Withdrawn May 16, the resignation is resubmitted May 22.

May 27. Vaino Johannes Sukselainen (Agrarian) forms a non-Socialist coalition government, but resigns Oct. 18 on loss of a confidence vote.

Nov. 29. Rainer von Fieandt forms a nonparty government.

Ireland

Feb. 12. The Dáil Eireann is dissolved following a vote of nonconfidence in the government of Prime Minister John A. Costello (Fine Gael, elected June 2, 1954).

Mar. 5. The Fianna Fáil is victorious in general elections.

Mar. 20. Eamon de Valera (Fianna Fáil) is elected Prime Minister by the Dáil.

Spain

Dec. 20. Secretary Dulles confers with Chief of State Francisco Franco in Madrid.

Sweden

Oct. 26. The government of Premier Tage Erlander (Social Democrat) resigns following the withdrawal of Agrarian party ministers. An all-Social Democratic cabinet headed by Mr. Erlander is inducted Oct. 31.

Switzerland

Jan. 1. Dr. Hans Streuli succeeds Dr. Markus Feldmann as President of the Swiss Confederation for 1957.

THE COMMONWEALTH OF NATIONS

Commonwealth Meetings

June 26-July 5. The Commonwealth Prime Ministers meet in London.

Sept. 28-Oct. 1. The Commonwealth Finance Ministers meet at Mont Tremblant, Que. (See text, sec. 22.)

Canada (see text, sec. 22)

Apr. 4. E. Herbert Norman, Canadian Ambassador to Egypt, commits suicide following release by the U.S. Senate Internal Security Subcommittee of testimony linking him with Communism.

May 31. The mid-Canada radar warning line is officially stated to be in operation.

June 10. The Liberal party loses its 22-year majority in the House of Commons as national elections give the Conservatives 110 seats, Liberals 104, Cooperative Commonwealth Federation 24, Social Credit 19.

June 17. The Liberal government of Prime Minister Louis S. St. Laurent (inducted Nov. 15, 1948) resigns. A Conservative government headed by

John Diefenbaker as Prime Minister in inducted June 21. Sidney E. Smith becomes Secretary of State for External Affairs Sept. 13.

July 31. The Distant Early Warning Line across northern Canada enters full operation.

Aug. 1. Canada and the U.S. announce plans to integrate their North American air defenses.

Oct. 7-8. The U.S.-Canadian Joint Committee on Economic Affairs meets in Washington.

New Zealand

Sept. 20. Keith Jack Holyoake (National party) succeeds Sidney G. Holland (National party) as Prime Minister.

Nov. 30. The Labor party wins a slight majority in parliamentary elections.

Dec. 12. Walter Nash (Labor party) heads a new cabinet as Prime Minister and Minister of External Affairs.

Union of South Africa

Apr. 2. The British naval base at Simonstown is turned over to the South African Government.

(See also "The United Nations.")

Pakistan (see text, sec. 15)

June 10. Prime Minister H. S. Suhrawardy completes a three-day visit to Afghanistan.

July 10-12. Prime Minister Suhrawardy confers with U.S. leaders in Washington. A communiqué is issued July 13.

Oct. 11. Prime Minister Suhrawardy (Awami League, inducted Sept. 12, 1956) resigns following the resignation of Republican party ministers. Ismail Ibrahim Chundrigar (Muslim League) takes office Oct. 18 as Prime Minister in a coalition government.

Dec. 11. Prime Minister Chundrigar resigns and is succeeded Dec. 16 by Malik Firoz Khan Noon (Republican).

India (see text, sec. 15)

Feb. 4-Mar. 12. Elections to the national and state parliaments are generally favorable to the Congress party, but the Communists score heavily and form a government in the State of Kerala Apr. 5.

May 13. Dr. Rajendra Prasad (Congress party) begins a second five-year term as President following election by the State Assembly May 10.

The Kashmir Problem (see text, sec. 15)

Jan. 26. The accession of the State of Jammu and Kashmir to the Union of India becomes effective under Indian law. (See further "The United Nations.")

Ceylon

June 7. An agreement covering the transfer to Ceylon of the British bases at Trincomalee (Oct. 15) and Katunayaka (Nov. 1) is signed in Colombo.

Ghana (see text, sec. 16)

Mar. 6. The former colony of the Gold Coast achieves independence within the Commonwealth as the State of Ghana. Kwame Nkrumah (Convention

People's party) remains as Prime Minister; the Earl of Listowel succeeds Sir Charles Arden-Clarke as Governor-General Nov. 13.

Malaya (see text, sec. 18)

Aug. 31. The Free and United Federation of Malaya achieves independence as the tenth state of the Commonwealth. Sir Abdul Rahman becomes Paramount Ruler (Yang di-Pertuan Agong) for a five-year term; Tengku (Prince) Abdul Rahman continues as Prime Minister.

Cyprus (see text, secs. 9, 26)

Mar. 28. Archbishop Makarios is released from detention in the Seychelles Islands and appeals to the EOKA terrorists to cease operations. (See further "The United Nations.")

THE COMMUNIST WORLD
(See also "People's Republic of China.")

Jan. 1-4. Communist party chiefs from the U.S.S.R., Bulgaria, Czechoslovakia, Hungary, and Rumania meet in Budapest.

June 22. The Council for Economic Mutual Assistance is revealed to have held a five-day meeting in Warsaw.

July 28-Aug. 11. The Sixth World Festival of Youth and Students is held in Moscow.

Nov. 16-19. World Communist leaders meet in Moscow following celebrations of the 40th anniversary of the Bolshevik Revolution on Nov. 6. (See text, sec. 23.)

Dec. 26-Jan. 1, 1958. A Communist-influenced "Asian-African Solidarity Conference" with nongovernmental representatives from 40 states and colonies is held in Cairo. (See text, sec. 26.)

The U.S.S.R. (see text, secs. 10, 23)

Jan. 20. A nuclear test is detected and announced by the U.S. Atomic Energy Commission. Further tests are announced as occurring Mar. 8 and Apr. 3, 6, 10, 12, and 16.

Feb. 15. Andrei A. Gromyko succeeds Dmitri T. Shepilov as Minister of Foreign Affairs.

May 4. J. J. Kuzmin is named a First Deputy Premier and Chairman of the State Planning Commission.

May 7. An economic reorganization plan involving establishment of 92 (later changed to 105) economic regions is outlined by Communist party secretary N. S. Khrushchev and goes into effect July 1 after approval by the Supreme Soviet.

June 6-13. Khrushchev and Premier N. A. Bulganin visit Finland.

July 3. The Communist Party Central Committee announces the removal from positions of party leadership of an "antiparty group" comprising G. M. Malenkov, L. M. Kaganovich, V. M. Molotov, and D. T. Shepilov; also the installation of a new 15-member party Presidium in which Marshal G. K. Zhukov is a full member.

July 4. The Presidium of the Supreme Soviet announces the removal of Molotov and Kaganovich as First Deputy Premiers and of Malenkov as Deputy Premier. Molotov and Malenkov also lose their ministerial portfolios.

July 5. The Presidium of the Supreme Soviet announces the removal of

Mikhail G. Pervukhin and Maxim Z. Saburov as First Deputy Premiers and the appointment of Alexei N. Kosygin as Deputy Premier together with A. I. Mikoyan and J. J. Kuzmin.

July 9-16. Khrushchev and Bulganin visit Czechoslovakia.

Aug. 7-14. Khrushchev and Mikoyan head a Soviet delegation to East Germany.

Aug. 22. A nuclear weapons test of "substantial size" occurs at the Siberian proving ground and is reported Aug. 23 by the U.S. Atomic Energy Commission.

Aug. 26. Moscow announces the successful test of an intercontinental ballistic rocket.

Sept. 24. A nuclear explosion in the megaton range north of the Arctic Circle is reported by the U.S. Atomic Energy Commission.

Sept. 25. Moscow announces that the Sixth Five-Year Plan for 1956–60 will be abandoned at the end of 1958 and replaced by a Seven-Year Plan for 1959–65.

Oct. 4. The world's first artificial earth satellite ("Sputnik I") is launched as part of the Soviet participation in the International Geophysical Year 1957–8.

Oct. 7. The U.S.S.R. announces the successful test (on Oct. 6) of "a mighty hydrogen war head of a new design."

Oct. 10. A small nuclear explosion north of the Arctic Circle is reported by the U.S. Atomic Energy Commission.

Oct. 26. Moscow announces the appointment of Marshal Rodion Y. Malinovsky as Minister of Defense, succeeding Marshal Zhukov. Zhukov's dismissal from the Communist party Central Committee and its Presidium are announced Nov. 2.

Nov. 3. A second artificial earth satellite ("Sputnik II") carrying a dog is launched.

Nov. 6. Khrushchev addresses a special meeting of the Supreme Soviet and calls for East-West talks.

Dec. 10. Premier Bulganin proposes a "summit conference" in letters to President Eisenhower and other heads of government. (See text, sec. 28.)

Dec. 14. Dmitri F. Ustinov is named a Deputy Premier.

Dec. 28. Another nuclear weapons test is carried out at the usual site in Siberia.

Albania

Apr. 11-17. Premier Mehmet Shehu and Communist chief Enver Hoxha visit Moscow.

Bulgaria

Feb. 20. Joint government and party declarations on relations with the U.S.S.R. are signed in Moscow.

July 16. The dismissal is announced of Georgi Chankov, Dobri Terpeshev, and Janko Panov from their high party positions. Chankov's replacement as a First Deputy Premier is announced July 17.

Dec. 22. Parliamentary elections produce a 99.92 percent vote for the official Fatherland Front list.

Czechoslovakia

Nov. 13. President Antonín Zapotocký dies and is succeeded Nov. 19 by Communist party First Secretary Antonín Novotný.

Hungary (see text, secs. 10, 24)

Mar. 28. Joint governmental and party declarations on relations with the U.S.S.R. are signed in Moscow.

May 27. An agreement on the "temporary" stationing of Soviet troops in Hungary is signed in Budapest.

(See further "The United Nations.")

Poland (see text, secs. 10, 23)

Jan. 20. The Communist-dominated National Front is overwhelmingly endorsed in general elections.

June 7. A $48.9 million economic aid agreement with the U.S. is signed in Washington, with provision for further aid totaling $46.1 million under an agreement signed Aug. 14.

Rumania

Feb. 3. Parliamentary elections are held for a single list representing the People's Democratic Front.

July 4. Miron Constantinescu and Iosif Chisinevsky are dismissed from their high party positions.

The "German Democratic Republic"

Jan. 7. An East German delegation reaches agreement with Soviet authorities in Moscow on current military, economic, and international matters.

Aug. 7-14. Communist proposals for German reunification are endorsed by Khrushchev on a visit to East Germany.

Oct. 7. President Wilhelm Pieck is designated for a second four-year term by the East German parliament.

Yugoslavia (see text, secs. 10, 23)

May 14. Resumption of U.S. military aid shipments, suspended in 1956, is announced in Washington.

Aug. 2-3. President J. B. Tito meets Khrushchev in Rumania.

Dec. 4. A five-year economic plan for 1957–61 is approved by the parliament.

THE MIDDLE EAST AND SOUTH ASIA

General (see text, secs. 13, 25)

Jan. 5. President Eisenhower's message on the Middle East (see "The United States.")

Jan. 19-20. The Premiers of Iran, Iraq, Pakistan, and Turkey meet in Baghdad and agree to support the American Middle East program.

Jan. 19. The heads of state or government of Egypt, Jordan, Saudi Arabia, and Syria reach agreement in Cairo on repudiation of the "vacuum theory" concerning the Middle East and on replacement of the British subsidy to Jordan.

Feb. 25-28. The same leaders meet in Cairo to hear a report on King Saud's visit to the U.S. (below), and adopt a declaration of "positive neutrality."

Mar. 12-May 8. Ambassador James P. Richards, special presidential representative under the U.S. Middle East resolution, visits Lebanon, Libya, Turkey, Iran, Pakistan, Afghanistan, Iraq, Saudi Arabia, Yemen, Ethiopia, the Sudan, Greece, Israel, Libya, Tunisia, and Morocco.

May 11-17. A reconciliation between Saudi Arabia and Iraq is effected as King Saud pays an official visit to Baghdad.

June 8-13. King Saud pays an official visit to Jordan.

Oct. 9. Khrushchev accuses the U.S. of inciting Turkey to attack Syria. The U.S. denies the charge Oct. 10 but emphasizes its determination to stand by Turkey.

Oct. 13. The presence of Egyptian forces in Syria is disclosed by the Egyptian-Syrian Joint Command.

Oct. 16. Syria and the U.S.S.R. ask the U.N. Assembly to consider the alleged Turkish threat to Syria. The demand is dropped Oct. 31.

The Baghdad Pact (see text, sec. 15)

Mar. 22. The decision of the U.S. to join the Baghdad Pact Military Committee is announced in Bermuda.

June 3-6. The Council of Ministers meets in Karachi and the U.S. formally joins the Military Committee.

The Arab-Israeli Conflict (see text, secs. 12, 25)

Jan. 7. Israeli military forces complete their withdrawal to the east of El Arish, Egypt.

Feb. 20. President Eisenhower says the U.N. has no choice but to exert increased pressure on Israel to withdraw completely behind the armistice lines.

Mar. 1. Israel announces its forces will be withdrawn from the Gaza Strip and Gulf of Aqaba area. Withdrawals are completed Mar. 8 as the U.N. Emergency Force assumes control.

Mar. 14. Egypt takes over the civil administration of the Gaza Strip from the U.N. Emergency Force.

(See further "The United Nations.")

The Suez Canal Problem (see text, secs. 12, 25)

Apr. 10. The Canal is declared open to all but the largest vessels following clearance operations by a U.N. salvage team.

Apr. 24. A unilateral statement setting forth Egypt's position on the future regime of the Canal is deposited with the United Nations.

(See further "The United Nations.")

Egypt

July 3. Elections are held to the 350-member Majlis al-Umma or national parliament. Run-off elections take place July 14.

Nov. 19. An agreement with the U.S.S.R. on political, economic, and military questions is negotiated in Moscow by War Minister Maj. Gen. Abdel Hakim Amer.

Iraq

Feb. 4-16. Crown Prince Abdul Illah pays an informal visit to the U.S.

June 8. Premier Nuri al-Said resigns. Ali Jawdat al-Ayyubi heads a new cabinet June 19.

Dec. 10. Premier Ali Jawdat resigns and is replaced Dec. 15 by Abdel Wahhab Marjan as head of a new cabinet.

Israel

Mar. 14. The U.S. announces resumption of economic aid discussions following Israel's withdrawal behind armistice lines.

Oct. 28. President Itzhak Ben-Zvi is elected by the Knesset to a second five-year term.

Dec. 31. Premier David Ben-Gurion resigns but is asked to head a new coalition government.

Jordan (see text, secs. 13, 25)

Mar. 14. The Anglo-Jordanian alliance treaty of 1948 is terminated pursuant to an exchange of notes in Amman.

Apr. 10. The government of Premier Sulayman al-Nabulsi (formed Oct. 29, 1956) resigns at the request of King Hussein. A new cabinet headed by Hussein Fakhri al-Khalidi is installed Apr. 15 but resigns Apr. 24 amid popular disturbances.

Apr. 25. Ibrahim Hashim forms a new government as the U.S. Sixth Fleet is dispatched to the Eastern Mediterranean to protect Jordan's independence and integrity. Acceptance of an emergency U.S. grant of $10 million is announced Apr. 29.

May 26. Syrian troops who entered the country in November 1956 are withdrawn.

July 4. The last British forces leave Jordan under the agreement of Mar. 14.

Lebanon

June 9, 16, 23. The pro-Western government parties are victorious in parliamentary elections.

Aug. 18. Premier Sami al-Sulh forms a new cabinet with Charles Malik remaining as Foreign Minister.

Saudi Arabia

Jan. 30-Feb. 8. King Saud confers with the President and other U.S. leaders in Washington. Agreement on increased U.S. aid and a five-year extension of the Dhahran base agreement (to Apr. 1, 1962) is formalized Apr. 2.

Syria (see text, secs. 14, 25)

Feb. 26. Numerous politically prominent Syrians are sentenced at the conclusion of a sensational treason trial.

July 24-Aug. 7. Defense Minister Khalid al-Azm heads a delegation to Moscow and secures broad promises of economic aid.

Aug. 13. Syria expels three U.S. Embassy officials allegedly implicated in an anti-Syrian plot. The U.S. next day declares the Syrian Ambassador *persona non grata*.

Aug. 17. Gen. Afif Bizri becomes Chief of Staff of the Army.

Oct. 28. A preliminary economic and technical assistance agreement with the U.S.S.R. is signed in Damascus. The formal agreement is signed in Moscow Dec. 11.

Yemen (see text, sec. 14)

Nov. 10-20. Following repeated clashes in the area of the Yemen-Aden frontier, Crown Prince Seif al-Islam al-Badr discusses outstanding issues with Great Britain on a visit to London.

Dec. 30. The Crown Prince reaches Moscow in the course of a tour of Communist capitals.

Muscat and Oman (see text, sec. 14)

July 19-Aug. 15. An independence movement by tribesmen professing loyalty to the Imam of Oman is quelled with British assistance by forces loyal to the Sultan of Muscat and Oman.

Iran

Apr. 3. Premier Hussein Ala (appointed Apr. 9, 1955) resigns and is succeeded by Dr. Manouchehr Eghbal.

Afghanistan

July 17-31. Mohammed Zahir Shah makes a state visit to the U.S.S.R.

Nepal (see text, sec. 18)

July 7. The government of Premier Tanka Prasad Acharya (People's party, formed Jan. 27, 1956) resigns. A new government headed by Dr. K. I. Singh (United Democratic party) is inducted July 26.

Nov. 14. The resignation of Premier Singh and the assumption of direct authority by King Mahendra are reported.

AFRICA
(See text, sec. 16.)

General

Feb. 28-Mar. 21. Vice-President Nixon visist Morocco, Ghana, Liberia, Uganda, Ethiopia, the Sudan, Libya, and Tunisia.

Libya

May 24. Premier Mustafa Ben Halim resigns and is replaced May 26 by Abdul Majid Kubar.

June 30. A military assistance agreement with the U.S. is signed in Tripoli.

Morocco

Nov. 23. Forces of the unofficial "Moroccan Liberation Army" open a campaign in the Spanish colony of Ifni.

Nov. 25-27. King Mohammed V makes a state visit to Washington.

Tunisia

July 25. The National Constituent Assembly proclaims Tunisia a Republic, deposes the Bey, Sidi Mohammed al-Amin Pasha, and unanimously elects Premier Habib Bourguiba as President. (See further sec. 26.)

Algeria
(See "The United Nations.")

Ethiopia

Oct. 10. Ethiopia's first general elections conclude as 210 members are elected to a new Chamber of Deputies.

Ghana
(See "The Commonwealth of Nations.")

Colonial Africa

Mar. 31. Elections for territorial and provincial assemblies are held in French West Africa, French Equatorial Africa, and Madagascar.

U.N. Trust Terrtories

Mar. 6. *British Togoland*—The trusteeship agreement for Togoland under British Administration is terminated as the territory achieves independence as part of the new state of Ghana.

Union of South Africa
(See "The Commonwealth of Nations.")

ASIA AND THE FAR EAST

The Colombo Plan

Oct. 7-24. The Consultative Committee for Economic Development in South and Southeast Asia holds its ninth annual meeting in Saigon. (See text, sec. 18.)

The ANZUS Treaty

Oct. 4. The ANZUS Council holds it regular meeting in Washington.

Southeast Asia Treaty Organization

Mar. 10-13. The SEATO Council holds its third annual session in Canberra. (See text, sec. 18.)

Sept. 4. Pote Sarasin (Thailand) is installed as SEATO's first Secretary-General but resigns Sept. 22 to become Prime Minister of Thailand.

Burma (see text, sec. 18)

Mar. 1. U Nu replaces U Ba Swe as Prime Minister.

Mar. 11. U Win Maung is unanimously elected President by the Parliament, succeeding Ba U.

Mar. 21. A $25 million U.S. development loan is announced.

Thailand (see text, sec. 18)

Feb. 26. The government party of Premier Pibul Songgram is victorious in partial parliamentary elections.

Sept. 17. The Pibul government is overthrown in a military coup engineered by the Army Commander-in-Chief, Marshal Sarit Thanarat. Pote Sarasin is installed as Premier Sept. 21.

Dec. 15. Anti-Communist candidates are generally successful in new elections to fill 160 seats in parliament.

Malaya
(See "The Commonwealth of Nations.")

Singapore

Apr. 11. An agreement envisaging early independence within the Commonwealth is signed in London.

Vietnam (see text, sec. 18)

May 8-11. President Ngo Dinh Diem of the Republic of Vietnam makes a state visit to Washington.

July 6-Aug. 30. President Ho Chi Minh of the "Democratic Republic of Vietnam" tours Communist countries in the Far East and Europe.

Cambodia (see text, sec. 18)

Apr. 7. Prince Norodom Sihanouk begins his fourth premiership, succeeding San Yun (inducted Oct. 15, 1956).

June 21. Prince Norodom Sihanouk resigns. A new cabinet headed by Sim Var is approved by the National Assembly July 26.

Nov. 20. The Sim Var cabinet offers its resignation but remains in office.

Laos (see text, sec. 18)

May 30. Prime Minister Prince Souvanna Phouma (inducted Mar. 21, 1956) resigns.

Aug. 9. The National Assembly approves a new coalition government headed by Prince Souvanna Phouma.

Nov. 18. The National Assembly approves a revised government headed by Prince Souvanna Phouma and including two representatives of the Communist-led Pathet-Lao movement.

Indonesia (see text, secs. 18, 26)

Mar. 14. The government of Ali Sastroamidjojo (Nationalist, installed Mar. 24, 1956) resigns as President Sukarno proclaims a nationwide state of war and siege to assist in coping with widespread autonomy demands in the outer islands.

Apr. 9. An "extraparliamentary" cabinet of experts takes office under the leadership of Premier Djuanda.

June 15. A 45-member National Council to advise the government is established by the President and formally installed July 12.

Nov. 30. An unsuccessful attempt is made to assassinate President Sukarno.

Dec. 1. Measures against Dutch nationals and interests are initiated following Indonesia's unsuccessful appeal for United Nations support in the "West Irian" question. (See below.)

The Philippines (see text, sec. 18)

Mar. 17. President Ramón Magsaysay is killed in an airplane accident and is succeeded by Vice-President Carlos P. Garcia (Nationalist).

Nov. 12. President Garcia and Diosdado Macapagal (Liberal) are elected to four-year terms as President and Vice-President respectively and are inaugurated Dec. 30.

Republic of China (see text, sec. 17)

May 23. The U.S. Embassy and Information headquarters in Taipei are wrecked and 13 Americans injured in anti-American riots.

People's Republic of China (see text, sec. 17)

Jan. 7-Feb. 6. Premier Chou En-lai visits the U.S.S.R., Poland, Hungary, Afghanistan, India, Nepal, and Ceylon. An important joint policy declaration is issued in Moscow Jan. 18. (See further secs. 3, 10.)

Feb. 27. Chairman Mao Tse-tung discusses contradictions in Chinese society in a speech to the Supreme State Conference which is published June 18.

Aug. 22. The State Department announces that representatives of 24 U.S. news-gathering organizations will be permitted to visit China on a trial basis.

Aug. 23 ff. Forty-two young Americans visit China on invitation of the Communist regime.

Nov. 6 ff. Mao Tse-tung visits Moscow to celebrate the 40th anniversary of the Bolshevik Revolution. (See text, sec. 23.)

Mongolian People's Republic

May 10-15. A delegation headed by Premier Yumzhagil Tsedenbal visits Moscow and concludes an agreement on Soviet economic aid.

Aug. 17 ff. Premier Tsedenbal visits the U.S.S.R. and Eastern Europe.

Japan (see text, sec. 19)

Jan. 16. A five-year agreement on limitation of cotton textile exports to the U.S. is announced in Washington.

Feb. 23. Premier Tanzan Ishibashi (Liberal Democrat, installed Dec. 23, 1956) resigns and is replaced Feb. 25 by Foreign Minister Nobosuke Kishi (Liberal Democrat).

May 20-June 4. Premier Kishi visits Burma, India, Pakistan, Ceylon, and Taiwan.

June 19-21. Premier Kishi confers with the President and other U.S. authorities in Washington. Agreement on withdrawal of U.S. ground combat troops in Japan is announced June 21.

July 10. Premier Kishi forms a new government with Aiichiro Fujiyama as Foreign Minister.

July 11. The U.S. Supreme Court upholds the waiver of jurisdiction by the U.S. to Japan in the case of Specialist 3/C William S. Girard.

Aug. 1. The last U.S. combat division in Japan is officially disbanded preliminary to withdrawal of U.S. ground combat forces.

Sept. 23. Foreign Minister Fujiyama confers with Secretary Dulles in Washington.

Nov. 18-Dec. 8. Premier Kishi visits Australia, New Zealand, South Vietnam, Cambodia, Laos, Malaya, Indonesia, Singapore, and the Philippines.

Nov. 19. A Japanese court finds Specialist 3/C Girard guilty of bodily injury resulting in death and imposes a three-year suspended sentence.

Dec. 6. A five-year commerce and navigation treaty with the U.S.S.R. is signed in Tokyo.

Dec. 8. A preliminary reparations agreement with Indonesia is signed in Jakarta.

Korea (see text, sec. 17)

June 21. The U.N. Command announces that in view of Communist violations of the Armistice it will not be bound by restrictions on the introduction of new matériel into South Korea.

(See further "The United Nations.")

THE WESTERN HEMISPHERE
(See text, secs. 20, 21.)

General

Apr. 24-26. U.S. armed forces exhibit modern assault techniques before Latin American observers in Panama and the Canal Zone.

May 7. The Inter-American Committee of Presidential Representatives concludes a week of closed sessions in Washington and approves a report released May 25.

Aug. 15-Sept. 4. The Economic Conference of the Organization of American States is held in Buenos Aires, with all Western Hemisphere republics except Venezuela participating.

Nov. 14. The Council of the Organization of American States unanimously elects José A. Mora (Uruguay) as Secretary-General and William Manger (U.S.) as Assistant Secretary-General.

Central America

Feb. 26. Treaties establishing a free trade zone and a system of regional industries are approved by representatives of Costa Rica, Guatemala, Honduras, Nicaragua, and El Salvador at a meeting in Guatemala.

Apr. 25. Honduras complains that Nicaraguan forces have invaded its territory. The Council of the Organization of American States appoints a five-man investigating commission May 2, and hostilities cease May 3. An agreement to submit the boundary dispute to the International Court of Justice is signed in Washington July 21.

South America

May 13-30. The chiefs of staff of Argentina, Brazil, Paraguay, and Uruguay discuss common defense problems in Buenos Aires under the auspices of the Inter-American Defense Board.

Argentina

July 28. Elections to a constituent assembly produce a majority in favor of constitutional reform.

Bolivia

July 19. President Hernán Siles Zuazo reorganizes the leadership of the governing National Revolutionary Movement following a victory over left-wing elements which had sought to seize control.

Brazil

Jan. 21. A U.S.-Brazilian agreement on construction of a guided missile tracking station on Fernando de Noronha Island is initialed in Rio de Janeiro.

Chile

Mar. 3. Congressional elections result in a strengthening of the moderate parties.

Apr. 2-3. Serious riots occur in Santiago.

Colombia

May 8. President Gustavo Rojas Pinilla (installed June 1953) is reelected by a specially convoked assembly to a four-year term beginning in 1958.

May 10. Gen. Rojas is ousted by a military junta headed by Maj. Gen. Gabriel Pario.

Dec. 1. A constitutional amendment establishing conditions for return to civilian government is approved by plebiscite.

Dominican Republic

May 16. President Hector B. Trujillo (inaugurated Aug. 16, 1952) is reelected unopposed for a five-year term and is inaugurated Aug. 16.

Guatemala

July 26. President Carlos Castillo Armas (inaugurated March 1956) is assassinated by an alleged Communist. Vice-President Luis Arturo González López succeeds him as Provisional President.

Oct. 20. Presidential and congressional elections result in an apparent victory for government candidate Miguel Ortiz Passarelli.

Oct. 24. A three-man military junta takes control and invalidates the elections following demonstrations on behalf of Gen. Miguel Ydígoras Fuentes.

Oct. 26. The military junta is dissolved as Guillermo Flores Avendano is installed as Provisional President and promises new elections.

Haiti

Feb. 4. Provisional President Joseph Nemours Pierre-Louis (installed Dec. 12, 1956) resigns and is replaced Feb. 11 by Franck Sylvain following his election by the Senate and Chamber of Deputies.

Apr. 2. Provisional President Sylvain resigns and is replaced Apr. 6 by an Executive Council of 13 ministers. The Council collapses Apr. 24 but resumes authority May 3.

May 21. The Executive Council is dissolved as an army administration takes control under Brig. Gen. Léon Cantave.

May 26. Daniel Fignolé forms a provisional government as Gen. Cantave resigns.

June 14. Provisional President Fignolé resigns at gun point and is replaced by a three-man military junta under Brig. Gen. Antonio Kébreau.

Sept. 22. Presidential and congressional elections are held by the military junta. The victorious presidential candidate, Dr. François Duvalier, is inaugurated Oct. 22.

Honduras

Sept. 22. Elections to a constituent assembly, held under the authority of a military junta, give the Liberal party 36 out of 58 seats.

Nov. 15. The Constituent Assembly designates Dr. Ramón Villeda Morales (Liberal) as President. He is inaugurated Dec. 21.

Mexico

Mar. 7. A civil aviation agreement with the U.S. is concluded in Mexico City.

Nicaragua

Feb. 4. President Luis A. Somoza de Bayle (installed Sept. 1956) is elected to a five-year term and inaugurated May 1.

Venezuela

Dec. 15. President Marcos Pérez Jiménez (installed Dec. 1952) is designated for a new five-year term (beginning April 19, 1958) in a national plebiscite which also approves a new Congress.

British Guiana

Aug. 12. Factions of the People's Progressive party capture a majority of the elective seats in the Legislative Council.

THE UNITED NATIONS

Membership

Mar. 8. Ghana is elected as the 81st U.N. member state.
Sept. 17. The Federation of Malaya is elected as the 82nd member state.

Security Council

Jan. 24. The Council reaffirms its position on the Kashmir problem. (See text, sec. 15.)

Feb. 20. A proposal to send Council President Gunnar Jarring to India and Pakistan in connection with the Kashmir question is defeated by the 80th Soviet veto.

Feb. 21. A modified proposal to send Mr. Jarring to the subcontinent is adopted. The report of his mission is released Apr. 30.

Mar. 7. The Council unanimously recommends Ghana for U.N. membership.

Apr. 26. The Council takes note of the Egyptian declaration on the regime of the Suez Canal. Two further meetings on the Suez Canal situation are held May 20 and 21. (See text, sec. 12.)

May 23, 28. The Council discusses a Syrian complaint of Israeli actions in the Lake Hula area.

Aug. 20. The Council declines to consider Arab charges relating to British intervention in Muscat and Oman. (See text, sec. 14.)

Sept. 5. The Council unanimously recommends Malaya for U.N. membership.

Sept. 9. Recommendations of the Republic of Korea and the Republic of Vietnam for U.N. membership are defeated by the 81st and 82nd Soviet vetoes. Also rejected are the applications of North Vietnam and the Mongolian People's Republic.

Sept. 26. The Council unanimously recommends Dag Hammarskjold for a second five-year term as Secretary-General beginning in April 1958.

Oct. 1. The Council agrees on the election of two incumbent and three new members of the International Court of Justice.

Dec. 2. The Council votes 10-0 to send Dr. Frank P. Graham on a mission to India and Pakistan in connection with the Kashmir problem.

General Assembly

Jan. 2-Mar. 8. The Assembly holds the second part of its 11th Regular Session in New York under the presidency of Prince Wan Waithayakon of Thailand, adopting the following resolutions among others:

Jan. 10. Resol. 1132 (XI)—Establishing a five-nation observation committee on Hungary. (See text, sec. 10.)

Jan. 11. Resol. 1010 (XI)—Reaffirming U.N. objectives in Korea.

Jan. 19. Resol. 1123 (XI)—Asking for a report on Israeli withdrawals from Egypt within five days. (See text, sec. 12.)

Jan. 23. Resol. 1039 (XI)—Urging contributions for Hungarian refugees.
Resol. 1046 (XI)—Establishing a commission to examine the situation in French Togoland.

Jan. 29. Resol. 1040 (XI)—Approving a convention on the nationality of married women.

Jan. 30. Resol. 1015 (XI)—Appealing to South Africa to negotiate with India and Pakistan on the treatment of its Indian population.
Resol. 1016 (XI)—Calling upon South Africa to revise its racial policies.

Feb. 2. Resol. 1124 (XI)—Calling on Israel to complete its withdrawal behind the armistice demarcation line. (See text, sec. 12.)
Resol. 1125 (XI)—Favoring deployment of the U.N. Emergency Force on the Egyptian-Israeli armistice demarcation line. (See text, sec. 12.)

Feb. 14. Resol. 1011 (XI)—Requesting further disarmament discussions by the Disarmament Commission and Subcommittee. (See text, sec. 11.)

Feb. 15. Resol. 1012 (XI)—Expressing hope for a peaceful, democratic and just solution in Algeria. (See text, sec. 16.)

Feb. 20. Resol. 1041 (XI)—Asking the Social, Humanitarian and Cultural Committee to complete the draft covenants on human rights in time for adoption at the 1958 session.

Feb. 21. Resol. 1043 (XI)—Inviting all states to promote wider cultural and scientific cooperation.
Resol. 1105 (XI)—Requesting that a conference on the law of the sea be convened in March 1958.

Feb. 26. Resol. 1013 (XI)—Favoring resumption of negotiations for a peaceful, democratic and just solution of the Cyprus problem.
Resol. 1030 (XI)—Requesting further study of a legal framework for the proposed Special U.N. Fund for Economic Development.
Resol. 1055 (XI)—Reiterating views on South West Africa.
Resol. 1064 (XI)—Inviting administering authorities to submit deadlines for self-government or independence for trust territories.

Feb. 27. Resol. 1090 (XI)—Inviting voluntary financial contributions for the U.N. Emergency Force.
Resol. 1100 (XI)—Increasing 1957 budgetary appropriations to $50,815,700.

Feb. 28. Resol. 1017 (XI)—Requesting the Security Council to reconsider the membership applications of the Republics of Korea and Vietnam.
Resol. 1018 (XI)—Authorizing continued assistance to Palestine refugees.

Mar. 8. Resol. 1118 (XI)—Admitting Ghana to U.N. membership.

Sept. 10-14. The Assembly reconvenes to consider the report of its Special Committee on the Problem of Hungary and adopts the following resolution:

Sept. 14. Resol. 1133 (XI)—Reiterating views on the Hungarian question. (See text, sec. 24.)

Sept. 17-Dec. 14. The Assembly holds its 12th Regular Session in New York under the presidency of Sir Leslie Munro of New Zealand, adopting the following resolutions and decisions among others:

Sept. 17. Resol. 1134 (XII)—Admitting the Federation of Malaya to U.N. membership.

Sept. 24. Resol. 1135 (XII)—Postponing discussion of Chinese representation. (See text, sec. 24.)

Sept. 26. Reelecting Dag Hammarskjold as Secretary-General. (See text, sec. 24.)

Oct. 1. Electing Japan, Canada, and Panama to Security Council membership for 1958–59.

Oct. 14. Resol. 1136 (XII)—Postponing consideration of a charter review conference.

Resol. 1137 (XII)—Recommending a maximum assessment per member of 30 percent of the annual budget.

Oct. 25. Resol. 1143 (XII)—Establishing a good offices committee on South West Africa.

Resol. 1144 (XII)—Regretting the nonmembership of the Republics of Korea and Vietnam. (See text, sec. 24.)

Nov. 14. Resol. 1148 (XII)—Requesting the Disarmament Commission to continue its work. (See text, sec. 24.)

Nov. 19. Resol. 1150 (XII)—Adding 14 members to the Disarmament Commission. (See text, sec. 24.)

Nov. 22. Resol. 1151 (XII)—Providing for financing of the U.N. Emergency Force. (See text, sec. 25.)

Nov. 26. Resol. 1155 (XII)—Requesting establishment of an Economic Commission for Africa.

Resol. 1159 (XII)—Approving liquidation of the U.N. Korean Reconstruction Agency as from June 30, 1958.

Resol. 1165 (XII)—Continuing the office of High Commissioner for Refugees for five years. (See text, sec. 27.)

Resol. 1166 (XII)—Urging that European refugee camps be closed by the end of 1960.

Resol. 1178 (XII)—Deploring South Africa's failure to modify its racial policies.

Resol. 1179 (XII)—Appealing to South Africa to negotiate with India and Pakistan on treatment of persons of Indian origin.

Nov. 29. Resol. 1180 (XII)—Calling for the reunification of Korea. (See text, sec. 24.)

Dec. 10. Resol. 1184 (XII)—Expressing hope for a solution in Algeria. (See text, sec. 26.)

Dec. 12. Resol. 1191 (XII)—Requesting funds for Palestine Arab refugees. (See text, sec. 25.)

Dec. 13. Resol. 1207 (XII)—Reiterating views on attainment by trust territories of self-government or independence.

Resol. 1211 (XII)—Expressing hope for restoration of normal conditions in French Cameroons.

Dec. 14. Resol. 1212 (XII)—Recommending a surcharge on Suez Canal traffic to defray costs of clearance. (See text, sec. 25.)

Resol. 1219 (XII)—Establishing a Special Fund for technical assistance projects. (See text, sec. 27.)

Resol. 1223 (XII)—Assessing the U.S. 32.51 percent of the 1958 budget.

Resol. 1230 (XII)—Establishing a 1958 budget of $55,062,850.

Resol. 1236 (XII)—Calling on all states to strengthen international peace and friendly relations.

The following resolutions are among those failing of adoption:

Oct. 31. Establishing a commission to investigate the Syrian-Turkish border situation. (See text, sec. 25.)

Nov. 29. Asking negotiations on the West Irian question. (See text, sec. 26.)

Dec. 14. Asking self-determination for Cyprus. (See text, sec. 26.)

Economic and Social Council

Apr. 16-May 2. The 23rd Session of the Council is held in New York.

July 2-Aug. 3. The first part of the 24th Session is held in Geneva.

Dec. 10, 13. The 24th Session is resumed in New York.

Trusteeship Council

Mar. 14-May 15. The 19th Session of the Council is held in New York.

May 20-July 12. The 20th Session is held in New York.

Sept. 12-20. The Seventh Special Session is held in New York to consider the problem of Togoland under French Administration.

Disarmament Commission

Mar. 18-Sept. 6. The Subcommittee of the Disarmament Commission meets in London. (See text, sec. 11.)

Sept. 30. The Disarmament Commission meets in New York and transmits the report of its Subcommittee to the General Assembly and the Security Council.

Other Activities

Apr. 8-18. The Scientific Committee on the Effects of Atomic Radiation meets in Geneva.

June 3. The Committee on Arrangements for a General Conference for the Purpose of Reviewing the Charter meets in New York and decides to recommend consideration of charter review by the 1959 session of the General Assembly.

Oct. 10. The Eighth U.N. Technical Assistance Conference in New York receives pledges of $30,249,314 from 75 countries toward the 1958 Expanded Technical Assistance Program.

Specialized and Related Agencies

May 7-27. W.H.O.—The Tenth World Health Assembly meets in Geneva.

June 5-27. I.L.O.—The 40th International Labor Conference meets in Geneva. (See text, sec. 27.)

July 29. I.A.E.A.—The International Atomic Energy Agency comes into being with the completion of ratification by the U.S. and 25 other member states. (See text, sec. 7.)

Aug. 14-Oct. 3. *U.P.U.*—The Universal Postal Union holds its 14th Congress in Ottawa.

Sept. 23-28. *I.B.R.D./I.M.F.*—The Boards of Governors of the International Bank for Reconstruction and Development and the International Monetary Fund hold their 12th annual meeting in Washington. The election of Libya, Malaya, Morocco, and Tunisia increases the membership of the two institutions to 68.

Sept. 27. *I.F.C.*—The Board of Governors of the International Finance Corporation holds its first meeting in Washington. (See text, sec. 27.)

Oct. 1-23. *I.A.E.A.*—The International Atomic Energy Agency holds its First General Conference and First Session in Geneva. (See text, sec. 27.)

Oct. 17-Nov. 30. *GATT*—The Contracting Parties to the General Agreement on Tariffs and Trade hold their 12th regular session at Geneva, with Ghana and Malaya participating as the 36th and 37th members.

Nov. 2-22. *F.A.O.*—The Food and Agriculture Organization holds its plenary conference in Rome, increasing its membership to 77 by the admission of Ghana and Malaya and the readmission of Poland.

Aug 24–Oct 9 U.S.A. which discussed postal Union help Dry Up Congress in Geneva.

Sept 21–22 U.S.A.A. (U.S.?) The Republican Congress of the ... dinner for Reconstruction and Reconstruction and the Division Court Monday and hold their fall supper meeting at Washington. The officials of Union Africa, Asia and Turkey between the neighbourship of the two nations to us.

Sept 27 U.S.A. The Second Congress of the International Finance Corporation held its first meeting in Washington 1947 (1957?).

Oct. 16-23 A week, an International Annual Simple Meeting holds at the General Conference and Food Supply of Europe. Last week ...

Nov. 5 Moscow U.S.S.R. addressing Peru to the General Agreement on Tariffs and Trade held their first regular session at Geneva and Union and Kenya participation at the dark and with telephone.

Nov. 23-30 F.A.O. The Food and Agriculture Organisation begins its annual conference in Rome, assessing its membership to 19 by the adoption of China and Sudan, and the readmission of Poland.

INDEX

drawals, 58, 245-6; Japanese-American Committee on Security established, 247; discussion of Okinawa problem, 247-8; of war criminals and vested assets, 248; of Asian development, 248-9; of East-West trade, 248-9; of Japanese free world trade, 249; of U.S. trade barriers, 249-51; Export-Import Bank loans, 251; austerity program initiated, 251-2, 348; commercial treaty with U.S.S.R., 252; second Kishi visit to Southeast Asia, 252-3; reparation settlement with Indonesia, 252-3; relations with Korea, 253; election to Security Council, 253, 320; general outlook, 253-4

Jarring, Gunnar V., mission to India and Pakistan, 197

Johnson, Joseph E., 355

Jordan, 31, 32, 45, 157; political trends, 43; U.K. military withdrawals, 96; Egyptian-Syrian subsidy, 182; alliance with U.K. terminated, 182; and U.S. Middle East resolution, 175-6; leftist coup forestalled, 182-3; receives U.S. aid, 185-6, 191; Egyptian-Syrian war of nerves, 331; clashes with Israel, 332

Judd, Walter H., 351

Kádár, János, 30, 119, 317

Kaganovich, L. M., and Soviet power struggle, 30, 115, 122-3; downgraded by Khrushchev, 125-6

Kashmir, developments in, 197-8; Soviet and U.S. attitudes, 198

Kennan, George F., 363

Kennedy, John F., on Algeria, 205; on Sputnik, 360-1

al-Khalidi, Hussein Fakhri, 183

Khan Noon, M. F., becomes Prime Minister, 195

Khrushchev, Nikita S., 25, 33; visit to Yugoslavia (1955), 121; to Asia (1955), 215; at 20th Party Congress (1956), 10-11, 123; on East-West relations, 12; in Soviet power struggle, 11, 30, 32, 115, 122-3; on relaxation of tensions, 102; appears on U.S. TV program, 123, 347; industrial decentralization plan, 125;

meat, milk, butter plan, 125, 309; visit to Finland, 125; ousts party rivals, 90, 125-6; visit to Czechoslovakia, 126; meeting with Tito, 126; visit to E. Germany, 129; statements on Dulles and E. Europe, 127; on proposed Zhukov visit, 128; on disarmament, 130; on nuclear tests, 145; on Eisenhower Doctrine, 177; on Sputniks, 300; Chinese Communist attitude, 221; interview with J. Reston, 147-8, 305-8, 327; threatens Turkey, 326; letter to European Socialists, 308, 328; ousts Zhukov, 309-10; announces improvement in Middle East, 310, 330; proposes summit conference before Supreme Soviet, 302, 312, 313, 363; interview with W. R. Hearst, Jr., 301; addresses Supreme Soviet, 367

Kishi, Nobosuke, becomes Prime Minister, 241; political views, 243-4; visit to Southeast Asia, 248; visit to U.S., 244-51; second visit to Southeast Asia, 252-3

Kissinger, Henry A., 51

Knowland, William F., 43

Korea, 20, 24, 32, 50, 96, 134; armistice in, 212-14; Communist aims, 214, 216; U.N. suspends armistice provisions, 222; relations with Japan, 253; debate on U.N. membership, 320; U.N. resolutions, 321

Krishnamachari, T. T., visit to U.S., 200

Kubitschek, Juscelino, 271

al-Kuwatli, Shukri, 188; at Cairo conference, 179

Kuznetsov, V. V., 323

Labouisse, Henry R., 334

Lacoste, Robert, 205-6

Laos, 234; developments in, 237

Latin America, 32, 68; attitudes toward U.S., 258-9; Communist threat in, 259-60; relations with U.S., 262-4; and U.N., 263, 338; military defense problems, 264; U.S. military displays, 264-5; South American military consultations, 265; issue of U.S. arms shipments, 265-6; intra-Latin American conflicts, 266; dic-

sion, 324; in F.A.O., 356; proposal for atom-free zone, 365
Pote Sarasin, becomes SEATO Secretary-General, 233; becomes Thai Prime Minister, 234
Prío Socarrás, Carlos, 272

Quarles, Donald A., on U.S. military policy, 47-8, 51-2

Radford, Arthur W., quoted, 59; on trusting the Russians, 23; on U.S. military posture, 50; on Mutual Security Program, 66; on Latin American defense, 264
Randall, Clarence B., 349-50
Reciprocal Trade Agreements Program, 69; extension prospects, 70, 350
Refugees, U.N. action on, 352; see also Hungary and Palestine
Reston, James, interview with Khrushchev, 147-8, 305-8, 327
Richards, James P., mission to the Middle East, 44, 45, 174-5, 180-81, 186, 193
Riddleberger, James W., 314
Rio de Janeiro Conference (1954), 278, 282
Rio Pact, see Inter-American Treaty of Reciprocal Assistance
Robertson, Walter S., 77; on Communist China, 217
Rockefeller, John D., III, 68
Rojas Pinilla, Gustavo, ouster of, 268-9
Romulo, Carlos P., 325
Rubottom, Roy R., 283
Rumania, 316

as-Said, Nuri, 195
St. Laurent, Louis S., retires as Canadian Prime Minister, 287
St. Lawrence Seaway, progress of, 294-5
El Salvador, 266, 274
Sandys, Duncan, visits Washington, 29, 97; reorganizes British defense planning, 94-5
Sarit Thanarat, coup d'état of, 234-5
Sarraj, Abdel Hamid, 14, 188
Saud, King, U.S. visit, 78, 178-9; reports to Arab leaders, 179; in Jordan crisis, 185; visits Iraq and Jordan, 186; receives U.S. arms, 191; in Syrian crisis, 192-3; in Syrian-Turkish crisis, 328-9
Saudi Arabia, 162; political trend, 7; and U.S., 31, 156; and Gulf of Aqaba, 162, 170; and Eisenhower Doctrine, 165, 176, 178; U.S. base agreement renewed, 179; Richards visit, 181; in Syrian-Turkish crisis, 327, 329; complaints against Israel, 332
Scandinavia, and European integration, 106; see also country names
SEATO, 6, 46, 213, 216; evaluations of, 230-2; annual report, 231; Council meeting (Canberra, Mar. 10-13), 230, 232-3; military problems, 231-2, 234; subversion problems, 232; economic problems, 232-3; political attitude, 232
Shepilov, Dmitri T., replaced as Foreign Minister, 123; and Soviet power struggle, 122-3; downgraded by Khrushchev, 125-6
al-Shishakly, Adib, 188
Sihanouk, Norodom, 237
Siles Zuazo, Hernán, 73, 272
Singapore, 79, 97, 234; progress toward independence, 235-6, 337; Kishi visit, 252
Singh, K. I., 238
Smith, Earl E. T., 273
Smith, Sidney E., becomes Canadian External Affairs Secretary, 287; on East-West negotiations, 294
Somaliland, 111
Somoza, Anastasio, 267, 268
Somoza de Bayle, Luis, 268
Southeast Asia, Communist aims in, 216; conditions in, 230-41; military threat to, 233-4; economic problems, 240-41; Japanese interest in, 241-2, 248, 252-3
Southeast Asia Collective Defense Treaty, see SEATO
South West Africa, U.N. consideration, 354
Souvanna Phouma, 237
Spaak, Paul-Henri, 2; becomes NATO Secretary-General, 101, 106; and